Realignment in American Politics

Realignment in American Politics

TOWARD A THEORY

Edited by
Bruce A. Campbell and Richard J. Trilling

University of Texas Press, Austin and London

Copyright © 1980 by the University of Texas Press
Printed in the United States of America

All rights reserved

Library of Congress Cataloging in Publication Data

Main entry under title:
Realignment in American politics.
  Bibliography: p.
  1. Elections—United States—Addresses, essays, lectures. 2. United States—Politics and government—Addresses, essays, lectures. 3. Elite (Social sciences)—United
States—Addresses, essays, lectures. I. Campbell, Bruce A.,
1944–   II. Trilling, Richard J.
JK1967.R33 1980   329'.00973   79-13510

ISBN 0-292-77019-7

Requests for permission to reproduce material from this
work should be sent to Permissions, University of Texas
Press, Box 7819, Austin, Texas 78712.

To the memory of V. O. Key, Jr.,
in acknowledgment of our debt

Contents

Preface

Change draws attention. When that change has social, political, and economic consequences, and when it appears to be regular and substantial, scholars and social commentators are drawn to its study. This is a book about change. The phenomenon that absorbs the contributors to this volume is the massive and sudden electoral change that seems to define what V. O. Key, Jr., called critical elections. Key's seminal pieces on the significance of critical elections gave birth to the study of realignment, and realignment was for many years regarded as an electoral phenomenon only. Slowly, scholars came to realize that the massive and sudden electoral change of realignment was accompanied by change among elites, either within governmental bodies or within political parties. Indeed, the significance scholars attributed to the phenomenon of realignment derived from its ability not only to describe a change among the masses but also to describe both elite responsiveness (or the lack thereof) to mass electoral change and the policy consequences of mass electoral change.

Realignment, then, is a concept applicable to the study of the whole democratic process—that process by which the desires of the public are translated into public policy. This is not to say that scholars have yet developed a full-blown theory of realignment. Such a theory would have to explain how and why sudden and massive electoral change occurs, how and why such change affects elites, how and why such change gets translated, when it does, into public policy.

This book presents a series of essays devoted to the exploration of these large theoretical questions: what exactly are realignments, how and why do they occur, what is the nature of elite change that is part of or is caused by realignments, and how do realignments affect public policy? No single essay can tackle the broad range of these questions; each chapter deals instead with a small piece of the puzzle. Together we hope to assemble that puzzle, at least in its broad outlines, so that future researchers can elaborate upon the concept of realignment and can deal more directly with the interrelationships of its many pieces.

We believe our effort is the first to present an integrated theory of realignment, however preliminary it may be, that follows the concept from mass electoral behavior to elite behavior to policy change. All the essays in this book save one appear in published form for the first time. It was fortunate that such a wide range of scholarly interests could be brought together in a common publication; yet it is indicative of the power of the concept of realignment that it should draw together scholars with such far-reaching substantive interests. It is clearly time to integrate the many approaches to the study of realignment. Despite the diverse nature of the essays in this volume, they all share this common theme.

Even this volume, however, does not include essays on realignment within states or across nations or on the manifestations of realignment within political parties. The study of realignment is still too much a study of the American national electorate or, perhaps, the American national polity. Wherever possible, we have tried to present the discussion of realignment in its most general form. A general theory of realignment will clearly need testing in times and places different from twentieth-century American national politics.

This book is written for scholars and social commentators interested in American social and political phenomena and for students in the fields of political science, public policy, history, and sociology. We also hope that students of comparative politics and of social movements will find the volume particularly enlightening.

Realignment in American Politics evolved out of the early efforts of Trilling to expand the theoretical focus of the concept of realignment. He conceived the structure of the book and commissioned most of the chapters. Campbell assumed the editorial tasks as the revised chapters were being prepared for review, when other professional demands prevented Trilling from continuing. Seven of the thirteen chapters were written especially for this book, and all the others were revised substantively to suit its theme.

Several of the chapters in this volume make use of data provided by the Inter-University Consortium of Political and Social Research. These data were originally collected by the staffs of Michigan's Survey Research Center and Center for Political Studies.

None of these institutions or individuals is responsible for the analyses or interpretations contained herein.

We would like to thank the various contributors for their patience and unfailing willingness to revise and polish their work. In addition, Sharron DeVane and Leah Wilds turned in their usual outstanding job of preparing the manuscripts, and Hammond Law provided assistance with the bibliography.

BAC
Athens, Georgia

RJT
Durham, North Carolina

PART I

Issues in the Study of Realignment

I

Toward a Theory of Realignment: An Introduction

RICHARD J. TRILLING and BRUCE A. CAMPBELL

ISSUES IN THE STUDY OF REALIGNMENT

We are attracted to the study of realignment for a number of reasons. The prominence of the concept in political science first evolved from its application to electoral behavior. The change connoted in the concept quite clearly involved alterations in electoral outcomes and/or in the group bases for such outcomes. That is, to "realign" means to "ally oneself with a *different* group, cause, etc. . . . to join again with a *different* set of others in a cause." When significant numbers of voters thereby form new and relatively permanent electoral coalitions, important consequences for the party system and for the public good soon follow, or so it seemed.

The glamour of the concept—and it has its glamour—derives from its application to dramatic, sudden, and otherwise inexplicable change. Originally, such change involved patterns of voting in the electorate. More recently, and particularly in this volume, the concept has expanded to include changes in the composition and behavior of elites and in the form taken by public policy.

The intellectual attractiveness of the concept—demonstrated by the persistent and growing attention it demands among scholars—comes from its impact on democratic theory. Realignment can be seen as a "constituent act" (Burnham 1970: 10); it is a mode of behavior by which the electorate seeks to exercise its sovereignty over government. Historically, realignments have affected the nature of government leadership, the realms in which government action is appropriate, and the directions which government policy output takes. If democracy means that voters have control over government, a critical realignment is the voters' most significant instrument of that control. The change in party support resulting from realignment enables the government to produce those policies which complete citizen control.

The concept of realignment, then, has some important implications for democratic theory in general. A common view of the democratic process pictures it as a continuous phenomenon, in which popular sovereignty forms a constant basis of legitimacy for the decisions of government. Some critics who claim that democracy does not exist in such a form have jumped to the untenable conclusion that democracy therefore does not exist at all. Realignment offers a middle ground. Studies included in this volume and elsewhere seem implicitly to redefine democracy as a process which is more continual than continuous; more periodic than constant; more sudden, dramatic, abrupt, shattering, and monumental than smooth and incremental. The essential element —citizen control of government—exists only in a potential form most of the time. Realignment translates this control into kinetic form, and it is the fact that control *can* occur that makes a system democratic. Thus, the study of realignment leads us to a new conception of democracy. It sees control in democracy as operative only at times—specifically, at times of crisis, when electoral passions are aroused. While this image does not imply the sort of crisis government suggested by Pomper (1977), it could properly be called crisis democracy.

What emerges from recent scholarly attention (see, for instance, Burnham 1970; Sundquist 1973) to the concept of realignment is still an immature theory which articulates the often vague links among the social and economic environments, mass and elite political behavior, and governmental policy. The typical process seems to work in the following way. (1) A social and/or economic crisis arises. (2) The crisis intensifies political debate and politicizes society and (3) manifests itself electorally in relatively sudden, massive, and permanent transformations of the coalitional bases of the party system. (4) This electoral change produces unusually high rates of personnel turnover within parties, elected bodies, and, to lesser extents, bureaucracies and the courts. In turn, and finally, (5) governmental institutions implement policies designed to resolve the original crisis in accordance with the interests of the newly established electoral majority.

This embryonic theory of realignment subsumes five major concepts, each of which deserves our attention. The first is the *stimulus* which triggers realignment. Clearly, since realignment is a relatively rare phenomenon, the sorts of stimuli which bring it about are also highly unusual. Specifically, a realignment-triggering stimulus is one (or, more likely a set of stimuli) which confronts the electorate with the perception that what it wants the government to do, in some area of critical importance, is not what the government is doing. For the sake of simplicity in later discussion, we will use the term "discontinuity" to refer to this perceived lack of fit between voters' policy desires and government's policy outputs.

The key element here is the meaning of the phrase "critical importance." While we cannot provide a precise definition at this stage, we can say that a stimulus is critically important, in the context of realignment, if it generates a motive for behavior which is more important than the habitual and traditional motive of party loyalty, among large numbers of people.

The second concept of realignment theory is *decomposition.* Decomposition is the weakening or dissolution of the traditional psychological bonds, the feelings of loyalty which link individuals to parties. In the aggregate, it takes the form of a greatly increased lability in the partisan division of the vote from election to election. The phenomenon of decomposition is not necessarily an end in itself: it seems most productive, in fact, to see it as a transitional phase. Decomposition opens several doors to change. Which door the electorate passes through depends on numerous factors, to which we shall turn our attention shortly.

Issue voting is the third concept of importance in realignment theory. This much used notion has acquired an unfortunate proliferation of meanings. For present purposes, we choose to view it as very closely related to decomposition. Decomposition, by definition, means the reduction in the importance of party loyalty as a factor in the vote choice. As party loyalty declines in importance, the role of the issues and the candidates must necessarily rise. Decomposition and issue voting therefore exist in a reciprocal relationship.

We hasten to point out that this concept is a broad one. Issue voting for many people may be far from the sort of rational assessment of one's own and the candidates' positions which is proposed by RePass (1971), among others. For most people, in fact, it is more probably a negative reaction, a feeling that the present incumbents haven't measured up and that the opposition ought to be given a chance. Thus, the "true" issue voting of RePass represents but a small fraction of this broader concept.

The fourth concept is *realignment.* As presented by McMichael and Trilling in the next chapter, realignment is a durable and sugnificant redistribution of party support. It may occur over a relatively short period of time, in which case we speak of critical realignment, or it may continue over a period of decades, in which case we are dealing with secular realignment. These two sorts of realignment differ in far more than the time element, however. The entire nature of the causal processes which underlie change is different, as the discussion by Seagull in chapter 4 makes clear.

It should also be noted that realignment *may* result from decomposition but that this is not a foregone conclusion. While decomposition is a necessary precursor of realignment, realignment is not a necessary consequence of decomposition. There are, in fact, three possible ways in which the instability of the decomposition phase can be resolved. The first is depoliticization, an end to party politics. In essense, this outcome represents the perpetuation of decomposition. The second is a return to the status quo ante, the reemergence of the original distribution of party support after a period of instability.

The third outcome, realignment, subsumes a number of possible patterns of change. In a two-party system, realignment is conventionally taken to mean the replacement of one of the parties by the other as the dominant, or majority, party. It is also possible for a realignment to occur without the emergence of a new majority party, however, as in the case where a noncompetitive minority party becomes a competitive minority party.

In a multiparty system, the meaning of realignment has never been carefully defined. There are several possible patterns of change which fit the definition, however. One cluster of changes preserves the original set of parties but shifts their relative strengths. The most important party might retain its status after a realignment, for instance, but it might be obliged to accept a new party into its governing coalition. Or the major party could decline in status, losing control of government to one of the former opposition parties.

A second set of changes involves the emergence or disappearance of parties. Realignment could split old parties, or it could force parties to consolidate. The most significant changes of this kind involve the fractionalization of a two-party system into a multiparty system and the consolidation of a multiparty system into a two-party system.

Clearly, any number of combinations of changes in party

strengths might fall under the definition of realignment in multi-party systems. As the theory of realignment is extended into this domain, there will be a need to limit the concept to some sub-set of all possible patterns of change. Perhaps an approach which defines realignment as any change involving the shift of some minimum proportion of the electorate might prove fruitful.

At this point, it seems appropriate to ask what the likelihood of each of these major outcomes is, given decomposition. Would we expect to observe realignment, depoliticization, or a return to the status quo ante, and what factors could we use to predict the outcome? Obviously, the answer depends on which national system is under discussion, so let us limit our present remarks to the American case. The most probable result of decomposition in this country is either realignment of the type which preserves the present two-party system or a return to the status quo ante.

The depoliticization outcome represents a much less attractive hypothesis for reasons which are grounded in socialization and information theory. In the first place, party loyalties are usually attitudes which can be traced to early experience in the family. The stability displayed by this identification over time has been attributed to the child's deep-seated desire to achieve a close re-lationship with its parents and, as time passes, this stability is solidified by habit and tradition. In the second place, party loyalty serves as a remarkably efficient information processor in the po-litical world. Without it, the task of evaluating political stimuli on their content and merit would overwhelm even the most dili-gent citizen. On both counts, the abandonment of party loyalty would entail a high cost for the average citizen, and this reduces the likelihood of such an outcome, in spite of repeated demonstra-tions of discontinuities between public desires and the behavior of the parties in the formulation of policy.

The first of these arguments may also be marshalled against another of realignment's possible outcomes, that of fractionaliza-tion into a multiparty system. A multiple-party outcome is even less stable than the depoliticization outcome, however. On the one hand, it retains the concept of party loyalty, assuming only that a new pattern of loyalties will emerge. On the other hand, it flies in the face of all the institutional factors present in our structure of government which favor a two-party system. While significant third parties have emerged from time to time in our history, multi-partism has never proved stable, and loyalties have eventually shifted back into the familiar two-party structure, although, to be sure, the subsequent parties have often differed from the antecedent ones.

The final concept of our developing theory of realignment is *elite responsiveness*. What are the ways in which parties move from supporting certain policy stands to supporting certain others? Two processes must obviously be considered. The first is the replacement of elites. This occurs must readily among leaders elected to short terms, but even those appointed for life are replaced eventually. In theory, replacement of elites following a realignment results in policy decisions which are more in tune with popular desires than was previously true.

The second mode of elite responsiveness arises from changes in the decision patterns of old elites who are not replaced. There are at least two possible reasons for such changes. Clearly, many elites view themselves as delegates who follow the instructions of their constituency—they will shift once the changed desires of their constituents become known. Second, elites change as a response to the threat which a realignment entails. This may be a threat of the loss of office. It may also be a threat to life-tenured decision makers like Supreme Court justices, who fear that decisions which fly in the face of a unified public will result in a lessening of their or the institution's legitimacy.

In sum, these five concepts link into a theory which gives us at least a crude ability to understand and to predict realignment. Figure 1.1 illustrates the process. Of all the stimuli which impinge upon the electorate, a small subset will have the three necessary characteristics: a discontinuity is revealed, a critical issue is involved, and a significant number of people are concerned. On the rare occasions when all three criteria are satisfied, we would predict that decomposition will occur.

Once decomposition has come about, the critical question from the point of view of realignment theory is whether and how the voter-party policy discontinuity is resolved. For reasons discussed above, we would expect that a resolution would eventually occur. It may happen in two distinct ways, however. On the one hand, the old majority party can shift its policy positions to accommodate the electorate's newly expressed desires. Or, on the other hand, the old minority party (or a new party which replaces one of the parties of the prerealignment system) could adopt the electorate's position and either take over the dominant position or at least become more competitive than it previously was. The first of these outcomes ap-

FIGURE 1.1. A schematic model of the decomposition-realignment process

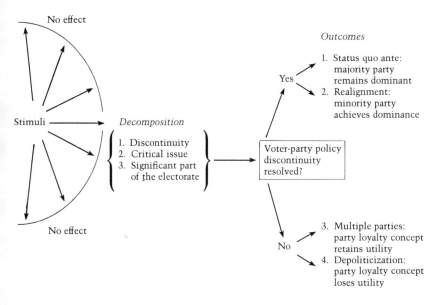

pears as the status quo ante in figure 1.1; the second is the realignment outcome.

We must also consider what happens should the voter-party policy discontinuity not be resolved. In this case, two outcomes are also possible. The multiple-party scenario will be the predicted result if party loyalty remains a useful concept in the electorate, for reasons either of the preservation of a socialized tradition or of information processing. Should party loyalty lose its utility, then the fourth outcome—depoliticization—becomes the prediction. These two alternatives are considered at some length by Campbell in chapter 5.

The sketch in figure 1.1 is a simple one and fails to do justice to the complexities of the real world in a number of ways. While, in times of crisis, demands upon the government may be relatively clear and intense, many obstacles threaten the completion of the process of realignment. The process may be aborted anywhere along the way—because the severity of the crisis ebbs by itself, or because party leaders waffle on the critical issues long enough to deny meaningful choice to voters, or because electoral change lacks the clarity and magnitude to transform the party system, or because institutional factors cause personnel turnover or policy change to lag substantially behind social and economic and electoral change, or because entrenched officials effectively engage in obstructionism, or because subsequent social and electoral conditions offset or reverse the realignment. Thus, the responsiveness of the political system to the needs and wishes of the people (that is, the ability of the system to resolve discontinuities) is put to a severe test by that crisis which prompts a realignment.

Clearly, responsiveness is a keystone to the theory of realignment which pervades the analyses in the chapters that follow. The set of social and political situations referred to as realignments increases the number of demands on the government. The willingness, ability, and techniques with which elites and governmental institutions respond to these demands determine whether the process of realignment will be completed and whether the voters' control will be maintained. It may seem logically inconsistent to claim that voters "control" government when elites and institutions may or may not respond to voters' concerns. There is no guarantee that any set of elites will implement these concerns, but we assume, with Key and Dahl, that the most effective and most likely means of control is the party-electoral system. Consequently, the measure of voters' control is the extent to which elites and institutions do respond; mass behavioral change which redirects or articulates a new set of concerns thus constitutes a "constituent act."

THE ORGANIZATION OF THE BOOK

The process of realignment involves both mass behavioral change (in such a manner that demands upon the government are clearly conveyed to elites) and elite responsiveness to and implementation of such demands. This distinction offers a means of organizing the chapters that follow. Realignment was first studied as a phenomenon of the masses, in which what is realigned is the sets of voters supporting each political party (see Key 1955, 1959). Part II thus discusses the nature and characteristics of mass behavioral change during realignment. The impact of this change on elites and governmental institutions provides the focus of part III. At the same time, the organization of the book reflects an attempt both to eliminate the murkiness about the concept of realignment and to extend the theory of realignment to new topics. The latter objective is achieved most directly in part IV, where we present two studies of the interrelationships of realignment and public policy.

Definition and Method
The two chapters remaining in part I address definitional and methodological issues and also expand our theoretical discussion. McMichael and Trilling sift among the many characteristics of electoral realignment for those attributes which together are necessary and sufficient for a workable and productive definition. Their analysis assumes that an electoral realignment occurred around 1930, develops a model of necessary and sufficient attributes of realignment, and confirms the model with aggregate data. The authors then develop two theories of realignment which amplify some of the remarks made earlier in this chapter. The first deals with the causes and effects of critical realignment; the second expands the discussion of the relationship between realignment and democracy in America.

The study of political realignments has raised a number of difficult methodological issues. Nexon addresses two of them in chapter 3: the first is the specification of what a realignment is, and the second involves the problem of causal inference in the study of realignment. In the former instance, Nexon employs the definition proposed and validated by McMichael and Trilling. Working from that base, he discusses a number of operational measures and advances a set of elections which he identifies as critical. In the latter instance, he points out how our present uncertainty regarding the identification of realigning elections casts any causal inference based on simple correlations into a certain shadow of doubt. He exhorts us to continue to work on theoretical generalizations which are not based on this particular statistic.

Realignment among Voters
The chapters in part II reflect two different though equally prevalent approaches to the study of electoral realignment. The approaches are somewhat contradictory, and their differences emerge clearly in the debate between Strong (1963) and Converse (1963).

The older approach, introduced by Key (1955, 1959), regarded realignment as the *behavioral phenomenon of an aggregate, the electorate*. This approach fell into disuse with the development of survey research techniques but has been revived with the work of Burnham (1965, 1968, 1970) and Seagull (1975). The second approach, made possible by the advances in survey technology, focuses on individual attitudinal bases of electoral change and is epitomized by Campbell's classification of presidential elections (1966a). Thus Key, Strong, and Ladd (Ladd and Hadley 1975) and their followers would proclaim an electoral realignment in the South since World War II, while Converse, Beck (1977), and other students of survey research still search for it.

While the attitudinal approach offers a more satisfactory explanation of individual behavior, its reliance on party identification is inadequate "in a period or region of rapid change in basic loyalties . . . [when] every *other* indicator of change would shift first, so that those relying on party loyalty [identification] would be the last to perceive what was happening" (Price 1968: 121; emphasis in original). But the behavioral, aggregate approach, which perceives such rapid change, can only *suggest* how and why individuals react to social crises. Thus the study of realignment poses a real methodological dilemma, which is discussed at some length by Nexon.

In the tradition of aggregate analysis, part II opens with the Seagull chapter, which pursues the theoretical status of "secular realignment." Electoral realignment can be accomplished over a relatively short period of time, in which case it is manifested in one or two successive critical elections, or over a longer period of time, with unilateral net partisan effects, in which case it is referred to as a secular realignment. The important distinction is originally V. O. Key's, but the drama, discontinuity, and suddenness of critical elections have drawn the attention of scholars away from the concept of secular realignment. It may very well be that secular realignments are not only the more common form of realignment but also a relatively common form of electoral change. Seagull proposes that secular dynamics, arising basically from demographic origins, may act not only to facilitate but also to impede realignment. In the former case, he cites the realignment to Republicanism which has slowly overtaken southern whites over the past twenty-five years and which is grounded in the vast social and economic changes which have occurred in the region during that time. In the latter case, Seagull discusses the emerging youth culture, a demographic change which has worked against the establishment of stable party loyalties in the electorate. Rather than realignment toward an equilibrium, the young have produced a dealignment of uncertain duration.

In chapter 5, Campbell shifts to an emphasis on survey data and individual attitudes. His chapter attempts to resolve the dilemma which separates the aggregate and individual approaches by focusing on the South over the twenty-four-year period for which survey data now exist. Changes in the partisanship of the South have been several times more rapid during this period than in the rest of the country. While the existence of a realignment during the 1970s remains a dubious proposition for the nation as a whole, realignment *has* occurred in this region (Campbell, 1977a).

This fortuitous occurrence permits a revealing analysis of how individuals react to the forces and situations which produce realignments. Campbell suggests that decomposition does not necessarily mean a rejection of parties but may simply lead to a period of confusion, after which a revival of party loyalties may be expected (although not necessarily in the former distribution).

Lehnen, in chapter 6, also focuses on a unique sector of political reality in order to reveal the workings of the realignment process. In contrast to Campbell, however, Lehnen chooses a slice of time rather than territory. He concentrates on Watergate, and he asks whether these events had an effect on the public's support of party government as a whole and whether they produced fundamental changes in affiliation with the two-party structure of political competition. His findings, also based on survey data, show that the Watergate crisis had a profound effect on attitudes toward public policy outcomes and the actions of incumbents. However, the allegiances of the public to the system of party government and its present bipolar structure remained virtually undisturbed. In conclusion, Lehnen cautions us not to assume that all attitude change observed in the mass public is related to realignment. In the context of the comments on a theory of realignment presented above, Watergate gave us a set of stimuli which involved a critical issue and which involved large portions of the electorate, but it failed to present a case of discontinuity between public desires and party programs (that is to say, they were not perceived in partisan terms).

Chapter 7, by Converse and Markus, closes out part II. This analysis is focused on the recent updating of the original Michigan panel study of 1956 to 1960. The earlier study formed the basis for much of the theoretical status of the party identification concept, since it provided the first longitudinal evidence of the great stability of that attitude. The more recent measurements, taken in 1972, 1974, and 1976, hold considerable interest because of the political ferment of recent years and because of the various claims that a realignment (or a dealignment) has or will shortly come about. Converse and Markus, in this preliminary analysis, demonstrate that the stability across time of individual party loyalty (for those who hold such loyalties) is virtually no different now than it was twenty years ago. The impact of this finding on our thinking about realignment cannot fail to be great.

These four chapters all present significant contributions, but still more could and should be done in the study of mass behavioral change in times of realignment. The aggregate approach has the obvious advantage of being less bound by time or place (Ranney 1962), but it is certainly inadequate in comparison to survey research for the study of individual motivation. Yet the advantages of survey research are just as clearly limited to times or places for which data are available. Since the theory of realignment regards the occurrence of realignment as relatively infrequent, and the availability of survey data is limited to the present political generation, the study of the motivational bases of realignment must await further realignments and further data.

These difficulties mean that we cannot answer, at least for some time, the following questions: How do the critical issues of a realignment affect the attitudes of voters? Campbell et al. (1960) argue that issues cannot affect voting unless voters perceive differences between candidates and parties on the issues. At what point do the issues of realignment begin to affect voting?

Why do some issues prompt realignment, while others do not, and how and why do some issues transcend the realm of short-term electoral phenomena and cause long-term effects? Is an electoral realignment the result of a two-step process in which at least two issues that might otherwise have only short-term effects reinforce each other in successive critical elections to transform the party-electoral system, as the McMichael-Trilling chapter suggests?

How do the reactions of the parties to the issues of a realignment affect voters? If parties fail to take distinguishable stands on the issues, how can voters vote on the issues? (See Sundquist 1973.)

Do the images voters have of the parties determine first their voting choices and later their party identifications? Historical and survey research data suggest such a role but do not yet confirm it. (See Kleppner 1970; Sellers 1965; Trilling 1976b.)

Do voters feel estranged from the entire political system or only from the incumbent party by a critical issue which prompts realignment? What is left to be realigned if voters, in larger numbers all the time, are alienated from the party system? How can voters respond to the institution of political parties when those institutions lose much of their function and activity through lateral entry and increased citizen reliance on media?

Realignment among Elites

If the answers to such questions await further research, part III of this volume illustrates how the impact of mass behavioral change on elites and governmental institutions can be productively pursued in the present. This section begins with a set of two chapters on the Congress. In chapter 8, Seligman and King note that, when new forces take over after a realignment, new patterns of political eligibility and recruitment are created. These new patterns lead in turn to changes in the composition of Congress and in legislative policies. The predominant sort of postrealignment change is from older to younger representatives, with the consequent establishment of new parochialisms favoring a more urbanized and technological constituency.

While Seligman and King concentrate on the nature of personnel turnover in the postrealignment period, Brady, in chapter 9, concentrates on the success which new congressional majorities have had in implementing a new political agenda, particularly after the critical elections of 1896 and 1932. This penetrating analysis is grounded in a theory of the dynamics of congressional decision making and, specifically, of party government in the House. Party government—the existence of partisan majorities capable of enacting clusters of policy changes—is usually inhibited by two major factors: the presence of major party-constituency cross pressures and the nature of the committee system. Brady demonstrates that realignment diminishes the forces of both of these factors and shows that, at the same time, levels of party voting in the House rise.

It is clear from these analyses that electoral change must directly affect the set of incumbents to guarantee their responsiveness. Furthermore, if it is true, as Mayhew (1973) and Burnham (1975a) have argued, that elected officials are becoming more and more insulated from their constituencies, most particularly through the mechanism of assured reelection, there is reason to fear that even the disruptive experience of a realignment, this ultimate constituent act of a democratic electorate, will have little impact on policy.

In chapter 10, Meier and Kramer shift from elections and elected officials to the bureaucracy. They examine the various influences which exist in the environment of a bureau, including not only the electorate, executive, legislature, and judiciary but also suppliers, allies, rivals, beneficiaries, and regulatees. The critical assumption examined by these authors is that elected officials have some impact on the outputs of the policy-making process. Or, viewed in the obverse, their concern is to assess both the abilities of the bureaucracy to prevent elections from influencing the policy process and the motives it might have for doing so.

Six characteristics of a bureaucracy appear to limit the influence of the electorate and elected officials: rational slow response, size, professionalism, the merit principle, clientele relationships, and cohesion. Critical elections and realignment provide the most promising opportunities for breaching these obstacles for two related reasons. First, a critical election will result in a large-scale change in the bureaucracy's environment. Both those groups which make demands on the bureaucracy and those which previously supported and defended the bureaucracy will be altered. Second, realignment means that new patterns of demands and support will probably be lasting, and a bureaucracy which might be able to resist change over the short term will be much more likely finally to succumb and institute the required policy changes. Meier and Kramer examine in some detail the links between the bureaucracy's sources of strength, on the one hand, and the changes wrought by critical elections, on the other. They make it clear that in times of realignment strong incentives exist for bureaucrats to be responsive to citizen demands, and yet equally strong institutional factors may inhibit their responsiveness, delaying if not completely postponing the fulfillment of these demands.

Chapter 11, the final chapter in part III, considers the role which the Supreme Court plays in critical elections. The traditional view of the Court in the context of realignment has centered on its legitimacy-conferring function. Adamany points out, however, that the Court's decisions are more likely to go against the policies of the administration brought to power by a realignment, since the Court's tenure makes it the last bastion of the prerealignment philosophy. Thus, if anything, the Court would be expected to delegitimate the policies of the new majority coalition.

Adamany casts considerable doubt on the notion that the Court does either one of these things. Rather, he concentrates on the role the Court plays at the center of the majority coalition in the *pre*realignment phase, in shaping the coalition's stance on the high-intensity issues which ultimately provoke critical elections. The role of the Court is not seen as one which encourages or inhibits policy change in the wake of a realignment—it is placed much more directly within the process which creates the realignment. Employing a wide-ranging analysis of the Court's major decisions over the history of the Republic, Adamany demonstrates that, in three of the four major realigning periods, the Court played a significant role in shaping the policies of the majority party which led ultimately to defeat and realignment. And, in two of the four converting periods (when there was significant realignment, but the majority party did not lose control), the Court allied itself with the majority party's presidential wing to define the policies around which the new majority coalition eventually formed.

The Impact of Realignment on Policy
Finally, despite the intellectual attractiveness of the concept of realignment, we still know surprisingly little about its long-term political significance. If realignments redefine the political agenda and affect political elites, presumably public policy will eventually change in perceptible and measurable ways. Yet the two essays in part IV, by Stewart and Hansen, constitute the first serious attempts to determine the empirical relationship between realignment and public policy.

Stewart, in chapter 12, presents a case study of the passage of the federal income tax in 1913. An income tax had been imposed by the Democratic Congress in 1894, amid great conflict and rancor. Less than a year later, in fact, the tax was struck down by the Supreme Court. Yet, by 1913, an amendment to the Constitution permitting such a tax had been ratified, and the tax itself was instituted in an atmosphere of bipartisan consensus.

Stewart's analysis links this striking reversal to the realignment of 1896. His explanation examines the crosscutting pattern of support for the income tax, on the one hand, and for the two major parties, on the other. Prior to 1896, nearly all the pro–income tax radicals were Democrats. This reflected the class-based appeal made by the Populist-Democratic coalition at that time and made the income tax appear to be an element in the coalition's broader effort to conduct a thorough overhaul of the country's system of economic organization. The 1896 election and subsequent realignment destroyed this coalition, however, and replaced it with the Progressive movement. The important consequence of this change was to homogenize the two parties with respect to various measures of industrial development. The patterns of congressional recruitment described by Seligman and King in chapter 8 are much in evidence here. Variation existed between the parties after 1896, but it was significantly smaller than the variation within the parties. There were pro–income tax radicals within *both* parties in 1913. Thus, a conservative realignment permitted popular demands for an income tax to be accommodated. The crosscutting of economics and party membership provided the conservative power-brokers in Congress the support they needed to allow a diplomatic reversal of policy.

The final chapter, by Hansen, also examines realignment and public policy. Her subject is also tax policy, but the focus is much broader, encompassing the question not only of the type of tax to be used but also of the level of taxation.

Hansen begins by setting aside the three traditional modes for explaining tax policy—war, economic development, and demands for new services—which she views as important but incomplete interpretations. She moves beyond these to introduce factors associated with politics, parties, and elections. In an interpretation reminiscent of Brady's, she finds that significant changes in tax policy follow when one party controls both houses of Congress and the White House. This party unity in the wake of a realignment has often coincided with an atmosphere of economic crisis, which compounds the likelihood that significant changes in tax policy will take place in such a period. However, Hansen goes on to warn us that the motives for parties to take opposing stands on tax policy have diminished markedly in the past decades. Substantive tax reform which would significantly shift the burden of taxes toward the upper-income brackets is unlikely because of the same dynamic which permitted the institution of the income tax in 1913: both major parties possess an influential upper-income constituency. We lack a major labor or socialist party which could support such reform.

REALIGNMENT RESEARCH

By almost anyone's definition, realignments are rare. And if our claim is correct—that there can be a significant lag between the onset of social crisis and the implementation of policy designed to resolve that crisis—it may be very difficult to establish empirically and trace the steps by which realignment proceeds. Yet, at the same time, the Stewart and Hansen essays demonstrate that the rarity of the phenomenon of realignment does not mean that *data* about realignment are necessarily rare. Historically, much information exists with which scholars can evaluate the concept of realignment.

Furthermore, the switch from studying the aggregate behavior of the electorate to studying the attitudinal bases of individual behavior was accompanied by a switch in attention from state electorates to the national electorate. Numerous veins of realignment data wait to be mined in the history of individual states and in the timing of changing electoral and policy patterns among the states. The potential contribution to the study of realignment offered by the availability of state data should not be underestimated. Not only do states significantly increase the number of cases available for study, but they offer natural controls for such socioeconomic conditions as level of industrialization, rate of unemployment, and cultural diversity. The diffusion of the process of realignment among the states might seem to reduce the number of truly independent cases available for study, but this methodological difficulty can be turned into an asset, since the diffusion process itself may very well help explain the process of realignment. Comparative state case studies offer the opportunity to test such propositions about realignment as the following: socioeconomic groups most affected by the crisis which prompts realignment will be the first groups to manifest their discontent electorally (from the McMichael-Trilling chapter); realignment creates conditions within the legislature that facilitate the building of partisan majorities capable of enacting clusters of policy changes (from the Brady chapter); and states in which bureaucrats have the greatest incentives to respond to citizen demands in times of crisis will experience greater bureaucratic responsiveness than states with bureaucrats having fewer incentives to respond (from the Meier-Kramer chapter).

Not only are states potential sources of relatively independent data for the study of realignment, but the study of electoral and policy change at the state level during the process of realignment offers an opportunity to understand the American federal system better. No known work presently examines the role of realignment in transforming governmental relationships, though Key's work on state politics (1967) suggests the relative immunity of state political systems from national forces. Furthermore, the relative responsiveness of different levels of government in times of social crises would further enhance our understanding of the representative nature of the American federal system.

We offer the reader this recommendation: the study of realignment needs to examine significant actors other than the voters and significant settings other than American national politics. Together these points suggest that the study of realignment needs to make use of new kinds and sources of data. Unfortunately, even the chapters in this volume do not explore subnational (or, of course, crossnational) examples of realignment as fully as possible. Extending the theme of Key's seminal paper, we would like to suggest that realignment plays a critical role in a representative political system at all levels, and we would argue that the discipline needs to break from its traditional ways of studying realignment in order to appreciate the full significance of this phenomenon.

Finally, we would argue that only a broadened understanding of the representative system—broadened by consideration of the concept of realignment—can help us deal with the ever increasing alienation of Americans from their political system. But even here we find reason to go beyond the traditional concept of realignment. Seen from a certain perspective, the findings of Hansen, Brady, and Meier and Kramer suggest that realignment may even now be fading as "the ultimate constituent act" of a democratic electorate. The increasing influence of incumbency in Congress, the increasing size and inaccessibility of the bureaucracies, and the increasing homogenization of the parties around centrist policy positions all constrain the effect which a realigning election can have on policy. Perhaps this is why the electorate has shown such enthusiasm in recent years for the mechanism of the referendum. California's Jarvis-Gann initiative, while not a critical election in the traditional sense, can certainly be seen as a constituent act by an electorate which was frustrated in its attempts to achieve meaningful reform through more conventional means. A general theory of realignment must contain a place for the referendum process as well.

2

The Structure and Meaning
of Critical Realignment: The Case
# of Pennsylvania, 1928–1932

LAWRENCE G. McMICHAEL and RICHARD J. TRILLING

One of the basic tenets of political thought in this country is the idea that the American form of democracy has survived so long because of the ability of its party system to absorb the intense conflict and critical change which have developed on occasion in its complex society. Ironically, the electoral system was engineered by men who actually opposed the formation of political parties. However, since the inception of the electoral system, political parties have proven to be the *sine qua non* in the process of absorption of critical social conflict. A ruling party possesses distinctive patterns of governmental policy output, of leadership and recruitment of leaders, and of support among various social groups (Chambers and Burnham 1967; Sorauf 1968). Relatively quick conversion from one social and political agenda to another is accomplished by major changes in the balance of party strength in the electorate, which produces a shift from one ruling party to another and, sometimes, will generate an entirely new party system to accommodate the changed agenda. The change itself is known as a partisan realignment, and the few elections in which the change is executed are known as critical elections. These occasions of intense partisan conflict and decisive change in the party system have thus taken on great analytical importance in the study of American politics and have received much recent scholarly attention.

The most noted pioneer in the field of change between party systems is V. O. Key, who published "A Theory of Critical Elections" (1955) and "Secular Realignment and the Party System" (1959). Key introduced the term "critical election" and popularized the word "realignment." Since then, there have been several variant forms of his concept, including the "realigning elections" offered by Pomper (1968) and Campbell (1966a), the "critical realignments" used throughout Burnham's work (1970), Pomper's "converting election" (1968), and the like. The close relationship among the underlying concepts probably accounts for the proliferation of vocabulary. Nevertheless, the lack of some more precise terminology doubtless adds confusion to the discussion of this complex phenomenon. Thus, the delineation of terms is as much a prerequisite for sensible analysis as is their definition.

Key initially proposed the concept of a critical election as a certain type of election in which voters are "deeply concerned," electoral involvement is "relatively quite high," and "the results of the voting reveal a sharp alteration of the preexisting cleavage within the electorate" (1955: 4). He added that the alteration tends "to persist for several succeeding elections." Writing a decade later, Campbell (1966a: 74) specified three more characteristics of what he called "realigning elections," changing Key's term but not the essential concept. Campbell asserted that, in this type of election, "popular feeling associated with politics is sufficiently intense that the basic partisan commitments of a portion of the electorate change, and a new party balance is created." With this, he made the subtle but firm and tremendously important connection between critical or realigning elections and the party system. He implied that Key's "cleavage within the electorate" is transmitted into "basic partisan commitments" and that this is what is altered. Campbell (1966a: 74) also proposed that "realigning elections have historically been associated with great national crises" and that "political polarization of important segments of the electorate," usually sectional or class-related, is likely to increase.

Pomper's discussion (1968: 104) of critical elections includes a distinction between realigning and so-called converting elections based on whether a new majority party is formed or whether the majority party of the previous party system is victorious and recreates its majority status. He identifies the key factor in both of his categories as "a change in a party's support" and defines this as a change in the party's relative strength in each state (1968: 105). Burnham (1970: 7–8) notes that critical elections "are characterized by abnormally high intensity," with the upheaval typically visible in the party conventions, by increased ideological polarizations within as well as between parties, and by high voter turnout. Finally, Sundquist (1973) provides a thorough historical examination of the many examples of realignment in American political history and amplifies the essential role of parties and party elites in accomplishing or forestalling the realignment.

These scholars as a group comprise the principal but by no means complete (Burnham 1964; Ginsberg 1972; Jahnige 1971; King and Seligman 1974; Ladd et al. 1971; MacRae and Meldrum 1960; Price 1971; Seitz 1974; Shively 1971–72; Ward 1973) body of theory of critical elections, and it is logical to look at them for a definition of the phenomenon. Since they have built upon each other's work, some type of distillation of their thoughts into a meaningful and unambiguous definition is in order.

DEFINITION OF TERMS

Above all, it must be clear what is being defined. The subsequent discussion will attempt to define the term "critical election." By doing so, we consciously set aside the competing concepts of re-aligning and converting elections. The frequently used term "re-aligning election" unfortunately maximizes the probability of confusion with realign*ment*, a related but distinct event on which we shall shortly focus our attention. In addition, Pomper's term, "converting election," makes a distinction which is less useful in light of history and theory, although Adamany's analysis of the Supreme Court does make use of it (see chap. 11).

Once we have chosen to use "critical election" as the term which embraces the type of phenomenon being discussed, a second problem of definition arises. The chief scholars in this field tend to define their subject implicitly by stating its characteristics rather than what, in fact, it is. The problem here is indeed subtle—it is often very difficult to distinguish conceptually between what something is and what its characteristics are. Nevertheless, the definition of a critical election is an excellent example of the unmanageable situation which may result if the problem is ignored. Suppose that a critical election is defined by a composite of its common characteristics. An election would then be critical if all the following obtain: the voters are deeply concerned; turnout is high; the results show a significant and durable change in the partisan cleavages of the electorate; it roughly coincides with a great national crisis; ideological polarizations increase within and between parties; the tensions are visible in the national party conventions; and the voting patterns of the states change.

In this definition there are seven determinants of a critical election, each of which can be supported by historical evidence to be a common characteristic of the elections generally regarded as critical. However, suppose an election occurred wherein all the determinants appeared except high turnout. Any reasonable analyst would consider the election to be critical, but by the proposed definition it would not be a critical election. Should one therefore narrow the list to two or three determinants? This also fails to provide a solution.

If a definition is constructed, on the other hand, such that the presence of any one of the seven determinants is sufficient for an election to be critical, that definition is clearly too broad. The presidential election of 1952 coincided with America's controversial involvement in Korea and with the infamous Red Scare at home, both of which were notable national crises. Yet no one considers the election of 1952 to be critical.

Considering these difficulties, it seems advisable to differentiate between what will be the definition and what are the characteristics of a critical election. Among the characteristics which have been discussed, one stands out as the most important. Key recognized this in his first article on the subject (1955: 4): "[P]erhaps this is the truly differentiating characteristic of this sort of election, the realignment made manifest in the voting in such elections seems to persist for several succeeding elections." Although he points out the "truly differentiating" nature of this one characteristic, he fails to establish it as a definition per se. Even less understandable is his failure to make the connection between the party system and the cleavages and realignments he mentions. This link is obviously quite important not only in developing a definition but in placing it into a body of theory. Taking these factors into account, let us state a provisional definition which will serve as a starting point for discussion:

> A critical election is an election which displays clearly in its outcome most or a major portion of the elements of a partisan realignment in progress at the time.

This definition has several features. We see that the display of a partisan realignment in voting *is* a critical election, as distinguished from other characteristics. It alone is sufficient for a critical election and without it, no matter what other characteristics appear, an election cannot be critical. Superficially, this feature may appear to present the same problem as the other possible definitions. We intend to demonstrate that this is not the case. It is clear, however, that this definition of critical elections rests squarely on the concept of realignment. The development of our argument therefore requires that we define realignment.

Defining realignment presents many of the same difficulties as defining a critical election, with the additional consideration that we no longer have the option of treating "critical election" as a known term and using it to specify the definition of realignment. One of these shared difficulties is to clarify what is being defined. Several uses of this term occur with regularity in the literature on the subject, including "electoral" realignment, "partisan" realignment, "secular" realignment, and "critical" realignment.

The first two of these modifiers have little importance. Since some type of joint party-electoral system forms the context for our entire discussion, all realignments are assumed to be electoral in nature. In a similar manner, the notion of anything other than a partisan realignment has little utility, at least for the purpose of the present discussion. It is technically possible to have some type of realignment which does not affect the party system, however—a notable shift in the age of voters would be an example. Thus, the distinction may be useful in certain circumstances, and we add some precision by specifying "partisan" realignment in our definitions.

The two remaining concepts, "secular" and "critical" realignments, do have great meaning for us. We shall turn our attention to that distinction in a moment.

First, however, we shall set out a general definition of partisan realignment. In 1960 Schattschneider, one of the most perceptive scholars of politics, referred to realignment implicitly as "a change in the party alignment, the way the two parties divide the nation" (1960: 89). Working from this crucial conceptualization of realignment as change, Campbell points out the utility of conceptualizing a realigning era, implying that the change to which Schattschneider referred has a substantial time dimension and does not occur in one or two elections (1966a: 75). Most recently, Sundquist has defined realignment as "an organic change in the party system" and further defines an organic change as a relocation of the line of party cleavage dividing the electorate (1973: 6). All three of these scholars share the idea of party alignment, which can be thought of as the distribution of party support within the electorate.

> Thus, a partisan realignment is a significant and durable change in the distribution of party support over relevant groups within the electorate.

At this point, Campbell's notion of a time dimension can be employed to distinguish between "secular" and "critical" realignments. Key (1955: 204) introduced the concept of secular realignment as "a substantial category of persons, defined by a common characteristic, demographic or otherwise, [moving] over a long period of time toward partisan homogeneity." He is simply referring to a progressive change in a particular area of the distribution of party support, not significant in any one or two elections but important over a long stretch. Critical realignment, on the other hand, is a realignment constrained by a time factor; that is, a substantial amount of the change must take place within a relatively short period. Burnham (1970: 10) speaks of "short, sharp reorganizations of the mass coalitional bases of the major parties." The basic difference between secular and critical realignments is the time factor, but the contrast goes far deeper. In particular, the two distinct processes of change are the product of two equally distinct etiologies. Critical realignment, since it occurs within a short period of time, must be caused by extremely salient, highly valenced issues—in short, by a crisis. Secular change, on the other hand, may continue over decades. Its causal structure must therefore arise from totally different sorts of issues—not volatile crisis-centered issues but issues which endure (Campbell 1977a).

This distinction in the definition of realignment can be brought to bear upon the definition of a critical election. Since the definition of a critical election requires that it display *most* or a *major portion* of the elements of a partisan realignment, the realignment involved cannot be of a secular nature, because by definition a secular realignment is significant only over a long period of time and will not reveal a major portion of its total magnitude in any one election. Within this reasoning, the previous assertion that the definition of a critical election will be neither too broad nor too constrained can be supported. It is clear from the definition of realignment that the crux of the entire matter is durable change in the distribution of party support or, simply, change between party systems. The initial concept of a critical election was based on the manifestation of this change in the outcome of a particular election. Therefore, it is not only reasonable but logically necessary that a critical election be an election in which a critical realignment is primarily displayed. To eliminate this condition is to dissociate the concept of critical elections from change between party systems.

From these definitions, further theoretical questions can be approached. First, the nature of the change in support involved in realignment can be expanded. Party support can be conceptualized as a continuous version of the vote. The party support at any given moment would be the partisan result of an election held at that moment. Support for a particular party is an ongoing condition of the electors: it does not appear on election day and vanish in the interim. In this regard and in others to be mentioned later, it is closely related to the survey research concepts of party identification and party image. It is preposterous to suppose that such qualities of the electorate exist only when ballots are being cast. Certainly salience may vary, but it is fundamental that party support, like identification and image, is continuous. Thus, any changes in party support are continuous processes, not discrete phenomena from one election to the next. Support translates into votes in an election, and thus elections gauge the relative strengths of party support at a particular point in time.

> Realignments are periods of flux in the continuous process of change in party support, whereas critical elections are demonstrations of that change at specific times.

It has been established by definition that critical elections cannot exist without critical realignment. Since support translates into votes, it is equally clear that a critical realignment cannot exist without a critical election. The two phenomena are distinct but mutually dependent. Whether a realignment is critical or secular, that is, the time it takes for the bulk of the change to take place, does not affect the continuity of the change. Graphically, a critical realignment would represent only an increase in the absolute value of the slope resulting from a constricting of the time segment on the horizontal axis. Substantively, it can be argued that the distribution of party support does not form one pattern at one moment and another instantaneously following that moment. Regardless of the severity of the change, it must always be continuous.

This deduction raises the question of the proper temporal bounds within which a realignment would be critical. A precise answer may not be possible. However, Burnham (1970: 26) has shown that interrealignment party systems last approximately 30 to 38 years.[1] Up to the 1930s, there were roughly 140 years of electoral history and four party systems separated by three critical realignments. Using Burnham's estimations, each critical realignment was executed in approximately 7 years.[2] Thus, it seems that a reasonable period within which a realignment is critical would be 10 years, involving at most three critical elections, probably fewer. This limitation is also consistent with the definition of a critical election in that a major portion of the change could not be spread over more than three elections.

Two important questions about the nature of critical realignment remain: what underlies the process of change in party support, and what results does this change have in other areas of the system? With regard to the former, since votes are the measure of support at any moment, a logical extension would be that the same variables which scholars have shown to have great impact on partisan choice in an election would also have impact on party support more generally. Two attitudinal variables which we shall consider are party identification and party image. Campbell et al. (1960) have defined party identification as a psychological tie between voters and their political party. The concept is one of the chief tools of voting behavior analysis because of consistent findings that the direction of voters' identification correlates highly with their partisan choice in an election. Moreover, party identification is extremely stable, usually seen as a long-term force in the voting decision, and provides the basis for the "normal vote" or the outcome of an election determined solely by the balance of party identification (Converse 1966, but see Brody 1975 and Dobson and St. Angelo 1975).

Since party identification usually correlates so highly with the vote, it is logically a major component of party support as well. In terms of realignment, it follows that a durable change in party support would be associated with a similar change in party identification. However, this change does not necessarily apply to the normal vote. In a time of realignment, the normal vote would remain the same if the number of identifiers changing to a given party is equal to the number leaving that party for the other. Nevertheless, empirical evidence relating party identification to the vote would make realignment unthinkable without a change in the electors' party identification. The question is whether change in party identification precedes realignment as a cause or follows it as an effect.

This question has been addressed with some recent research. Individual-level data are obviously necessary. Although the last universally recognized critical realignment on the national level was in the early 1930s and no survey data are available for this period, some current work on voting behavior can be brought to bear on the issue. Ladd and Hadley point out that defining the party in the electorate by means of self-perceptions of party identifications may be quite inaccurate in times of rapid social and political change (1973: 22). They provide evidence that changes in identification can lag significantly behind permanent changes in voting behavior. Their findings lead to the tentative conclusion that changes in party identification would follow critical realignment and would thus be a result, serving to reinforce the new patterns of voting behavior.

If there is at least substantial doubt concerning the utility of party identification in explaining the vote during times of realignment, then the question of what underlies the realignment is still open. The recently explored concept of party image helps fill the gap. The concept is defined as the gross mental image which the voter has of each party (Matthews and Prothro 1966a: 378). The authors of *The American Voter* have established that the image which a voter has of political objects, including party, plays an intervening role between party identification and voting behavior (Campbell et al. 1960: 81–83). It explains part of the deviation of voting behavior from party identification; as the clarity and salience of the image increase, deviation becomes more likely. Thus, party image would be crucial during critical realignment when deviations are massive. Additionally, there is evidence that party image is important in the process of changing party identification which is expected to follow realignment (Trilling 1975b). It would have a particularly heavy impact on the voting behavior and subsequent party identifications of new groups of voters entering the electorate without clear previous commitments. The important role of party image in realignment is consistent with previously stated characteristics of critical elections. Their tendency to coincide with major national crises is explained by the fact that party images should be strongest in times of national crisis and behavioral deviations from identification would be most probable. It is indeed unfortunate that survey data did not exist for the twenties and thirties. This sketch of the role of party image must await future events to be tested rigorously.[3]

In summation, it has been established that a realignment is a durable and significant redistribution of party support. A critical realignment is a realignment in which the bulk of the redistribution takes place within reasonably defined time limits. A critical election is an election which initially displays most or a major portion of the elements of a critical realignment in its results.

For this framework to become really useful requires more definite specification of such terms as "durable," "significant," "bulk," and "major portion." The study of a realignment will provide, to a certain extent, this further specification. But strict numerical precision, as is often the case in social-science research, may be too much to expect. In addition to these definitions, it must be emphasized that the work of scholars in this field has produced a number of important indicators, characteristics, and correlates of realignment. Deep concern and high turnout among the voters, the presence of a severe national crisis, evidence of increasing ideological polarizations between and within parties, and major shifts in governmental policy output are evidence of realignment and should not be ignored. But the firm definition of basic concepts will allow a more precise and meaningful study of the realignment phenomenon itself.

METHODOLOGY AND APPROACH

This part of our chapter contains two sections. To begin, the analysis will be based on the *assumption* that there was a critical realignment around the year 1930.[4] What will be sought is a confirmation that the proposed definitions of critical election and critical realignment are not only logically sound but are descriptively accurate in light of empirical data. In addition, various indicators of these phenomena will be developed and their utility tested. As a testing ground for these definitions and indicators, the state of Pennsylvania has been chosen. Several reasons underlie this choice. First, this state was used by Burnham in his prominent and somewhat controversial study of the subject (1970: 34–70). The use of only one state makes in-depth analysis easier by reasonably limiting the amount of data. Yet Pennsylvania is sufficiently large, with its sixty-seven counties used as units of analysis, to provide confidence in the findings. The state also has a heterogeneous population, with several large metropolitan centers and a substantial rural population. The only disadvantage of restricting the analysis to one state is that such a strategy will not provide very satisfactory data if the thrust of the issues or cleavages around which the changes in distribution of party support hinged were primarily sectional (i.e., North vs. South) or otherwise not salient to citizens of the chosen state. But there is much evidence to indicate that the cleavages which were important in the realignment of the 1930s were particularly relevant to Pennsylvania.[5] Additionally, certain indicators pertinent to realignment which are derived from the concept of the "normal vote" are more useful with a data base smaller than the nation as a whole. These arguments will become clearer with the development of indicators and procedures to be used in the first section of the analysis.

Basically, the confirmation of the definitions and indicators presented in the preceding section of this chapter requires the same logic and procedures which would be used if the occurrence of realignment were being tested. Only the underlying assumption changes. Instead of assuming that the definitions and indicators are valid, the occurrence of realignment is assumed. Thus, the observation of a significant and durable change in the distribution of party support, occurring fairly rapidly, will be taken as evidence confirming the validity of the definitions and indicators. From this hypothesis, the development of these indicators of the change in distribution of party support can proceed.

Since critical elections display critical realignments, all the indicators will be based on aggregate election data. The first and simplest indicator is the *percentage received by one of the major parties of the two-party vote over time.* Although it is not theoretically necessary, it is expected that the redistribution of party support will benefit one party more in relation to the other. It has been pointed out that the transfer of support between parties could balance out, leaving the normal vote essentially the same. This type of balance in a realignment has not occurred on a major scale in U.S. history;[6] however, the larger and more heterogeneous the population, the more probable is such a balance, since forces affecting party support may cancel each other out. Obviously, Pennsylvania is smaller and less heterogeneous than the entire United States. Hence, it is expected that an untouched normal vote is even less likely in the smaller data base.

Thus, realignment should be accompanied by notable changes in one party's percentage of the two-party vote. Since historical evidence documents the fact that the Democratic and Republican parties constituted the only major parties both before and after the 1930s, our interest is in their relationship to each other, as measured by percentages of the two-party vote. In this chapter, the Democratic percentage will be observed.

Minor parties should not be ignored, however. Their role as precursors of realignment and as possible "halfway houses" in the redistribution of party support has been suggested (Burnham 1970: 26–30; Key 1958: 290). In addition, an increase in support for minor parties would at least indicate an increased dissatisfaction with one or both of the major parties as instruments of political action in periods of unrest, when such action is desired. Thus, the total minor-party percentage of the total vote will also be examined over time as a second indication of realignment.[7] This indicator is certainly less definitive than others because "major" third-party activity is expected to precede realignment, and increases in the more constant, smaller minor parties' strengths are expected to coincide with realignment.[8]

Of the two indicators discussed so far, the percentage of the two-party vote can point to a redistribution of party support. The other indicator, minor-party activity, points mainly to the unrest and potential volatility in the electorate which should accompany realignment. Remembering that realignment is defined as a significant and durable change in the distribution of party support, we would like to develop a less ambiguous indicator of this latter type of change. It is possible to refine the first indicator by differentiating between types of counties in Pennsylvania and by examining variability within different groups of counties. This categorization will be done on an urban-rural index which is the same as the one used by Burnham (1970: 40). Certainly a durable increase in the percentage of Democratic votes in urban areas and a corresponding decrease in rural areas would be fairly clear evidence of a change in distribution of party support. The question of different behavior in different types of counties will be explored in more detail in the third section of this analysis.

A third and very powerful indicator of a change in distribution is the technique of autocorrelation (zero-order correlation coefficients measuring the strength of the linear relationship of the counties' voting patterns of one year with the patterns of the following year) used by Burnham (1970: 57–58) and by Pomper (1968: 105–107). Normally these correlations are high, above +.7. A major shift in the distribution of party support among the counties in a particular year would be indicated by an abnormally low coefficient. If the shift is durable, the coefficients for the following years would maintain strong readings. If a realignment occurred, according to the proposed definition, a relatively sharp drop in correlations is expected around the turn of the decade.

If these tests, particularly that involving the third indicator, reveal the realignment we assume occurred around 1930, a great advance has been made in confirming the validity of the proposed definitions and in developing useful indicators.[9] In addition, throughout the analysis we shall be able to derive substantively interesting propositions about the process of realignment. In a concluding section, then, we shall draw together these propositions and offer a theoretical perspective on the phenomenon of realignment.

THE VALIDATION OF DEFINITIONS:
THE PRESENCE OF REALIGNMENT

The purpose of this section is to examine a critical realignment and to evaluate the definitions and indicators which have been proposed. According to the definitions, critical realignment has occurred if there has been a reasonably sudden, significant change in the distribution of party support over relevant social groups. The realignment would be reflected in critical elections, since elections measure the level of party support at any given time. There are two ways in which the change in the distribution of party support can be conceptualized. Realignment does not necessarily imply a change in the mean of the distribution, which is roughly equivalent to the normal vote. However, a change in the mean *is* a change in the distribution and constitutes realignment if it is substantial and permanent. Thus, one model of realignment is a shift in the mean of the distribution corresponding to a similar change in party support among all social groups. A second model is a decrease in some groups and a parallel increase in others, which leaves the mean virtually the same as before the realignment. These models will be referred to as Model 1 and Model 2 respectively. (The mean and the shape of the distribution can of course both change.)

With these models in mind, an examination of the data can begin. The first indicator is the mean Democratic percentage in the two-party vote.[10] It has been hypothesized that a relatively sharp break in Democratic percentages over time will occur around 1930. This break would be analogous to a change in the normal vote which is evidence of a critical election and a critical realignment. As shown by figures 2.1 and 2.2, this hypothesis is surely confirmed. In the presidential elections of 1924 and 1928, the mean

FIGURE 2.1. Mean Democratic percentages of the two-party vote in Pennsylvania presidential elections

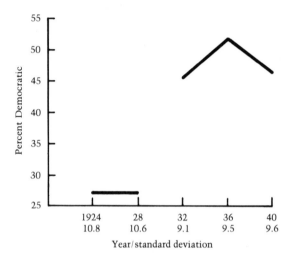

FIGURE 2.2. Mean Democratic percentages of the two-party vote in Pennsylvania congressional elections

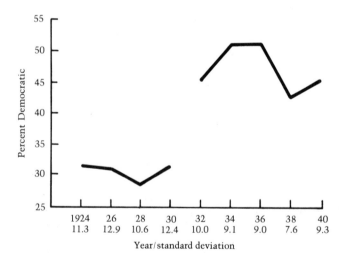

Democratic percentages are both under 30 percent. In the elections of 1932, 1936, and 1940, the percentages are over 45 percent in each case. The break occurs between 1928 and 1932 and indicates, quite preliminarily, that 1932 was a critical election. The congressional elections produce similar results. The means for the congressional elections from 1924 through 1930 are all close to or less than 30 percent. From 1932 through 1940, all the means are over 45 percent, except for that of 1938, which is not a major deviation from the pattern. The break here is between 1930 and 1932 and again points to 1932 as a critical election. In both congressional and presidential elections, the normal vote appears to have changed by about 15 percent entirely between one election and the next. Thus, the Democratic fortunes were sharply, substantially, and relatively permanently raised in 1932.

At this point, it is important to ask exactly what these figures say about the change in the distribution of party support which is requisite for a realignment and a critical election. So far, the analysis certainly provides no real insights into a change in the *shape* of the distribution over the relevant social groups. However, it does indicate a change at least in the mean of the distribution. Thus, even if the shape remains the same, the distribution of party support before 1930 is not the same as the distribution after 1930, since the Democratic percentage has increased among some if not all social groups. This pattern of change is depicted in Model 1 (figure 2.3).

These data suggest that Model 1 applies after 1930 and the distribution, at least in terms of the Democratic percentage has been pushed upward. In general, this is an upward push of approximately fifteen percentage points, which is judged to be substantial and which occurs fairly sharply. Therefore, the proposed definitions are provisionally validated, since they generate data consistent with the stated assumption that a critical realignment did in fact occur in the early 1930s.

A brief explanation of the trend of minor-party shares of the total vote confirms the timing of realignment. Although this percentage says nothing directly about the change in distribution of party support, it has been hypothesized that the shares will increase in critical elections because of negative voting. In other words, if the thrust of realignment was anti-Republican, the anti-Republican vote in a critical election would convert in a nearly one-to-one manner into a pro-Democratic vote. The gap in the one-to-one

FIGURE 2.3.   Distribution of party support: Model 1

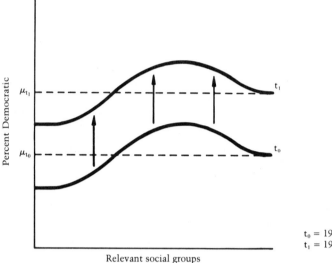

t_0 = 1928 and before.
t_1 = 1932 and after.

Relevant social groups

conversion represents votes against the Republicans but not for the Democrats and would be reflected in increases in minor-party percentages. These increases must be carefully distinguished from increases associated with a major third-party movement. The latter type of movement, which is expected to precede realignment, would represent a rising tide of dissatisfaction with the major parties.

The data shown in figures 2.4 and 2.5 confirm both hypotheses. In both presidential and congressional elections, there is a peak in minor-party percentages in 1932. There is, of course, a much higher level of minor-party percentages in 1924, which is associated with the La Follette Progressive movement. This result is hardly startling, since Key's theory of third-party movements as precursors of realignment is primarily based on this era (Key 1958: 289–290). The significant finding here is the peak in minor-party percentages in 1932, when there was no major third-party movement. This peak is further evidence that 1932 was a critical election.

Another powerful and often used indicator of electoral change

FIGURE 2.4. Mean minor-party percentages of the total vote in Pennsylvania presidential elections

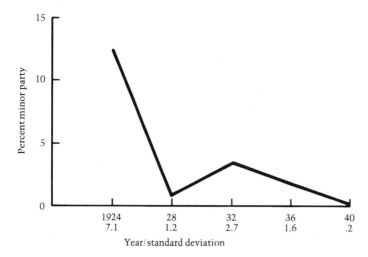

FIGURE 2.5. Mean minor-party percentages of the total vote in Pennsylvania congressional elections

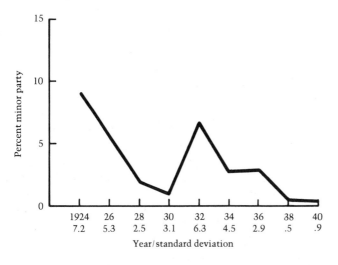

FIGURE 2.6. Autocorrelations of the two-party vote in Pennsylvania presidential elections

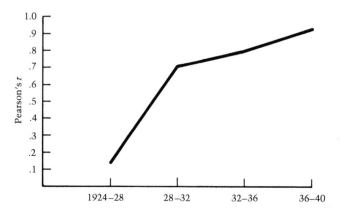

FIGURE 2.7. Autocorrelations of the two-party vote in Pennsylvania congressional elections

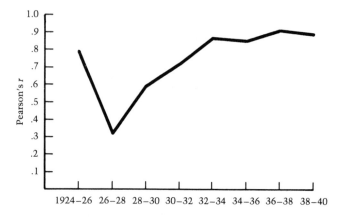

is the series of year-by-year autocorrelations. The patterns of county partisanship at two points in time are correlated to see if the patterns of one election persist to the next. Autocorrelations for both presidential and congressional elections are presented in figures 2.6 and 2.7 respectively. From Pomper's (1968: 105–108) and Burnham's (1970: 39, 57) work, it is known that, during periods of electoral stability, values of Pearson's r should be greater than .7 and are usually around .8 or .9. It has been hypothesized that r should take on an abnormally low value around 1930 as evidence of electoral discontinuity. Again, the data confirm the hypothesis. For presidential elections, the correlation between the Democratic percentage in 1924 and 1928 is very low compared with that of other years. These data are essentially the same as those presented by Burnham, who uses a more expanded time frame and provides evidence that the autocorrelations for the years before 1928 were also quite high (i.e., 1924 with 1920 and 1920 with 1916 are both greater than .8) (1970: 57).

The same analysis used on year-by-year congressional elections also identifies 1928 as the election with an abnormally low correlation coefficient. After 1928, the correlation coefficients climb to a new period of stability, leaving a breaking point at 1928. Again, it is important to ask exactly what the correlation coefficients say about the distribution of party support. Unlike the Democratic percentages of the two-party vote, the correlation coefficients do not provide any information about the level of the mean of the distribution. They do, however, provide evidence of a change in the shape of the distribution. A significantly low coefficient would indicate that the shape of the distribution of party support in one year is different from the shape in the previous year. High coefficients would indicate that the shape of the distribution remains basically intact over the years correlated. It is important to consider that, although the shape of the distribution may change, the mean may remain the same. Therefore, the discontinuity in these data suggests that Model 2 applies around 1928 and that the shape of the distribution at least has changed without indicating a change in the mean. This phenomenon is illustrated in figure 2.8.[11]

There is an apparent conflict between the correlation analysis and the mean Democratic percentage analysis which leads to the question of which election was critical, 1928 or 1932. It has been found that there was a significant change in the shape of the distribution of party support in 1928 without a change in the mean of the distribution and that there was a significant change in the mean in 1932 without a change in the shape of the distribution. This problem can be resolved felicitously if we propose that the following model of realignment applied during this era. Around 1928 there were pressures which brought about a change in the order of Democratic support among a variety of relevant social groups, although the mean level of this support remained low. And around 1932 the general level of support rose among all social groups, yet the order of support newly instituted in 1928 was maintained. Thus, a two-stage process of realignment is proposed in

FIGURE 2.8.   Distribution of party support: Model 2

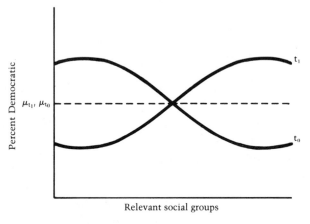

t_0 = Before 1928.
t_1 = After 1928.

which the shape of the distribution of party support changes first (as illustrated in fig. 2.8), and this newly shaped distribution is then pushed upward soon afterward (as illustrated in fig. 2.3).

To test this two-stage model empirically, the horizontal axis of the graph of distribution of party support, so far labeled "relevant social groups," must be more precisely defined. Any social variable can be attached to this axis, whether interval, ordinal, or nominal. Thus, the distribution of party support over members of certain occupations, over members of various age cohorts, over residents of different areas, or over counties with different degrees of urbanization can be investigated. Obviously, there is a good deal of overlap among the relevant social variables, and thus in reality the distribution can be best conceptualized as a multidimensional, multivariate distribution. However, to facilitate manageability, the distribution of party support over one important social variable —categories of counties on an urban-rural index—will be investigated. According to the proposed model, a change in the order of strength of Democratic support among the urban-rural categories is expected in 1928. Then, in 1932, an upward thrust is expected in all categories of counties. The data for this analysis are presented in table 2.1. The two categories with the highest Democratic support in 1924—rural and semirural—have the lowest Democratic support in 1928. The lowest category of Democratic support in 1924 is metropolitan areas, and these areas become the highest in 1928. In 1932, there is a general rise in the Democratic support for all counties, maintaining the approximate order of 1928. In 1932, rural areas increase above urban and semirural areas only temporarily, returning to the bottom in 1936. The congressional vote reveals a similar inversion and increase in the Democratic percentage between 1926 and 1938. Thus, the inversion of the order of support and the overall increase in the level of support occur at different times within the realignment.[12]

In summary, the data generated by the definitions and indicators allow the conclusion that a realignment occurred around 1930. This realignment took the form of a two-stage change in the distribution of party support. The first stage followed the scheme illustrated in figure 2.8, and the second stage followed the scheme illustrated in figure 2.3. The final result of the realignment was a distribution similar to the one illustrated in figure 2.9. The first stage in the change of distribution occurred around 1928 and was almost wholly reflected in the 1928 elections. This is consistent with the rise in 1928 of ethnic and religious cleavages. The second

TABLE 2.1. Comparisons of Democratic Support

Type of County	Presidential Elections Percent Democratic (Rank)			
	1924	1928	1932	1936
Rural	35.8 (1)	23.7 (4)	47.7 (2)	47.0 (4)
Semirural	28.0 (2)	23.8 (3)	44.6 (4)	50.5 (3)
Urban	24.0 (3)	31.8 (2)	45.9 (3)	55.2 (2)
Metropolitan	19.1 (4)	45.2 (1)	51.2 (1)	63.6 (1)

Type of County	Congressional Elections Percent Democratic (Rank)			
	1926	1930	1934	1938
Rural	36.8 (1)	33.8 (2)	49.9 (4)	41.6 (4)
Semirural	31.0 (3)	30.5 (3)	50.1 (3)	41.8 (3)
Urban	31.8 (2)	34.1 (1)	53.2 (1)	44.2 (2)
Metropolitan	18.3 (4)	25.2 (4)	51.6 (2)	51.4 (1)

FIGURE 2.9. Distribution of party support

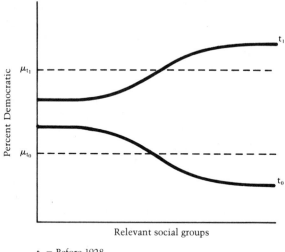

t₀ = Before 1928.
t₁ = After 1932.

stage occurred around 1932 and was predominantly reflected in the elections of that year. This stage, presumably associated with the economic collapse and with the perceived poor Republican performance, would be expected to have a relatively uniform effect on the electorate. By the proposed definitions, then, the elections of both 1928 and 1932 would be critical elections. Since critical elections and realignment have both been detected, it can be concluded that the definitions as proposed are accurate and operationally meaningful. Similarly, the indicators based on these definitions provide some interesting insights into the process of realignment during the late twenties and early thirties.

CRITICAL REALIGNMENT:
A THEORETICAL PERSPECTIVE

The purpose of this concluding section is to review some of the findings presented earlier, compare them to the conclusions of other political scientists, and suggest possible theoretical implications about the nature of realignment and its causes and about the place of realignment in a larger theory of American democracy. The logical starting point of theory building is the identification of necessary concepts. In this study of realignment, two fundamental concepts were introduced. First is the idea of social groups or groups of people with a similar characteristic or interest. This concept is accepted as a given and does not require detailed discussion here. It is assumed that the electorate can be divided into numerous politically relevant social groups. Second is the concept of party support. Party support is specifically identified as the potential strength of a given party in an election at any moment in time. The partisan results of an election, therefore, constitute a measure of party support at that moment. The important difference between election results and party support is that party support is an ongoing condition of the electorate, a continuous variable, whereas election results are certainly discrete. It is also important to note that any additional concepts used to analyze voting behavior can be applied equally well to party support. Those mentioned in this study include party identification and party image.

Using the two fundamental concepts of social groups and party support, the more complex concept of a distribution of party support can be developed. If the electorate is divided into a number of relevant social groups, each group will have a level of party support—that is, party support is distributed over relevant social groups. The completion of this concept requires that the dimension of time also be included. Since party support is continuous over time, the distribution of party support is also continuous over time. Given this concept, critical realignment has been defined as a change in this distribution. This definition is qualified by three conditions: the change must be significant in relation to the universe of social groups under consideration; it must be long-lasting; and it must occur fairly rapidly.

Before placing this concept of critical realignment into a theory, there are some inherent characteristics of the concept which need discussion. This study has demonstrated that the concept can be applied well to state-level data. But the important question remains as to how well this concept fits levels above and below the state. This consideration ties in closely to the problem of continuity. On the one hand, the social groupings of the electorate will correspond to reality more closely if the groupings themselves are minutely defined. A division into three or four social groups is an obvious oversimplification of the electorate. The more numerous these social groups become, the more closely this part of the graph will approach continuity. On the other hand, if the electorate is broken into social groups so minute that the number of individuals in each group is severely limited, there will not be continuity along the axis of party support. If there are only two individuals in a group, that group can have only three levels of party support: 0, 50 percent, and 100 percent. In general, if N equals the number of individuals in a group, that group can have $N + 1$ levels of party support. One hundred members per group would allow any unit percentage of party support, which is sufficiently close to continuity for most analytical purposes. The conclusion to be reached from this analysis is that the concept of realignment is appropriate for any area with a sufficient population to provide 100 or more individuals for each social grouping employed. Substantively, this concept could be used to analyze the electoral behavior of any major city, most sizable counties, any state, or the nation as a whole. But an analysis based on this concept may falter in lesser municipalities such as townships and small towns. In effect, realignment is a macropolitical, rather than a micropolitical, concept.

There is another approach to the conceptualization of realignment, initially proposed by Schattschneider (1960: 62–78) and further developed by Sundquist (1973: 11–25). This concept pictures society divided by a "line of cleavage" which is also a rough division of the electoral coalitions of the parties. Presumably, supporters of one party would fall on one side of the line and supporters of the other party would fall on the other side. It is this approximate separation which persists over time, and the relocation of this line indicates realignment. The logic of this concept relies on the ability of an individual to support either one party or the other and to fall either on one side of the line or the other but not on both sides. This reasoning is not compatible with the concept of a distribution proposed here. Unlike an individual, the decision of a group to support a party is not a yes-no decision but a matter of degree. There is no line of cleavage among social groups which fits onto the distribution.

To choose between the two concepts, the distribution seems to be the more useful for three main reasons. First, the use of a line or lines of cleavage is an oversimplification of the situation in the electorate. It assumes that individuals as members of groups will behave with their group's interest at heart. Thus, if there is a cleavage between the interests of two clusters of groups, each represented by a party, the individual members of a group will fall on one side of the line of cleavage and vote for one party. There is an immediate problem of an individual who is a member of two groups, each of which falls on an opposite side of the line of cleavage. Even disregarding the problem of overlaps, this assumption is dubious in light of current theories of group behavior (Olson 1971). Thus, the electorate would have to be considered as a body of individuals divided by a line of cleavage and not as a composition of groups. Second, then, the potential explanatory power and analytical importance of groups are all but lost with the Schattschneider-Sundquist concept, because implicitly they regard the electorate as a collection of individuals rather than of groups. Third, the distribution concept leads directly to operational statements allowing the distribution itself to be measured. The line of cleavage, on the other hand, is extremely difficult to operationalize meaningfully. The debate, in essence, is between continuity and discreteness. Measurements and tests are always discrete, even when continuity is the ideal. The argument is that the concept of a distribution is closer to a continuous reality than that of the line of cleavage.

If the concept of realignment as developed in this essay is at variance with the one used by Schattschneider and Sundquist, it nevertheless is quite compatible with four theoretical propositions derived from but extending the work of these and other scholars. The first such proposition considers realignment as a phenomenon caused by social readjustments and party response, with effects on the entire range of voting behavior. This proposition begins with the assertion that there are certain social changes accompanied by building tension among certain groups in the society (Burnham 1970: 9, 66–67; Sundquist 1973: 29–30, 276). These tensions are usually in the form of a divergence of interests among various clusters of groups. This divergence may involve a specific issue, such as Prohibition, or a more diffuse grievance. The result is some type of objective cleavage to which different groups react differently. Sundquist considers such a cleavage specifically issue-related, which cuts sharply across society. He emphasizes that profound social changes are not adequate to produce realignment but must give rise to political issues (1973: 276). The political issues polarize society; they force groups to move to one side or the other of the cleavage. This situation is only true if one accepts Sundquist's implicit definition of groups as bodies of individuals either for or against a particular issue (1973: 11–14). When one does this, Sundquist's analysis becomes tautological: groups move to one side or the other of an issue cleavage because they are either on one side or the other of the issue. It is more analytically useful to define groups according to demographic or socioeconomic variables and to assess how they react to an objective cleavage. It is also important to note that such an objective cleavage can result purely from increasing relative strengths of one group over another.[13]

This discussion becomes clearer when a second proposition is considered: the political parties respond in some way to the cleavage. There are several alternatives to this response. The parties themselves may diverge, whether intentionally or not, with the divergence corresponding to the cleavage of interest. Such was probably the case in 1928. There was a perception among the old American WASP groups that the increasing power of the ethnic groups was against their interest. Al Smith's candidacy reinforced this perception. Pennsylvania's most ethnic counties rose sharply in Democratic support around 1928 as a result of Smith's campaign, and the least ethnic counties declined just as sharply. Yet no group of counties achieved a level of Democratic support over 40 percent. The ethnic counties were not as much *for* the Democrats because of Smith as the nonethnic counties were *against* the Democrats. The objective cleavage of interest, paralleled by a divergence of the parties' images, does *not* produce a yes-no, on-one-side-of-the-line-or-the-other situation. The response of even the most directly involved groups perceiving a clear cleavage is a matter of degree.

The 1932 election further illustrates this point. There was obviously no cleavage of the simple form, pro or anti-Depression. Some groups were more afflicted by the economic hardship than others. These groups had more of an interest in ending the Depression than the others, although everyone was against it. Here was a cleavage in interests to which the most affected groups reacted the most strongly. The Democrats' image of activism presumably appealed most to these groups in light of the minimal improvement brought by the Republicans' conservative policies. The data from Pennsylvania confirm the proposition that the counties most affected by the Depression responded with the most Democratic support. This question of how different groups perceive a cleavage and how strongly they react to it in terms of their images of the political parties is fertile ground for further research (see Trilling 1976b: chaps. 5–7).

If the parties do not separate over the cleavage, they must both remain on one side or the other. If the voters do not see the parties as meaningfully distinct with respect to a cleavage, then they must be close together. Sundquist points out that a party response which puts the two parties together in the eyes of the electorate, whether by intention or by inaction, establishes a climate conducive to a third-party movement (1973: 289). This seems to have been the case with the Whig party before the Civil War. Research concerning this type of party response will certainly be useful both in clarifying the perceptions and reactions of social groups when the major parties provide no alternative and in determining the roots of significant third-party activity.

The third theoretical proposition is that a major social change and a divergence of interests act together with some type of party response to cause a critical realignment. The redistribution of party support among social groups need not be accompanied by higher electoral participation. One would expect that social dislocations and tensions would produce high intensity and consequently high turnout in elections occurring during a realignment. But a more appropriate measure of the intensity of an election during a realignment may be the difference between levels of party support. Since turnout itself can be suppressed by some exogenous factor, the decisiveness of the election results, reflected by the gap between the levels of party support for the two major parties, may be a more appropriate indicator of intensity.[14] Decisive results which are the reverse of the well-established levels of support, such as in 1932, are surely a clear indication of a high-intensity election, since strong, unilateral partisan forces are necessary to produce such a reversal. It is entirely possible that such intense, unilateral partisan forces can suppress turnout among voters loyal to the disadvantaged party. Therefore, it can be very misleading to equate high intensity with high turnout; critical elections are expected to be high-intensity elections but not necessarily high-turnout elections.

The fourth proposition, developed elsewhere by the present authors, is that the realignment causes certain changes relating to party identification and the core-periphery structure of the electorate. These changes seem to follow the realignment and reinforce the new distribution of party support. This last proposition, which has received the least scholarly attention, certainly deserves much more careful investigation.

At this point, we can address the larger, normative question about the role of critical realignment in the American democratic polity. Schattschneider has advanced the brilliant argument that the requirements of a democratic system of government dictate not the number of decisions the people should make but how important those decisions should be: "A good democratic system protects the public against the demand that it do impossible things" (1960: 140). Many commentators and political analysts look upon the American system with despair because of their unrealistic expectations. Schattschneider criticizes these analysts for expecting 215 million people to act the same way and make the same kind of decisions as one monarch or as a small group of legislators (1960: 141). In a mass democracy, one *cannot* expect the people to make governmental decisions on a day-to-day basis, or even occasionally, concerning a plethora of small matters. Instead, Schattschneider concludes, the people should, on occasion, make a few immensely important decisions which guide the general policy output of the government.

Within the framework of this argument, the concept of critical realignment becomes quite important. A general theory can be constructed as follows: the occurrence of critical realignment is a decision of the electorate which directly guides the functioning of the government. This theory rests on the one basic assumption that realignment is a constituent act, a choice of voters. This assumption (Burnham 1970: 9–10, 68–69) can be logically deduced from the fact that a change in the distribution of party support is essentially a composite of decisions by many individuals, influenced as they may be by group interests, either to change their party support or not to support any party. However, the definition of realignment requires only a change in the distribution, which could result from the coercive removal or authoritative enfranchisement of a particular social group. An example of the coercive removal of a group from the electorate is the suppression of black voting in the South, which was commonplace until fairly recently. Although the critical realignments at the national level do not seem to be associated with such changes by force, the assumption of a constituent act certainly deserves further investigation.

Beyond this assumption, there are three propositions which must be true in order to confirm the theory. First, critical realignments must occur in reality. Sundquist (1973: 39–217) provides evidence that critical realignments have occurred in many states and in the nation at various points in history. Second, critical realignment must be a rational act of the electorate. A minimum degree of rationality implies that, where there is a clear divergence of group interests and corresponding partisan alternatives, groups do not react randomly or act against their perceived interests. Our earlier analysis demonstrates that this minimum amount of rationality was apparent in the realignment around 1930 in Pennsylvania. Third, and most important, realignment must cause the government's policy output to flow in a direction consistent with the electorate's decision. It is implicit in Schattschneider's argument that the realignments of the 1890s and 1930s had such an effect on the national level. Burnham (1970: 9) contends that realignments are "intimately associated with . . . transformations in large clusters of policy." King and Seligman have provided further evidence of this link:

> Institutional change in Congress, to the extent that it is reflected in declining retirement rates and increasing seniority, has not been incremental, but constitutes periodic or cyclical responses to the new issues, outlooks, recruitment patterns, and voting identification that gave rise to the critical elections of 1896 and 1932. (1974: 12)

These authors further suggest that

> . . . the changes in the membership of congressional elites that result from critical elections play a significant part in congressional policy direction. Although we have not proven that new members of Congress elected during a critical election are responsible for legislative innovation, we have shown that they are catalysts for such innovation. To say that critical elections are turning points includes not only what "starts" them, but also what policy changes the new electoral coalitions *make possible* as a result of the changed complexion of congressional alignments. (1974: 43)

Nonetheless, there has yet to be a systematic analysis of the changes in governmental policy output and their relation to critical realignments. Such a contribution would surely be worthwhile and would add to the plausibility of this theory.

Thus, two theories of realignment have been suggested. The first involves a set of propositions which deal with the causes and effects of critical realignment in an electoral universe. The second deals with the importance of realignment to democracy in America. Data have been provided which support various propositions from these theories, but it is clear that some critical lacunae remain. It has been suggested where research is needed most. These theories seem particularly important and deserving of rigorous treatment now, since only recently have scholars begun to change the lines of their thinking about American history and politics to include such dynamic relationships over time.

NOTES

Note: All data reported in this chapter were provided by the archive of the Inter-University Consortium of Political and Social Research at the University of Michigan.

1   For discussion of the apparent periodicity of American electoral realignments and of the role of realignments in American political history, see Chambers and Burnham (1967), Sundquist (1973), Ward (1973), Jahnige (1971), Price (1971), Ginsberg (1972), and Seitz (1974).

2   Calculations are as follows: (1) 30 years per party system × 4 party systems = 120 years; (2) 140 years (1793–1933) − 120 years = 20 years; (3) 20 years ÷ 3 realignments = ca. 7 years per critical realignment. These calculations, of course, apply to critical realignment at the national level. Such temporal limitations may not be appropriate at other levels, where elections may occur more frequently. In the mathematical sense of limits, however, these estimations still apply. It is expected that critical realignments at a lower level with a smaller electorate would take no more time than critical realignments at the national level. Certainly, changes in distribution of party support would become significant sooner in a smaller electorate.

3   For research into the concept of party image, see Black and Rabinowitz (1974), Kessel (1968: chap. 9), Matthews and Prothro (1964, 1966a: 369–404, 1966b), Meisel (1973: 63–126), Pomper (1975: chap. 7), and Trilling (1975a, 1975b, 1976b).

4   This point is well established, and thorough documentation is hardly necessary. See Burnham: "There is an extremely sharp post-1929 break in the Pennsylvania data with the preceding structure of electoral politics" (1970: 54–55). See also Sundquist: "The realignment of the 1930s came suddenly" (1973: 183).

5   The work of other scholars indicates that the initially important cleavage may have been of an urban-rural nature, later taking on economic or class overtones. These cleavages certainly overlap, to a great extent. See Sundquist (1973: 200–204) and Jahnige (1971).

6   Apparently the forces prompting realignment have overwhelmingly favored one party over the other, in the manner suggested by Campbell (1966b), who argues that forces of partisanship typically are reinforced by forces of stimulation to produce surging electoral landslides.

7 As calculated in this chapter, the minor-party vote equals the total vote minus the two-party vote. Thus, it includes "scattering" votes as well as votes cast for minor parties appearing on the ballot. The formula for the percentage is as follows:

$$\text{minor-party percentage} = \frac{\text{total vote} - \text{major vote}}{\text{total vote}}$$

8 Major third parties are those described by Burnham (1970: 28). Examples are the Populists of Bryan in the 1890s, the La Follette Progressives in 1924, and perhaps the American Independents (Wallace) in 1968. The smaller, more constant minor parties are the Socialist, Communist, and Labor parties. Since a general increase in minor-party activity is a characteristic of realignment, not an integral part of the proposed definition nor crucial to the analysis, the indicator described here does not differentiate between types of minor parties. An increase in such activity, regardless of the type of minor party involved, is only further evidence of a suspected realignment. It is by no means proof.

9 Burnham (1970) uses several other tests for realignment, including a discontinuity variable technique (p. 13), a t-test for difference of means (p. 14), and the construction of a pseudo Z-score (p. 42). These methods were not used in this study because of the lack of the sufficiently long time dimension required for the meaningful application of these tests.

10 The statistics employed by these indicators are straightforward and produce results which are easily interpreted. However, one caveat remains: the meaning and the suddenness of change in distribution of party support are both subjective judgments.

11 The low correlation between 1924 presidential voting and 1928 presidential voting is not the result of La Follette's personal influence in 1924 or Smith's in 1928. Congressional correlations are strong between 1924 and 1926 (.79) but weak between 1924 and 1928 (.47) and between 1926 and 1928 (.32), then strong again in pairwise comparisons beginning with 1928 to 1930, thus pointing to the critical breaking point in 1928.

12 Again the possible special influence of La Follette and Smith on these data can be dismissed. Pairwise presidential voting correlations are strong through 1920 to 1924, weak between 1924 and 1928 (.06), and strong again beginning with the 1928 to 1932 pair, as reported by Burnham (1970: 57, table 3.8). La Follette's influence on these data is not distinctive, since 1924 correlates with 1920 as 1920 does with 1916; Smith's influence is not distinctive, since 1928 correlates with 1932 as 1932 does with 1936.

13 Thus, if the ethnic groups were increasing in numbers because of higher birthrates, as Lubell argues, the old American WASP groups may have perceived a potential loss of political dominance or an erosion of their value system as a result. This situation would produce an objective cleavage in the interests of certain groups to which the WASP groups may have reacted more strongly than the ethnic groups. Here there is no *real* political issue but a divergence of interests to which different groups react differently. See Lubell (1965: 29–35).

14 The results of the 1972 election, however, indicate that even this proposed indicator is not infallible.

3

Methodological Issues
in the Study of Realignment

DAVID H. NEXON

While any particular study of some phenomenon believed to be associated with realignment will have its unique set of methodological problems, two methodological issues seem to have particular importance in this volume and will be addressed in this chapter. The first is the specification of which phenomena are to be considered realignments; the second is the problem of inferring causation in the study of realignments.

The first issue is particularly crucial. No discussion of competing theories of the causes or consequences of realignment can proceed very far without resolving it. Unfortunately, most studies of realignment have proceeded without much attention being paid to defining realignment in a very precise way, and, more important, the reasons the individual researcher has had for considering particular elections or periods to be examples of realignment have seldom been specified. One influential study, for example, has deduced causes of realignment from a series of historical case studies; nowhere in this otherwise excellent book, however, is there any systematic discussion of the reasons the author had for believing that the elections he chose *and not others* were examples of realignments (Sundquist 1973).

This problem of specification becomes even more critical when we move from discussions of the causes of realignments to their consequences. A number of authors, for example, have recently made longitudinal studies of such phenomena as judicial behavior, output of public policy, and so on, and have concluded that the regularities they found were associated with realigning elections. Obviously, one cannot take such findings very seriously without deciding that the periods identified as being associated with greater than average changes in the dependent variables were in fact realignments.

In this chapter, I discuss operational measures of realignment and, in view of these measures, abstract from the literature a judgment about which elections should be considered realigning. I will make some comments on the measurement of secular realignment, but most of my focus will be on realigning elections—what Mc-Michael and Trilling, in the previous chapter, call critical elections. After identifying critical elections, I will return to the second issue noted above—the problem of inferring causation.

DEFINITION AND MEASUREMENT OF REALIGNMENT

McMichael and Trilling abstract from the relevant literature a definition of realignments as durable and significant redistributions of party support. They say that "a critical realignment is a realignment in which the bulk of the redistribution takes place within reasonably defined time limits," while critical elections are elections which "display" most or a major portion of the elements of a critical realignment. To rephrase this definition slightly, a critical election might be defined as an election in which the correlates of habitual party support change in a widespread, systematic, and relatively abrupt way.

Two general types of changes in party support can occur. First, the relative support given to each party by demographic or opinion groups in the population can change. Second, the proportion of the total population supporting each party can change. One example of the first case would be a situation in which Catholics moved disproportionately to the Democratic party, while Protestants moved disproportionately to the Republican party. If these changes were of equal absolute magnitudes (implying, of course, that the Catholic movement was stronger in percentage terms), the overall percentage of the population supporting each party would not change. The 1960 election seems to have been the occasion of a movement of exactly this type (Nexon 1970). In the second case, the proportion of the population supporting each party would change, but the relative support given to each party by various groups would remain about the same. An example of this kind of critical election might be the election of 1932, in which there seems to have been a general swing toward the Democrats throughout the society. It is probably the case that most critical elections exhibit both types of changes.

This definition of a critical election as one in which there are sharp changes in the correlates of party support seems rather straightforward, except for two problems. First, most discussions of critical elections imply that they involve changes in party support that last for at least several elections. This distinction grows largely out of theoretical work by the Michigan Survey Research Center that distinguished between short-term and long-term components of the vote (Converse 1966). The short-term component was a response to particular issues or personalities of the current election, while the long-term component was associated with party identification and set the contours of the "normal vote" that would occur in the absence of short-term forces.

This distinction is important. The Eisenhower elections, for example, involved a short-term movement to the Republican presidential candidate. The correlates of party identification did not change, however. Moreover, Eisenhower's sweeping electoral success was not, except for the 1952 election, carried over into any comparable movement to the Republicans at the level of congressional voting. Here, with personal candidate factors far less important, the normal vote asserted itself, and the Democrats controlled both houses of Congress after 1954 throughout the Eisenhower years.

No writer on the subject of realignment would characterize the Eisenhower elections as critical. These elections would be distinguished from true realignments on the grounds that their effect was not durable and that the normal vote did not change during these years.

The criterion of durability, unfortunately, poses a theoretical problem. First, it suggests that we can identify realignments only retrospectively. More seriously, it seems intuitively somewhat unreasonable in terms of some of our beliefs about the causes of realignment. The reader will notice that I define a critical election as one in which the correlates of *habitual* party support change. Habitual party support might be considered the normal vote or the long-term component of the voting act. Suppose we have something that, by all criteria but durability, appears to be a realigning election. There is a change in the correlates of party support as measured by the relation of the vote to various demographic and opinion variables. More striking, the change is not confined to the vote alone but is reflected both in a change in the correlates of party identification and in party images. If no further major events occur, we would expect this to be a realigning election that would set the contours of the normal vote for a generation or more.

But let us suppose that, a year after the election, a major depression strikes. The parties take opposing stands on the best way to deal with it, and these stands create a new dimension of issue cleavage in the public. In the next presidential election, the correlates of party support again change dramatically, and this change fixes the contours of the normal vote for many years. In this situation, the first election would not, by a definition that relied on durability as a necessary criterion, be classified as critical. Yet, if not for the accident of the depression, the first election would undoubtedly have had a durable impact on the normal vote and would have been classified as realigning. It is rather strange to define an event not in terms of its inherent qualities but in terms of subsequent occurrences completely independent of the event.

If we allow for the possibility of a critical election that does not result in *durable* change in the correlates of party support, we could define critical elections as systematic changes in the correlates of party support that would be expected to be enduring in the absence of other subsequent changes. This revised definition, however, presents a second problem. How could we measure party support in a way that would pick up such a change? Clearly, the most obvious measure of party support—the vote—will not tell us whether a change could be expected to last, since the vote is produced by both short-term and long-term forces.

An obvious alternative would be to examine not only the correlates of the vote but the correlates of party identification and to use the latter as our primary criterion of the occurrence of a realignment. This would avoid the problem of measuring durability, since party identification is relatively independent of short-term forces. Unfortunately, this measurement presents two problems. First, as McMichael and Trilling point out, some scholars believe that shifts in party identification lag behind shifts in the vote. This is almost certainly true in that the full impact of a shift in party identification will not be apparent until several elections after the realignment, since such a shift affects the younger voters most strongly and they become a larger proportion of the total electorate as time passes.[1] On the other hand, based on the experience of the 1964 realignment, a sharp shift in the correlates of party identification almost certainly occurs at the time of the realignment, even if the total shift will not reach its absolute magnitude for some years (Pomper 1972).

The second problem with employing party identification as the primary indicator of durable party support is that it is obviously unusable in the era before opinion polls. This is the most serious objection to employing it, since most of our studies of realignment must draw on historical materials where our basic datum on party support is the aggregate distribution of the vote.

Given these difficulties, I would take the position that we should regard realignments as having taken place when either of the following occurs: (1) there is a durable change in the correlates of the vote; (2) there is a change, durable or not, in the correlates of party identification. For periods in which no poll data are available, sharp changes in the vote which do not endure should be considered cases of possible realignment on which other sources of evidence should be brought to bear. Given this position, what methods have been used to identify realignments and what results have they produced?

THE IDENTIFICATION OF CRITICAL REALIGNMENTS

There have been two attempts to identify realignments across the whole span of U.S. history. Each used different methods to identify realignments, and each came to somewhat different conclusions. The first, by Walter Dean Burnham, compares the average vote for the Democrats in each possible set of five continuous presidential elections to the average vote in the five succeeding presidential elections (Burnham 1970). The midpoint of this combined set of ten is moved up one election at a time, so that all possible sets of ten continuous elections are compared. Where there is a sharp, discontinuous break in the average, indicating that there has been a sudden shift of the vote which endured in some form for at least five elections, Burnham concludes that a realigning election has occurred. His statistics show four elections resembling realignments: 1856, 1876, 1896, and 1932. Of this group, Burnham dismisses 1876 as a true realignment on the grounds that it was associated with the overthrow of Reconstruction. It was not so much that there was a shifting of loyalties to the Democrats on the part of the population—rather, the Democratic vote was artificially depressed by the Federal occupation of the South until that year.

Burnham's method is obviously well adapted to identifying realignments that dramatically change the party balance and endure over the course of at least five elections. However, it does not reveal coalitional shifts within the parties that do not dramatically affect the party balance.

The second attempt to identify realignments, conducted by Gerald Pomper, avoids some of the problems of the Burnham method while producing problems of its own (Pomper 1967). Pomper compares the percentage of an individual state's vote for the Democratic presidential candidate in a particular election with the same state's vote in the previous election. From the results of this comparison for all the states, a correlation statistic, Pearson's r, is computed. In cases where the correlation between an election and its predecessor is strikingly low, Pomper concludes that a realignment has probably occurred. He also considers such supplementary data as the correlation with the average vote in the preceding four elections. Particularly valuable is his technique of generating a correlation matrix of each election against every other election. This matrix is then inspected for elections which appear to be weakly correlated with previous elections and strongly correlated with subsequent elections, suggesting a durable shift in the vote.

Pomper's method is well adapted to identifying changes in each party's coalition where the groups shifting are more concentrated in some states than in others. Because of the way Pearson's r is computed, a change in the overall proportion of the population supporting each party will not be picked up by this statistic if the decline or the increase in support is evenly distributed among the states. Thus, Pomper's method will not capture the second type of realignment discussed previously—a task to which Burnham's method is well adapted—but will identify some of the changes in party coalitions that escape Burnham's methodology.

Pomper's method has several problems associated with it. First, as noted above, it will not pick up changes in party support that are due to uniform changes throughout the population. Second, it will not identify changes in party coalitions, except where the shifting groups are differentially distributed between the states. Finally, while Burnham's method risks missing a realignment that is rapidly superseded by another realignment, Pomper's method makes the equally serious error of risking the belief that a short-term swing of the vote is really a realignment. This error is a possibility because Pomper bases his classification of elections primarily on a comparison of the correlation of the vote with the immediately preceding election.

Relying primarily on the method of comparing each election to its immediate predecessor, Pomper shows the elections of 1836, 1896, and 1960 to 1964 to be converting and those of 1864 and 1928 to 1932 to be realigning (1967: 562). (The distinction between converting and realigning elections is not relevant to the present analysis and will therefore be neglected.) His and Burnham's results, based on their different methods of identification, obviously disagree in several respects. Pomper classifies 1864 as realigning, while Burnham thinks the Civil War realignment occurred in 1856. Pomper also, unlike Burnham, classifies 1928 as realigning, and he ignores 1876, which Burnham's statistics pinpoint. Both agree that 1896 and 1932 are realigning elections. There is no necessary disagreement between Pomper and Burnham over 1836, 1960, and 1964. Burnham's method requires data on five elections before and after a presidential election before he can identify it as realigning: these data do not exist for 1836, 1960, and 1964.[2]

Why do Burnham and Pomper identify a different election as being the base of the Civil War realignment? It is easy to see why Burnham does not identify 1864 as a realigning year. The Democrats received about 45 percent of the vote that year, a drop of less than 3 percent from their 1860 total and almost exactly the same vote they received in 1856. The 1868 percentage was less than 1 point higher than the Democratic vote of 1860. Clearly, 1864 did not represent much of a long-term shift in the overall percentage of support enjoyed by the Democrats. On the other hand, Pomper's data make it clear that the coalitional base of the Democrats' support changed dramatically from 1860 to 1864. The correlation between the 1860 state-by-state percentage and the vote in 1864 was only .55 in the northern states that held elections in both years. The correlation of the 1868 vote with the 1864 vote, however, was a high of .84.

The 1856 case is more curious. Burnham finds a shift because the Democratic percentage of the major-party vote dropped in that year from an average of around 50 percent in the preceding five elections to around 46 percent in the five elections from 1856 on. It is surprising that Pomper's figures show no realignment, however, considering that 1856 was marked by a tremendous furor over the Kansas-Nebraska Act, an issue which seemed to pit North against South, and by the rise of the Republican party, whose basic *raison d'être* was to oppose the expansion of slavery.

What seems to have happened is that, while the election did have a powerful effect on the political parties, the components of that effect did not show up fully in Pomper's statistics. First, there were widespread intrastate shifts in Democratic support. Obvious-ly, Pomper's state-by-state correlations would not pick up these shifts. Second, much of the net change in the vote was not reflected in the Democratic totals but resulted from the demise of the Whigs. It seems unreasonable not to regard as a critical election one that sees the elimination of a major party and the rise of one major and one minor new party. But Pomper's figures are based only on the state-by-state vote for the Democrats. Although there was some regional variation in this state-by-state vote, it was not as great as it would have been had the Republicans provided the Democrats' only opposition. Thus, in the North, the Democratic vote dropped from about 49.8 percent in 1852 to about 42.5 percent in 1856. In the South, the Democratic vote increased from 55.3 percent to 58 percent. In the North, most of the votes the Demo-crats did not get went to the Republicans (40.5 percent), with a smaller group going to the American party (17 percent). In the South, the Republicans got virtually no votes, but the American party polled about 42 percent. Thus, it is clear why Pomper and Burnham get different results for these two years, and it seems reasonable to call both 1856 and 1864 realigning elections.

The 1928 election is another area of disagreement between Pomper and Burnham, with only Pomper showing a realignment. Again, the reason for the disagreement is not mysterious. While the Democrats' share of the two-party vote was higher than that of the preceding two elections—about 40 percent versus about 34 percent in 1924 and 36 percent in 1920—it was less than they got in 1916 and fades into insignificance compared to the Roosevelt years. Thus, Burnham's figures would not show realignment. On the other hand, states and population groups moved in very dif-ferent directions in 1928. Thus, Pomper's figures show 1928 stand-ing out fairly sharply from the elections that preceded it (Pearson's *r* of .77 with the 1924 election). It is not clear, however, whether 1928 should be considered a short-term swing of the vote or a re-alignment. Pomper's correlation matrix shows that 1928 is weakly correlated not only with the elections that preceded it but also with the elections that followed it.

1960 is a similar case. Extending Pomper's matrix forward from 1964 shows 1960 to be weakly correlated with both preceding and subsequent elections. As noted previously, poll data show an in-crease in the proportion of Catholics identifying with the Demo-crats; this increase is partly washed away by the 1964 election.

There is nothing ambiguous about the 1964 case, however. Independent calculations by the author reveal that, using Pomper's methodology, the 1964 election is weakly or negatively correlated with preceding elections and highly correlated with the 1968 and 1972 elections. Poll data show that the 1964 election is associated with a marked increase in the proportion of liberals on civil rights and welfare policies who identify with the Democrats (Pomper 1972).

One election which is identified by neither Pomper nor Burnham as a realigning one but which may have that character is the election of 1936. Some evidence suggests that this election marked a dramatic shift along class lines, with lower-class groups moving to the Democrats and upper-class groups moving to the Republicans. Pomper's figures might not reveal such a shift because of his focus on interstate movements, while Burnham's figures might also fail to reveal such a realignment if the net effect of the shift was to leave the overall balance unchanged. The evidence suggesting that such a movement did occur is fragmentary but persuasive.

First, Burnham's own investigation of the relationship of the vote to such demographic characteristics as Catholicism and urbanism suggests that the Democratic majority of 1936 was quite different from that of 1932. In Pennsylvania, in 1932, the percentage of the variance of the vote by county explained by the proportion Catholic and the proportion urban is a near zero 1.5 percent; in 1936 and 1940, the percentages explained are a substantial 29.7 and 26.4. As Burnham himself says, in Pennsylvania at least, "the pattern [of the vote] in 1932 corresponds much more closely to that of the Democratic percentages in 1916–24 than to . . . those of 1936 and 1940" (1970: 56). A detailed discussion of Pennsylvania data generally supporting the conclusion that the 1936 election involved a further realignment may be found in the McMichael and Trilling chapter in this book.

Moreover, as Burnham points out, strong inferential evidence is provided by the *Literary Digest*'s famous debacle. As students of polling know, the *Literary Digest*'s predictions were based on a massive sample drawn primarily from telephone books and lists of automobile owners. Since wealthy people were more likely to have telephones and automobiles than the less well off, there was a strong upper-class bias to the sample. This made no difference in the accuracy of the prediction as long as the vote was not divided along class lines but would be disastrous given today's well-known Democratic advantage among the lower classes. The *Literary Digest* was very accurate in 1932, but it predicted a Landon victory in 1936 and shortly thereafter went out of business. George Gallup, using a scientifically selected sample and knowing the *Digest*'s sampling procedure, not only predicted the election much more accurately but was even able to predict by how much the *Digest* would be wrong (Gallup 1940).

It seems fair, then, to classify the elections of 1836, 1856, 1864, 1896, 1932, and 1964 as realigning elections. The 1928, 1936, and 1960 elections fall in the category of possible realignments. Of this group of nine elections, all but 1928 and 1960 were strikingly marked by the adoption of clearly differentiated and unusually polarizing issue positions by the two major parties. In both 1928 and 1960, on the other hand, the Democratic presidential candidates shared an unusually polarizing personal characteristic (Catholicism).

These classifications of realigning elections are based primarily on data analyses by Burnham and Pomper. The methods used by these two authors do not, of course, exhaust the techniques available for identifying realigning elections. The other statistical technique most prominently used has been factor analysis. MacRae and Meldrum (1969) carried out such an analysis on county-level voting data from Michigan, Illinois, and New Hampshire for the realignments of the 1890s and the 1930s. Their conclusion, interesting in light of the discussion of the 1936 election above, was that both the 1928 election and the 1936 election loaded more heavily on a factor they called New Dealism than did the 1932 election.

The most likely advance in our ability to classify historical elections as realigning or not realigning, however, will come, it seems to me, not from the application of different statistical techniques but from more finely disaggregated data sources, such as county-level election returns. Correlation networks drawn from county-level data may reveal that there have been more realigning elections than we currently believe to be the case. If county-level or lower election returns are linked to such demographic data as county-level census materials, we may discover, through the examination of the partial slopes of regression equations predicting the vote, that there are changes in the party support of particular population groups which are significant enough to warrant classifying a particular election as a realignment, even if these changes occur in the absence of any net changes in party support for the population as a whole.[3] In any event, those who seek regularities in either the causes or the consequences of realignment should be prepared to defend their choice of the elections they choose to view as realigning. In the absence of additional analysis, the list I have abstracted from the data presented by Pomper and Burnham would be a good starting place.

THE IDENTIFICATION OF SECULAR REALIGNMENTS

Following the discussion by McMichael and Trilling, a secular realignment would be defined as a change in the correlates of party support or in the distribution of party support that occurs gradually over a long time span. As in the case of critical elections, such realignments can be of several types. In the first type, the population as a whole moves toward one party or another, so that the overall party balance is shifted, but the relative strength of a particular party among various groups is unchanged. In the second type, the relative strength of one party among particular groups is unchanged, but groups that incline to a particular party over time represent a larger portion of the electorate, thus shifting the party balance in favor of one party or the other. In the third case, groups move slowly in different directions so that, over time, the elements making up each party coalition change.

There are a number of ways in which such changes can presumably occur. First, they can occur as the aftermath of a critical realignment. For example, the realignment moves either the population as a whole or specific groups toward a particular party. The movement continues, but at a slower pace, after the critical realignment, because the party identification of older individuals is less malleable than that of newer voters. As the older individuals die off and the newer voters become the majority, the division established by the realigning election increases in absolute strength, although the rate of change is much smaller than it was at the time of the critical election (Campbell et al. 1960: 153–156).

A second sort of secular realignment would be a case in which groups identifying with a particular party were a more rapidly growing segment of the electorate than were groups identifying with the other party. For example, between 1868 and 1896, the Republican national advantage was essentially wiped out and the parties reached a situation of parity. This was partly the result of changing control of the franchise in the South, with Reconstruction overthrown and black political participation increasingly limited. In the North, however, the same trend was evident as groups (particularly Catholics) and areas that were traditionally Democratic had a faster rate of population increase than the rest of the country (Kleppner 1970: 16).

Finally, secular realignment might occur—although it has never been documented that it does occur in this way—if one party, in the absence of any critical election, developed an image that was more attractive to some groups than to others. As time went by, newer voters from those groups would disproportionately favor that party as they entered the electorate and replaced older cohorts less likely to change their party support.

Any of these three types of changes could be responsible for a secular realignment. Clearly, in order to measure such changes, we would have to measure *between* critical realignments. If we simply compared the party support of the electorate or of particular groups at two arbitrarily selected points in time, we would not know whether the differences we found were the result of secular realignment or of an intervening critical election. Hence, the measurement of secular realignment involves a prior identification of critical realignments.

Once the period between critical realignments is identified, it is possible to measure the existence of secular realignment. For the population as a whole, this task is not too difficult—an analyst simply plots the results of each election during the period (or polls of party support, if available) and draws a trend line through the measurements. A slope of the line could be plotted, and the average change over time would correspond to this slope. Plotting a line is necessary because each measurement (election) would be a mixture of both short- and long-term forces. The trend line would represent the long-term force of secular realignment.

For measurement of the realignment of particular groups, the measure that seems most appropriate to me would be the plotting of a trend line for the partial regression slopes associated with each group in each election during the period between critical elections. For example, one could use the partial slope associated with Catholicism (whether measured from poll data or ecological correlation). The trend in the value of this partial slope over time would tell us to what degree being a Catholic was an increasingly good predictor of a vote for or an identification with the Democrats, for example. This would be equivalent to measuring the extent to which Catholics were moving to the Democratic party over time.

In the case where the proportion of the total electorate favoring a particular party changes solely because adherents of a particular party come from groups which are increasing more rapidly than others as a proportion of the total population, it should be the case that the partial slopes association with particular groups stay the same over time but the proportion of the electorate favoring a particular party changes. If this situation arises, the analyst can examine census data and electoral data to see if the groups and geographical places favoring the growing party are in fact increasing more rapidly than the population as a whole.

INFERRING CAUSATION IN THE STUDY OF REALIGNMENTS

With a few exceptions, studies concerned with the causes or consequences of realignments have been restricted to noting an association between the incidence of realignment and a change in either the predictor or the dependent variable. This is all right as far as it goes, except for two problems. First, as noted earlier, identification of critical realignments has varied with particular analysts and may well change as our data sources become better. Hence, any simple correlation between critical realignment and some other phenomenon is on somewhat shaky ground. Second, there are many phenomena that seem to be partly but not perfectly associated with the incidence of critical realignments. A correlation is interesting for exploratory purposes but does not tell us whether it is an associated phenomenon or the realignment itself which is the causal or dependent variable. Obviously, as we move beyond exploratory studies, we will become increasingly interested in a theoretical understanding of any relationships we find.

There is no easy formula for arriving at and testing such theoretical statements. In general, analysts will have to think through the mechanisms that are most likely to be operating. They will then need to devise measures to test the operation of these mechanisms across several realignments. David Brady's chapter in this volume is an excellent example of such a procedure—I hope we will see other such efforts in the near future. Realignments are particularly appropriate phenomena for application of this style of analysis, since they are important events with possible impacts on many areas of the political system and are also repeated events that can be examined for common elements.

NOTES

1   One recent study, in fact, concludes that, for the bulk of the population, party identification *never* changes. Realignment is due solely to new voters entering the electorate (Nie et al. 1976).

2   There were, of course, five presidential elections prior to 1836, but estimates of the popular vote were not published until 1824 and, even in that year, the presidential electors were chosen by the state legislators—not the voters— in over half the states. Subsequent events make it clear that Burnham's methodology would not show either 1960 or 1964 to be a realignment.

3   In using such data one must, of course, be aware of possible mistakes arising from the so-called ecological fallacy. An argument that the importance of this fallacy for theory construction is often overstated may be found in a recent article (Hanushek et al. 1974).

PART II

Mass Behavioral Change

4

Secular Realignment:
The Concept and Its Utility

LOUIS M. SEAGULL

Secular realignment is an important tool for comprehending the dynamics of American electoral politics. The purpose of this chapter is to bring attention to the phenomenon, to demonstrate its central importance to the general phenomenon of electoral realignment, to show its relationship to critical realignment, and to indicate the manner in which secular dynamics can also work against realignment.

Briefly, the argument of this essay is that critical realignment has received undue and possibly inappropriate attention. A critical realignment is sustained by issues which have the capacity to rupture and supersede older cleavage patterns for some period of time. By contrast, the secular or long-term dynamics of electoral change have been celebrated less often, perhaps because they are less dramatic. Such realignment is not based on crisis issues, at least not in the attention-grabbing manner of critical realignment. However, secular dynamics have been important features of electoral realignment, both as a facilitating and as an inhibiting factor.

REALIGNMENT: CRITICAL AND SECULAR

Realignment is an electoral change which persists or is institutionalized. While the term "critical realignment" has received the bulk of scholarly attention, it is well to remember that Key's seminal articles suggested two routes to electoral and party realignment—the critical (Key 1955) and the secular (Key 1959). The popularity of the study of critical realignments has directed attention away from secular realignment dynamics and has raised expectations, during the past decade and a half, of a kind of realignment which has probably not occurred.

Secular realignment is a change of a different sort. It is not rapid, compressed, intense, periodic, or issue-oriented (Burnham 1970: 6–11)—it is gradual, slow, and emphasizes the group basis of the vote. Key wrote of the increasing political homogeneity of the groups in a population:

> We may presuppose the existence of processes by which categories of people, under specified conditions, gradually approach political homogeneity. This process may or may not be associated with introduction of new population elements. . . . The odds are that some objective change in the status of a group of persons is the condition most frequently associated with such a long-term partisan shift. (1959: 204)

As an analytical tool, secular dynamics constitute a double-edged sword. On the one hand, the dynamic is one by which groups attain political homogeneity. This development will be illustrated in our interpretation of the youth culture and its impact on American politics. On the other hand, secular realignment may involve the breakdown of formerly homogeneous groupings. In this instance we shall discuss migration patterns which bring about changes in population composition. The changing American South provides a good example of this dynamic.

As ideal types, critical and secular realignments are distinct; in reality, they both contribute to electoral realignment. The critical realignment of the 1930s was feasible, in part, because migration produced an ethnic swelling of northern urban populations and the emerging political consciousness of these groups. The presidential campaign of Al Smith in 1928 and the conflict between wet and dry forces over Prohibition represented the divergence between new and old groups in American politics. Samuel Lubell's observation that the Roosevelt revolution of 1932 was anticipated by the Smith revolution of 1928 is entirely to the point (1965: 49).

In an analogous fashion, the realignment of the more durable phase of the new southern Republican vote was primarily a phenomenon of secular realignment produced by the selective immigration of homogeneous groups. The migration of blacks out of the South and the migration of better-off whites into the region in the decades after World War II produced a context in which it was possible to alter the formerly one-party South politically. Moreover, the durable phase of the new southern Republican vote, the white-collar-based vote, persisted on the presidential level from 1952 to 1960 and emerged again in 1968 despite the shifting emphases on the issues (Seagull 1975). It is also true, however, that the secular realignment of the recent southern Republican vote can be interpreted, as Sundquist does (1973: 8), as the aftershock of the earlier New Deal critical alignment in the North.

These major examples of electoral change are not offered to suggest the importance of secular dynamics exclusively: critical election components were present also. But they are not present in any sense exclusively or alone. The complete story of realignment comprises both critical and secular dynamics.

It is important to emphasize that, while slow change attends secular realignment dynamics, it is not the slowness of change which is the essential characteristic of secular realignment. Rather, population shifts, the social-group basis for political choice, and the identity of the individual with these groups are at issue. And while these groups are often social in character, having an ethnic or even a geographic basis, they can also be political in their own right. Party identification, for instance, has meaning and relevance to the voting decision, and this is the sort of group basis which can sustain the direction of long-term political choice, even if not premised directly on class or ethnicity.

In an ideal type analysis, it is possible to view the critical and secular realignment dynamics in terms of essential and differing characteristics. Realignment via the critical route is initiated by some sharp convulsion in the body politic and is given final form by some issue of major importance to the citizenry. Realignment via the secular route need not be issue-based at all but can be a reflection of gradual sociological change. Migration patterns have expressed this latter sort of change in the past, but these are simply the expression of the more fundamental phenomenon—the saliency of group membership for voting. In any evaluation of the potential for realignment, therefore, the major assumptions of either route must be kept in mind. The critical election route emphasizes the importance of issues in determining the vote; the secular route stresses the social bases of the vote independent of particular issue concerns.

THE PLACE OF ISSUES IN REALIGNMENT THEORY

Any analysis of the prospects for realignment, secular or critical, has to confront the new role of issues in public opinion. That the public is more aware of issues, that there are new issue concerns, and that the public manifests greater ideological constraints are not in dispute. What is problematic, however, are the implications of issues for the party system. The contributions of issues are more complex, subtle, and varied than recognized heretofore.

One of the hallmarks of critical realignment seems to be a new and intense issue polarization. Accordingly, the potential for critical realignment has attracted much attention from a number of political scientists since 1964, when first the issues of race and later the "social issue" more generally seemed to dominate public opinion. But realignment has not occurred during this period. The most that can be said is that the cleavages of the older New Deal alignment have become attenuated and electoral behavior has become unstable. Of course, issues have played an important role in this evolution. Sundquist suggests that the newer issues—race, Vietnam, the social issue—have weakened the hold of older economic and ethnic polarizations by crosscutting these oppositions (1973: 314–331). More recently, the authors of *The Changing American Voter* suggest that these newer sorts of concerns are not conducive to stable partisan commitment (Nie et al. 1976: 105). Citizens may be unhappy about these newer issues and problems but do not expect that they are amenable to correction by either party or by government itself. Thus, the same sorts of concerns which have weakened an older alignment are themselves incapable of stimulating and supporting a new one.

This does not deny a role for issues in contemporary election analysis. However, it does place them in a different perspective, for the issues of real importance to the citizenry may not be the substantive policy concerns posed in the public opinion surveys. Instead, the important issue may be whether one is comfortable with the candidates, trusts them, and likes them as persons. Personality and image come to dominate the citizenry's evaluation of the candidates. Only after this anchor of affect is set are the more specific policy issues brought into line with the fundamental choice. Rationality, therefore, may be less the case of an issue-oriented electorate picking a candidate who is in line with its positions on issues than one of picking a candidate because of affect and then justifying this choice in terms of selective issue positions. Presidential electoral politics, therefore, has become less the politics of issues and ideologies than it has that of soothing, of feeling good.

The phenomenon of selective perception is not new in election analysis. The authors of *Voting* observed that voters will perceive the policy positions of their candidates to be in line with their own policy preferences, even when this is not actually the case. Similarly, voters tend to refuse to acknowledge issue differences between themselves and their candidates (Berelson et al. 1954: 220). But the antipolitics tendencies dominant since the mid 1960s were not present in 1948, when the surveys for *Voting* were taken. In an age of stronger partisan commitment, the citizenry could more easily espouse a candidate and a series of issue positions than is the case today. In the current period of antipolitics and dealignment, it is entirely plausible to expect the citizenry to pick candidates on the grounds of comfort and confidence, not on the grounds of party or issues. Disillusionment with problems and issues becomes a resource for the image candidates.

The argument that candidate choice often comes first and then determines the issue perception, position, and imagery by the voter is reinforced by recent research on the impact of television in the electoral campaign (Patterson and McClure 1976). The authors of *The Unseeing Eye* found that, irrespective of TV viewing, Richard Nixon's image rose among pro-Nixon voters and fell among pro-McGovern partisans. "Among people who preferred Nixon, his image showed a 35 percent improvement and McGovern's image a 28 percent decline. This happened among people exposed to many of the candidates' ads and to those seeing few commercials, if any" (1976: 111). A similar pattern for McGovern partisans, irrespective of party, was recorded.

There is an unfortunate tendency to reify issues, particularly the policy position ones, in juxtaposition to images. This is unfortunate because it is impossible to separate the two, given the power of the communications media, particularly television, to convey both simultaneously. A televised debate between presidential candidates conveys both issues and imagery in the same communication. At the same time that the viewer hears the candidates' positions on taxes, foreign policy, or whatever, she or he also receives some sense of their personality, leadership qualities, and intelligence. And, once again, there is no reason not to presume that it is these latter concerns which come to the fore in the voter's mind and, in this age of antipolitics, lead to electoral choice.

SECULAR REALIGNMENT IN RECENT EXPERIENCE

The argument that the comprehension of recent American politics owes more to secular than to critical election dynamics ought not to be startling if attention is confined to the period since World War II. During this time, the New Deal electoral alignment has not been replaced by a new political alignment. Indeed, two of the period's major electoral phenomena—the extension and working through of the New Deal alignment and the extension of antiparty and dealignment tendencies—are very much the outcome of secular dynamics. In order to gain a perspective on both of these phenomena, aspects of the American South since 1952 and of the youth culture are highlighted.

The Southern Republican Vote

The rationale for durable political change in the American South lies in the anomaly of the position of the once solid Democratic South in the Democratic party as this party was recast by the New Deal alignment. Between 1928 and 1936 this party, which had once been agricultural, nativist, and southern and western in character, underwent a realignment to new bases in the ethnic and labor sectors in the northern industrial cities. More important, the role of the government in economic life became the basis for ideological differentiation between the Republican and Democratic parties: the Democrats became the party of activist interventionist government, while the Republicans became the party of preservation and resistance to this intervention.

The southern political elites, particularly in Congress, began taking sides on the new ideological divide in the late 1930s. Electoral protest against the changing Democratic party was manifest in the Dixiecrat revolt of 1948. The major Republican manifestation of this revolt did not appear until 1952, when the Eisenhower candidacy cracked the once solid South. Different dynamics, however, differentiated unstable electoral protest from durable Republican development in the South. Secular dynamics were the bases of the durable Republican presidential vote in the South, the vote that persisted from the same bases in at least several elections.

The years between 1952 and 1960 were ones of vast social and economic change in the South. This was the beginning of a catch-up period in which the South entered national economic life. Population swelled. The southern economy advanced and became complex. Migration out of the South was disproportionately black; migration into the region was disproportionately white and Republican. In retrospect, also, the pressures and agitation of civil rights activity, devoted mainly to school desegregation, were mild in comparison with those of the decade which followed.

Population movement, a key secular dynamic, was an important component of socioeconomic change during this period in the South. But the region's political response, even in its Republican manifestation, has not been of a consistent and stable quality in all respects. This suggests that not all Republican voting can be understood as realignment, be it secular or critical. In its more stable manifestation, new Republican voting in the southern states has been based in the counties with higher white-collar populations. These are also the counties which have sustained new economic development and have been the magnets for population in-migration as well as population shifts from the more rural South. From 1952 to 1960 and again in 1968, the new Republican vote in these states was concentrated disproportionately in these white-collar counties (Seagull 1975).

But in 1964 and 1972 a different pattern prevailed. These were years of record Republican presidential voting strength. At times such as these, the vote transcended the contours of its more usual white-collar base and spread throughout these states. In these two years, the southern Republican vote resembled more the characteristic response of a political movement than that of a durable partisan tendency. During these years, the southern states' Republican votes were swelled by the temporary support of groups and sectors not ordinarily Republican. The politics of these temporarily Republican segments owed more to the specific campaign situations than to any partisan commitment. The short-term focus and immediate response of these temporarily Republican groups stamp their reaction as a surge movement rather than as a durable partisan tendency or even as one of the more durable forms of social movement.

An important difference in the context of the southern Republican tendencies in 1964 and 1972 must be noted as well. In 1964, the Deep South Republican vote soared at the same time that it plummeted outside the South. Indeed, even in the border South states, it declined from previous levels. These patterns served to highlight the unusual southern Republican response in that year. But, in 1972, the southern Republican vote was high at the same time that the national Republican vote also peaked. In this latter year, the southern Republican response, although different from the previously dominant southern pattern, was not unique in the context of the national political response. The joining of the southern response to the national response in 1972 reflects the movement character of the national pattern in that year. Political currents, then, ran outside their usual boundaries both in and out of the South.

Just as the varieties of electoral change in the South can be understood from the perspectives of realignment theory, so too can realignment theory be illuminated by the recent southern experience. The dynamics of surge movements, critical realignment, and secular realignment have all been manifest, sometimes simultaneously. Aside from the southern black electorate, which appears to have undergone a critical realignment to Democratic loyalty in 1964 in response to the specific issues of civil rights, the dominant dynamics of recent southern electoral politics have been secular. The indications of secular realignment in the white-collar sector, measured on the aggregate level (Seagull 1975), are consistent with more recent research on secular change measured on the individual level. Campbell has demonstrated that civil rights had a great impact on the party attitudes of blacks but not on those of whites: "For whites, the forces of change have not been unique and identifiable events. They arise instead from the increasing strain between the policies of integration and federal power which the national Democratic party has come to espouse, and the attitudes of many Southern whites which oppose them" (1977b: 749–750). Secular dynamics among southern whites have realigned southern partisanship with national patterns, thereby "correcting" the anomaly which once persisted between the former partisanship of southern whites and the position of the Democrats elsewhere.

The Youth Culture

An assessment of the youth culture illustrates a different outcome of secular dynamics. Unlike the southern example, which contributed to party realignment, the secular dynamics of the youth culture work against durable partisanship. This second expression of secular change—the assertion of group consciousness and the tendency toward a common value climate—has run counter to traditional forms of partisanship (Seagull 1977).

The phenomenon of youth was first recognized at the turn of the century. In 1904, G. Stanley Hall identified "adolescence" as a period of life intervening between childhood and adulthood. The adolescent was one who did not move directly from childhood into the work force, as had been the case for generations before, but instead continued schooling in the high schools (Coleman 1974: 112). Much later, in 1968, Kenneth Keniston identified "youth" in a similar fashion. He argued that, just as industrial society made the phenomenon of adolescence available to a large number of children, so postindustrial society has made "youth," the next stage in the life cycle, available to increasing numbers of the population. This time it was the university and graduate school experience which served to defer entry into adult occupational roles (Keniston 1968: 264ff.).

The single greatest characteristic which separates those in their late teens and early twenties today from their counterparts in earlier decades is mass secondary and higher education (Seagull 1971: 92–93). The decade between 1960 and 1970 was one of expanded educational attainment. Moreover, during the same period, when an increased proportion of young people attended college, the absolute number of young persons in this age segment jumped appreciably. Samuel Lubell has noted that "the 1964 count of eighteen-year-old males stood at roughly 1,401,000. Just one year later the figure had jumped 35 percent, to 1,897,000, continuing at roughly that level in the years after" (1970: 182–183). This bulge in the population, which presumably was approximated for females also, reflected the baby boom of the two previous decades. This demographic fact can only accelerate the retirement bulge in the population, anticipated for the beginning of the twenty-first century.

The concentration and segregation of many of these young people in educational institutions in record numbers in the 1960s account for their special group consciousness, an important secular dynamic. Richard Flacks has written:

> The rise of mass higher education is one of the most significant and dramatic changes in American society—if for no other reason than that it has created "youth" on a mass scale by segregating seventeen to twenty-one year olds in large numbers from other social groups and keeping them from full-time participation in the labor force. (1971: 36)

Similarly, some three decades previous, Theodore Newcomb explored the powerful effects of peer groups on attitude conversion of a population of college women in the 1930s (1943). Coming from upper-middle-class, conservative families, these women became liberal and favorable to the New Deal program in the Bennington College environment. In both the 1930s and the 1960s, therefore, the separation and concentration of youths in educational institutions facilitated the effects of peer groups on the members of a given age segment. Of course, in the 1960s, education took place on a much larger scale.

The recognition of youth as a distinct social type is reflected in the recent acceptance of the generational model in accounting for the political behavior of youths. This model implies that the political patterns of youths which differ from those of their parents are not temporary phases but, instead, will likely continue as this group ages. The model need not imply that youths' political response is monolithic; indeed, it is entirely plausible that there are different segments within the young, such as college youths and working-class youths. What is implied by the model, however, is that those in a given age group are affected disproportionately and durably by external factors which condition their behavior.

During the period of *The American Voter*'s dominance on the interpretation of American electoral behavior, the life-cycle model was favored over the generational one in accounting for and predicting the evolution of youthful patterns which differed from those of older citizens. In particular, according to the life-cycle interpretation, new voters who claimed to be independent instead of Republican or Democratic and whose opinions may have been more liberal than those of older citizens would fall into more routine patterns—that is, following those of their parents—as they aged. More recent analyses indicate that the new patterns of youth are not altered back into the traditional mold with age (Abramson 1975: 123–125; Nie et al. 1976: 234–242). The implication of this changed pattern of behavior is that generational change, which is a secular dynamic, becomes a vehicle by means of which new values and patterns are introduced into the polity.

Perhaps the major contribution of youths to the party system is negative in character. Youths' unwillingness to identify with either of the major parties is a manifestation of noncommitment to them. Past analyses have considered a change in party identification to be a critical component of realignment. Clearly, there is an essential relationship between the strength of party identification and voting participation. Conversely, as Irving Crespi suggests, "the proportion of voting-age Americans who call themselves independents rather than identifying with a political party has risen sharply during precisely the period in which voting turnout has declined" (1977: 291).

Since 1968, more than half of those eighteen to twenty-four years of age have claimed to be independent in party identification. And, unlike the pattern in decades past, this proportion is remaining high as this group ages. Without an attitudinal commitment to the parties, realignment does not seem feasible. It is by these patterns that the secular dynamics of the youth culture run counter to realignment.

The common denominator of youths is their tendency toward conformity within particular segments. Youths are not understood to be one large, homogeneous, conforming population—instead, there are a plurality of youth segments. What they share is a reliance on their peers for support and approval. This "other-directed" need to conform to relevant peers is not surprising, for youth, as a stage in life, is a stage in limbo. That there are behavioral patterns and roles clearly associated with childhood and adulthood is obvious, but the accepted patterns for adolescents and youths are less clearly delineated and surely less clearly understood. To complicate things, the social status of the average teenager is one of dependence, be it to parents or school. In so many ways he or she is an adult, except for this one. He or she is not autonomous: thus, it is understandable that youths should turn to their peers for psychic support and approval. This is made all the easier in the educational institutions, the high schools and especially the colleges, where youths are concentrated and segregated from others.

The importance of youths' attention to peer groups is consistent with the argument that in modern society the character of socialization is extrafamilial. This evolution of socialization dynamics has been elaborated in David Riesman's classic, *The Lonely Crowd* (1950). His analysis of emerging socialization by "other direction" as opposed to "inner direction" dynamics corresponds to the increased importance of peer groups instead of parents as sources of social and political learning. A major implication of this tendency is that youth, in some sense, becomes a self-fulfilling prophecy. What is incipient among some youths tends to be adopted by increasing numbers of them. This is why the notions of a "youth culture" and a "youth market" have become distinct phenomena in the past few decades.

The major political consequence of youth has been its contribution to attitudinal change in the society more generally. What Daniel Yankelovich has termed the "New Values"—moral norms, social values, and self-fulfillment—have "spread from a small minority of privileged college students to the mainstream of college youth, and from college youth to the noncollege majority of young workers, housewives, high school students" (1974: 6). It is in this sense, then, that it is possible to speak of youth as expressing secular dynamics. The evolution of society has contributed to the establishment of the social type "youth." In turn, this type "youth" has been a vehicle by means of which basic changes in the society and the polity have taken place.

The recognition of youth as the cutting edge of value change in society gives this population type an importance aside from any question of numbers which may be raised. This is a major consideration, given the recent attention to the aged in the polity. No one questions that the aged represent an important number of votes, often concentrated geographically. But the aged are not the source of attitudes and values in a modern society—if anything, they often adopt the values and styles of youth. The appeal and outlook of youth are not the province of the young alone.

CONCLUSION

The two routes to realignment—the critical and the secular—comprise very different realignment dynamics. Of these, secular realignment includes two different modes, both of which deal with the group bases of the vote. But, for one, population migration is the key: the political response of a sector or region changes as the flux of population alters the society. For the other, groups can assert or attenuate a common political response, even in the absence of migration patterns. The new southern Republican vote illustrates the first mode, that of population flux; the political and cultural homogeneity of youth represents the second, that of sheer group influence.

In the past, realignment has been considered important to the party system; indeed, party realignment was held to be an essential requisite to a party system which met society's needs. To the extent that the direction of secular dynamics today runs counter to the model of realignment as a constituent act proposed by Burnham (1970) and discussed by Trilling and Campbell in chapter 1, we must consider the possibility that this phenomenon does not bode well for traditional modes of democratic governance. Secular realignment among the young is introducing a new form of political competition, which, essentially, is politics without parties. This politics of appealing directly to the voters with the skills of the marketing and advertising expert gives a new way of bridging the gap between the citizenry and their governors.

While the decline of party politics may mean the end of realignment as it is currently conceived, the outlook need not be at all pessimistic from the point of view of democratic theory. The diminished influence of institutionalized party structures will mean the removal of a layer of insulation which previously existed between the popular will and policy outputs. While *partisan* realignment will no longer occur, realignment of electoral opinion will certainly endure and should be more easily converted into changes in the policy decisions of government.

5

Realignment, Party Decomposition, and Issue Voting

BRUCE A. CAMPBELL

Those observing the American electorate over the past couple of decades just *know* that something important is going on. If they are inclined to look at contests for the presidency, they will doubtlessly notice that the New Deal coalition, which brought the Democrats their resounding White House victories of the 1930s and 1940s, has lost most of its political vitality. They will also notice that sixteen of the twenty-four years prior to 1977 passed with a Republican on Pennsylvania Avenue. If they are inclined, as I am, to look at partisan self-identification, they will see that *both* the Democrats and the Republicans lost about one loyalist in every six between 1952 and 1976 (in the aggregate, of course) and that, where there were three independents in 1952, there were *five* in 1976.

These changes present political scientists with an unavoidable obligation. We cannot escape the fact that the American electorate is currently in a period of flux. Like the center fielder who sees the fly ball coming, we haven't got much choice: either we catch the ball, or we drop it; either we explain what is going on, or we surrender and let history do the explaining in its own good time.

This book presents a collection of efforts to explain realignment and to develop prognoses from those explanations. My own contribution occupies a fairly small space in the total landscape, so let me be fairly careful at the outset to define what I am going to do. There are three terms in the title of this chapter: issue voting, decomposition, and realignment. The first has a reasonably straightforward definition: issue voting means that individuals make a choice among competing candidates according to some kind of calculus which involves a comparison between their own and the candidates' issue positions and (presumably) the choice of the candidate who is "closer." Since our concern in this chapter does not lie with issue voting per se, I will leave the matter here.

Realignment presents a bit more of a problem because of the variety of ways it has been used in the past and the extent to which the concept has entered the popular lore. For present purposes, I do not conform to the usage of McMichael and Trilling, who in chapter 2 focus on *critical* realignment. By realignment, I mean *any* shift in the partisan identification of the electorate. This definition reveals a further aspect of my analysis. While we are concerned with macrolevel "whither the electorate?" sorts of questions, my approach also contains an implicit and unavoidable microlevel element: what is the nature of the party identification concept? It is my feeling that only through an understanding of one can we arrive at an understanding of the other.

Finally, decomposition needs definition. By this I simply mean the shift of former partisan identifiers to an independent identification. As we shall presently see, this simple concept takes on great additional meaning as we attach other elements to the definition. For instance, the meaning of decomposition for the future of party identification as a viable attitude in the American electorate varies greatly according to our assumptions about the forces which produce it. But much more on this in a moment.

Decomposition is really the key concept in the analysis presented below, because it seems to me that the main actors in the drama of realignment which we are currently observing are the independents. Most particularly, I am especially interested in those independents who have shifted into that identification from a former loyalty to one of the two major parties—those whose partisanship has actually decomposed. Knowing the reasons for these shifts lies at the very center of the task of revealing the nature of realignment.

The plan of attack which I propose to follow is fairly simple. The first step lays out the problem. A review of recent work on realignment (at least the realignment of my narrow definition) indicates that four major questions must be answered in order to achieve a satisfactory understanding of the phenomenon.

Once these questions have been confronted and discussed, a second step becomes necessary. There is considerable diversity in the literature concerning the interpretation of the changes observed in the current period—and much controversy surrounds the interpretation of the decomposition phenomenon. Initially, I have attempted to reconcile what I see to be the two major strands of

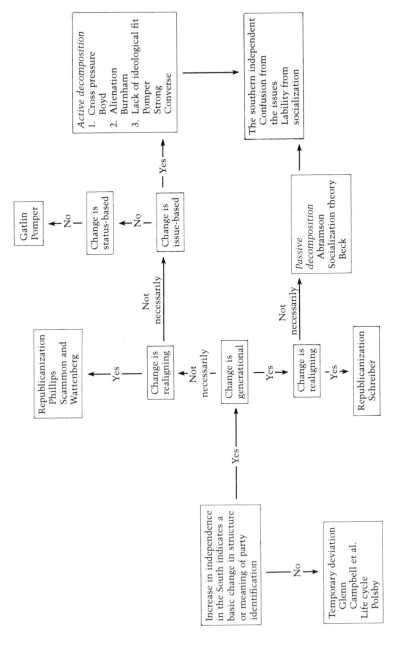

FIGURE 5.1. A schema of approaches to the phenomenon of southern independence

theory about decomposition—which I have called active and passive decomposition. Subsequently, I offer an interpretation of recent change which presents decomposition in a new light, one, incidentally, which I believe is more adequately supported by the evidence.

One final note of introduction. My comments on realignment are intended to apply to the American electorate as a whole. For reasons which I have outlined below, I have chosen the South as the arena in which to test my ideas. It is my belief, however, that the theoretical orientations developed in this chapter have general relevance.

A CLASSIFICATION OF THE REALIGNMENT PHENOMENON

Recent studies of party identification can be classified according to how four major questions are answered. (1) Does the recently observed increase in independent identification indicate a basic change in the meaning or structure of party identification? (2) Is change generational? (3) Is change realigning? (4) How have the issues affected change?

Figure 5.1 contains a schema which lays out these major questions, as well as the major answers which have been developed in response. The first step in the short review is the demonstration of the assumption underlying the schema of figure 5.1: an increase in independent identification has in fact taken place among native white Southerners since 1952.[1]

Table 5.1 presents these data, revealing the shift in partisanship which has by now become a familiar part of studies on voting behavior. As noted, these data eliminate the effect of in-migration, and the effect of out-migration on partisan change has been shown to be minimal (Campbell 1977a). Clearly, the major increase in independent strength has been provided in the aggregate, at least, by the decline of Democratic strength. The Republicans, on the other hand, have not as yet managed to attract many new loyalists. While Democratic strength has fallen from about 75 percent to about 50 percent, the Republicans have augmented their strength from about 15 percent to only about 20 percent. The remaining change has accumulated in the independent category.

This observation has triggered analyses which have concentrated on one or more of the four major questions presented above. The

TABLE 5.1. Party Identification of White Native Southerners, 1952–1976

Party Identification	1952	1956	1960	1964	1968	1972	1976
Democratic	73.4%	70.3%	65.2%	69.8%	50.6%	50.1%	51.3%
Independent[a]	13.2	15.3	17.8	17.4	36.0	30.7	29.8
Republican	13.5	14.4	17.0	12.8	13.4	19.2	19.0
Total	100.1%	100.0%	100.0%	100.0%	100.0%	100.0%	100.1%
	(349)	(358)	(465)	(299)	(328)	(591)	(520)

Note: These and all subsequent data are from the election studies of Michigan's Survey Research Center and Center for Political Studies as provided by the Inter-University Consortium of Political and Social Research.
[a]Includes independents leaning Democratic or Republican.

most basic of these questions is whether the patterns documented in table 5.1 do in fact indicate a lasting change in the structure or meaning of partisan identification in the South. In spite of the preponderance of agreement that this question should be answered in the affirmative, there are dissenting voices. The traditional approach is of course presented in *The American Voter* (Campbell et al. 1960). The basic thesis of the Michigan school is that party identification is a stable attribute, not given to large change in the aggregate except in convulsive circumstances, such as the Depression or the Civil War. Following this line of thought, the increase in independent identification must be seen as a temporary condition which obscures a more normal partisan division which will eventually reemerge.

To be sure, the *American Voter* model of voting has borne its share of criticism as outdated and time-bound (Burnham 1974b; but also Converse 1974). It is significant, therefore, to note two more recent studies which also suggest that no basic, long-term change in partisanship has come about among white Southerners. Polsby (1969), in his review of Phillips' *The Emerging Republican Majority* (1969), observes the increase in independents nationwide and maintains that it is explained by the increasing size of the younger cohorts of the electorate produced by the postwar baby boom, cohorts which "affiliate and vote at a much lower rate than their elders." He goes on to suggest that these are life-cycle differences, implying that the normal balance will be restored once this unusually large cohort of young voters ages.

The second analysis deals directly with independents in the South. Glenn focuses on the massive shift to independence which occurred during the 1966 to 1968 period (1972).[2] He attributes this change to the emergence of George Wallace, and his analysis reveals that, contrary to Polsby's supposition, Southerners of all ages participated. Since Glenn is writing in 1972, he is able to include data from 1971, three years after the candidacy of Wallace. His data show that, while there was an increase of 23.9 percentage points in the independent category in the South between 1965 and 1969, by 1971 two-thirds of that increase had disappeared. He concludes that the changes of the 1960s did not represent a permanent gain in independence, nor was there evidence to suggest any substantial movement of independents into the Republican party. In the end, while the bases of his conclusion are more elaborate, Glenn concurs with Polsby in an affirmation of the essential *American Voter* position.

It may well be that Polsby and Glenn will have the last laugh in this matter. However, we now have the additional data points of 1972 and 1976.[3] Some evidence of Glenn's finding does appear, as many Wallaceites of 1968, who fell into the independent category because they mistook it for American Independent, moved back to an identification with one of the two traditional parties of 1972. Nevertheless, we cannot conclude from table 5.1 that the Wallace phenomenon explains the observed patterns. Wallace may well have catalyzed the potential which had built up among white Southerners to break with the Democratic party, but he neither defined nor limited it. About three-quarters of the 1964 to 1968 increase in the independent identification remained in 1976.

This brings us simultaneously to the second and third questions: is change generational, and is change realigning? Figure 5.1 shows that two basic positions exist on the question of whether change is generational, that is, whether contemporary youths differ basically from what contemporary adults were like when they were young. One set of analyses concludes that change is indeed generational; a second set either concludes that change is "not necessarily" generational or fails to treat the question at all.

We begin our review of this second section of the schema with the latter group: those who do not necessarily see change to be produced by generation-related factors (see the upper part of figure 5.1). We come immediately to the question of realignment. This is simply the issue of whether the South is becoming a basically Republican bastion or whether the outcome of partisan change is still in doubt. Those authors who have supported the view that change is realigning and that a Republicanization of the South is coming about are, significantly, engaged more in topical commentary than in theoretical exegesis. Neither Phillips (1969) nor Scammon and Wattenberg (1970) make any use at all of the concept of party identification. This fact makes their cases considerably less useful for our purposes.[4]

Of much greater interest is the path (moving to the right along the upper part of figure 5.1) in which increasing independence is not necessarily attributed to generational change and in which the question of realignment is also held in abeyance. At this point we confront the final question: what role do the issues play in all this? The possibility exists, of course, that the issues have not brought about the shift to independence. Rather, demographic factors such as shifting socioeconomic status may have been responsible. This path has been explored by Gatlin (1975), who concludes that status has not influenced the distribution of partisanship in the South. Pomper (1972) has also considered the possibility of demographically induced change and finds no evidence to suggest that changing levels of education have brought about realignment. We come then to the most often traveled path in the schema of figure 5.1. The outcome labeled "active decomposition" contains a number of analyses which are characterized by a rejection of the generational change hypothesis (or which, at least, do not rest on a generational explanation of change), a refusal to make a commitment to the prospect of realignment, and a conviction that the issues of the current period have had something to do with the changes observed in table 5.1. More specifically, all these analyses maintain in one way or another that the increasing salience of political issues (and candidates) is dissolving the glue which, during the 1950s, held the vote close to partisan identification. This has been signaled, in the South at least, by an increasing rejection of the traditional Democratic loyalty in favor of the uncommitted independent identification and by the notable successes of Republican presidential candidates since the 1950s. The movement away from hard party loyalty into a state of greater fluidity, as a result of the action of contemporary issues and candidates, is the process of active decomposition.

Needless to say, in spite of these common elements, the approaches listed in the active decomposition category are diverse in their detail. Boyd, for instance, deals with the important concept of cross pressure (1969). His analysis shows that the likelihood of defection from one's declared party is a function of inconsistencies of party, issue, or candidate orientations.

Boyd's approach is closely related to the notion of ideological fit, which has been explored by a number of authors. This concept simply reflects the dilemma faced by the southern white who has a tradition of Democratic loyalty but, during the 1960s, found the national platforms of the party to be increasingly repugnant. In Converse's words, "It has long been obvious that the historical link between the South and the Democratic Party has become quite implausible from the ideological point of view" (1963: 196).

Pomper, in a major analysis, discovered that southern whites have changed most markedly over the twelve years from 1956 to 1968 in their ability to identify the Democratic party as the more liberal party in the area of civil rights (1972). He cites this evidence to support his thesis that 1964 was a critical election, in that voters began to respond to the specific issues presented to them and to align their partisan loyalties far more closely to their policy preferences.

Strong is another who has interpreted southern politics using the concept of ideological fit (1971). He focuses on economic as well as racial issues, but the essential conclusion is the same: white Southerners will vote for their economic or racial preferences before they will vote for their party, if the two come substantially into conflict.

The third major version of active decomposition which we shall note in this review is Burnham's alienation thesis (1969 and elsewhere). Once again, the common themes that change is not due to generational differences and a refusal to predict realignment characterize this work. Burnham's interpretation of his evidence involves the central idea that the party system has become entirely inappropriate as a conveyer of public desires into the governmental realm. The sudden awareness and involvement of southern whites accompanying the 1968 election produced, as Glenn has noted, large numbers of independents. Rather than expecting an eventual drift of alienated southern whites into the republican party (or back into the Democratic party), however, Burnham speaks of a phenomenon of disaggregation or a complete breakdown of party loyalty. Ultimately, he predicts a politics with neither parties nor party identification.

In sum, the upper branch of figure 5.1 represents a model of change in which all members of the electorate (rather than only the young) are subject to some dynamic which is pushing them away from a loyalty to the Democratic party. A few analysts believe that this movement is simply the first step in wholesale conversion to a Republican hegemony. However, the dominant view withholds judgment on this question, preferring simply to establish a partisan decomposition without projecting whether, or in what form, a recomposition may eventually come about.

The active decomposition view also subscribes to the notion that the increased salience and popular awareness of the issues of the recent past are in some way responsible for the increased penchant for the independent identification. Although this basic concept is cast in a number of different ways, its common theme is that the policy desires of native white Southerners diverge with increasing moment from what is being offered by the platforms and candidates of the national Democratic party. We can see the pejorative image of the "habitual" or "dependent" partisan of the

1950s being replaced by a more aware individual of the 1960s and 1970s, one who votes in accord with personal issue preferences.

The lower branch of figure 5.1 takes a rather different view of change in the southern electorate. This position is based on the conclusion that change has come about through the mechanism of generational turnover rather than as an effect which reaches out to touch all members of the electorate. One of the most prominent presentations of the generational hypothesis is made by Abramson (1976), who shows that the overall decline in major-party identifiers results largely from generational change. In other words, the increase in independent identification among the young is not merely a result of their stage in the life cycle but reflects the uniqueness of their time in history.[5]

If we choose to accept the generational interpretation, the second question involves whether the observed change can be expected to produce realignment. Schreiber is one scholar who suggests that this may be the case for white Southerners (1971). His analysis shows that, in 1968, southern white independents possessed the strongest preference for Nixon, with Wallace following in second position. He extrapolates these facts to conclude that white Southerners will soon accept the southern strategy of the Republicans and will be led by the cohort under thirty into a position of loyalty to the Republican party.

Schreiber is probably the most forceful in presenting the view of Republicanization through the mechanism of generational change.[6] The alternate path, to which Abramson subscribes and which is developed most extensively by Beck, suspends judgment on the issue of realignment. The fundamental idea upon which Beck's analysis rests is that socialization patterns have been responsible for the ungluing of young Southerners from their traditional loyalty to the Democrats (1977). In this theory, partisan loyalty is strongest among those whose politically formative years were spent in a period of realignment. Hence, the bulk of the older electorate in 1978 (those born between 1905 and 1923) could be considered to be members of a realignment generation. Because of their historical experience, their sense of loyalty to the Democratic party should be especially strong. On the other hand, those who came into the electorate since the New Deal realignment (those born between 1924 and 1935) lack this personal sense of urgency. Their partisanship is much less determined by history and thus remains more open to change with the flow of contemporary events.

Beck concludes that the socialization of this cohort is such that they are now "ripe for realignment." One presumes that the children of the latter group, who began to enter the electorate in about 1964, will be riper still.

Contemporary issues are important in Beck's theory, but in a way quite different from the active role they play in the Burnham-Pomper interpretation. For Beck, the major dynamic underlying change is not the issues but, rather, the shift in socialization experiences. For this reason, I have labeled this interpretation of change "passive decomposition." The primary condition for change is a socialization experience which does not occur during a period of realignment. Socialization alone is not sufficient, however. Change will occur only if the issues become strong enough to catalyze the potential already present in the realignment-prone generation.

A RECOMBINATION OF ACTIVE AND PASSIVE DECOMPOSITION

It is clear that the existence of a large number of independents in the South has led to two basic and distinctively different theoretical approaches. Pomper, on the one hand, supports active decomposition and maintains that, because of their heightened awareness of politics, voters tend increasingly to choose their partisanship on the basis of a clearer perception of partisan differences. This leads in turn to the image of the independent as one who can find satisfactory representation on a number of issues in neither of the major parties and, therefore, rejects them both.

Beck, on the other hand, attributes independence to the socialization experiences of the current young cohort in the South. Since they grew up in an environment free from crisis realignment, their motive to defend the Democratic party is considerably weakened. This passive decomposition is fed, to be sure, by contemporary issues which disfavor the Democrats, but the basic explanatory concept for change is socialization.

My goal in this section is to attempt a reconciliation between these two positions and to apply that reconciliation to the task of understanding the remarkable increase in the incidence of independence among native white Southerners. I pursue this task in two steps. First, I suggest that decomposition should not be viewed dichotomously but, rather, should be conceived as a single,

FIGURE 5.2. A combination of the active and passive decomposition approaches to realignment: the issue-voter model

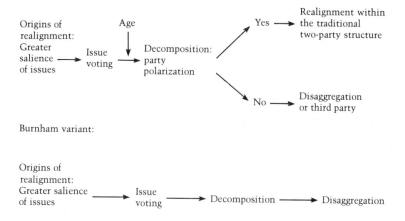

Burnham variant:

unitary process in which the active and the passive components interact. I see active decomposition as a process which acts upon all members of the electorate but, by virtue of the mechanism of passive decomposition, simply moves at a more rapid pace among the young. The basic model which emerges from this sort of theorizing can be depicted along the lines sketched in figure 5.2.

Virtually all the authors cited in the previous section agree that current changes in partisanship have their origins in the increased salience of issues at the national level which occurred during the 1960s. This has led in turn to an increase in issue voting. As the voters begin to seek out candidates who meet issue-based criteria, they come to realize that their party fails to provide them with a reliable guide. They therefore choose to abandon the party as an organizing stereotype in the political realm (the decomposition step). This relationship between issue voting and decomposition is mediated, according to Beck, by the age variable. The transfer of the former into the latter will proceed with relative ease among the younger and middle-aged (those ripe for realignment), while the direct experience with the Depression and New Deal realignment in the socialization of older voters will inhibit their abandonment of party loyalty.

Once decomposition comes about, an external variable enters the fray. The lack of party-voter fit on the issues has produced decomposition—therefore, the resolution of the decomposition hinges on whether the parties can reestablish a fit with their client electorates. If, at some future time, the two major parties manage to polarize, that is, to rearrange their issue positions to fit the desires of the electorate, we should expect a return to the traditional two-party structure, perhaps with some alterations in the strength of each of the parties among the voters. If, on the other hand, the parties fail to reestablish a fit with the issues, one of two outcomes appears most likely. First, we might expect third parties to form. After all, the electorate has traditionally accepted cues from political parties, and political elites nearly always align themselves with party organizations. The temptation to replace a defunct Republican or Democratic party with a Conservative party would be more than most political elites could resist, especially if the fruits of electoral victory were the reward.

However, some analysts take the position that, if the major parties fail to polarize in necessary ways, the electorate will abandon parties altogether. This outcome has been labeled "disaggregation." Not only has the electorate become cynical about the Democrats and the Republicans, so the argument goes, but it has discovered that it can survive without them. My own inclination is to doubt this prognosis. After all, party identification plays a role other than that of a conveyer into government of the voters' desires on the issues—it also reduces the psychological cost of keeping up with an increasingly complex political world. Like any stereotype, party loyalty permits the quick and efficient processing of enormous numbers of political stimuli, since no stimulus demands understanding beyond the datum of which party stands pro and which stands con.

In spite of my doubts, however, disaggregation has attracted a certain amount of attention recently. The Burnham variant of figure 5.2 represents an extreme position. As I read Burnham, disaggregation may come about no matter what the parties do. The electorate has already crossed its Rubicon when it arrives at the decomposition stage. According to this view, we can look forward to the prospect of an electorate without parties.

The Confusion Hypothesis
The second step in our task of understanding the increase in southern independence involves a reconceptualization of the active decomposition position. Pomper's work suggests, as we noted above, that independence is the result of a movement from con-

fusion to clarity as the parties and issues sort themselves out in identifiable ways. Given clear choices based on the issues, the electorate will make them. To support this point of view, Pomper (1972) advances data showing that, of individual white Southerners who can distinguish between the two major parties, the Democratic party has come to be viewed quite clearly as the liberal one.[7]

My own interpretation is just the opposite. The increased popularity of the independent identification is best explained, I feel, by the fact that the political space of native white Southerners has become vastly more complex and intransitive during the past several years. The racial politics of times gone by made political judgments extraordinarily easy for white Southerners and formed the basis for a half century of Democratic hegemony in the region. Today, the issue of race is intermingled with issues of social, economic, and international affairs. Neither party has managed to create a clear appeal to the native white constituency.

My hypothesis, therefore, is that the increasing complexity of southern politics has led to a *reduced*, rather than an increased, ability to place oneself in terms of partisan loyalties. Specifically, the huge increase in the independent category which many have observed among native white Southerners does *not* represent the outcome of an increased clarity of political perceptions and a consequent rejection of the Democratic party on issue-based grounds. Rather, I predict that decomposition has been produced by increased confusion, which has arisen in turn from the impenetrable political complexities with which Southerners are now faced.

In keeping with my theoretical orientation which integrates the dynamics of active and passive decomposition, I predict that the effect of increasing confusion should be reflected most profoundly among the young: the individuals who do not have the sense of loyalty to the Democrats which the Depression and the New Deal forged in the elders.[8] These loyalties, if my view is correct, should allow the latter group to remain steadfast in a world of conflicts, where the younger individuals fail to see the justification of continued attachment to the Democrats. This view of realignment appears in figure 5.3.

In this figure, the importance of distinguishing between issue voting and confusion as the dynamic underlying decomposition becomes manifest. If we look over to the right side of the figure, we see differences from figure 5.2. In the first place, there is no supposition that the voters, once they have reached the decom-

FIGURE 5.3. An alternate model of the combination of the active and passive decomposition approaches to realignment: the confused-voter model

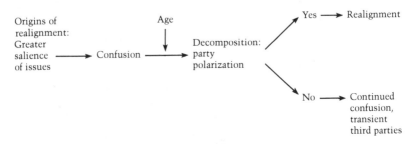

position stage, have abandoned parties permanently. There is no automatic disaggregation outcome, as in the Burnham variant of figure 5.2. In fact, there is no disaggregation outcome at all.

Should the parties polarize successfully, the outcome is the same as it is under the assumption that decomposition is produced by issue voting. The only difference is that, instead of polarizing to fit a specific matrix of issue desires, as they must to satisfy issue voters, the parties must make the political choices clear in the mind of the electorate. This may well be a more difficult task than that envisioned in figure 5.2. Parties may succeed in staking out their positions on the issues but still fail to resolve the confusion in the electorate. This is true because, as I have hypothesized, confusion arises only partly from the parties' failure to present clear alternatives. Mainly, the voters are confused because politics has become too complicated. There is little the parties can do about that.

One must assume that both major parties are trying diligently to find that combination of positions which will appeal to the bulk of the southern white electorate. If one of them does achieve this, and if the electorate manages to break through the mysteries and complexities of contemporary political life, we can expect a realignment to come about.

If the parties fail to stake out identifiable positions, then, presumptively, realignment will not occur. The most likely outcome, in my mind, is a continuation of the confusion. This implies two things. First, third parties may and probably will arise from time to time. I would, however, expect them to be transient, rallying voters for a short time, then disappearing. Unlike the issue voters which Burnham proposes, confused voters have not necessarily rejected the two major parties. They have not necessarily turned cynical about the abilities of one party or the other to represent their interests—they are simply confused about which one it will be. For these people, I would expect the traditional appeal of a Democratic-Republican alignment in partisan competition, if only by virtue of its familiarity, to dominate over a long-term preference for a third party.

The second implication emerges when we ask ourselves what the eventual outcome of continued confusion might be. I feel that confusion is an inherently unstable condition. There are strong motives within the individual psychology which strive to obtain the knowledge necessary to give structure to the world. In the absence of a meaningful polarization by one of the major parties, I would expect that the voters would slowly come to grips, of their own accord, with the complexities of the political world. In other words, they would slowly develop into issue voters.

In sum, one of the two outcomes proposed in figure 5.3 appears to be in the offing. If one of the major parties manages to fit its appeal to the bulk of the electorate in an understandable way, that party will reap the benefits of a realignment. If this does not occur, a period of continued confusion will follow. The main characteristic of such a period will be great lability in voting for president, as the voters shift first to one alternative, then to another. Eventually, however, the period of confusion will end. At that point, the electorate will evolve into the model presented in figure 5.2: an issue-voter electorate. The prognoses for the future are then those which I discussed in the previous section.

ANALYSIS

The first step in the investigation of the hypothesis is the subdivision of the native white southern electorate into two age cohorts.[9] Table 5.2 presents the distribution of partisan identification in this group from 1952 to 1976. The data corroborate a number of the points made above. First, as the authors of *The American Voter* observe, the younger cohort starts out in 1952 with a higher incidence of independent identification. As time passes, and as the younger cohort ages, however, the expectation that the rate of independence will decline and partisan loyalties will be established in their place is not fulfilled (Converse 1969). Instead of this life-cycle change, the generational pattern which Abramson discusses

TABLE 5.2. Party Identification of Native White Southerners, by Age, for Seven Presidential Years

Age Cohort	Party Identification	1952	1956	1960	1964	1968	1972	1976
Younger cohort, born between 1924 and 1935	Democrat	67.4%	68.8%	63.4%	57.1%	53.2%	53.5%	58.1%
	Independent	21.2	20.4	24.4	25.4	34.2	29.7	35.1
	Republican	11.5	10.8	12.2	17.5	12.7	16.8	6.8
Total		100.1%	100.0%	100.0%	100.0%	100.1%	100.0%	100.0%
		(52)	(93)	(123)	(63)	(79)	(101)	(74)
Older cohort, born between 1905 and 1923	Democrat	73.9%	74.7%	65.2%	74.0%	52.3%	65.0%	58.5%
	Independent	14.5	13.9	15.5	15.4	33.6	17.5	24.4
	Republican	11.5	11.4	19.3	10.6	14.0	17.5	17.1
Total		99.9%	100.0%	100.0%	100.0%	99.9%	100.0%	100.0%
		(165)	(166)	(233)	(123)	(107)	(183)	(158)

becomes manifest. The young move progressively away from a Democratic partisanship, while adherence to the independent label increases apace. Republican loyalties increase less rapidly over the entire period.

Among the older individuals, there are signs that Democratic loyalties are weakening as well. However, Beck's prediction that these loyalties should be much more resistant to change is not clearly borne out. While the older cohort is substantially more partisan than the younger one, at both the beginning and the end of the time period, there is great instability in between. In 1964, a pro-Democratic reaction is seen, and, in 1968, there is a flow of nearly a quarter of the total group out of the Democratic ranks. The clear inference is, of course, that these movements are manifestations of a very profound reaction to the Goldwater and Wallace candidacies of those years. Whatever the case, the presumably stable realignment socialization of this group has been seriously compromised.

One additional point concerns the election of 1964. Pomper has labeled this a critical election for southern whites, but table 5.2 suggests that the situation may be a good deal less clear. Key's criteria for critical realignment demand that a sharp and enduring shift in partisan loyalties come about (1955). While sharp movements did occur in 1964, they have not endured in any clear way, particularly in the case of the older cohort. The pattern revealed here is much more reminiscent of Key's lesser-known concept of secular realignment (1959; see also Campbell 1977b and Seagull's discussion in chap. 4).

Table 5.2 has indicated what other investigators have previously documented:[10] the phenomenon of partisan change in the South must be understood in the context of generational turnover. While the older cohort has shown a surprising instability in its partisan loyalties, it remains quite clear that the tendency to report an independent-party identification is strongest among the young. Our next step is to demonstrate that the increasing popularity of the independent identification is not a function of increased political clarity. I shall attempt to show that independence is the reaction of an electorate which has been overwhelmed by a profusion of crosscutting issues and that this reaction is strongest among those who have no solid traditional loyalty in which to seek refuge.

My basic approach to this question involves an examination of the same variables treated by Pomper—the questions which tap

TABLE 5.3. Average Intercorrelation of Five Opinion Scales for Native White Southern Partisans and Independents, by Age, for Four Presidential Years

Groups	1956	1960	1964	1968
All partisans	.20	.22	.21	.29
Young independents	.22	.21	.46	.21
Old independents	.24	.17	.30	.22
N	372	275	305	335

opinion in each of six issue areas.[11] The first test which I shall conduct is a simple measurement of the extent of organization, or structure, which exists in the way southern whites view these issues over time. If the independent category has in fact been swelled by the addition of voters who have rejected the Democrats on the basis of clearly perceived issues, then, as we move from the early 1950s to the late 1960s, we should find that the independents, of all groups, have increased the level of organization in their views on the issues to the greatest extent.

Table 5.3 displays the results of this test. Here, we have placed the average intercorrelation (tau betas) of five of the six issue positions (foreign aid was omitted on logical grounds from the cluster of issues). Most generally, one of Pomper's basic points is confirmed. Among partisans in the native southern electorate, the coherence with which issues are viewed increases somewhat over time. From an average intercorrelation of .20 in 1956, the figure for 1968 has advanced to .29.

To confirm the active decomposition hypothesis, the data must show independents to be more able than partisans to structure their political worlds, particularly in the latter half of this time period. Clearly, nothing of the sort has occurred. Goldwater's candidacy did crystallize the independents' views of the issues in 1964, but 1968 brought a return to the pre-1964 levels of coherence. In relative terms, at the beginning of the period, independents displayed a slightly greater structuring of the issues than did the electorate as a whole, but by 1968 their views were somewhat *less* structured. This result cannot easily be explained if we assume that the ranks of the independents have been augmented by highly issue-aware individuals who reject the Democratic party on ideological grounds.

The second test of our hypothesis also centers on the issue variables, this time considered singly. Pomper bases a good deal of his argument on the fact that, among those who chose either the Democrats or the Republicans as the more liberal party with respect to each of the six issues, the proportion choosing the Democrats increases markedly in 1964 and is generally maintained in 1968 (1972: 425). I have replicated this approach, with two important differences.[12] First, Pomper employs a set of rather fine filters to arrive at the respondents who are used to estimate the extent to which the Democratic party is seen as liberal. Only those who identify one or the other party as liberal are considered. The result gives very high proportions, especially after 1960. Of course, Pomper does not mean to suggest that, in 1968, 79.6 percent of *all* southern whites saw the Democratic party as liberal in the area of school integration (1972: 425). Nonetheless, his figures are misleading. In table 5.4, I have calculated the proportion of *all* native southern whites able to identify the Democratic party as liberal on each issue. This gives a more accurate estimate, in my opinion, of the extent to which political information has penetrated the electorate.[13]

The second difference in my calculations is simply the control imposed for age and party identification. Once again, if the independent group is the most informed, follows the issues in voting choices, and rejects party attachments, these should be the people most able to identify the position of each party on the six issues. If, on the other hand, the independents decline to enlist in the partisan ranks because of confusion and a lack of clear indications that either party is suitable, this group should be least able to identify the party positions on the issues. Furthermore, this characteristic should be most evident among the young, whose inexperience hampers their evaluation of the political world even further.

Consider first the data in table 5.4 relating to the entire native white southern group. Pomper reported that 1964 was a critical year, in that a good deal of focus was brought to bear on the parties' issue positions. My analysis shows this to be true for native white Southerners mainly in the case of the two race-related issues—school integration and fair employment practices. Of course, this is scarcely surprising, given the nature of the 1964 campaign. In three of the other four issue areas, a more gradual increase in the identification of the Democrats as the liberal party has taken place between 1956 and 1964. In the case of government guarantee of employment and medical aid, and in aid to

TABLE 5.4. Percentage of the Native Southern White Electorate, by Partisanship and Age, Naming the Democratic Party as Liberal on Six Issues in Four Presidential Years

	School Integration			
Groups	1956	1960	1964	1968
All South	7.8 (375)	7.9 (479)	35.1 (305)	35.5 (335)
Younger Democrats	14.1 (64)	9.0 (78)	50.0 (36)	35.7 (42)
Younger independents	5.3 (19)	3.3 (30)	31.3 (16)	33.3 (27)
Younger Republicans	0.0 (10)	13.3 (15)	27.3 (11)	50.0 (10)
Older Democrats	9.7 (124)	7.9 (152)	38.5 (91)	39.3 (56)
Older independents	4.3 (23)	0.0 (36)	26.3 (19)	36.1 (36)
Older Republicans	0.0 (19)	22.2 (45)	23.1 (13)	26.7 (15)

	Aid to Education			
Groups	1956	1960	1964	1968
All South	14.7 (375)	28.2 (479)	36.1 (305)	23.9 (335)
Younger Democrats	18.8 (64)	39.7 (78)	44.4 (36)	33.3 (42)
Younger independents	10.5 (19)	3.3 (30)	31.3 (16)	22.2 (27)
Younger Republicans	0.0 (10)	0.0 (15)	18.2 (11)	10.0 (10)
Older Democrats	16.9 (124)	31.6 (152)	46.2 (91)	25.0 (56)
Older independents	8.7 (23)	19.4 (36)	36.8 (19)	19.4 (36)
Older Republicans	0.0 (19)	22.2 (45)	7.7 (13)	13.3 (15)

	Medical Care			
Groups	1956	1960	1964	1968
All South	14.7 (375)	31.5 (479)	42.0 (305)	34.9 (335)
Younger Democrats	23.4 (64)	43.6 (78)	50.0 (36)	42.9 (42)
Younger independents	5.3 (19)	40.0 (30)	50.0 (16)	22.2 (27)
Younger Republicans	0.0 (10)	60.0 (15)	36.4 (11)	30.0 (10)
Older Democrats	17.7 (124)	32.2 (152)	44.0 (91)	42.9 (56)
Older independents	8.7 (23)	8.3 (36)	42.1 (19)	38.9 (36)
Older Republicans	0.0 (19)	24.4 (45)	7.7 (13)	0.0 (15)

Groups	*Job Guarantees* 1956	1960	1964	1968
All South	18.9 (375)	33.2 (479)	43.0 (305)	33.1 (335)
Younger Democrats	28.1 (64)	55.1 (78)	50.0 (36)	52.4 (42)
Younger independents	10.5 (19)	40.0 (30)	25.0 (16)	22.2 (27)
Younger Republicans	0.0 (10)	6.7 (15)	36.4 (11)	10.0 (10)
Older Democrats	21.0 (124)	38.8 (152)	60.4 (91)	35.7 (56)
Older independents	0.0 (23)	8.3 (36)	36.8 (19)	25.0 (36)
Older Republicans	0.0 (19)	17.8 (45)	15.4 (13)	13.3 (15)

Groups	*Fair Employment Practices* 1956	1960	1964	1968
All South	8.3 (375)	13.4 (479)	38.4 (305)	31.9 (335)
Younger Democrats	10.9 (64)	15.4 (78)	50.0 (36)	40.5 (42)
Younger independents	15.8 (19)	26.7 (30)	37.5 (16)	25.9 (27)
Younger Republicans	0.0 (10)	0.0 (15)	36.4 (11)	0.0 (10)
Older Democrats	8.1 (124)	12.5 (152)	48.4 (91)	35.7 (56)
Older independents	0.0 (23)	2.8 (36)	36.8 (19)	33.3 (36)
Older Republicans	0.0 (19)	24.4 (45)	15.4 (13)	6.7 (15)

Groups	*Foreign Aid* 1956	1960	1964	1968
All South	9.3 (375)	11.1 (479)	36.7 (305)	27.8 (335)
Younger Democrats	23.4 (64)	15.4 (78)	55.6 (36)	26.2 (42)
Younger independents	5.3 (19)	6.7 (30)	37.5 (16)	11.1 (27)
Younger Republicans	0.0 (10)	0.0 (15)	18.2 (11)	30.0 (10)
Older Democrats	8.1 (124)	9.2 (152)	42.9 (91)	42.9 (56)
Older independents	0.0 (23)	19.4 (36)	31.6 (19)	30.6 (36)
Older Republicans	0.0 (19)	8.9 (45)	0.0 (13)	20.0 (15)

education, the focusing seems to have begun in 1960. The foreign aid issue more closely resembles the racial issues in that the increased focus appears in 1964.

Naturally, the selection of the entire group as the base for these percentages, rather than only those identifying one or the other party as liberal, changes the basic message quite markedly from what Pomper presented. The average proportion identifying the Democrats as liberal in 1964, as reported by Pomper for all six issues, was 79.8 percent. In table 5.4, the corresponding figure is 38.6 percent.

A second difference emerges when the entire group is used as the base. In Pomper's table, the shifts toward the identification of the Democrats as liberal, which took place in either 1960 or 1964, were generally maintained in 1968. The average proportion making such an identification declined only from 79.8 percent to 76.4 percent in this four-year period. Considering the entire native southern white electorate, however, the decline is from 38.6 percent in 1964 to 31.2 percent in 1968, a shift of nearly one-fifth. This indicates (as we have already seen in the analysis of table 5.3) that the enhanced ability of these voters to identify the issue positions of the two parties rests in large measure on the extraordinary nature of the 1964 campaign, rather than on a more general phenomenon of increasing information and awareness.

Moving into the body of table 5.4, we can examine the behavior of young and old independents relative to either Democratic or Republican partisans. Two consistent patterns emerge. First, from 1964 to 1968, the independents *decline* in their ability to name the Democrats as the liberal party in ten of the twelve cases. While it is certainly true that the independents are much more able to identify the liberal party in the 1960s than they were in 1956, there seems to be no trend to increase that particular competence after 1964. In fact, in five of the twelve instances, the choice of the Democrats declines by over 10 points between 1964 and 1968. In accord with our hypothesis, this decline is nearly three times as great, on the average, for the younger independents than for the older. The former group fell 12.6 points in its rating of the Democrats as liberal, while the latter group declined just 4.5 points.

The second set of comparisons is between the Independents and the Democratic identifiers.[14] There are forty-eight independent-Democratic pairs in table 5.4, and in only three of these do the independents exceed the Democrats' ability to name the

Democratic party as liberal.[15] In all the other cases (save one tie), the independents are less clear about the identity of the liberal party than are the Democrats. In 1968, across all six issues, the average proportion of Democrats identifying the Democratic party as liberal was 37.6 percent. The corresponding level among independents was 27.2 percent.

Generational differences emerge in these figures as well. When only the younger cohort is considered, the difference in the independent and Democratic averages is over 15 points. The average ability of the younger Democrats to name their party as the liberal one is 38.5 percent, while the comparable figure among the younger independents is only 22.8 percent. The similar difference for the older cohort is 6.4 points. The older Democrats' percentage is 36.9, and the older Independents', 30.6.

The suggestion of these data, clearly, is that the image of the southern independent as a relatively informed voter, who eschews partisan attachment on issue-related grounds, should be rejected. The southern independents are less clear about the parties' position on the issues than are Democratic identifiers, in some cases by considerable margins, and the clarity of their perceptions has declined from 1964 to 1968.

CONCLUSION

This analysis has attempted to demonstrate two basic points. First, the theoretical diversity found in the literature regarding the increasing numbers of independents among southern whites is unnecessary and inappropriate. We have seen that the move toward the independent identification exists among both young and old. Because of generational differences, however, the young are somewhat more responsive to the forces which move people out of a Democratic attachment. These differences in generation are linked in turn to differences in the basic socialization experience. The adult cohort was socialized primarily during the height of the Depression–New Deal realignment, while the young cohort came into the age of political awareness after that period. Consequently, the motivational force of partisanship is not nearly as strong in the latter group, for whom a Democratic loyalty would tend to be simply a question of tradition and habit, not rooted in direct experience with the Depression. The present approach combines the ideas of active and passive decomposition and sees them as operating interactively in the contemporary South.

The second major point of this analysis has been to investigate the nature of the decomposition phenomenon. A number of writers have attached a rather high level of meaning to the progressive increase in the proportion of the electorate which calls itself independent. The central theme of their work is that an increased clarification of parties' issue positions, brought about by an increased salience of issues in general, has produced the realization among many southern Democrats that their loyalties have been misplaced. This increased focus in the political world has therefore led many individuals to reject a Democratic loyalty in favor of the independent identification. This is what I have called the issue-voter model.

This hypothesis was tested in two ways. If the independents of the South do in fact conform to the model proposed above, we should be able to discern a greater increase in coherence in their various issue positions than is true in the rest of the electorate. We examine the average intercorrelations among the positions taken on five issues and found that, among independents, the trend ran in precisely the opposite direction. Since the supposedly critical year of 1964, independents show less interrelation in their issue positions than do partisans, rather than more.

The second test of the issue-voter hypothesis involved the extent to which native white Southerners could identify the Democrats as the liberal party in six issue areas, between 1956 and 1968. If the issue-voter model is correct, the independents should be the most sensitive to such matters, since it is precisely on these grounds that large numbers of them have supposedly left the Democratic party. The findings once again do not confirm this hypothesis. The southern independents of both age cohorts are nearly universally less able to identify the Democrats (or either the Democrats *or* the Republicans, as it turns out) as the liberal party than are those individuals who maintain an attachment to the Democratic party, and, moreover, their ability to do this declines markedly from 1964 to 1968.

While it is clear that the level of awareness among all Southerners of the parties' issue positions was given a considerable boost by the campaign of 1964, it does not appear correct to attribute any special possession of issue awareness to southern independents. However, if the hypothesis of increased clarity among independents is to be rejected, how does one explain the undeniable phenomenon of decline in partisan loyalty? I suggest that the movement into the independent category is produced predominantly by young voters who do not have well-seated traditional loyalties and who have been confronted rather suddenly by a political world which is a good deal more complicated than it once was. Prior to 1960, the Democratic party platform in the South confused no one. The only issues of importance were states' rights and white supremacy, and there were few reasons to doubt that the Democratic party defended both. The decade of the 1960s produced two things. First, the unquestioned position of the Democrats in the area of race was shattered; second, enormous economic development introduced entirely new issues into the politics of the region. The result of these developments has been to make politics in the South a good deal more multidimensional, intransitive, and confusing than it once was. Without long-standing reasons, grounded either in socialization or in ideology, for loyalty to the Democratic party, many young Southerners have withheld loyalty to either party, as a manifestation of their uncertainty about the political world. This is the major factor which has produced the massive increases observed in the independent group.

The implications of this are most interesting. The South is now peopled with large numbers of individuals who appear to have adopted a wait-and-see attitude. They have not rejected the party system—they have simply failed to find the cues necessary to guide them to one party or the other. This state of affairs may be resolved in any number of ways, as discussed at some length above. My analysis leads me to conclude that the most probable outcome is that these confused independents will eventually be absorbed back into the two-party system, in the process bringing about a greater balancing of the strengths of the Democrats and the Republicans in the South.

While this projection lacks drama, two arguments may be cited in its behalf. The first speaks to the assumption that today's independents will eventually come to identify with one of the major parties, rather than reject parties altogether. It is based upon the functional utility which partisan attachment has for the individual voter, coupled with my fundamental hypothesis that the political world is far more complex now than it once was. The processing of political information is very expensive in terms of time and effort and is becoming more so with each passing year. This creates a very strong dynamic in the direction of partisan loyalty, since the evaluation of political information becomes manageable when it is viewed in partisan terms.

The second argument takes an institutional point of view and also stems from the hypothesis that the political world is increasing in complexity. In addition to creating numerous confused independents, this situation also creates opportunities for the Republican party. This is true because the possibilities for a second party to make an attractive appeal to the voters increases directly as the complexity of the political world increases. Since politics is no longer unidimensional in the South, the Republicans have been more able to find areas in the political space which the Democrats have been unable to cover. They should continue to expand their appeal among disaffected groups in the South until they, like the Democrats, reach the point where new recruits can be gained only at the cost of alienating old supporters. This process complements at the institutional level the one which I see the voters following at the individual level. The result should be a more competitive Republican party in a two-party South.

NOTES

Note: I would like to thank Gerald Pomper, Richard Trilling, and Paul Abramson for comments made on earlier versions of this paper. Ronald Newcomb provided able assistance with the data analysis. The data utilized in this study were made available by the Inter-University Consortium for Political and Social Research. They were originally collected by the staffs of the Survey Research Center and the Center for Political Studies. None of these institutions or individuals is responsible for the analysis or interpretations contained herein.

1   I have used the sixteen-state South (Deep South plus border South) in this analysis. This choice minimizes error produced by the Survey Research Center sampling procedures. I have also confined my attention to native white Southerners—that is, those who grew up in the South—thus eliminating the effect of in-migration.

2   It should be noted that Glenn does not control for in-migration.

3   I do not consider midterm election studies here, because the stimulus environment differs so radically that they are not really comparable to presidential elections.

4   Two reviews provide entertaining and informative commentaries on these works. They are Lamb (1972) and Price (1971).

5   Converse (1976) has recently published a rejoinder to Abramson which challenges the latter's conclusions on primarily methodological grounds. It appears that we can look forward to a continuing dialogue on this issue.

6   Glenn (1972) specifically rejects this interpretation.

7   In fairness to Pomper, an earlier table in his article documents that, in the
     national electorate, independents are the least able to perceive the parties'
     positions on the issues, compared to weak and strong partisans. However,
     his data also show that the perceptive abilities increase over the time period,
     and, in several instances, the increase of independents is greater than that
     displayed by strong partisans (1972: 418).

8   Beck (1977) notes that the racial basis of partisanship in the South dilutes
     the effect of the socialization theory, since his realignment generation is de-
     fined principally by its exposure to the welfare liberalism of the New Deal.
     Cassel, however, in an analysis of native white Southerners (1977), reveals
     change patterns which fit Beck's approach very nicely.

9   These two cohorts are established following Beck's socialization theory (1977).
     The older cohort contains those individuals who belong to the realignment
     generation of the Depression and the New Deal. The younger cohort, who
     were socialized primarily during and after World War II, is ripe for realignment.
     The birth year of 1923, which separates the two cohorts, was suggested by
     Beck in a personal communication.

10   This conclusion is demonstrated in great detail by Glenn (1972: 500–501).
     He breaks Southerners down into six age cohorts and shows that the incidence
     of independence is half as great in the oldest (15.6 percent for those seventy-six
     to eighty-five years old in 1971) as in the youngest (38 percent for those twenty-
     six to thirty-five years old in 1971). Schreiber (1971: 162–163) reports that, in
     1968, 60 percent of white Southerners twenty-one to thirty years old reported
     an independent identification, compared to 30 percent of southern whites over
     thirty.

11   The issues are (1) government aid to education, (2) government-sponsored
     medical care, (3) government job guarantees, (4) fair employment practices,
     (5) school integration, and (6) foreign aid. There are wording changes over the
     twelve-year period. These problems are treated at length by Pomper (1975:
     chap. 8).

12   I was unfortunately prevented from extending the analysis to 1972 by the fact
     that certain critical questions were omitted from the Center for Political Stud-
     ies instrument in that year.

13   Wolfinger and Arseneau (1974) present a similar correction, although it does
     not include the entire group.

14   It is clear that a comparison with the Republicans is less desirable because of
     the small frequencies. It is also obvious that the Republicans have their
     own problems with issue perceptions, a question which is beyond our present
     scope.

15   I also ran the table using the proportion of the respondents who named either
     Democrats or Republicans as liberal. The results are basically unchanged.

6

Realignment and Short-Term Crisis: A Case Study of Public Opinion during the Watergate Era

ROBERT G. LEHNEN

Because the preconditions are only vaguely understood, the assessment of ongoing or the prediction of forthcoming realignments is a risky business at best. Several writers have suggested that the United States of the late 1960s and early 1970s manifested symptoms of potential, if not actual, realignment. The conditions that are usually singled out are (1) the deviating elections of 1968 and 1972, won by the minority Republican party; (2) the dramatic increase in public conflict reflected in student demonstrations, urban disorders, and civil rights activity; (3) the assassination of major public figures; (4) the increase in issue-oriented voting since the 1964 Presidential election; (5) the emergence of George Wallace as a viable third-party candidate in 1968; and (6) the rise in political cynicism among citizens in the late 1960s. Clearly, these are interdependent phenomena, and some may be as much a symptom of political stress as a cause. It is safe to conclude, however, that, by the beginning of Richard Nixon's second presidential term in 1973, the United States had experienced a decade of dramatic political upheaval quite unlike the quiet Eisenhower years of the 1950s. The year 1973 also brought the beginning of a severe economic downturn, which could only contribute to the already high levels of political conflict.

It is in this context that Watergate emerged as an issue challenging the integrity of the American presidency. Scandal, corruption, and official wrongdoing are a common part of government in Washington, but the events associated with the Watergate break-in were different not only in scale but in kind, so much so that by late summer 1974 the House Judiciary Committee had taken the extraordinary step of recommending articles of impeachment.

Watergate, if taken in isolation of the theory of realignment, might be conceived simply as a scandal reminiscent of earlier episodes in the history of the presidency. But, taken in the context of other forces which have served as preconditions for realignment, Watergate assumes more significance. In the first place, it challenged long-standing assumptions about the legitimacy of the presidency. Second, it became tied to major officials in the Republican party in addition to the president, including cabinet officials, campaign directors, the White House staff, and officials in important governmental agencies. Thus, the *potential* of Watergate was to alter significantly how Americans felt about one and possibly both political parties and what they believed about the integrity of their system of government. Such changes combined with the already high levels of tension would lead to predictions of profound change in the latter half of the 1970s. To make such conclusions, however, requires that the dynamics of opinion during the Watergate period be better understood.

There are three questions to be addressed in assessing the significance of Watergate for American public opinion. First, what relationship does the well-documented negative public opinion toward Nixon have with support for the system of party government as a whole? Second, is an increase in negative evaluations the same as withdrawal of support? Finally, did the Watergate period produce fundamental changes in the public's affiliation with the two-party structure of political competition?

TWO LEVELS OF OPINION

It is important to distinguish two levels of opinion effects when speaking of the consequences of political events on public opinion —*systemic* and *temporal* effects. Systemic effects are changes in the attitudes, beliefs, and behavior associated with the existing political cleavages of a culture. Easton's concept of diffuse support identifies a type of systemic attitude (1965: 272). If Easton is correct, the consequence of changes in diffuse support can be profound. Miller (1974), for example, treats the increase in political cynicism as a system-related attitude by maintaining that continued declines in trust, as observed in the 1964 to 1970 period, would likely cause major public uprisings.

Temporal effects are attitude consequences associated with immediate public policy outcomes and other actions of incumbents. Such attitudes are highly variable and may be positive or negative, whereas systemic attitudes, by definition, are relatively stable and are not greatly affected by current events (cf. Lehnen 1976: chap. 4). Easton's concept of specific support is an example of a temporal effect. Citrin (1974) disagrees with Miller's position that certain measures of cynicism are indicative of system changes. He stresses the relationship of such measures to the performances of incumbents and concludes that declines in trust are not as directly related to system stress as Miller maintains. A similar disagreement in interpreting negative attitudes toward government, in this case attitudes manifested by English schoolchildren, is reflected in the exchange between Dennis et al. (1971) and two British political scientists, Birch (1971) and Budge (1971).

The conceptualization of the levels of effects is central to the task of interpreting political change manifested by public opinion. If the observed changes in public attitudes are conceived as temporal effects, then one must conclude that the Watergate era is merely a deviating period. A change in the incumbents and their policies will certainly restore "normal politics"—that is, politics determined by the dominant social parameters of the era. If, however, one views the changes as systemic effects, the conclusion will be quite different: the parameters affecting political conflict will have been altered and the political system will not revert to the politics of the past.

FOUR MEASURES OF OPINION

The difficulty, of course, lies in identifying suitable indicators of temporal and systemic effects. Most attitudinal measures combine elements of both temporal and systemic behavior but, in spite of this difficulty, some indicators are closer to being "pure" measures of one type of effect. The historical record created by the American Institute of Public Opinion (the Gallup Poll) starting in 1937 provides crucial information for judging the extent of systemic and temporal changes during the past forty years and establishing a baseline for evaluating the importance of the Watergate era. Three questions of particular interest are the party identification question, the presidential popularity question, and a question about the need for Nixon's removal from office asked during the 1973 to 1974 period. The text of these questions is reported in the appendix.

Wahlke (1971) has discussed a hypothesis regarding party-related systemic effects—what I shall call the "curse on both your houses" hypothesis. Wahlke suggests that periods of major political stress

may produce a withdrawal of support from all segments of government and may not be limited simply to the incumbent party. This
argument implies that the major contenders for political power
share the responsibilities of political failure, regardless of their
role in creating the crisis. Because his hypothesis suggests that the
major parties will lose support proportionally, their relative advantage will remain about the same. Thus, the change in support for
the party *system* is best measured by the Party Support Index (PSI):

$$PSI = \left(\frac{R + D}{T}\right) \times 100$$

$$(0\% \leqslant PSI \leqslant 100\%)$$

Where:
 R = the number of Republicans
 D = the number of Democrats
 I = the number of independents or "other-party" identifiers
 $T = R + D + I$

The PSI measure reports the percentage of respondents who identify with a major party and varies between 0 and 100 percent. A
decline in this measure would provide evidence of a major shift
in mass attitudinal support for the dominant contenders in the current party system.

A related measure of systemic change derived from the Gallup
party indicator is the Net Party Advantage Index (NPAI). This measure is defined as follows:

$$NPAI = \left(\frac{R - D}{T}\right) \times 100$$

$$(-100\% \leqslant NPAI \leqslant 100\%)$$

The NPAI measure varies between −100 percent and +100 percent. It is negative when the Democrats have an advantage and
positive when the Republicans do. A zero value means that both
parties are proportionately equal. The NPAI indicator is a net percentage difference measure and thus is sensitive to shifts in partisan
advantage. Since the 1930s, the NPAI has mostly been negative
because the Democrats have been the dominant party (Converse
1966). There has been some variation in the net party advantage
over short periods of time, but the general trend of the NPAI has
been relatively stable over the past forty years. This finding implies
that the standard party identification questions repeatedly asked
by the major polling organizations probably measure systemic attitudes relating to party competition rather than temporal opinions

about specific party actions. For this reason, the NPAI measure is treated as a measure of systemic attitudes. Major shifts in the NPAI lasting over four years are probably systemic ones, whereas fluctuations of shorter duration are changes induced by short-term phenomena. Another reason for conceiving of the NPAI measure as a systemic measure is that an enduring shift in partisan advantage implies a radical shift in the political advantage of the dominant party. Correspondingly, the minority party could cease to perform an effective opposition role, and thus new competitors such as third parties could enter the scene.

A second item asked by the Gallup Poll has been the presidential popularity question, "Do you generally approve or disapprove of the way [president's name] is handling his job as president?" Unlike the party question, the item is closely tied to the time of its administration, to incumbent behavior, and to current events. It is very much a temporal measure responsive to public moods (Mueller 1970, 1971, 1973; Stimpson 1976). Current policies, international crises, the economy, and the incumbent president's style all play a role in shaping public response to the popularity question.

A measure of popularity that captures changes in public moods is the Net Presidential Popularity Index (NPPI):

$$\text{NPPI} = \left(\frac{A - D}{T}\right) \times 100$$

$$(-100\% \leqslant \text{NPPI} \leqslant 100\%)$$

Where:

A	=	the number approving
D	=	the number disapproving
NO	=	the number having no opinion
T	=	$A + D + NO$

The NPPI, like the Net Party Advantage Index, is a net percentage difference measure; a negative score represents net disapproval, and a positive score represents net approval. One would hypothesize an abnormally strong decline in popularity during the Nixon term, characterized by fluctuations associated with short-term events. The replacement of Nixon with Ford should reveal a correspondingly sudden increase in the approval measure followed by a decline in Ford's popularity after a few months in office.

The final Gallup question referred to in the following discussion is one regarding whether Nixon should leave or be removed from office. This is an important question, since it represents a "bottom line" assessment of Nixon's involvement in Watergate. The complicated Watergate issue went far beyond the limited question of who entered the Democratic party headquarters in the Watergate office complex and why it was burglarized. The issues and their ramifications were intricate, and the public evidence available at the time of the polling, though voluminous, was incomplete and contradictory. Thus, a question which asked about Nixon's removal required the respondent not only to weigh public evidence on the various issues but also to draw upon inner values about the presidency and Richard Nixon. In the end, the respondent's decision had to be either "yes" or "no."

Response to the removal question provides an important insight into not only how the public judged Nixon but also what they felt about the presidency. The general response to the question early in the Watergate period was against removal, suggesting that the American people accepted the legitimacy of the office and preferred to err in favor of Nixon. As will be demonstrated, responses to this question are difficult to interpret, however, and, because this is the case, they will be interpreted in the context of the other indicators described above.

In order to measure public judgments about the removal question, the Removal Index (RI) was defined as:

$$RI = \left(\frac{N - Y}{T} \right) \times 100$$

$$(-100\% \leqslant RI \leqslant 100\%)$$

Where:

N = the number of no responses (against removal)
Y = the number of yes responses (for removal)
NO = the number of no-opinion responses
T = $N + Y + NO$

This measure is also a net percentage difference measure. A dramatic decline in conjunction with the other measures would be evidence that fundamental values regarding the presidency were being questioned. It is essential, however, that changes in this measure be juxtaposed to the party indexes, since a change in the removal index without corresponding changes in one of the party indexes would raise serious questions about the systemic, though not the temporal, implications of such opinion change.

A final point should be made regarding the scoring of the four indexes of opinion. In each instance, the scoring is defined such that a decline in the measure means a net unfavorable response for the incumbent president, the Republican party, or the political system. Thus, a decline in the measures means public opinion became more Democratic, more unaligned with the major parties, more disapproving of the president, or more in favor of removal.

PUBLIC OPINION DURING THE WATERGATE ERA

The Watergate period is a complicated one combining a central issue involving Nixon's conduct in office with a dozen peripheral issues relating to illegal acts of subordinates, abuse of power, corruption in government and business, and unethical behavior. Because of the complexity of the issues associated with the period, it is necessary to define three phases of the Watergate era: (1) the period defining the issues to be resolved, (2) the period in which the evidence was assembled and evaluated with respect to the questions, and (3) the judgment stage in which preliminary or final decisions were made about the central questions. The discovery stage began in June 1972, when the break-in became public, and continued until the early summer of 1973. The commencement of the Senate investigations (the Ervin Committee) with televised hearings in midsummer 1973 began the evidential stage, which continued until the summer of 1974 and the convening of the House Judiciary Committee (the Rodino Committee) hearings on articles of impeachment. The decision stage began in that summer and continued to 1979, as manifested by court actions, congressional investigations, and legislative decisions. Although the periods clearly overlap, these divisions are useful for analytical purposes. It is the second and third stages that present the critical period for analysis.

During the discovery stage, several changes in public opinion occurred that set the stage for the evidential period and made the Ervin hearings of 1973 a significant event. The most important of these was the creation of "Watergate" as a public issue. It was during this period that public awareness increased dramatically to the point that, by May 1973, over 90 percent of the American people had heard of Watergate (*The Gallup Opinion Index* 1973, 1974; Sniderman et al. 1975; Weaver et al. 1975). Thus, the evidential stage proceeded in front of an attentive public responsive to the Watergate issue and informed of continuing developments via the national press.

In spite of the high saliency of the Watergate issue to the average citizen, there was little change during the entire evidential phase in the proportion of citizens attributing various levels of complicity to Nixon. Starting a few weeks prior to the 1973 hearings, Gallup asked a question about the president's involvement and continued the question throughout the following year (see table 6.1). The most telling point of table 6.1 is that there was no major shift in the public aggregate judgment of Nixon's guilt or innocence during the entire year. This was the period when the White House tapes were discovered, the resignations of the special prosecutor and the attorney general occurred, the transcripts were made public, and the president made several televised speeches regarding Watergate matters. Yet the distribution on the involvement question derived from the June 19, 1973, Gallup Poll is essentially the same as that for May 1974, almost one year later. The massive publicity and communication of evidence apparently had had little net effect on systemic public attitudes.

This pattern is borne out by a look at the Net Party Advantage Index and the Party Support Index for the period 1973–1974 (fig. 6.1). During the two-year period, the NPAI averaged −19 percent or slightly below the average for 1937–1976. It showed a slight shift toward the Democratic advantage, as illustrated by the regression equation for the period:

$$\text{NPAI} = -15.5 - .07X$$

where X is the time in weeks ($X = 0$ is the first week of January 1973). The regression equation shows that the weekly shift was only −.07 percent or about −3.6 percent a year. Over a long period of time, such a trend could produce important changes, but the critical realignment theory explains system restructuring by sudden, dramatic change, not evolutionary change. While Watergate thus shifted the partisan advantage slightly more to the Democrats, it is not sufficient on this basis alone to argue that Watergate caused a critical realignment.

The data regarding the effect on support for the major parties show no decline in support for the two-party system (fig. 6.1). The regression line for the PSI is PSI = 67 percent, which is 6 percent below the forty-year average. There was no statistically significant variation associated with time in office for the period 1973 to 1974 and the level of the PSI. The highest percentage

TABLE 6.1. Public Perceptions of Nixon's Involvement in Watergate, 1973–1974

Here are four statements concerning President Nixon's connection with the Watergate affair. Will you tell me which one comes closest to your own point of view.

	June 19, 1973	July 3, 1973	July 31, 1973	August 14, 1973	October 30, 1973	January 1974	May 1974
1. Nixon planned the Watergate "bugging" from the beginning.	8%	8%	8%	8%	10%	9%	8%
2. Nixon did not plan the "bugging" but knew about it before it took place.	27	30	29	25	32	26	26
3. Nixon found out about the "bugging" after it occurred but tried to cover it up.	35	34	37	40	34	36	40
4. Nixon had no knowledge of the "bugging" and spoke up as soon as he learned about it.	17	15	15	22	14	17	14
5. No opinion[a]	13	14	11	6	9	12	12
Total	100%	101%	100%	101%	99%	100%	100%
Sample size	(1,566)	(1,544)	(1,513)	(1,547)	(1,550)	(1,591)	(1,543)

Note: The survey date represents the beginning date of the survey. Most surveys require one to two weeks to complete, but some studies require as much as one month.

[a] The "No opinion" category includes respondents who were not coded because they had not heard of Watergate or had "No opinion" on a prior filter question. These respondents usually comprised less than 3 percent of the total sample.

FIGURE 6.1. Attitudes toward political parties, presidential popularity, and the question of presidential removal from office, 1973–1974

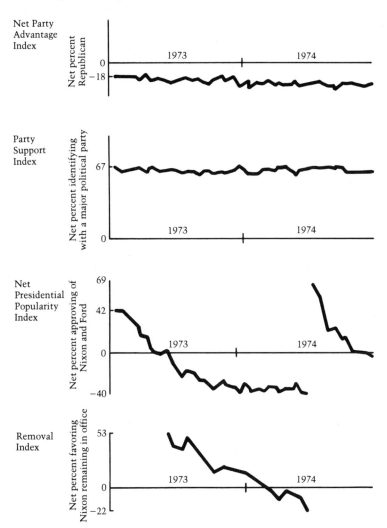

SOURCE: *The Gallup Opinion Index* 1973, 1974.

among the forty-five polls taken during the two years was 71 percent of a national sample identifying itself as Republican or Democrat, and the lowest was 62 percent. In sum, Watergate had no effect on party support attitudes either.

If the systemic measures were stable during the Watergate period, the measures of public approval were not (fig. 6.1). The general trend of the popularity index (NPPI) was downward, the high of +42 percent occurring in the first poll taken after Inauguration Day of 1973. The low point of −40 percent was recorded in the last Gallup Poll taken during the Nixon administration (July 30, 1974). During this period, the change in popularity is steadily downward, with brief interruptions for such major events as Soviet leader Leonid Brezhnev's visit and televised presidential speeches (cf. Stimpson 1976).

When Ford assumed office in August 1974, his popularity was at a high (+53 percent) for the 1973 to 1974 period, but, by March 1975, his popularity had fallen precipitously to −6 percent. Thus, the mood of the public changed dramatically in a matter of weeks, where presidential popularity was concerned, but the system-related attitudes remained stable.

The question of presidential removal poses some interesting contrasts. Figure 6.1 shows that, even though the question's general trend was downward during the middle Watergate period, it was well into 1974 (April) before more people felt Nixon should leave office than believed he should remain. The general acceptance of Nixon's complicity and the movement toward the conclusion that he should leave office are in marked contrast to the responses to the involvement question (table 6.1). One finds little change in how people judge the evidence, but there is a steady movement toward acceptance of the idea that the president should leave office.

There are two confounding facts that compromise the clarity of these findings. For one thing, Gallup began explaining the meaning of impeachment in his surveys beginning with the April 1974 poll. Hence, the decline in this measure is probably associated with enhanced respondent understanding of the impeachment process. Furthermore, a Harris Poll taken just before the House Judiciary Committee met in July 1974 shows that 48 percent had negative feelings toward the proceedings and only 36 percent were positive (Lehnen 1976: 166). Less than two months before Nixon resigned from office, a plurality of the American public viewed the constitutionally prescribed impeachment proceedings with suspicion. The American public showed little change in how it judged the facts regarding Nixon's involvement, and many Americans gave the president the benefit of the doubt or accepted the presumption of his guilt even to the very end. It was only *after* the House Judiciary Committee had voted in favor of articles of impeachment that a majority of citizens expressed approval of the committee's action (Lehnen 1976: 166).

One cannot avoid the conclusion that systemic attitudes were not altered dramatically by the Watergate era. These imperfect and incomplete measures do not compromise the judgment that temporal opinions were buffeted by the gales of scandal blowing from Washington, but the American public's underlying attitudes toward the system remained intact.

AN EXPLANATION OF THE STABILITY OF SYSTEMIC ATTITUDES

The realignment theory and the social structure theory of political conflict both imply that partisan differences are based on status differences. Voting studies in western countries have repeatedly demonstrated the importance of income, education, and other status indicators as predictors of differences in party alignments (cf. Allardt and Rokkan 1970; Campbell et al. 1960), and most explanations of the realignment process incorporate observations about extreme changes in social structure as contributing factors. Thus, industrialization in the latter half of the nineteenth century produced major changes resulting in the elections of 1892 and 1896, and the Great Depression affected the 1928 and 1932 elections.

Social status variables, particularly education, have also been related to policy attitudes, but the interpretation of the "education" effect in this context has been different. Where policy attitudes—that is, temporal attitudes—are concerned, education is usually a surrogate for issue salience and political knowledge. Status variables are especially poor predictors of *positions* on policy issues, although they often show a statistically significant association with issue salience. When status influences are considered in conjunction with measures of saliency and political information, the role of the former is substantially reduced.

This last point is especially crucial, since Gallup also administered the involvement question (see table 6.1) at selected intervals during the 1973 to 1974 period. The involvement question can be conceived as two separate items: a salience measure, "Do you have an opinion about Watergate?" and an information measure, "How do you characterize the president's role in Watergate?" One would expect the salience and information dimensions to be associated less with the Party Support Index than with the Net Party Advantage Index because of the issue content associated with party choices.

The temporal measures, the popularity and removal measures, should be strongly associated with the levels of saliency and information, and status should have lesser effects. This prediction is derived from the definitions of systemic and temporal attitudes. Systemic attitudes are a reflection of social conflict structured by status; hence, status should predict differences. Temporal attitudes are responsive to current events, incumbents, and policy outputs and thus are more dependent on saliency and information factors.

Six Gallup surveys, beginning in June 1973 and continuing through May 1974, contain the proper *combination* of status, involvement, party, popularity, and removal questions. Four of these surveys were done in the summer of 1973 during the Ervin Senate Committee hearings, one in January 1974, and another in May 1974. The first four surveys will be analyzed as a single problem, since they are spaced every two to three weeks and isolate significant events of that summer in their intervals. The June 19 survey occurred prior to the committee's hearing; the July 3 study measured the initial reaction to the televised hearings; the July 31 survey occurred after the White House tapes had been discovered and legal moves had been initiated to obtain them; and the August 14 study came after Nixon made a televised speech about "executive privilege" regarding the tapes and disavowed any role in the break-in. Since the total number of interviews in these six surveys is 9,299, the data base for the analysis is unusually abundant.

The effects included in the regression equation are as follows:

Status effect: An index which is based on income and education, dividing the sample into lower, middle, and upper thirds.

Saliency effect: This term is a comparison between those who had "heard of Watergate" and expressed an opinion and those who did not.

Perceived Involvement Effect: Gallup presented four choices regarding Nixon's involvement. The effect is estimated only for those expressing an opinion.

Time Effects: These effects were included only for the summer 1973 surveys.

The equation used to predict attitudes is:

Estimated Attitude = General Mean + Status Effect + Saliency Effect + Nixon Involvement Effect Given Salient Opinion + Time Effect

The statistical effects are summarized in tables 6.2 and 6.3 for party, popularity, and removal attitudes. The estimate for any combination of characteristics may be computed by adding the effect in the manner described in the above equation. Note that the Perceived Involvement Effect is present only when the respondent expressed an opinion (Saliency Effect), and Time Effects are modeled for four surveys only.

Party effects: Table 6.2 reports the centered regression effects on the Net Party Advantage and Party Support indexes for the six polls. The regression means represent estimates with the effects of status, saliency, and the respondent's information accounted for. Looking at the NPAI, one finds that the mean varies between −13 and −17 percent, which is essentially constant. The status variable has an important and uniform effect on party advantage; the difference associated with status is ±12 to ±15 percent for this period. This statistic implies that the low status group was between 12 and 15 percent less supportive of the Republican party, whereas the high-status group was between 12 and 15 percent more supportive.

The saliency of Watergate also had an effect on party advantage, indicated by the fact that *respondents expressing an opinion about Watergate were less Republican.* The nature of the judgment a respondent held about Nixon's involvement also produced large differences in the NPAI. As might be expected, those who judged Nixon guilty from the beginning ("he planned it") were least supportive of the Republicans, and those who believed Nixon "told all" were most Republican. There was little change in the magnitude of the effect for the involvement responses over the period analyzed.

One may estimate a group's Net Party Advantage Index score by summing the effects listed in table 6.2. In January 1974, for example, high-status respondents who believed Nixon planned Wa-

TABLE 6.2. The Effects of Social Status and Perceptions of Presidential Involvement on Support for Political Parties, 1973–1974

Response Categories	Net Party Advantage Index			Party Support Index		
	June 19–Aug. 14, 1973	Jan. 1974	May 1974	June 19–Aug. 14, 1973	Jan. 1974	May 1974
General Mean	–15%	–17%	–13%	64%	62%	66%
Effects of status						
Low	–12%	–12%	–15%	–5%	–4%	–6%
Middle	0	0	0	0	0	0
High	+12	+12	+15	+5	+4	+6
Effects of holding an opinion						
Expressed opinion about Nixon	–6%	–5%	–7%	–3%	–7%	–5%
Expressed no opinion about Nixon	+6	+5	+7	+3	+7	+5
Effects of perceived involvement (given opinion expressed)						
Nixon planned Watergate from the beginning	–33%	–29%	–23%	0%	0%	0%
Nixon did not plan Watergate but knew ahead of time	–20	–23	–27	0	0	0
Nixon found out later but covered up	+3	0	0	–2	–5	–6
Nixon had no prior knowledge and spoke up as soon as he learned	+50	+52	+50	+2	+5	+6
Effects of time (June 19 to August 14, 1973, only)						
Nixon planned Watergate from the beginning						

	1,543	1,590	6,166		1,590	1,543
August 14, 1973			0			0
Nixon did not plan Watergate but knew ahead of time						
June 19, 1973	0%		0%			0%
July 3, 1973	0		0			0
July 31, 1973	0		0			0
August 14, 1973	0		0			0
Nixon found out later but covered up						
June 19, 1973	0%		0%			0%
July 3, 1973	0		+3			0
July 31, 1973	0		0			0
August 14, 1973	0		−3			0
Nixon had no prior knowledge and spoke up as soon as he learned						
June 19, 1973	0%		0%			0%
July 3, 1973	0		0			0
July 31, 1973	0		0			0
August 14, 1973	0		0			0
No opinion						
June 19, 1973	0%		0%			0%
July 3, 1973	0		0			0
July 31, 1973	0		0			0
August 14, 1973	0		0			0
Number of cases	6,166	1,590	1,543	6,166	1,590	1,543

Note: Net Party Advantage Index = net percentage Republican.

tergate had an NPAI score of −39 percent. This estimated NPAI was computed as follows:

$$\text{NPAI} = \text{Mean} + \text{Status} + \text{Saliency} + \text{Involvement}$$
$$\text{NPAI} = -17\% + (+12\%) + (-5\%) + (-29\%) = -39\%$$

Thus, the difference between Republican and Democratic support for this group was −39 percent: *R* percent − *D* percent = −39 percent.

The Party Support Index shows that the normal percentage identified with a party ranged from 62 to 66. Status had a small but uniform effect of ±4 to ±6 percent. The low-status respondents were less identified (more independent) than the high-status respondents. The saliency of the controversy also affected party support by lowering it from 3 to 7 percent. The most unexpected finding, however, arose with respect to the effects that a respondent's opinion about Nixon's involvement in Watergate had on the PSI. *What citizens thought about Nixon's role had little impact on their support for the two-party system.* The only exceptions are relatively small but consistent. Those who believed a cover-up occurred were somewhat less supportive, whereas those who felt Nixon "told all" were a bit more supportive of the party system. In general, the people least identified with political parties were low-status respondents who perceived a cover-up. In May 1974, the estimated PSI for them was only 49 percent: 66 percent + (−6 percent) + (−5 percent) + (−6 percent) = 49%.

The short-term effects of the first major public investigation of Watergate can be assessed from the polls conducted between June 19 and August 14, 1973. Table 6.2 shows that the Senate hearings had no effect on either the Net Party Advantage or the Party Support indexes. A preliminary summary of related studies of the Senate hearings also reflects this same conclusion: the hearings had small and probably insignificant consequences on existing public attitudes (Lang and Lang 1975).

EFFECTS OF WATERGATE ON THE TEMPORAL MEASURES

Table 6.3 reports the regression results for the temporal measures, the popularity and removal questions, in a format similar to that of table 6.2. Examining the popularity item first, one immediately finds important contrasts to the party measures. In the first place, the mean scores consistently decline over the period, reflecting the drop in popularity illustrated earlier in figure 6.1. A second and more important contrast is the diminishing effect that status had over this period. By 1974, the status variable had no explanatory power with regard to popularity responses. The salience and involvement questions, however, had large effects, and the magnitude of differences increased throughout 1973 and early 1974 for the saliency dimension. In 1973, the saliency effect was ±12 percent but had increased to ±17 percent by May 1974. By this time, the only people with a favorable view of the president were those believing he had "spoken up." Their NPPI score was 57 percent: $-20\% + (-17\%) + (94\%) = 57\%$.

Similar results are present for the removal question. The mean removal score declined during this period, indicating a trend in favor of Nixon's removal, and status ceased to have a significant effect. The effects of saliency increased over time, and the involvement question continued to differentiate attitudes.

DISCUSSION

If any conclusion is evident, it is the finding of stability in the systemic public attitudes. Except for a small shift (.07 percent per week) toward the Democratic party during the 1973 to 1974 period, there is no major change in the NPAI or the PSI over a two-year period. The social status indicators explain the most variation in systemic variables, suggesting that these attitudes are most likely associated with the underlying structure of American society. Attitudes about day-to-day events, as reflected by the variables associated with the saliency of Watergate and specific explorations of presidential involvement, have much lower associations with the NPAI and the PSI.

Yet Watergate did produce dramatic changes in attitudes, changes which were confined to attitudes about popularity and presidential removal. Presidential popularity consistently fell during Nixon's term and then reached a new high after Ford assumed office. Similarly, the public's acceptance of a Nixon resignation or impeachment increased, but, ironically, the proportion of Americans who believed that the president had prior knowledge of or covered up the facts about Watergate did not change significantly. Status differences do not explain these temporal attitudes, but the saliency of Watergate and the judgments respondents made about the af-

TABLE 6.3. The Effects of Social Status and Perceptions of Presidential Involvement on Popularity and Attitudes toward Removal, 1973–1974

Response Categories	Net Presidential Popularity Index			Removal Index		
	June 19–Aug. 14, 1973	Jan. 1974	May 1974	June 19–Aug. 14, 1973	Jan. 1974	May 1974
General mean	−5%	−19%	−20%	+43%	+21%	+2%
Effects of status						
Low	−6%	0%	0%	−14%	−7%	0%
Middle	0	0	0	−3	0	0
High	+6	0	0	+11	+7	0
Effects of holding an opinion						
Expressed opinion about Nixon	−12%	−13%	−17%	−11%	−16%	−17%
Expressed no opinion about Nixon	+12	+13	+17	+11	+16	+17
Effects of perceived involvement (given opinion expressed)						
Nixon planned Watergate from the beginning	−59%	−56%	−47%	−76%	−78%	−63%
Nixon did not plan Watergate but knew ahead of time	−31	−29	−33	−10	−26	−38
Nixon found out later but covered up	0	−15	−14	+27	+14	0
Nixon had no prior knowledge and spoke up as soon as he learned	+90	+100	+94	+59	+90	+101
Effects of time (June 19 to August 14, 1973, only)						
Nixon planned Watergate from the beginning						

June 19, 1973	0%	+16%
July 3, 1973	0	0
July 31, 1973	0	0
August 14, 1973	0	−16
Nixon did not plan Watergate but knew ahead of time		
June 19, 1973	+17%	+11%
July 3, 1973	0	0
July 31, 1973	−8	−11
August 14, 1973	−9	0
Nixon found out later but covered up		
June 19, 1973	+18%	+7%
July 3, 1973	+11	0
July 31, 1973	−17	−9
August 14, 1973	−12	+2
Nixon had no prior knowledge and spoke up as soon as he learned		
June 19, 1973	0%	0%
July 3, 1973	0	−6
July 31, 1973	0	0
August 14, 1973	0	+6
No opinion		
June 19, 1973	+11%	0%
July 3, 1973	0	0
July 31, 1973	0	0
August 14, 1973	−11	0
Number of cases	6,166 1,590 1,543	6,166 1,590 1,543

fair do. Yet a respondent's position on the president's involvement does not explain her or his support for the two-party system.

In sum, the American public held attitudes at two nearly independent levels. At the temporal level, they demonstrated severe and extreme reactions to information about official misconduct, and judgments about this behavior were buffeted by changing events. At another level, the public maintained a set of allegiances to the party system in near isolation from the turmoil of the Watergate controversy.

The short-term time effects for the summer of 1973 further confirm the observation that systemic attitudes are only slightly affected by current events while temporal ones fluctuate widely. During this eight-week period, systemic measures were unchanged by the Senate hearings, but the temporal ones changed substantially. This change is observed primarily for respondents with "middle" positions, less so for those who believed Nixon "planned Watergate" or "spoke up as soon as he learned." This fact reflects a well-known finding of attitude research that extreme attitudes are most resistant to change. The respondents who believed the cover-up explanation were faced with a subtle decision about how much complicity was Nixon's and, therefore, were most affected by the hearings. The lowest point for Nixon's popularity during the hearings occurred after the tapes were made public and Special Prosecutor Cox began steps to obtain them (July 31, 1973, survey). But the very next survey (August 14) conducted after a nationally televised presidential speech shows an increase in both temporal measures.

Because of the nature of temporal attitudes, it is doubtful that such negative levels of support, as manifested by the popularity and removal questions, would have resulted in mass reactions directed against "the system." Even if Nixon had remained in office and a full impeachment proceeding had taken place, it appears unlikely that the system would have become unstable. The reason is simple: such events probably would not have changed the underlying systemic attitudes held by most citizens.

Unfortunately, too many social scientists fail to make the distinction between temporal and systemic attitude changes and often premise their predictions of dire consequences on the basis of observed changes in the former. It is entirely feasible and conceptually sound to recognize that mass publics operate at several levels of awareness. When one reads in Harris Poll and Gallup Poll reports about "dramatic changes" or "challenges to the system," one is probably observing the more easily noticed and readily measured temporal attitudes. Identifying the systemic attitudes that are tied to system-changing behavior and developing measures for them should be a first priority. Until such attempts are made, attitude research will muddle through an analytical morass.

To say that temporal attitudes have little immediate impact on the political system is not to say that they are politically unimportant. Although revolutionary responses may not be the normal public reaction to extreme dissatisfaction with incumbents and their policies, depression, distrust, alienation, contempt, cynicism, disinterest, and withdrawal of participation are. Because most scholars of democratic processes would judge these behavioral consequences unacceptable, they can hardly afford to ignore them. It is time to put aside the distractions created by the promise of finding "revolutionary" changes and structural realignments and to confront the consequences that day-to-day politics have for most citizens.

APPENDIX

Party identification question: In politics, as of today, do you consider yourself a Republican, a Democrat, or an independent?
  1. Republican
  2. Democrat
  3. Independent
  4. Other party
  0. No code or no data

Presidential popularity question: Do you approve or disapprove of the way Nixon is handling his job as president?
  1. Approve
  2. Disapprove
  3. No opinion

Leave question (form 1): Do you think President Nixon should be impeached and compelled to leave the presidency or not?
  1. Yes, should
  2. No, should not
  3. No opinion

Leave question (form 2) (After an explanation of impeachment and a preliminary question): *Just from the way you feel now, do you think his actions are serious enough to warrant his being removed from the presidency or not?
  1. Yes
  2. No
  3. No opinion
*Used after March 1974.

7

Recent Evidence on the Stability of Party Identification: The New Michigan Election Study Panel

PHILIP E. CONVERSE and GREGORY B. MARKUS

Throughout the current debate on realignment, its existence, its rate of progress, and its various possible outcomes, the behavior over time of one central concept—party identification—holds the key to understanding. After all, realignment implies the dissolution of old party loyalties and their replacement with new ones or with no loyalty at all. Because of the dynamic nature of the process, however, the numerous analysts of the sequence of national election studies generated by the Center for Political Studies at the University of Michigan have been frustrated for some time by the lack of long-term panel linkages—the reinterviewing of the same respondents—in successive replications of the basic study design. The period of the 1976 presidential election marked the completion of the first large-scale panel segment, stretching back to 1972, since the original four-year panel was completed in 1960. This new batch of panel information constitutes the fresh and important data base which has seemed to us worth a preliminary report.

Of course, the study of electoral change has scarcely withered on the vine for lack of full longitudinal studies in the interim. The more normal and inexpensive cross-time design, consisting of independent samples at each biennial national election, has greatly enriched our understanding of the range of variation in American electoral processes since the completion of the first electorate panel in 1960, in part because the intervening period has been one of political change of sufficient magnitude to be plainly visible without the extra sensor of a genuine panel design. On the other hand, however, it is exactly this high degree of change that has put an increasing premium on the advent of a new round of panel data. It will be helpful background for much that follows if we review, with a brevity which verges on oversimplification, the chief findings from the original panel and the subsequent challenges to those findings provoked by new independent cross-section data from the 1960s and early 1970s.

THE ORIGINAL 1956 TO 1960 PANEL AND LATER FINDINGS

Considering only the major contours of the panel data from the 1956 to 1958 to 1960 sample, one brute fact which could have arisen only from long-term longitudinal data was the discovery that, *at the individual level*, the stability of party identifications in the 1956 to 1960 period vastly outstripped the stability of individual positions on even the most stable of the major political issues of the period. Such stability of party identification had been suspected for some time on the basis of the noteworthy inertia of marginal distributions for the variable in independent cross-section samples throughout the 1950s. In fact, that suspicion, along with the provisional supporting evidence in marginal distributions, had been central in some of the major theses of *The American Voter* (1960). However, inertia of marginals, or minimal net change, is not at all incompatible with the possibility of high rates of *gross* change or rapid individual-level "turnover." Indeed, while time-series data on distributions of mass opinions on major political issues were somewhat more truncated because of the flux of salient issues from one election to the next, where repeated cross-section measurement did exist for political issues the marginals were often as inert as in the 1950s as those for party identification.

Therefore, it was particularly striking to discover that beneath the net stability of party identification lay a very marked degree of gross or individual-level stability, whereas the inertia or net stability of opinion distributions on major political issues concealed an equally surprising degree of individual-level turnover which appeared to be almost a Brownian motion. Let us be careful not to overstate the case. It was not, of course, true that party identification was *perfectly* stable for individuals over the 1956 to 1958 to 1960 panel observations, in the sense that all individuals located themselves in the same one of seven possible categories in each ensuing measurement. Substantial numbers changed to an adjacent location on the continuum, and a very few appeared to move long distances (five to seven "slots") across the continuum. Similarly, it was not true that the individual-level data on issue positions showed no stability whatever, in the sense that correlations between issue positions at two points in time fell all the way to zero. For one thing, there was significant variation from issue to issue, in patterns that seemed decodable; and, in any event, even the issues with the greatest individual-level turnover showed some significant degree of continuity (as indexed by continuity or stability correlations departing reliably above zero).

Nonetheless, the contrasts in stability between party and issue positions remained absolutely stark. If we square the comparative continuity correlations to erect a vocabulary of temporal covariance permitting ratio comparisons to be made, it can legitimately be observed that party identifications appeared to be over three times as stable at the individual level as positions on even the most stable of the major issues measured, over four times as stable as the modal issue, and more than six times as stable as the least stable of the issues available for comparison!

These are not trivial differences, and we would find it hard to be impressed with any theory of the dynamics of these political attitudes which failed to encompass such contrasts. A theoretical implication of these contrasts seemed to be that party loyalties had a considerable primacy in the attitude systems involved. In the 1950s, at least, issue positions appeared to be aligned only weakly with partisanship, in the minds of the voters in any event. Perceived linkages between parties and issues were, by and large, vague and contradictory as well. We opined at the time (*The American Voter*, pp. 179–183) that a major cause of the confusion might be that "actual" party differentiation on the major issues seemed to be at a low ebb in the mid fifties, a guess that later proved to have some merit. However, in the modest degree that partisanship and issue positions did covary, the contrasts in stability from the panel data suggested that it was likely that these issue preferences were more often brought into line with prior partisanship than the reverse. Once again, there is no need to exaggerate the case: it was not claimed that the causal flow was absolutely unidirectional. Surely issue positions could affect partisanship for occasional individuals at any time, and at some time occasional junctures might affect larger fractions of the population. But it seemed well-nigh impossible to square the panel contrasts in party and issue stability with a model in which the preponderant causal flow was, in any intermediate term, from issue position to partisanship, at least in the late 1950s.

Cross-Sectional Sample Findings from the 1960s

Although no full-blown panels of the national electorate were followed in the 1960s, there was ample sign of major trends in these matters by the middle years of the decade. While change was rapid on many fronts, some of the most impressive evidence involved the party-issue nexus.

Burnham (1968) noted that, after a lengthy period in which the aggregate distribution of party identification had remained nearly constant, the first signal change began in the middle 1960s with a rising proportion of the electorate refusing to report identification with either party and insisting on being classed as independents, thereby swelling the neutral middle of the party identification continuum as it stretches from strongly attached Democrats through independents to strongly attached Republicans. This apparent erosion in feelings of party loyalty among American voters, caught at an incipient stage by the first Burnham accounts, has since proceeded majestically in the same direction for close to a decade and certainly must rank by now as a change of massive magnitude. Such erosion of popular partisanship has fit nicely with Burnham's broader views as to the progressive "decomposition" of the traditional party system in the United States and has become the subject of a torrent of literature analyzing the trend away from partisanship in more detailed fashion or speculating as to its implications for an impending partisan realignment of major order.

Where issue positions of the public are concerned, Nie (with Anderson, 1974) has advanced some provocative analyses suggesting that, soon after 1960, voter policy preferences began to take on a much firmer muscle tone than was characteristic of data from the 1950s. This change is largely, although not exclusively, indexed by an apparent marked increase in the cross-sectional correlations among issue positions in the 1960s, as opposed to their feeble level of the preceding decade. The reality of the issue trends charted by Nie has been subject to somewhat more controversy than attends the brute empirical facts of erosion in party loyalties, since some (e.g., Bishop et al. 1978) have suggested that the changes may be more an artifact of shifts in question format in the Michigan series than true secular change. However this matter may be resolved, the Nie thesis has strong face validity at least, since increased public attention to policy cleavages is almost another way of describing the onset of political turbulence of the type characterizing American politics for the past dozen years.

Moreover, the Nie thesis receives supplementary support from changes observed in the domain of party-issue linkages, as well as linkages between partisanship, issue positions, and voting decisions. For example, Pomper (1972) pointed out that voter perceptions of party differences on policy issues had taken on a notably greater degree of clarity by 1964 than had been true in the first panel period of the late 1950s. The citizen was more likely to detect differences between the parties on major policy matters, and the alignment between personal partisanship and issue preferences had heightened as well. In the most exhaustive recapitulation of all these trends, Nie, Verba, and Petrocik (1976) have more recently shown that the election-by-election correlations between party identification and final voting decision, as compared with issue-vote correlations, came to look quite different in the period after the early 1960s than they had in the 1950s: the apparent weight of partisanship in the voting decision had undergone a significant decline, while the apparent weight of policy preferences showed a marked advance.[1]

Again, the magnitude of these trends, as well as their durability into the 1970s, remains subject to scholarly dispute (see, for example, Margolis 1977 on Pomper). Similarly, the longer-range import of the differences before and after the early 1960s is subject to basic disagreement. Some see these changes as secular and permanent or even accelerating in the future. Others see one or the other political period as the American norm, interrupted by an era of aberration. Still others see the two periods as local minima and maxima, with a putative normal lying somewhere between.

Nevertheless, some of the component changes are beyond dispute as empirical facts, and the total circle of changes, taken as a gestalt, has a great deal of intuitive appeal. The parts fit together with admirable consistency and, moreover, enjoy a very intelligible correspondence with impressions most of us who lived through both periods would have harbored in any event.

It is against this backdrop that the advent of the new 1972 to 1974 to 1976 panel version of the Michigan election series is particularly welcome. After all, the trends cataloged since 1960 have all been developed on successive cross-section replications, without the longitudinal tracing of the same individuals over time. This is not to say that there is anything spurious about these trends: the movements of marginal distributions and drifts in correlation coefficients estimated within each slice of time would certainly have been duplicated (apart from sampling error and variation due to population replacement) if panel studies had been persistently run throughout the era since 1960.

However, one precious class of information—the continuity or individual-level stability of the key variables—cannot be squeezed from the independent-replication design. In fact, it cannot even be deduced from other attendant slice-of-time facts with much reliability, as we shall shortly see. And, given the intervening work on electoral change, some of the first-cut expectations as to how the new panel data might look are extremely straightforward. That is to say, one of the most dramatic surprises from the 1956 to 1960 panel was the vastly greater individual stability of party identification, relative to that for individual issue positions. And the most compelling evidence of massive change since 1960 involves a major destabilization in partisanship and at least some advance in attentiveness to, and judgmental dependence upon, personal policy preferences. In short, party is down, and issues are up. The main question to be asked of the new panel data would merely seem to be "By how much?"

PLUS ÇA CHANGE . . .

Although it might be more fun to keep the reader in suspense, it will serve our purposes best to reveal the general answer rapidly, for its explication can easily occupy us for the rest of this chapter. The general answer, to be read with exquisite attention given to the conditioning clauses, is as follows. Where party and issues are concerned, and *with respect to those facets of change which a panel design is uniquely equipped to illuminate,* our first-cut explorations show that *the 1972 to 1976 panel data are very nearly a carbon copy of those from the 1956 to 1960 panel!* That is, the individual stability of party identification, both absolutely and relative to that for policy preferences, is just about as great for the latter period as for the former.

We shall spend most of the rest of this essay trying to clarify just what these initial results do and do not mean. One thing they do not mean is that no change has occurred over this period. A severe handicap in approaching problems of change consists of the first simplistic assumption that change with respect to a given variable is monolithic: either the variable changes or it doesn't, in which case we might not want to call it a variable. Such a statement sustains some merit if we specify it much more closely, as we might by insisting that we are referring only to the mean or central tendency of the variable. Then it is undoubtedly true that either the mean has changed or it has not, although, even here, some changes in mean which are numerically identical between two time points can have a vastly different portent for the future, and these differences can often be diagnosed. But, more generally speaking, change is multifaceted, even if we are addressing the same variable in its behavior over time.

These multiple facets of change, even with respect to a single variable, are recognized in more formal treatments of process. Although the distinctions are looser than one might like, processes are described as "strictly stationary," only "weakly stationary," or "not stationary at all," according to whether all, some, or none of the moments of the univariate distribution are constant. Thus each moment is, unto itself, a facet of change. As we shall presently see, there are still further facets of change with respect to a single variable, in addition to the moments, and it is one of these which shows unexpected constancy or stationarity.

It is exactly because impressive changes are known to have occurred in the party and issue variables that the panel discovery of any points of stationarity is particularly exciting. These stationary aspects may not be at all exciting by themselves, especially if our attention is riveted on the occurrence of change, since they represent the antithesis of change. However, in a period in which multiple facets of change are occurring, the localization of some points of stationarity is theoretically pregnant in diagnosing the nature of the processes underlying the total manifold of observations. To paraphrase Archimedes, these points give us "a place to stand" from which other facets in flux can be evaluated.

THE CASE OF PARTY IDENTIFICATION

We can profitably turn to the case of party identification over the comparative 1956 to 1960 and 1972 to 1976 time segments for concrete examples of the varied facets of change. All too frequently, contradictions appear to arise in the treatments of change carried out on the same variables by different scholars, simply because different aspects of change are being addressed, for quite different purposes. This potential for confusion is particularly virulent as we approach the panel feature of these change data, so careful description is important.

The most obvious facet of change in a single variable based on aggregated observations over time is the displacement of the mean of the distribution from one reading to the next. Several authors dealing with the first panel have examined changes in the central tendency of the party identification variable in the 1956 to 1960 period. There are various ways such change can be indexed in addition to obvious integer scoring of the conventional seven-point scale and taking an actual mean. One can deal, for example, with the Democratic (or Republican) percentage of the total sample or of the more restricted set of those who identify with one party or another. If, for example, we examine the marginal distributions of party identification in the panel years in terms of the Democratic percentage (strong or weak) of all *identifiers*, we find values of about 60 percent for 1956, 64 percent for 1958, and 61 percent for 1960. For 1972 the value is 63 percent, for 1974 65 percent, and for 1976 63 percent. These are forms of change. The differences from observation to observation are not very large, but they can be made to seem larger by focusing on smaller and smaller fractions of the population, properly chosen. Thus, for example, the biggest difference in the adjacent observations above is the gain from 60 percent to 64 percent between 1956 and 1958. If, instead of considering all identifiers, we focus our attention on *strong* identifiers, we find that the Democratic proportion of such identifiers shifted from 58 percent in 1956 to 70 percent in 1958, for a change of twelve percentage points. However, we succeed in amplifying the apparent change mainly by disregarding well over half the sample in each year.

All the above statements of change can be conceived as referring to shifts in the mean or central tendency of the party identification distribution, as one facet of change. The shifts are customarily small. If we stick to the Democratic percentage of all identifiers, the median biennial displacement over the whole election study series runs below 2 percent. On the other hand, unless they can be thought of as sampling error, these differences in themselves warrant that party identification is not perfectly stable down to the last voter. Although they are typically small enough to lie within the tolerances of plausible sampling error, it has long been clear that these shifts are quite systematic, moving nicely in tune with national short-term tides favoring one party or the other.

For example, the three biennial shifts since 1952 which exceed 3 percent are all associated with landslide presidential elections. More impressively still, first differences in these Democratic percentages among identifiers from one biennial election to another show a resounding correlation of .75 with first differences in the Democratic fraction of House seats after the corresponding elections since 1952. Clearly, although these shifts are slight, we are not dealing with mere sampling error in this facet of party identification change. Indeed, Brody (1977), in working with the 1956 to 1958 and 1972 to 1974 segments of the panel studies, focuses a great deal of his attention on these shifts, showing within the panels themselves that shifting has political meaning in terms of other attitudinal dimensions.

How important these slight displacements are theoretically and practically depends entirely on the more specific class of questions one wishes to ask about change. Certainly for any problems of short-term changes in political tides they are a crucial indicator, although it must be recognized that a disproportionate share of these swings comes from people who do not vote in any event. Their statements of party identification are less "abiding" than those of regular voters, and they are thus more sensitive to shifts in the short-term political winds.[2]

On the other hand, if one's research interests concerning change are longer-run in their perspective, these small shifts are not of gripping interest. This is not simply because they are small but, rather, because their nature as short-term oscillations around a mean value has historically been quite clear. If the Democratic percentage shifts by 4 percent between two biennial elections, as it did between 1956 and 1958, this is not likely to be an intriguing harbinger of fundamental partisan change, because the odds are extremely high (if not absolutely certain) that the shift will very rapidly be reversed. It is as though we were watching the tops of reeds growing in a shallow pond. Before an east wind, they tilt to the west. Before a west wind, they tilt to the east. When it is still, they stand in a middling position. From some points of view the motion is of interest, since it tells us which way the wind is blowing at the moment. From other points of view it is not of great interest, since we know the reeds are not moving in any absolute sense but are firmly anchored in a fixed position by their roots.

More technically speaking, the mean of the party identification distribution around which these small oscillations occur has been almost stationary for the past twenty-five years. We say "almost" because there appears to have been a glacially slow drift of the mean in a Democratic direction over this period, probably due to population replacement. Even in twenty-five years, the total ground covered is very small. This secular drift is small by comparison with the amplitude of the oscillations about that mean, even though these oscillations are in turn very small by comparison with the swings of the national popular vote.

It is important to recognize these oscillations about a nearly fixed mean for what they are in the panel data, to avoid misinterpretations of some of the changes they generate. Thus, for example, Brody (1977) discusses the counter intuitive finding that, in *both* the 1956 to 1958 and the 1972 to 1974 segments of the panel studies, Republican identifiers appear to be less "directionally stable" (i.e., more likely to move out of the Republican camp into at least an independent if not a Democratic identification) than Democrats, despite the fact that in most other times Republicans have seemed more anchored in their political behavior. This perplexing effect is almost certainly a function of the fact that both the 1956 to 1958 and the 1972 to 1974 segments bracketed major shifts in short-term partisan fortunes from the Republicans to the Democrats. Thus, even relatively labile respondents who claimed to be Democrats when current winds were favoring the Republicans (1956 to 1972) would have very little reason to stop being Democrats two years later, when the winds had then become more supportive. Presumably the reverse partisan contrasts would occur in temporal comparisons where the wind change was simply reversed.

While the mean of a distribution provides one facet of potential change in a variable, it scarcely exhausts the subject of change where that variable is concerned. Aside from such practical problems as ceilings and floors on measuring instruments, the variance of the distribution can move in total independence of the temporal behavior of the mean. The variance can remain stationary while the mean shifts dramatically, or the variance can shrink or expand dramatically while the mean is stationary. In fact, as we have seen, the most striking change in the party identification distribution since 1965 is a shrinkage of the variance by more than 10 percent, as fewer and fewer voters report strong identifications at the extremes, and more and more cluster toward the independent middle of the distribution. This is again a true change in the nature of party identification, a change which has appropriately been treated in the recent literature as having major theoretical interest. Yet this change has occurred quite rapidly in a period when the mean of the distribution has been to all intents and purposes a constant.

There is no need to do a panel study to monitor constancy or change in either the mean or the variance of a distribution. Successive independent cross-section samples can perform this task equally well. The information a panel study uniquely supplies involves the continuity in positioning of the same individuals over time. One index of such continuity is to calculate the proportion of the panel sample on the main diagonal (or the main diagonal plus one or two adjacent categories) of the cross tabulation of the same variable between waves. While such expressions are commonly used, they are rather weak summarizations not only because of the arbitrary nature of the category width that constitutes the "stable" diagonal but, more especially, because the proportions resulting are very strongly influenced by the total number of categories into which the variable is partitioned, so that comparisons across variables of different category "length" become nonsensical. An obvious improvement is to deal with a summary expression of correlation or regression.

We have approached the new panel data on party identification only after a lengthy detour through a consideration of changes in means and variances of distributions for a very simple reason: although novitiates are constantly confused by the fact, stability or continuity correlations formed on the same variable in two panel waves are as fully independent of temporal changes in the mean and variance of the distribution between the two time points as the mean and variance are independent of one another. That is to say, a continuity correlation can range from zero to perfection whether both mean and variance are constant or one or both shift dramatically between the two time points. This is true by the very construction of the standard product moment correlation coefficient, which in its calculation equates or normalizes the two means and variances, thereby controlling away whatever real change may have occurred with respect to those facets of the variable.[3]

Since continuity correlations can vary independently of changes in means and variances, they obviously tap still another facet of change. It is important to be clear just what facet that is. Clearly, it has to do with stability of individual-level positioning. What is important to remember is that it taps the stability of *relative* individual positions, not absolute ones, across a population. Let us imagine that political controversy surrounds the first suggestion of major investment in a space program. At the outset, some enthusiasts wish to invest a billion dollars a year, others wish to limit the investment to 500 million, and still others wish to have no program at all. Then a foreign power makes major strides in space, and concern about the competition shifts individual policy preferences in a more lavish direction. One possible form of the change is that response to the competition is very differential by person, with some initially enthusiastic observers now deciding they do not want to participate in a space race at all. Thus one extreme possibility is that, while the mean (in preferred dollar expenditure) has risen, there is no correlation between individual preferences over the two time points. But the polar opposite case is also a lively possibility, with no participant raising his or her personal ante by more than any other, thereby preserving the stability of relative preference locations on the dollar continuum. In the latter case, the continuity correlation would be perfect despite the marked change in mean preference.

While it is thereby technically quite possible that individual-level continuity correlations for party identification have remained at their high levels of the late 1950s despite the shrinking variance of the distribution, it would not intuitively seem very likely. After all, the descriptors commonly applied to the surge in independence talk of the "erosion" of these identifications and the "destabilization of partisanship." While such terms are entirely proper, they would certainly seem to imply a major unraveling of individual-level continuities in party preferences, even in the stability of relative locations. Moreover, at a less intuitive and more technical level, if error variances remain constant while true variances of a variable decline, then the magnitude of correlations involving the variable will be attenuated.[4] Thus, the natural shrinkage of observed variance of party identification might be expected on these grounds alone to dilute the continuity correlations correspondingly.

Some years back, we suggested that this might not turn out empirically to be the case with party identification (Converse 1975), since the only scrap of a national panel conducted during the 1960s—a couple hundred stray cases reinterviewed between 1964 and 1966—showed continuity correlations which were virtually identical to those estimated from the 1956 to 1960 panel, despite the fact that this panel overlapped into the period in which the variance of identification reports had begun to shrink palpably. Therefore, we are not entirely surprised to discover that the continuity correlations calculated for party identification from the new 1972 to 1976 panel are just about as high as they were in 1956 to 1960. In absolute terms they are a hair lower, but the difference is too slight for statistical significance. Probably the drop is in some degree real, as one would expect from the truncation of variance in the later period. However, the stunning fact is that the decline is simply vestigial: if one could say from the 1956 to 1960 panel that individual-level continuity correlations for party identification with a two-year time lapse ran in the low .80s, one can make exactly the same statement for the 1972 to 1976 panel.

For reasons that should be intuitively apparent, the magnitudes or continuity coefficients are specific to the size of the time interval elapsing between measurements. In processes of progressive (i.e., not cyclical) change, they can be expected to decline as the interval becomes more extended. Indeed, this property emerges clearly in the party identification data. The four-year correlations are less than those calculated for a two-year interval; and the latter are smaller than correlations formed for measurements separated by only a few weeks in time, as is the case when the party identification item is applied to the same sample in both the preelection and the postelection questionnaires. Therefore, continuity correlations in general have meaning only as they are tagged with some specific time interval. If we stick with the two-year correlations in order to encompass comfortably the data from the two-wave, 1964 to 1966 minipanel, we find the following raw comparisons:[5]

Best estimate of two-year continuity correlation,
1956 to 1960 period = .835
Estimate from the 1964 to 1966 minipanel = .836
Best estimate from the 1972 to 1976 period = .813

There are several ways of processing these raw continuity coefficients into more refined components. One of the easiest partitions, dependent on having at least three waves of measurement, is to break the raw coefficients into (1) a reliability component, reflecting the complement of the proportion of error variance, and (2) a "true" stability coefficient, reflecting the degree to which the measurement at two points in time would be correlated if there were no intrusion of unreliability. Such procedures have been described by Heise (1969) and further refined by Wiley and Wiley (1970). These manipulations rest, as always, on a series of assumptions about the character of the data and the attendant error structures. One of the less pleasing sets of assumptions—that the measurement reliability (Heise) or the absolute error variances (Wiley and Wiley) are constant from wave to wave in a given panel sequence—can be relaxed in the case of the 1956 to 1960 panel, where instead of three waves of measurement of party identification we can profit from five.[6] While it is regrettable that party identification was measured only three times in the new panel (1972 preelection, 1974, and 1976 preelection), there is sufficiently striking consistency between the two panels to reassure ourselves concerning various assumptions which must be made for the later batch of panel data. Also, of course, we can proceed no further with the mere two waves offered by the 1964 to 1966 minipanel, although the data presented above also give some assurance that we are dealing with process parameters which have a considerable stability in the intermediate term.

There are other assumptions embedded in calculations of the Heise or Wiley-Wiley type that are not entirely well met by the data. Thus, for example, there is reason to believe that both the measurement reliability and the true stability of the party identification item are less than nicely homogeneous over the population. In later, more complicated assays of these data, we shall take such characteristics into fuller account. Nonetheless, as first-cut approximations, it is worth seeing what can provisionally be estimated concerning the relative proportions of change due to unreliability, as opposed to "true change," in these longitudinal measurements.

Where they can be compared most fully (as in the five-wave panel), calculations of the Heise and Wiley-Wiley type give virtually identical estimates with these data. Both calculations agree that the main source of the slight decline in overall continuity between the two large panels is a slight increase in unreliability, exactly as one would expect if the main change in the data were a shrinkage in the true variance.[7] In both calculations, the decline in reliability is roughly from (a central tendency of about) .88 in the first panel to about .84 in the second.[8] Once this slight decline in reliability is set aside, as it is when we calculate the true stability coefficients, we find comparisons of the following sort as our best estimates for the two-year interval:

	1956–58–60	1972–74–76
Two-year stability (Heise style)	.951	.972
Two-year stability (Wiley-Wiley style)	.958	.972

The homogeneity of these estimates, both between calculation methods and more especially across two periods in which the nature of party identification has seemed so different, when other facets of change in the variable are considered, is very striking. There are a variety of ways in which the implications of these findings can be expressed. We shall postpone some of the broader theoretical implications until our conclusion. For now, we might briefly consider what the above data imply for the long-term staying power of party identifications at the individual level.

If we merely knew that the raw two-year continuity correlation for party identification was about .82 (as a period-free average), we might be tempted to conclude that, over a period of sixteen (2^4) years, we could expect only a continuity of .45 (or .82⁴), a value which would not be entirely impressive. However, if we trust the above estimates as to the proportion of observed change which is mere unreliability of measurement, we would expect the sixteen-year *observed* (i.e., error-attenuated) stability coefficient to look something like .73 (or .86 [.96⁴], where the .86 is the period-free reliability estimate) instead of .45. This is a vastly different picture of the long-term individual-level stability of the variable, especially as it is appropriate to square these two values, yielding a contrast in shared temporal covariance of .53 instead of .20. And we feel considerably less cavalier about cycling hypothetically over longer periods of time in this way once we have at least some shred of assurance, which the above data give, that the true stability of the party identification measure is remarkably close to stationary across two political periods in which, in other senses, it has been subject to major change.

SUMMARY AND CONCLUSION

Figure 7.1 provides a handy graphic summary of the continuity correlation information we have reviewed over the course of the preceding pages. In addition to the coefficients for party identification which we have discussed in some detail, we have included here similar continuity correlations for six of the major political

FIGURE 7.1.   Continuities in public response to parties, leaders, and issues

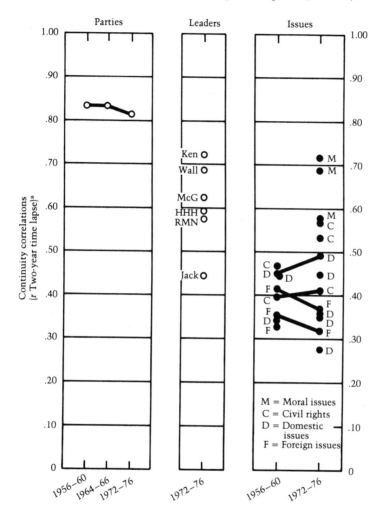

Note: Where items can be plausibly matched between panel segments, the respective data points are linked by a trend line.

[a]The whole figure is expressed in the currency of *two*-year continuity correlations. Where only four-year correlations are available, plausible two-year interpolations have been made to permit inclusion of a maximal number of items.

figures of the 1972 to 1976 period, as well as a number of the issues which were explored by the Survey Research Center/Center for Political Studies interviews in both the earlier and the later time periods.[9]

In a nutshell, this summary says that, apart from the emergence of some political cleavages having to do with traditional moral values in the later period,[10] there has been scarcely any change in the comparative continuity of party and issue positioning between the two eras, despite manifold reasons to expect not only change but change of major proportions. The individual-level continuity of party attachments continues to dwarf that for issue positioning in the 1972 to 1976 period, as it did in 1956 to 1960. And affections and dislikes for the most prominent political leaders of the epoch seem to show levels of continuity which—again apart from the moral issues—clearly lie between parties and issues.

One thing this summary does *not* mean is that the signs of weakening partisanship, as registered in change in the party identification marginals since 1965, have somehow been imaginary or meaningless. Such could scarcely be argued, and, for reasons developed earlier in this essay, the display in figure 7.1 does not even address this facet of change in any direct way. To be sure, there is a tiny decline in the continuity correlation for party identification in the later period, and we pointed out internal evidence to suggest that this decline can be traced almost exclusively to a shrinkage in the true variance of the party identification distribution, with both the true change parameters and the absolute size of the error variance remaining essentially constant. Hence the known weakening of partisanship does have its effect, albeit a very glancing one, even on the data of figure 7.1. What is important is the demonstration that the effect of such renowned changes on the continuity correlation is as light as it is or, to put the matter another way, that the gulf in continuity between party identification and issue positioning was so staggeringly large as originally observed in the late 1950s that even the major changes of the late 1960s and early 1970s have failed to close the gap in more than a barely discernible degree.

To reiterate, however, none of this is to deny that reported strength of party identification has declined in the past decade. Moreover, there is evidence that defection rates for given levels of identification strength have been higher in recent years than they were in the 1950s. Both changes independently attest to a weakening of partisanship in the electorate. Both are thoroughly documented, and both have had real and important effects on the operation of the American political system.

For many analytic purposes and prognostications, the weakening of partisanship can be more important information than the near constancy of continuity correlations summarized in figure 7.1. For other purposes, however, the reverse is true, and it remains for us to suggest what some of the genuine implications of the figure would seem to be.

One of these implications must certainly involve the nature of partisan realignments. The subject has captured uncommon scholarly interest not merely because of its obvious crucial importance in any theory of elections but also because of the seeming imminence of such a realignment after 1964 or so. Given past periodicities, the time was ripe. Much more to the point, several key ingredients associated with past realignments had begun to emerge.

Very crudely put, the most important of these ingredients was the outbreak of uncommonly galvanizing political turmoil, of the sort which certainly marked the late 1960s and early 1970s. More finely drawn, we have the excellent effort of Sundquist (1973) to reconstruct the internal dynamics of partisan realignment, with stress upon crucial emergence of important crosscutting cleavages which the leaderships of the extant traditional parties, bound to older cleavage lines, fail to articulate. Again, such ingredients were present par excellence by the late 1960s. That these new cleavages were gripping for common voters is attested to at least indirectly by the high continuity values associated in the new panel with items like busing and the life-style or moral issues. That these new issues posed cleavages which were truly crosscutting (i.e., relatively orthogonal to or uncorrelated with prior lines of party alignment) is clearly demonstrated by Miller and Levitin (1976: 82), who show the lack of much association between voter persuasions on the newer issues and their party identifications.

One must insist that the new issues be crosscutting ones to set the stage for a realignment, since otherwise the emergence of new issues more or less aligned with old ones would merely reinforce existing party differences. In the late 1960s and early 1970s, some Democrats were affronted by counterculture trends while others were not; likewise, some Republicans approved while others did not. What is important about these differential within-party affinities is that, if potent enough, they should produce changes in partisanship of a leapfrogging kind, disturbing the relative ordering of individuals on the continuum of partisan loyalties. However, it is exactly this possibility of leapfrogging that our continuity correlations are admirably designed to register, however insensitive they may be to other forms of change. And they give us the message that the leapfrogging type of change in partisanship was scarcely more prevalent in the 1972 to 1976 period than it had been in 1956 to 1960.

Of course, on the basis of the data shown in figure 7.1, we could not rule out the possibility that the individual-level stability of relative positioning might have suffered a major collapse in the 1966 to 1972 period, too late to be seen in the 1964 to 1966 mini-panel but too early to have registered in the new panel. Such a neat outflanking of our moments of panel measurement would be a bit implausible on the face of it, but we do in fact have data that make such a possibility still more implausible. In 1973, Jennings and Niemi (1975) reinterviewed the parents of their 1965 graduating high school students, who had originally been interviewed in 1965. These parents cannot, of course, be seen as a proper sample of the adult electorate. Having in common the fact of being parents of children typically eighteen years of age in 1965, they represent a somewhat homogeneous cohort, lacking in the newer and younger voters and, given their association with children not dropping out of high school, a shade higher than normal in social-class terms. It can be calculated that, if the Jennings-Niemi parent panel were in fact representative of the full electorate and followed the continuity parameters typical of our party identification data earlier shown, they should show a continuity correlation for party identification of .761 over an eight-year span. Their age and class bias would lead one to expect a slightly higher figure.

The observed figure for the party identifications of the Jennings-Niemi parents over the 1965 to 1973 interval is .791. Hence, if there were any limited period of collapse in the individual stabilities of party positioning from 1966 to 1972, it somehow miraculously left this particular age cohort untouched, since the relevant value observed here is right on target, and the period of observation perfectly spans the suspect era. But by now any attempt to defend a hypothesis of some hidden collapse of partisanship continuity between our measurements is beginning to get rather farfetched. It seems much easier to believe that the continuity correlations for party identification have been constant in an almost uncanny degree throughout the period of observation starting with the 1950s.

No doubt the manifest pressures represented by new crosscutting issues in the latter half of this period have served to increase hesitation about the expression of strong party loyalties. But there is no evidence whatever that these pressures have been strong enough to produce an actual leapfrogging change of individual locations on the partisan continuum.

The resistance of party identification to any unusual increase in individual instability during this period of shocks is impressive in its own right. Even when coupled with evidence of the considerable instability of issue positioning, however, this fact cannot in itself serve as a guarantee that such identifications are nearly always causally primary when partisanship is aligned with issue preferences. Among other things, it is worth keeping in mind the fact that there are only two major parties, whereas the number of political issues which may exercise one or another voter is legion. Thus it would always be possible, if indeed a bit strained, to imagine that the typical voter might be viscerally gripped by one issue out of some thirty, with very uncrystallized attitudes on the other twenty-nine. If party positions on such crucial but idiosyncratic issues remained constant over long periods of time, it would be possible that these policy preferences totally dictated party identifications, at the very same time that measurement over a dozen or so of the thirty potential issues might show very high aggregate instability, since only one voter in thirty would, on the average, be gripped by each.

While such a model remains conceivable, it is obviously not the most plausible reading of current data. The discrepancies in individual-level continuities between party loyalties on the one hand and issue positions on the other, particularly in view of what now seems to be the long-term constancy of these huge discrepancies, would seem to argue for an overwhelming primacy of the party term when party-issue congruence does occur.

The additional fact, also made clear by the new panel data, that reactions to political leaders display levels of continuity intermediary between partisanship and policy preferences, raises a number of further interesting possibilities. Such a data configuration may, for example, be suggestive of a significant margin for policy leadership available to major political figures, whereby admirers are quite susceptible to influence into taking on policy positions more congruent with those espoused by their heroes. Or, again, the greater continuity in evaluation of leaders than in issue positions may simply reflect the fact that party attachments anchor *both* leader assessments and issue positions but do so more effectively in the case of leaders, because the common voter can maintain much more firm and unequivocal cognitive links between parties and their most prominent leaders than between parties and positions on various issues.

This is obviously not the place to begin sorting out such possibilities. However, the first-cut results from the new Center for Political Studies panel are striking indeed. They already rule out some constructions which might be placed upon the electoral history of the past decade and begin to draw into focus a number of new research questions which, with more refined milling of the panel data, we may well be able to answer effectively.

NOTES

Note: The research on which this report is based was supported by National Science Foundation Grant SOC-7707537. We are also grateful to Jean Dotson, Maria Sanchez, and Peter Joftis for their aid in data preparation. This chapter is an abridgement of Philip E. Converse and Gregory B. Markus, "Plus Ça Change . . . : The New CPS Election Study Panel," *American Political Science Review* 73: 32–49. Reprinted by permission.

1   Presidential voting in the 1976 election seems to be the first major reversal of this trend.

2   For a more extended discussion of the significance of these oscillations, see Converse (1976: 126–130).

3   Obviously, one can restore some of this information in relatively compact form by shifting from correlation coefficients to raw or nonstandardized regression coefficients plus intercept terms. For some purposes this is exactly what one should do, although such statements operate in a metric-bound currency which can impede communication for those unfamiliar with the variable. For simplicity, we shall deal here with continuity correlations.

4   Note, however, that this expectation is contingent on an error variance which is gaining in size relative to the true variance. In the more general case, the continuity correlation is in theory independent of the variances of the component distributions.

5   Here, as at some other points in this essay, precise numbers of cases are difficult to provide, since the estimates are more often than not "synthetic," resting on multiple bases. Thus, for example, the value of .835 is based on an averaging of four different estimates available in the 1956 to 1960 panel for the correlation after about a two-year interval. While all these values are very similar in appearance, each is based on a rather different number of cases.

6   In addition to the full-blown fourth wave present on Inter-University Consortium for Political and Social Research tapes due to a full-sample application of the party identification item in the postelection as well as the preelection

study for 1960, a stray set of 165 cases were reasked the party identification question in the 1956 postelection study as well. Estimates from this mini-sample are, of course, less stable than their counterparts in the four other waves. However, where comparisons are possible, they are so gracefully consistent with what can be learned from the pre- and post-1960 waves that we do not have much hesitation in using them to yield the additional degrees of freedom provided by a fifth wave. Naturally, in all relevant calculations, we take account of the fact that the points of observation are very unequally spaced in real time.

7 Actually, our detailed calculations show not only no shrinkage in the error variance but, if anything, a slight absolute increase. Thus, the decrease in reliability (or the proportion of true variance to total variance) has a double source.

8 Throughout this essay we are providing mere "bottom line" estimates that conceal more detailed consideration of angularities in the data. These will be dealt with more explicitly in subsequent technical papers. One such angularity being momentarily ignored in this statement, although dealt with in our calculations, is the presence of some systematic progression of the unreliability term across waves of the same panel.

9 These two latter sets of correlations are discussed at length in Converse and Markus (1979).

10 The moral values which emerged in the 1972 to 1976 period (along with their two-year continuity correlations) were legalization of marijuana (.712), approval of abortion (.685), and approval of women's liberation (.577).

PART III

Elite Behavioral Change

8

Political Realignments and Recruitment to the U.S. Congress, 1870–1970

LESTER G. SELIGMAN and MICHAEL R. KING

One of the most enduring continuities in American politics over the past century may be found in the social and political profiles of members of the U.S. Congress. A contemporary senator or representative is typically a middle-aged male attorney of white Anglo-Saxon Protestant extraction. He was born in the state or district he represents, or he settled there shortly after graduating from a reputable law school. He represents one of the two major political parties and launched his political career as a state legislator, state's attorney, or some other state or local elected official.

The same profile would describe a congressman or senator of the 1870s, except that he would have received his legal training by reading law in apprenticeship to a practicing attorney, would have been a bit younger, and would have been somewhat more likely to have migrated into his constituency. Otherwise, the religious, ethnic, racial, sex, and occupational breakdowns of members of Congress have remained amazingly stable.

Thus, while in this century the United States has changed so profoundly, Congress has consistently included lawyers, business executives, and farmers who personify the values, outlooks, interests, and styles of their states and congressional districts (Harris 1969). Most of them have been the sons of successful middle-class families; a smaller number achieved middle-class status. But, while the office enjoys high status, our national legislators themselves are not held in high esteem by the public, perhaps because, to paraphrase Walter Bagehot's characterization of Sir Robert Peel, members of Congress and senators are regarded as "common men of uncommon ambition" (Davidson et al. 1966).

The uniqueness of the continuity in the occupational background of United States representatives and senators becomes evident when compared with the background of members of parliaments in other democratic countries. Wences' research on the occupational composition of parliaments in sixteen countries shows that, as voting participation has increased and suffrage has broadened, the proportion of business executives and attorneys in parliament has decreased and the proportion recruited from other professions and from labor and party bureaucracies has increased (1969). In the United States, perhaps because universal white male suffrage was achieved early in our history, the percentage of attorneys and business executives in Congress has not changed appreciably with the expansion of suffrage or with changing levels of voting participation.

Basic differences in the role of lawmakers in Congress as compared with legislators in other democracies doubtless also contribute to this continuity. The European lawmakers are more obedient to party discipline and therefore play less independent roles than do their American counterparts. Such role differences influence the selection of individuals of particular background and abilities.

Perhaps the continuity in the occupational background of members of Congress is something of an illusion, because it masks substantial increases in specialization *within* occupations. Obviously, the highly specialized farmers, businesspeople, or attorneys of today are a far cry from their counterparts of 1870, and the implications of such increased specialization merit closer study. But, in the face of such changes, the local attachments and parochial outlooks of members of Congress, particularly in the House of Representatives, persist.

There is evidence, however, that, during intervals of political realignment, the continuity in backgrounds is disrupted. New, younger members of Congress are elected whose political and occupational career paths differ from the customary ones (King and Seligman 1976). Such political realignment occurred in the last century during the periods surrounding the presidential elections of 1896 and 1932. At these times, substantial electoral changes took place. Regional patterns of party allegiance among the electorate shifted, elements of the active electorate lapsed into inactivity, and other segments began to participate consistently for the first time (Nie et al. 1976).

Concomitantly, some ambitious younger candidates of both parties at the state and local levels challenged members of the old guard. New patterns of congressional recruitment emerged as a result of intensified political conflict within congressional constituencies. Turnover in Congress increased as many of these younger people, whose background was of lower status and whose policy preferences differed from those of the incumbents they displaced, were elected. As a result of the impact of such newcomers on congressional coalitions, important changes in public policy occurred.

Thus, both continuity and discontinuity have characterized the backgrounds of the congressional elite over the past century. During the periods of realignment, turnover and change in background profiles have had special significance. Research on the periods *between* realignments has shown no consistent relationships among background variables, turnover, and roll-call behavior (King and Seligman 1976). *During* realignments, however, background factors successfully predicted congressional voting behavior, indicating that new legislators, elected in the midst of realignment, acted as a cohort (King and Seligman 1976), seizing opportunities presented by the realignment crisis to represent the interests of the disaffected.

In this chapter, both continuity and discontinuity in the backgrounds of members of Congress are investigated, and several explanations of this dual pattern are presented. In particular, we will examine the dramatic, short-run departures from such continuities which mark periods of realignment as well as their implications for patterns of congressional decision making.

POLITICAL REALIGNMENTS AND SHIFTS IN THE PARTY BALANCE IN CONGRESS

The usual turnover in Congress which occurs with each election causes only marginal change in the party balance. Party control of one or both houses of Congress may change, but such shifts reflect short-term reactions to current events and issues or the fluctuating popularity of the president. But, during realignment periods, the sizable turnover in Congress indicates profound change. The new people elected to Congress are the vanguard influence of new groups and signal the relative decline of older groups and interests.

Substantial turnover may occur in noncritical elections as well. For example, in 1920, the Republicans gained sixty-one seats, a 14.1 percent increase in their representation in the House. This is somewhat larger than the net gains and losses in 1896 and not too different from those which occurred in 1932 in the House of Representatives. But there are crucial differences in the character

FIGURE 8.1.   Turnover in Congress, 1872–1956, including the critical
elections of 1896 and 1932

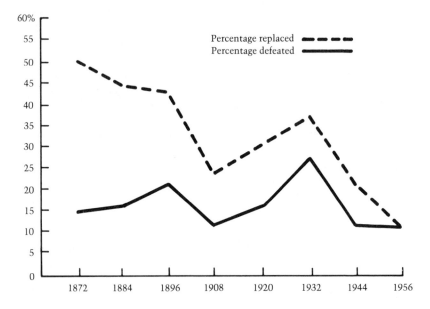

of such turnover in realignment and nonrealignment periods. During realignments, turnover is disproportionately attributable to the
defeat of incumbents, whereas instances of sizable turnover at
other times are due primarily to the retirement of incumbents.
This is illustrated in figure 8.1, which shows turnover in the House
of Representatives at twelve-year intervals, or every sixth congressional election since 1872, including the critical elections of 1896
and 1932. The data include measures of the percentage of members
replaced at each election as well as the percentage defeated. The
percentage replaced records turnover from all causes (e.g., defeat,
retirement, death), after controlling for the effects of reapportionment and the admission of new states (Fiorina et al. 1975). The latter measure indicates turnover owing to electoral defeat, either
through failure to secure renomination or through defeat by an opponent of the other party.[1] Clearly, the proportion of members defeated was greater in critical elections than in other elections. As
was noted, in 1920 a substantial shift took place in the party balance in Congress favoring the Republicans, but this was attribu-

table as much to retirement as to defeat. In 1920, an unusually large number of Democratic incumbents retired, to be replaced disproportionately by Republicans.[2] Thus, unlike other elections, turnover during realignment periods involves a high rate of electoral defeat.

In still another respect, turnover during political realignments differs from turnover at other times. The changes in the composition of Congress during realignments are more lasting and have more durable effects on congressional coalitions. The election of new legislators reflects changes in voting preferences, political opportunities, and recruitment patterns in a number of districts. As a result, the doors to Congress are opened to new elements. The persistence of the new voter loyalties and recruitment patterns until the next realignment creates and stabilizes a new coalitional balance in Congress.

The number of districts that must change in order to bring about shifts in the balance in Congress is surprisingly small. A shift of 15 to 20 percent from one party or coalition to the other has been sufficient to tip the scales and, in the process, to give the new members influence out of proportion to their numbers. Thus, durable changes in a relatively small number of districts, amplified through their effects on congressional coalitions, may be sufficient to affect the course of public policy.

CRITICAL ELECTIONS AND CHANGES IN POLITICAL AND SOCIAL BACKGROUNDS

Political realignments alter existing pathways to Congress in both parties. During realignments, by definition, one party gains more from the electoral shifts. But the issues that precipitated the realignment have generated battles *within, as well as between,* both parties, resulting in the ouster of incumbents by insurgent candidates who defeat them in the primary or at the local nominating convention. Although the usual turnover during realignment involves the defeat of incumbents of the old majority party by challengers from the other party, a substantial proportion of the turnover is due to the defeat of incumbents of both parties by insurgents from *within* their own ranks.

The changes in the background profile of Congress which result from realignment turnover set them apart from changes which occur at other times. *During critical elections, changes in background profiles cut across party lines, affecting both of the parties in similar ways, whereas, after nonrealigning elections, the background profiles of each party's congressional contingent change independently of one another.*

This crosscutting change can be illustrated by examining the socioeconomic and political background characteristics of winning and losing members of Congress in every fourth presidential election from 1872 to 1956. We collected information about (1) candidates' experiences in precongressional political offices (i.e., local, state, national); (2) the character of such offices (elective, appointive, party); (3) the average number of such offices held by each individual before election to Congress; (4) educational attainment; (5) age when elected to the Congress in question; (6) occupation; and (7) geographic mobility, that is, whether the members were elected from the region of their birth or from another region to which they had migrated.[3]

Each background characteristic was examined, and the change in the proportion of legislators who shared that characteristic attributable to the defeat of incumbents was noted for each party. In some instances, the increase or decrease followed the same direction in both parties, indicating changes that crossed party lines; in other cases, changes were in opposite directions. Figure 8.2 graphs the proportion of changes which were in the same direction in both parties as a percentage of *all* instances of change.

As figure 8.2 shows, political realignments disproportionately bring new people to Congress from both parties who have experienced common types of political apprenticeship and who share many socioeconomic characteristics. A change in relative political opportunities occurs in both parties, *especially within the former minority party.* The minority-party organization has been captured by dissidents in some constituencies, who acquire new influence and representation in Congress because of the shift in voter loyalty during the realignment. Some of the incumbent representatives of the old minority party are challenged within their own party, but most withstand the challenge and are reelected by the electoral tide which defeats many of their colleagues of the opposing party. Many incumbents of the previous majority party are defeated, not only by challengers of the opposite party but also by insurgents within their own ranks who share some characteristics with the newly elected in the other party. Thus, during critical elections,

FIGURE 8.2. Patterns of change in political and socioeconomic background characteristics in critical and noncritical elections

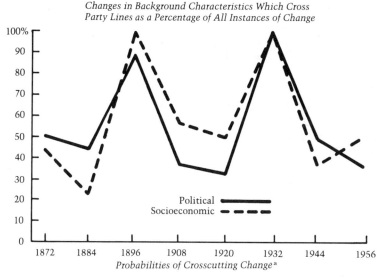

Changes in Background Characteristics Which Cross Party Lines as a Percentage of All Instances of Change

Political ——————
Socioeconomic ▬ ▬ ▬ ▬

Probabilities of Crosscutting Change[a]

Elections	P (crosscutting change)	
	Political	*Socioeconomic*
Critical elections		
(1896, 1932 combined)	>.999	>.999
1896	>.98	>.99
1932	>.99	>.99
Noncritical elections		
(1872, 1884, 1908, 1920,		
1944, 1956 combined)	<.95	<.95
1872	<.95	<.95
1884	<.95	<.95
1908	<.95	<.95
1920	<.95	<.95
1944	<.95	<.95
1956	<.95	<.95

[a]Probabilities were calculated by means of the binomial sign test. For a description of the procedures used, see the methodological note in the appendix. Cases where there was no change between the background characteristics of incoming and defeated members of Congress in one or the other party were not included in the calculations.

winners resemble other winners, losers resemble other losers, and both groups differ from each other, irrespective of party.

Change in Age and Education during Political Realignments

In many ways, the character of change in congressional backgrounds in every election is tied to the specific conditions and candidates involved. This is as true during realignment periods as at other times. Although changes in background cut across party lines during realignments, the specifics of such changes (e.g., whether the proportion of attorneys increases or decreases) are not uniform from one realignment to the next, with two notable exceptions. During realignment periods, the newly elected members of both parties are of lower status than the incumbents they defeat and are substantially younger than their opponents. These findings shed light on the changes that occur within each party during realignments and on the central role of the recruitment process as the touchstone of such changes.

The significant change during critical elections is *within* each party, and the crucible of the change is the recruitment process. A new generational set of candidates challenges the old guard within each party. The struggle of these generational cohorts to gain office becomes an ideological conflict. Younger insurgents and seasoned incumbents battle in each party as new candidates and new interests emerge. During each realignment, generational cleavages become more salient and are reflected in congressional turnover. *After each of the critical elections, the newly elected members were much younger than their defeated opponents.* This is not true of any of the other elections examined. Prior to the 1896 election, for example, the average age of the membership of the House in the Fifty-fourth Congress was fifty-five. After the 1896 election, the defeated congressmen averaged fifty-eight years of age, while the average age of the new congressmen elected to the Fifty-fifth Congress was forty-two. The age difference in 1932 was even more striking. The average age of the incumbents from the Seventy-second Congress who were defeated in 1932 was sixty-three and the incoming freshmen averaged forty-three years of age (Oleszek 1969).

To be sure, new members of Congress in any period are likely to be younger than incumbents. Oleszek (1969) found that the average age of legislators elected to the House of Representatives for the first time is between forty and forty-five. Prior service in state legislatures and local offices is common before people seek

FIGURE 8.3. Mean age of losing incumbents and winning replacements
in the House in every fourth presidential election, 1872–1956

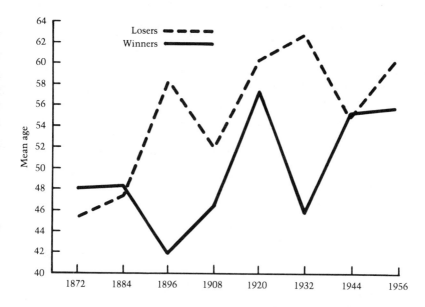

SOURCE: *Biographical Directory* 1961.

congressional office, which usually makes new candidates in their
forties. But our findings suggest that newcomers are sometimes
older on the average than the incumbents they replace. This was
true in 1872, 1884, and 1944. At other times, such as 1920, virtually no change occurred. When the mean age of defeated incumbents
and winning freshmen is plotted across the eight elections, it becomes clear that only during the critical elections were the newcomers substantially younger than the defeated incumbents (figure
8.3). These large age differences have special political importance
because they correspond with differences among members in political and social background and policy outlooks. The age changes
during realignments mark the advent in Congress of the kind of
political generation to which Mannheim referred, a cohort with
a particular policy outlook.[4]

This generational phenomenon is also associated with new opportunity for election to Congress of individuals of somewhat
lower social status. In the aftermath of critical elections, the new-

comers of both parties are, on the average, somewhat less educated than the defeated incumbents (fig. 8.4). In most of the other elections, increases in the social status of some candidates in one party were balanced by decreases in the other. Only in 1920 did the average educational attainment decline in both parties, but these changes were substantially smaller than those which occurred in 1896 and 1932.

Thus, during critical elections, changes in representation are not confined to shifts from one party to the other. The newcomers reflect changes in both parties in relative political opportunities in some constituencies. Some of the shifts in background profiles are idiosyncratic and indicate only the particular issues and interests in conflict in the realignment. Other changes affect both parties in common; the new legislators are younger and less well educated than the losing incumbents.

THE REALIGNMENT PROCESS AND PATTERNS OF POLITICAL CHANGE: THE CASE OF 1932

Political realignments are periods of significant change which often take a decade or more to come to fruition. The scholarly literature has tended to emphasize the dramatic events, personalities, and changes which mark "critical elections." This emphasis has obscured the longer and more subtle electoral, recruitment, and policy changes which characterize the realignment process. During the early years of a realignment, new interests acquire identity and organization, new leaders emerge to express these interests, and new issues are raised to compete, at first unsuccessfully, for public support. Faint harbingers of changes to come were discernible, for example, in the issues raised and in the electoral bases of the Granger movement and, later, the Greenback party of the 1870s and early 1880s. Continuity can be detected between these early roots and what occurred later by following the careers of particular Granger and Greenback leaders, classic professional mavericks, who disappeared from the political limelight with the decline of their following, only to reappear a decade or so later, espousing the same issues as leaders of the Farmers' Alliance or its political offshoot, the Populist party. At the electoral level, congressional constituencies where the Grangers and Greenbackers were strongest later supported Populist candidates disproportionately. The basic problems, interests, and issues remained the

FIGURE 8.4. Percentage of change in mean years schooling between losing incumbents and winning replacements in the House, for every fourth
presidential election since 1872, by party

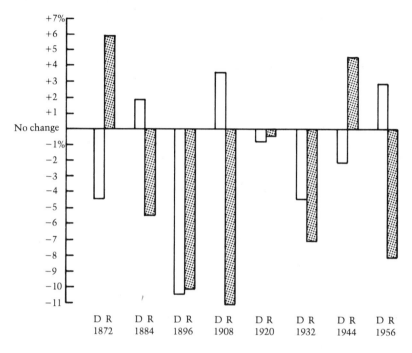

SOURCE: *Biographical Directory* 1961.

same in such constituencies; only the political vehicles used to
express them changed.

Similarly, the New Deal realignment had its roots in the Progressive movement, the increased militancy of organized labor and
farmers, particularly those affiliated with the American Farm Bureau Federation, and the first defections of northern blacks from
the party of Lincoln, all of which occurred in the 1920s and before.
The Great Depression catalyzed such discontent, and FDR mobilized these diverse groups into the concert of interests called the
New Deal coalition.

The New Deal era provides a clear illustration of the pattern
of change which occurs over the course of a realignment period.
In Congress, such changes were most pronounced in the years
between 1928, when the conservative Republican coalition was

still largely intact, and 1936, when the New Deal contingent in the House was largest. Figure 8.5 shows the net change in the number of Democratic seats in the House over the five-election period. As a result of the 1928 election, the Democrats lost thirty seats, as the Republicans increased their majority in the House. In the two elections which followed, the pendulum swung sharply in the opposite direction. The Democrats gained fifty-three seats in the 1930 election, sufficient to become the majority party, and added ninety-four more in 1932. The Democrats made only modest additional gains in the 1934 and 1936 elections. The bulk of the shift toward the Democrats occurred relatively early in the realignment period, in 1930 and 1932.

Figure 8.5 also indicates the number of seats which changed hands owing to the defeat of incumbents and to other types of turnover, such as retirement or death. Clearly, the defeat of Republican incumbents by Democratic challengers was responsible for most of the Democratic gains. Changes due to retirement or death favored the Democrats only in 1930 and 1932. Indeed, in 1934, instances where Republican incumbents died or retired to be replaced by Democrats were exactly balanced by instances which

FIGURE 8.5. Net change in the number of Democratic seats in the House, 1928–1936 elections, by type of turnover

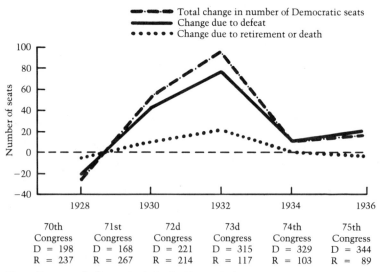

Note: Democratic figures include the Farmer-Labor party.
SOURCE: *Biographical Directory* 1961.

FIGURE 8.6. Percentage of defeated incumbents who failed to secure renomination, 1928–1936

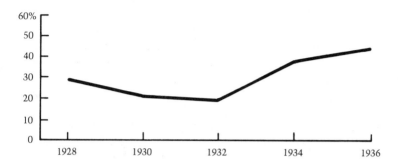

FIGURE 8.7. Democratic percentage of defeated incumbents who failed to secure renomination, 1928–1936

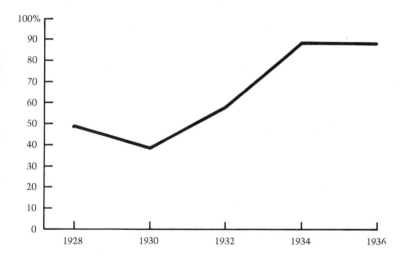

went in the opposite direction. In 1936, the Republicans actually gained a few seats in cases of turnover due to death or retirement.

As the realignment progressed, the focus of turnover due to defeat shifted from the Republican to the Democratic party. As figure 8.6 shows, the rate of turnover due to failure of an incumbent to secure nomination increased after 1932, until, by 1936, over 45 percent of all cases of defeat occurred in primary elections or party nominating conventions. As figure 8.7 indicates, this turnover was increasingly confined to the Democratic party, until, by 1934 and 1936, over 90 percent of all incumbents who were not renominated were Democrats. Thus, during the early years of the realignment, most instances of electoral defeat involved Democratic challengers defeating Republican incumbents. After 1932, however, substantial turnover occurred *within* the Democratic party. In increasing numbers, Democratic incumbents were ousted from their party's ticket by challengers who then went on to defeat their Republican opponents in the general election in most cases.[5]

Analysis of the social and economic backgrounds of winners and losers during this period sheds light on the significance of this intraparty turnover. Changes in background occurred in two distinct phases between 1928 and 1936. During the early years of the realignment (up through 1932), winning members of both parties tended to be substantially younger than the incumbents they defeated.[6] In 1932 in particular, this age differential was paralleled

FIGURE 8.8. Average age: losing incumbents and winning replacements, 1928–1936 congressional elections

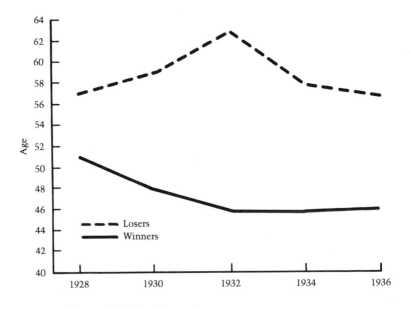

SOURCE: *Biographical Directory* 1961.

FIGURE 8.9. Percentage of members of Congress with college degrees: losing incumbents and winning replacements, 1928–1936 elections

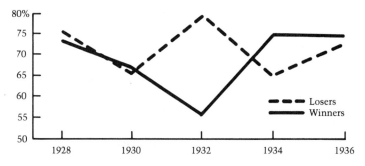

SOURCE: *Biographical Directory* 1961.

by marked differences in socioeconomic status. Winners tended to be of lower status than losers (see figs. 8.8 and 8.9). These changes also occurred in roughly equal proportions in both parties.[7] After 1932, the pattern changed. The age difference between winners and losers narrowed again until, by 1936, it had declined from a maximum of seventeen to ten years. Although it is not shown in figure 8.8, by 1938, the age difference had dropped to six years, precisely the figure which existed in 1928 at the onset of the realignment. Moreover, after 1932, newcomers were of higher social status (as measured by educational attainment) than defeated incumbents.

By 1936 and 1938, the socioeconomic background profile of members of the House had returned to that which prevailed before the realignment. Turnover within the Democratic party which occurred in 1934 and 1936 involved, more often than not, the defeat of lower-status, relatively young incumbents elected to Congress during the early years of the realignment (King and Seligman 1976). They were replaced by individuals who were also relatively young but who had more conventional socioeconomic credentials. The same was true of the substantial number of newly elected Republicans after 1932. In most instances, they ousted Democratic incumbents who had been among the wave of young, lower-status liberal Democrats elected in 1930 and 1932. *Thus, within the six years after the critical elections of 1932, the continuity in background that has been so much a characteristic of the American congressional elite over the past century had been restored.* However, the new legislators with different backgrounds had, during their short tenure, changed the direction of public policy. These changes are the subject of chapter 9.

SUMMARY AND CONCLUSION

This study has shed some light on patterns of continuity and discontinuity in the background of members of Congress during the past century. Change in background characteristics during realignment periods differs from change at other times. New issues and interests arise, representing the cumulative products of economic growth and social change which a new generation of aspiring political leaders articulate. Factional divisions intensify as leaders of these emergent interests organize to challenge the established coalitions, and the contests within and between parties become more intense. At the same time, voters turn out in higher percentages during realignment periods than otherwise and new voters are activated. Some voters change allegiance, while others lapse into inactivity as they confront cross pressures created by inconsistencies between old loyalties and new issues. The circulation of legislative and executive elites accelerates.

In a concomitant development, the new legislators differ in significant ways from their predecessors. Political realignments mark a generational change in the composition of Congress which goes hand in hand with changes in the structure of political opportunity and selection. Realignments bring new people to Congress of a younger generation than the incumbents of both parties. These younger men and women struggled with the old guard of their parties in their climb to Congress. The rise of such new elements upsets the coalitions in the electorate and in Congress.

The increasing average age of members of Congress during the past century or so and their longer average tenure have made generational turnover more significant. If the normal pattern had been followed, members of Congress would have become older than the median age of the electorate. Conventional beliefs notwithstanding, it is not certain that advancing age necessarily makes people conservative. It is more certain that a political generation shares a particular political frame of reference. Therefore, the arrival of new members in Congress renovates political perspectives and helps make Congress respond more sensitively to the ways in which political problems are perceived in the country. In this regard, it is important to note that, during the latter phase of the realignment of the 1930s, the new, higher-status winners were at the same time substantially younger than the average winners at the onset of the realignment in 1928. Thus, the generational aspect of the realignment persisted, although the socioeconomic profile of the House returned to its conventional pattern.

The most important characteristic of the realignment cohort, however, is that these newcomers, regardless of party, resemble one another and tend to agree on measures more than in the past, sharply divided Congress.[8] Consequently, generational change may be regarded as a circulation of elites that increases congressional responsiveness, albeit irregularly. The advent of new members also forces the older legislators to accommodate. As a result of the realignment, issues long dormant for lack of support resurface and legislation is enacted. Thus, after 1896 and 1932, a number of measures were enacted that had been placed on the congressional agenda during the previous decade.

A note of caution in conclusion. We cannot attribute changes in policy to one single characteristic of the new members. But we believe the common recruitment experience of cohorts leads to generational identification. Many factors are at work. It puts too much weight on recruitment and background influences to hold them solely responsible for the decision-making behavior of members of Congress. Particular changes in background variables may be associated with policy changes, though the chain of causal linkage is neither direct nor immediate. On balance, changes in background factors are indicative of changes in the parties, recruitment, opportunity, and new issues that culminate in realignments. *The new legislators and the new issues grow up together.* This crystallization of political outlooks is one of the factors which allows electoral realignment to bring about significant policy changes.

APPENDIX
METHODOLOGICAL NOTE

We used the binomial sign test as a means of characterizing gross patterns of change in background characteristics resulting from an election. Whenever the percentage of members of Congress possessing a given background characteristic changed in the same direction in both parties, the signs (+ or −) of the changes are the same. For example, if the percentage of farmers increases in both parties, the signs are + for both parties; if the percentage decreases, the signs are both −. Whenever changes occurred in different directions in the two parties, the signs are opposite. The proportion of like-signed *pairs of changes* (i.e., change in each of the *two* parties) to the total number of pairs of signed changes indicates whether the differences in the background profiles of the two parties increase, decrease, or change in a manner which crosscuts party lines in the aftermath of an election. The greater the proportion of like-signed pairs, the greater the incidence of changes which cut across party lines and affect both parties in similar ways.

Figure 8.2 graphs the number of like-signed pairs of changes as a percentage of all pairs of signed changes and indicates those elections where the probability is great that changes in background profiles cross party lines. Such probabilities show the odds of obtaining the observed number of like-signed pairs, assuming that change in background characteristics is random (i.e., P [like-signed changes] = P [unlike-signed changes] = .5).

NOTES

Note: An earlier version of this essay was presented at the annual meeting of the International Political Science Association, Munich, in August 1970.

1   The subset of members of Congress who were defeated was separated from those involved generally in turnover as follows. First, we examined the biography of each legislator involved in turnover in the *Biographical Directory of the American Congress 1774–1961* for statements explaining why the person left Congress. We then cross-checked these results with data from the Historical Election Returns archive of the Inter-University Consortium for Political and Social Research. Beyond this, we examined a lengthy array of other biographical sources, state election archives, and the like. We can be certain that all incumbents we have classified as "defeated" did in fact lose, either in the general election or through failure to secure nomination. We are virtually certain that all who lost a general election are included in the "defeated" category, but it is possible that we have failed to identify all who lost renomination bids, since state election data are of uneven completeness, and the records of some constituency nominating conventions have been lost.

2   See King and Seligman (1976) for a more detailed analysis of changes in these background characteristics during the realignments of the 1890s and 1930s.

3   These findings differ somewhat from those we reported earlier (King and Seligman 1976). The difference occurs in 1932, where we had earlier reported that the average age of defeated incumbents was seventy-one years and of incoming freshmen, fifty years. The reason for these differences arises from the fact that 1932 was the first election after the 1930 census. Congress had been reapportioned, many states had gained or lost representation, and, as a consequence, twenty-six incumbents had been forced to run against one another. The obvious effects of the reapportionment were to increase the rate of defeat of incumbents and to increase the average age of those defeated. The latter is due to the fact, as yet unexplained, that incumbents who were forced to run against one another as a consequence of reapportionment tended to be significantly older than the average age of all members of Congress. Consequently, we have omitted all instances of defeat arising from reapportionment from figures 8.3, 8.6, 8.7, and 8.8, where the age difference of increased turnover due to reapportionment would bias the findings. In the remaining figures, these defeated

members are included, since they do not differ in their other background characteristics from the remaining defeated incumbents.

4 In 1934, over 85 percent of the Democratic challengers who ousted Democratic incumbents at the nomination stage were successful in the general election. In 1936, the figure was over 90 percent.

5 See note 3 above, concerning the 1932 election.

6 See King and Seligman (1976) for a more detailed analysis of these status changes in 1932.

7 Of the Democratic incumbents who unsuccessfully sought renomination in 1934, over 92 percent were elected after 1928. In 1936, the figure was 100 percent.

8 See Brady and Lynn (1973); Fischel (1973); Ginsberg (1976); and King and Seligman (1976). The findings on policy change during realignments in Congress include some apparent inconsistencies. In contrast with the other studies cited above, Ginsberg's research suggests that policy change in the aftermath of the 1896 realignment was substantially less than that during other realignment periods and, indeed, no more substantial than that following many "normal" elections. Brady and Lynn explain this apparent anomaly by suggesting that the net result of the 1892 to 1896 realignment was a vindication of the Republican status quo which served to strengthen the majority (Republican) party in Congress and thereby to prevent policy changes associated with Bryan and Populism (1973: 15). However, the interpretation of such findings remains unclear. Viewed another way, Ginsberg's data suggest that the decade between 1893 and 1903 was indeed a major watershed in public policy. In terms of the issue areas Ginsberg examines, the "capitalism" dimension shifted from consistently "pro" to consistently "anti" during this decade, as did the "international cooperation" issue area. At the same time, government's stance toward "internal sovereignty," "universalism," and "ruralism" changed from basically unfavorable to basically favorable. Thus, while the *number* of enactments during this period was not as great as in other realignment periods, fundamental changes in the basic *stance* of the federal government did occur in more issue areas and with greater persistence afterward than in any other realignment periods examined by Ginsberg.

9

Elections, Congress, and Public Policy Changes: 1886–1960

DAVID W. BRADY

One of the most important questions regarding democratic politics concerns the nature of the relationship between popular choices in elections and the policies of the elected government. Normally this relationship is not strong or direct. However, a number of scholars have argued that, during realigning eras, there is a relatively clear-cut relationship between popular choices in elections and public policy (Burnham 1970; Sundquist 1973; Ginsberg 1976). The general thrust of the argument for this relationship is as follows. "During realignment periods discontented elements penetrated or replaced one or the other of the two major parties, altered the terms of partisan conflict and substantially increased the magnitude of choice available to the electorate" (Ginsberg 1976: 49). Under such conditions, there is in Schattschneider's (1960) term a "redefinition of conflict," and many voters make new decisions which realign the electorate and change the socioeconomic status patterns underlying the normal vote. When such changes in the electorate occur, as in 1856 to 1860 and 1932 to 1936, there is a concomitant shift in public policy or, in Burnham's words, "clusters of policy" (1970: 10). In sum, during realignment periods the political parties respond to tensions in the society by offering widely divergent policy alternatives, and the corresponding electoral results bring about a new majority alignment which forms the backbone of the policy changes. Thus, for example, in the New Deal realignment blacks and blue-collar urban ethnics were the electoral base that assured the future of Roosevelt's welfare-statist policies.

These changes in clusters of policy have until very recently been unmeasured. That is, scholars simply stated or assumed that significant policy changes occurred in 1860, or 1932 to 1936, and so on. While the assumption that policy changes of some magnitude did in fact occur in the New Deal or the Progressive Era is not unwarranted, political scientists were unable to deal with degree of change and area of change questions. That is, all that could be done was to study the 1932 to 1936 period as an era of policy change. The question of how much change occurred over time and in which policy areas change occurred was of necessity neglected. Fortunately, in an important work, Ginsberg (1976) has utilized content analysis in such a way as to measure policy change over time. Moreover, he has shown that during realignment periods partisan differences are substantial and under such conditions policy changes are also greater. In short, it does seem to be the case that, during realignments, the political parties do offer voters contrasting alternatives and that the electoral choices made by the public result in major shifts in public policy. There is, however, an important element missing from this description of realignments and changes in public policy—institutional linkages.

Intervening between elections and policy are representative institutions which at times distort, delay, and improve policy but always change policy preferences. One such institution, long noted for its ability to delay, distort, and change policy preferences, is the U.S. House of Representatives. The House's norms, division of labor, and rules all help shape policy—mainly in a conservative fashion—by making it easy for minorities to thwart majorities (Orfield 1975; Sundquist 1966; Burns 1963). Thus, it is difficult under normal conditions for major shifts in policy to occur. In reference to realignments and policy changes, the question is simple: what conditions are created during realignments such that the U.S. House of Representatives is induced to build majorities capable of passing clusters of policy changes?

The argument advanced in this chapter is that critical elections create conditions necessary for majority-party government in the House (Sorauf 1968: 333–337) and that major shifts in policy are adopted and legitimized by the new congressional majority party while the minority party—reduced in Key's (1966) terms to "stand patters"—futilely but cohesively objects. The skeletal argument, so ably presented by Seligman and King in the preceding chapter, is that, due to tensions in the society, the parties are forced to take divergent views on the issues associated with those tensions and that the realignment election(s) brings to the House a large number of new members who disrupt its established order. The "new" majority party then adopts the cluster of policy changes by party votes, and the linkage between elections and policy is recognizable as party government (Brady 1978).

Since the crux of the argument concerns the creation of the conditions for majority-party government in the House, it is necessary to specify how realignments contribute to majority-party strength in the House, that is, a cohesive majority party. In order to demonstrate how realignments contribute to majority-party strength, it is essential to identify the major constraints on party government in the House and to show how realignments reduce the effect of such constraints. The two major constraints on party government in the House are "frozen incumbencies" (Orfield 1975) and the decentralized nature of the committee system. If it can be shown that these two factors are constraints on majority-party rule and that realigning elections reduce their effect, it will be possible to develop and test a model of policy change which includes institutional linkages.

Congressional elections in the United States are normally determined by local factors. Thus, representatives who satisfy relevant local constituencies (Fenno 1977) are normally reelected. In Orfield's words, this "slow turnover of members causes Congress to be dominated by members with a vested interest in the organizational status quo. Sometimes it also isolates the legislative branch from changes in public attitudes" (1975: 306).

The fact that incumbents dominate elections means that a representative's relationship to constituents is paramount and, to the extent that national-party positions conflict with real or perceived constituent interests, there is cross pressuring. Cross-pressured representatives will often vote constituent interests, not party position (Miller and Stokes 1963). This relationship between member and constituency is so prominent that both parties' caucuses have formalized the representatives' right to vote constituent interests. Huitt sums up the political logic of this relationship nicely when he states, "If the member pleases [the constituency] no party leader can fatally hurt him; if he does not, no national party organ can save him" (1961: 335). In the modern House, a large number of representatives are cross-pressured; for example, southern Democrats from rural districts have constituency pressures not to vote with the Democratic leadership on certain welfare issues. During realignments, the number of such cross-pressured districts is reduced because the election results in a new congressional majority which is not tied to the same constituent interests as the majority it replaced. In short, realigning elections are characterized by a large number of switched-seat districts (Brady and Lynn 1973). Thus, across districts in the new majority party, there is a relative homogeneity of interests and issues and thus a reduction in cross pressuring. For example, in 1932 the new Democratic majority in Congress represented blue-collar and ethnic urbanites who were switching to the Democrats, and on welfare and governmental activism issues cross pressuring was nonexistent.[1]

The committee system is a drawback to party government because committee leaders immunized (until the Ninety-fourth House?) by seniority "are chieftains to be bargained with not lieutenants to be commanded" (Huitt 1954: 341). And their power to decide is based on the fact that committees have a continuous life of their own. Change in committee membership is "never complete and seldom dramatic" (Huitt 1954: 341). Under these conditions, committee norms and decision styles which determine public policy can be transmitted to the new members. Committees are normally stable both in membership and in norms, thus public policy decisions are gradual or incremental. Other work has shown that during realignments committee stability and continuity are affected by a drastic turnover in membership (Brady 1978), and, as Fenno has shown, "The two occasions on which the greatest amount of open dissatisfaction, threatened rebellion, and actual rebellion occurred coincided with the two greatest personnel turnovers . . . the tendency to rebellion increases as personnel turnover increases, the very stability of committee membership appears, once again, as a vital condition of [the style and content of decision making]" 1966: 226–227).

Realigning elections, as Ginsberg has shown, are characterized by partisan conflict and policy changes. The analysis presented below demonstrates that such elections result in abnormally large electoral turnover which results in committee instability, and the combination of these factors reduces the constraints on majority-party government in Congress. An example of how realigning elections create these conditions is the 1932 Roosevelt realignment. In 1932, nearly one hundred House seats shifted to the Democrats, and committee turnover was rampant. In 1929 Robert Doughton was twenty-fifth and last on the Ways and Means Committee, while in 1933 he was chairman. Of course, one example does not verify the model; however, the analysis which follows tests the generalizability of the model. What the example does show is that membership turnover can change committee stability rapidly.

THE MODEL

All the parts of the argument have been covered; what remains is to present the model in full. In certain electoral periods, the political parties offer widely divergent choices to the general electorate, and the electoral choice results in the election of a "new" majority party (membership turnover). The influx of new members disrupts the stability of the committee system, and the combination of these events produces a *cohesive majority party* which adopts the policy changes associated with the realignment, while the minority party opposes (i.e., party government). Figure 9.1 shows in causal model form the argument.[2]

However, it is possible that two other models might better explain policy changes. The second model posits a direct arrow from membership turnover to policy changes. The justification for such a relationship is straightforward: "The main impetus for change in the overall policy posture of the Congress comes in the new membership" (Clausen 1973: 231). In short, the new members could effect changes in policy directly as well as indirectly, through party voting. Figure 9.2 shows the model.

Another possibility is that there exists a direct relationship between committee instability and policy changes. That is, since committees in the House are responsible for shaping legislation, they may have a direct effect on policy changes. Thus the third model to be tested is shown in figure 9.3.

Since the three models are identical through the party strength variable, the formalization that follows does not repeat steps 1 through 4 for Models 2 and 3.

Model 1
$$X_1 = e_1$$
$$X_2 = b_{21}X_1 + e_2$$
$$X_3 = b_{32}X_2 + e_3$$
$$X_4 = b_{43}X_3 + b_{42}X_2 + e_4$$
$$X_5 = b_{54}X_4 + e_5$$
Where:
X_1 = partisan conflict
X_2 = membership turnover
X_3 = committee instability
X_4 = majority party strength
X_5 = policy changes

FIGURE 9.1. The first policy change model

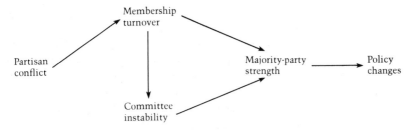

FIGURE 9.2. The second policy change model

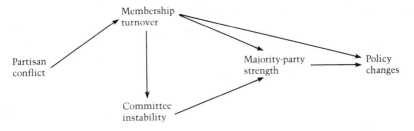

FIGURE 9.3. The third policy change model

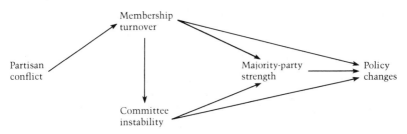

In Models 2 and 3 all variables are the same, and only X_5 differs, thus:

Model 2
$$X_5 = b_{54}X_4 + b_{52}X_2 + e_5$$
Model 3
$$X_5 = b_{54}X_4 + b_{53}X_3 + b_{52}X_2 + e_5$$

TESTING THE MODELS

Determining which of these models best explains policy changes involves operationalizing the variables and choosing a method for selecting from among the models. The entire discussion has focused on the effect of elections on policy changes over time. Thus, the data set must be a time series encompassing a number of policy changes, and the period chosen is 1886 to 1960. The 1886 date was chosen because, from Woodrow Wilson's *Congressional Government* (1885), we know that committees were by then important shapers of policy and, of course, committee instability plays a crucial role in each of the models. The 1960 date was chosen because Ginsberg's policy change variable ends in that year. This period includes the Fifty-first through the Eighty-sixth Houses and both the 1896 and 1932 realignments as well as the Progressive Era. Thus, it encompasses both change and stability and is sufficient to test the proposed models.

The first variable in the model (partisan conflict) is Ginsberg's measure of overall difference of issue positions between parties. Issue differences between the parties measure the magnitude of choices available to the electorate and were determined by a content analysis of all party platforms from 1844 to 1968. The higher the value, the greater the degree of choice the voter has. For a detailed exposition of the technique, the reader should refer to Ginsberg's original article (1972).

The membership turnover variable was operationalized by determining in each House the percentage of representatives elected from switched-seat districts. That is, those districts which changed the party representing the district were classified as switched seats, and the percentage of such seats was determined for each House.

Committee stability was operationalized as the total percentage of turnover on the Ways and Means, Rules, and Appropriations committees. These three committees have important implications for policy changes. For example, the addition of three members to the Rules Committee in the Eighty-seventh House generated a book and a number of articles on the policy implications of the change (MacKaye 1963; Peabody and Polsby 1963). It is safe to assume that, the higher the turnover on these three committees, the greater the instability and thus the greater the prospects for policy changes.

It should be noted that using these three committees is a conservative measure of committee instability. That is, these are the three most important committees in the House and as such they are more isolated from instability than are the other committees. Thus, the turnover levels in these committees are lower than turnover levels on other committees.

Since the argument of all three models is that membership turnover and committee instability are positively related to the majority party's ability to legislate, the measure of partisan strength combines both majority-party size and unity. Majority-party strength is measured by the size of the majority party times its average party unity score. For example, if in a given Congress the majority size was 60 percent and the average party unity score was 70, the score for that House was 4,200. In order to eliminate dealing with the large numbers involved, Z-scores were created.

The policy change variable is taken from Ginsberg's content analysis of the U.S. Statutes at Large. In this chapter, the policy scores on capitalism, labor, redistribution, universalism, and overall policy change were recorded. These categories are the same as those used to determine partisan differences in platforms. A brief description of the labor, redistribution, capitalism, and universalism variables follows:

Labor: a positive score signals legislation favorable to labor and labor organizations.

Redistribution: a positive score signals a reallocation of wealth in favor of the economically disadvantaged.

Capitalism: a positive score signals laws promoting the aggregation of wealth by business, financial, and mercantile elites.

Universalism: a positive score signals laws promoting equality of rights and privileges for domestic minorities.

Having formulated the models and operationalized the variable, it is necessary to choose a method for selecting among the models. I have chosen to test these models by using unstandardized regression coefficients after the mean has been subtracted from each variable in the set. Subtracting the means from each variable allows one to delete the "*a*" or intercept from the model, which simplifies writing the equations. The reader will note that the original formulation of the models did not contain intercepts. The use of unstandardized regression coefficients is preferable to path analysis because it reduces the effect of variance caused by the exogenous variable. As Duncan (1975) has demonstrated, it could happen that the structural parameters or coefficients of a model are identical in two or more populations under study. Yet, if only the variance in the exogenous variable(s) of the model differs from population to population, differences would in general be observed between the populations in all the standardized regression coefficients. That is, estimates of standardized coefficients will (in general) suggest that the populations differ in many ways when in fact they may differ in only one: the variance of the exogenous variable(s). The use of unstandardized b's greatly reduces the likelihood of this kind of error. Therefore the analysis which follows utilizes unstandardized b's, standard errors, and F-tests to determine which model works.

Each of the three posited models is identical through the first four equations; thus, the strategy is to test these relationships first. The specific argument is that partisan conflict which offers voters a wider choice of alternative policies will be positively related to membership turnover (the greater the partisan conflict, the higher the percentage of turnover in membership), and the higher the membership turnover, the greater the committee instability. The combination of new members and resultant committee instability increases the majority party's unity and its ability to legislate; thus, both committee instability and membership turnover should be positively related to the majority party's legislative strength. Figure 9.4 and table 9.1 show the results of this analysis.

The first stage of the model is confirmed by these results. In each instance, both the standard errors and the F-tests indicate an acceptable model. The F-tests were significant at the .05 or .01 levels, and in every case the standard error of the b's did not indicate instability in the relationships. Thus, during periods when voters are offered choices by the parties, the electoral outcomes result in more strength for the majority party in the House.

The test for which of the three proposed models best fits the policy change data is straightforward. Model 1 posits that only party strength has a significant direct effect on policy change, whereas Models 2 and 3 posit that membership turnover and committee instability (respectively) also have a direct effect on policy change. The first test of the models will be on overall policy changes as defined and measured by Ginsberg; further tests will be made using different policy categories. Figure 9.5 and table 9.2 show the results.

The results of the analysis show that both majority-party strength and committee instability are directly and significantly related to overall policy changes. Membership turnover was neither significantly nor positively related to overall policy change. Tech-

FIGURE 9.4. Electoral effects on majority-party strength, 1886–1960

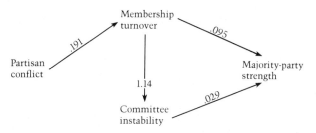

Note: The figures are *b*'s.

TABLE 9.1. Electoral Effects on Majority-Party Strength, 1886–1960

Relationships	b	SE	F[a]
Partisan conflict and member turnover	.191	.052	12.4[a]
Membership turnover and stability	1.135	.141	64.6[a]
Turnover and majority-party strength	.095	.031	6.8[a]
Instability and majority-party strength	.029	.009	2.5[b]

[a] Significant at .01.
[b] Significant at .05.

nically, none of the three proposed models fits the data for overall change. However, with regard to overall policy change, it is clear that party strength and committee instability are directly related to policy changes; thus, a model of overall change should include both party strength and committee instability as directly related, whereas membership turnover has indirect effects on policy through party. The fact that membership turnover had only an indirect effect on policy change was surprising, given the strong association found between new members and policy shifts in other research (Brady and Lynn 1973 : Fischel 1973).

The most likely explanation is that the dependent variable is a summary measure of change, and thus the effect of turnover on specific policy areas was masked. Moreover, since different realignments result in policy changes in different areas, it should be the case that party strength and committee instability as well as membership turnover have different effects on different policy areas. In order to determine whether there were different patterns for dif-

FIGURE 9.5. Effects of turnover, instability, and majority-party strength on overall policy change, 1886–1960

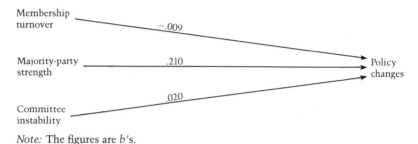

Note: The figures are b's.

TABLE 9.2. The Effects of Turnover, Instability, and Majority-Party Strength on Overall Policy Change, 1886–1960

Relationships	b	SE	F
Membership turnover	−.004	.001	.76
Committee instability	.020	.010	3.67[a]
Majority-party strength	.210	.070	10.11[b]

[a] Significant at .05.
[b] Significant at .01.

ferent policy areas, the same tests applied to the overall policy change variable were run on some of the specific policy change variables measured and defined by Ginsberg.

Rather than repeating the results for each test as was done above, the results are presented in a summary table. The criteria for significance were the same as was the case for the overall change variable, namely, a significant F ratio and a standard error of the *b* which was less than one-half the size of the *b*. Table 9.3 shows the results.

These results partially vindicate retaining membership turnover as an important variable. In the case of both redistributive policy changes and policy universalism, membership turnover in the House is significantly related and, in the case of redistribution, only turnover is significantly related. Party strength in the House was significantly related to three of the four policy areas and was the only variable related to labor policy changes. Committee instability was significantly related only to changes in the policy capitalism area. Thus, it appears to be the case that different sets of relationships between the independent variables account for changes in different policy areas. What has been shown is that various combinations of membership turnover, committee instability, and party strength do account for policy changes. In sum, when the electorate is offered policy choices and its response is to elect new majorities in the House, the congressional majority party's ability to legislate is increased and policy changes often result. It is also important to note that these relationships were shown to be associated with *policy changes*, and the same mechanisms can be used to prevent major policy changes, as was the case in the late 1890s. That is, the 1890s realignment resulted in a strengthened majority party which did not change policy but, rather, prevented the policy changes associated with Bryan and Populism. In effect, this electoral phenomenon, while consistent with the argument in this chapter, will not show up statistically because the policy change variable does not (and cannot as such) measure the prevention of change. And, as we all know, preventing change is often as important as change itself. The findings reported should be amended to include the fact that certain elections result in strengthened majority parties which, depending on circumstances, can either change policy or prevent change.

While the model developed in this essay fits the data for the 1886 to 1960 period, it cannot show in detail how realignments affect policy. Therefore, in the following section the realignments of 1896 and 1932 are examined in order to demonstrate that realigning elections create party government in the U.S. House of Representatives. The analysis of these two realignments will show that the constituency bases of the congressional parties were changed along a continuum which reflects the changes that were

ABLE 9.3. The Effects of Turnover, Instability, and Majority-Party Strength on pecific Areas of Policy Change, 1886–1960

olicy Area	Membership Turnover	Independent Variables Committee Instability	Majority-Party Strength
.edistribution	Significant[a]	Not significant	Not significant
Jniversalism	Significant[a]	Not significant	Significant[a]
abor	Not significant	Not significant	Significant
.apitalism	Not significant	Significant[a]	Significant[b]

[a] Significant at .05.
[b] Significant at .01.

occurring in the "party in the electorate" thereby diminishing constituency-party cross pressuring. These elections also effectively rearrange the committees of the House so that the party leadership is able to perform its function of organizing coherent majorities for legislative programs. Given these conditions, levels of party voting in the House rise, and party voting on the programs central to the policy changes is especially high.

THE 1896 AND 1932 REALIGNMENTS

The agrarian revolt that culminated in the critical election of 1896 was the product of the crises of industrialization. Western and southern farmers allied with western silver interests and sought to enlist the "toiling masses" of the industrial East and Midwest, thereby recapturing America from the foreign moneyed interests responsible for industrialization. The crisis of industrialization squarely placed an agrarian-fundamentalist view of life against an industrial-progressive view of life, and the issue positions taken on this division were polar (Burnham 1970; Jones 1964; Key 1958).

The specific issues that cut across party preferences in the 1890s were the gold-silver question, the protective tariff, and expansionism. These specific issues were subsumed under the more general "crisis of vulnerability" in which urban industrial interests were pitted against rural antiindustrial forces. The election of McKinley and the Republicans assured America's industrial future: never again would the agricultural interests capture a major party and come so close to winning control of the government. The crisis of vulnerability was resolvable only by the victory of one side or the other. Thus, the 1896 realignment answered the question of whether the northern and eastern industrial interests or the southern and western agricultural and mining interests would be victorious. The effect of the realignment was that it "eventually separated the Southern and Western agrarians and transformed the most industrially advanced region of the country into a bulwark of industrial Republicanism" (Burnham 1965: 25).

Sundquist's analysis (1973) of the voters who switched their allegiance to the Republicans during the realignment showed that those who switched were mainly northern, urban, and blue-collar, residing in the industrial East and Midwest. In contrast, Bryan did not increase the Democrats' support compared with that of

1892 in the rural Midwest and East; thus, the Democratic party after 1896 was essentially southern and border-state agrarian in its constituency base.

The political revolution that Franklin Roosevelt led was, unlike the 1896 realignment, the product of a single event—the Great Depression. The underlying issue dimension which separated and distinguished the parties was the question of whether the government would *actively* deal with the problems facing the country. Hoover and the majority of the Republican party came down against greatly increased governmental activity: "Economic depression cannot be cured by legislative action or executive pronouncement. Economic wounds must be healed by . . . the producers and the consumers themselves" (Myers 1934: 429–430). The Democrats, while not entirely sure in which direction to move, had formulated activist programs. John Garner, the conservative Speaker of the House, had advocated a $900 million federal public works program, a billion dollar Reconstruction Finance Corporation loan fund, and a $100 million mercy money fund. The Democratic platform in 1932 differed markedly from the Republican on issues regarding the aggregation of wealth, control over the distribution of wealth, and the exercise of governmental power. Ginsberg's 1972 content analysis of party platforms from 1844 to 1968 showed the above issues to be both salient to parties and divisive across them during the 1932 election. In sum, the parties differed markedly over the role the government was to play in curing the Depression. The Democrats favored active government involvement; the Republicans favored voluntarism and nonintervention.

The voters switching to the Democrats in the 1932 election came primarily from those groups most affected by the Depression: farmers and city dwellers. The farm depression of the 1920s had continued long after industry had recovered. The Republican leadership had done little to deal with the problem and seemed relatively unconcerned; President Coolidge commented: "Well, farmers never have made money [and] I don't believe we can do much about it" (White 1965: 344). This policy resulted in a number of farm protests, such as McNary-Haugenism, and may be viewed as a harbinger of the political revolution precipitated by the Depression. In fact, Sundquist (1973) suggests that these farm protests were an integral part of the realignment of the 1930s. We would expect the congressional Democratic party over the 1926 to 1932 period to reflect this change in voter sentiment.

The second and larger group of voters switching to the Democratic party is most readily identifiable by place of residence. The cities, populated by workers, ethnics, and blacks, moved into the Democratic column during this period. In such formerly Democratic cities as New York, the Republicans ceased to be competitive, while, in such cities as Boston which had voted for Al Smith in 1928, the Democrats became the dominant party from 1932 onward. Working-class ethnics and northern blacks were hard hit by the Depression and voted for the Democrats. We would also expect to see this change reflected in the congressional Democratic party.

Constituency Changes during Realignments
If realignments in the parties in the electorate are reflected in the composition of the congressional parties, then the constituency bases of the congressional parties should show dramatic shifts also. Accordingly, one would expect that, from the Fifty-third House to the Fifty-fifth, the congressional Republican party would suddenly come to overrepresent industrial and eastern constituencies. The shift in the congressional Democratic party during the New Deal should be toward northern industrial urban districts.

In order to test these hypotheses, the following data were collected for the 1896 and 1932 periods. The numbers of farmers and blue-collar workers were collected from the appropriate county sections of the 1890 census and mapped onto congressional districts. The number of blue-collar workers, the value added by manufacture, and the population density were collected from the appropriate county sections of the 1930 census and likewise mapped onto congressional districts. Since in both periods congressional districts varied in size, percentages were used. These percentage data were then arrayed and divided by mean and median and into quartiles. Table 9.4 presents the results of this analysis. The results in both cases show a dramatic shift in the constituency bases of the new majority congressional party. From the Fifty-third to the Fifty-fifth House, the percentage of Republican congressmen from labor districts increased from 44 to 79, while the ratio of increase in absolute numbers of Republicans from such districts was 1.91. In agricultural districts, the Republican percentage decreased by 3 percent over the period; the ratio of absolute change was .95. Moreover, the switch in the constituency base of the Republican party was also highly sectional, with over three-fourths of the Republicans being elected from the eastern and the north central regions by 1896. Analysis of the same figures for the congressional

TABLE 9.4. Shifts in Congressional Majority-Party Composition during the 1896 and 1932 Realignments in Percentages and Absolute Ratio of Increase

District Composition	1896 Realignment		Percentage Increase	Absolute Ratio
	53d Congress	55th Congress		
Republicans from:				
Labor				
Low	35%	31%	−4	.93
High	44	79	+35	1.91
Agriculture				
Low	40%	71%	+31	1.78
High	36	33	−3	.95
Region				
Dems. from southern and border states	47%	64%	+17	
Reps. from east and north central regions	62	76	+14	

District Composition	1932 Realignment		Percentage Increase	Absolute Ratio
	70th Congress	73d Congress		
Democrats from:				
Labor				
Low	57%	82%	+25	1.37
High	32	64	+32	1.97
Industry				
Low	54%	81%	+27	1.40
High	34	67	+33	1.89
Urban				
Low	53%	77%	+24	1.38
High	30	67	+37	1.96

Democrats showed a shift toward highly agricultural districts located in the southern and border states. In short, the 1896 realignment yielded two relatively homogeneous congressional parties, with distinct centers of gravity on both a sectional and an agricultural-industrial continuum.

During the 1932 realignment, Democratic gains were proportionately greater in urban, blue-collar, industrial districts than in more rural, less industrial districts. During the New Deal realignment, the Democrats increased their share of urban seats from 30 to 67 percent; in industrial and labor districts, the increase was from 34 and 32 percent respectively to 67 and 64 percent. The ratio of increase, which measures absolute change, shows that in each category the more urban, more industrial, more blue-collar the district, the greater the increase in Democratic strength. The effect of the Roosevelt realignment on the congressional Democratic party was to add a large number of legislators representing urban blue-collar districts to the solid rural, nonindustrial southern base that the Democrats had had since 1896. A secondary effect was to increase the Democrats' share of northern farm districts. This, of course, meant a corresponding reduction in the number of Republicans from urban and northern farm districts. Thus, the "New Deal" coalition so often studied in the party in the electorate was reflected directly in the composition of the congressional Democratic party.

In both realignments, the shifts in voter sentiment were reflected in the composition of the majority congressional party. These shifts created relatively homogeneous congressional parties, organized in effect around substantive partisan divisions of policy. Over time such stable "partisan alignments form the constituent bases for governments committed to the translation of the choices made by the electorate during critical periods into public policy" (Ginsberg 1976: 49). Under such conditions, there is a reduction in party-constituency cross pressuring because party and constituency are relatively homogeneous. Thus, if our analysis is correct, party voting should rise over the realignment period. However, before we test the party-voting hypothesis, it is necessary to determine the effect of realignments on the second obstacle to party government—the committee system.

Realignment and the Stability of the Committee System
In this section, it is argued that the effects of this second obstacle are substantially reduced—specifically, that the turnover rates on House committees during the realignments were drastic enough to disturb committee continuity and that the new members were more partisan than the members they replaced. The result of the realignments was the replacement of old committee members with new members more predisposed to partisan voting.

Demonstrating that committee continuity is drastically affected by realignments and that the change in membership results in more partisanship requires that (1) turnover on House committees during the realignments was high; (2) a substantial portion of the committee leaders in the Fifty-fifth (1896) and Seventy-third (1932)

Houses were not prominent immediately prior to the realignment; and (3) the new members of the Ways and Means and Appropriations committees, in particular, were more party-oriented than the members they replaced.

In order to demonstrate the drastic nature of committee turnovers in both realignments, membership lists from thirteen committees were collected for the Fifty-third through Fifty-fifth Houses and the Seventieth through Seventy-third Houses. A turnover rate for each of these committees was computed both over the whole committee and for the party components of each committee.[3] The turnover rates were computed by taking the number of holdover members on the committee and dividing it by the number of committee members. For example, in the Fifty-fifth House the Appropriations Committee had seventeen members, only six of whom had served on the committee in the Fifty-third House. The total turnover was 64.7 percent; conversely, the percentage of carryovers was 35.3 percent. Party turnover rates on these committees were arrived at in the same fashion and are included to demonstrate that the high turnover figures were not solely the result of changes in the relative positions of the majority and minority parties. Table 9.5 shows the results of this analysis for the thirteen committees.

The results are striking. The lowest of any of the rates of turnover was 50 percent. Excluding the Republicans on Rules, Ways and Means, Appropriations, and Merchant Marine, the lowest turnover rates were 60 percent. Thus, during both realignments all thirteen committees found themselves with majorities consisting of new members. Committee continuity was greatly disrupted. Comparing committee turnover during the realignments to turnover in the period immediately preceding them reveals that turnover was much greater during the realignment periods. The average turnover for the thirteen committees from the Fifty-second House to the Fifty-third was slightly over 30 percent, while the average turnover from the Fifty-third to the Fifty-fifth was over 80 percent. The same pattern holds for the 1930s realignment. Average committee turnover during the prerealignment Houses was slightly over 20 percent, while during the realignment it was over 80 percent. Comparisons with turnover figures for the modern House of Representatives reveal the same pattern (Fenno 1973). It seems clear that, no matter how turnover rates are computed, the 1896 and 1932 realignments effected drastic changes in committee composition.

Committee Leaders   Important components of the committee

TABLE 9.5. Percentages of Committee and Partisan Committee Turnover for Thirteen Selected House Committees in the 1896 and 1932 Realignments

Committee	1896 Realignment			1932 Realignment		
	Total Turnover	Dem. Turnover	Rep. Turnover	Total Turnover	Dem. Turnover	Rep. Turnover
Agriculture	100.0	100.0	100.0	85.2	89.5	75.0
Appropriations	64.7	66.6	50.0	74.3	67.0	85.7
Banking and Currency	76.5	88.9	62.5	79.2	81.2	75.0
Commerce	82.4	100.0	71.4	64.0	85.7	62.5
Education	100.0	100.0	100.0	85.7	80.0	100.0
Foreign Affairs	86.7	87.5	85.7	80.0	88.2	62.5
Judiciary	82.4	100.0	62.5	88.0	88.2	87.5
Labor	76.9	85.7	66.7	85.0	85.7	83.3
Merchant Marine	91.7	100.0	83.3	73.9	82.4	50.0
Mines and Mining	84.6	85.7	100.0	95.5	100.0	83.3
Public Lands	86.7	100.0	71.4	95.7	100.0	83.3
Rules[a]	80.0	100.0	50.0	67.0	62.5	75.0
Ways and Means	76.5	88.9	62.5	80.0	93.3	60.0

[a] During the 1890s realignment, the Rules Committee had only five members.

system, facilitating committee continuity and stability, are the seniority and specialization norms. Committee leadership positions become available relatively rarely; leaders are brought along slowly. A committee's leader serves on the same committee for long periods of time, acquiring expertise and becoming a keeper of committee norms and policy.

If in a very short time there are drastic turnovers in membership, one would expect the norms of seniority and specialization to be affected—specifically, during realignment periods committee turnover would be so drastic that many of the committee leaders in the realignment Houses would not have acquired much seniority. Any committee chairman in the Fifty-fifth and Seventy-third Houses who was either not on that committee in the Fifty-third or Seventieth Houses or who was below the median rank of seniority in those Houses was considered to have advanced rapidly to committee leadership. Obviously, a chairman in the realignment Houses who had not been on the committee two or three terms before could not have acquired either much seniority or much expertise in the intervening period.

During the period of the 1890s realignment, forty-nine House committees with more than five members were continuously in existence. Of these forty-nine committees in the Fifty-fifth House, twenty-eight, or 57 percent, had chairmen who were below the median seniority in the Fifty-third. Thus, thirty-nine of forty-nine committees, or 80 percent of House committees in the 1896 House, had committee chairmen who had not acquired much seniority and who were not likely to be subject-matter experts. Of course, at this time, the Speaker had the power to appoint committees and chairmen. Thus the effect of turnover, which gave the party leadership flexibility in appointments, was further enhanced by the Speaker's power to jump members to committee chairmanships. However, most of these thirty-nine committee chairmen were not the result of the Speaker's appointive powers.[4]

During the period of the 1930s realignment, there were forty-four House committees with more than five members, and analysis of these forty-four committees shows that, within the short period of three elections, eighteen of them acquired chairmen who were either not on the committee at all at the end of the Seventieth House or were below the median minority rank. Robert Doughton of North Carolina, for example, was the tenth-ranking Democrat, the last, on the Ways and Means Committee in January 1929; he was chairman of Ways and Means in January 1933. Representative Ragon of Arkansas was not a member of Ways and Means in the Seventieth House; he was the ranking majority member in the Seventy-third House. Representative Sabath of Illinois was not on the Rules Committee in the Seventieth House; by the Seventy-third House he was the fourth-ranking member. The influx of new members plus the high turnover on committees facilitated the kind of rapid committee advancement noted in the above examples.

Both important and unimportant committees in both realignment Houses had chairmen who had not acquired much committee seniority and were not keepers of the committee norms. The most obvious effect of the discontinuities in committee leadership was that the committee system became more flexible or pliable in providing party-voting cues. Committee leaders and members had not acquired the norms and expertise necessary to provide the committee with the voting cues so prominent in the modern House of Representatives. The negative effect of committee continuity on party voting was thus diminished.

The final stage of the argument concerning the committee system and party government entails demonstrating the increased partisanship of the new committee members. In order to do this, party support scores for majority-party members of the Ways and Means and Appropriations committees were computed for each of the seven Congresses. The score was computed by scoring one each time the member voted with the majority of his party on all roll calls in which a majority of one party opposed a majority of the other and converting the figure to a percentage of the total number of roll calls. For example, if out of twenty such votes a member voted with the majority of his party on eleven occasions, his support score was 55. Only majority-party members were analyzed because, of course, "clusters of policy changes" are voted through by a cohesive majority party.[5] In the Fifty-third House the average partisan predispositions of the Republicans on both committees was 65.5 percent while in the Fifty-fourth and Fifty-fifth realignment Houses the equivalent partisan predispositions were 85 and 86 percent respectively. Thus the influx of new members increased the committees' partisan predispositions. This finding would be strengthened if the new members were found to have higher support scores than the carryovers. The average partisan predisposition of the carryovers was 75.5 in the Fifty-fifth House, while the same figure for the new members (Fifty-fourth House plus Fifty-fifth) was 86.7. The average party support score for Democrats on the Ways and Means and Appropriations committees in the Seventieth House was slightly below 60 percent. In contrast, Democratic committee members' support scores in the Seventy-second and Seventy-third Houses were over 80 percent. Thus, as in the 1890s, the influx of new members increased the committees' partisan predispositions. However, in contrast to the 1890s, when the new committee members' party scores were compared to those of the carryover members, the results showed no significant differences. Nevertheless, the results show clearly that during both realignments the majority-party members of both committees became markedly more partisan.

Realignments and Party Voting

The realignments of the 1890s and 1930s resulted in shifts in the constituency bases of the new congressional majority parties and a drastic turnover in committee membership and leadership. If the thesis of this essay is correct, this combination of factors reduced constituency-party cross pressuring and disrupted committees' policy continuity, thereby enhancing the ability of the majority party to build partisan majorities. Given these conditions, there should have been a sharp rise in party cohesion and party voting. The hypothesis to be tested in this section is that the elimination of Huitt's two obstacles to responsible parties—constituency-member relationships and the continuity of the committee system—will have resulted in a sharp rise in party voting during both realignment eras.

To test this hypothesis, the percentage of roll calls in which a majority of one party opposed a majority of the other party as well as the party unity scores on majority versus majority roll calls were calculated for the Fifty-second through the Fifty-fifth and the Seventieth through the Seventy-third Houses. Further, for each of the Houses an average Index of Party Likeness (IPL) was computed by adding the IPL values for each roll call and dividing by the total number of roll calls in the House. The results should show a rise in party unity, a decline in the average Index of Party Likeness (an increase in party voting), and a sharp rise in the number of party votes. Table 9.6 shows the results of this analysis, using an Index of Party Likeness of 20 percent or less and a majority of one party versus a majority of the other party as measures of party voting.

The results substantiate the hypothesis. The party unity scores on majority versus majority votes rose from 79.6 to 93.3 for the Republicans during the 1890s, while the comparable figures for the

TABLE 9.6. Changing Levels of Party Unity and Party Voting over the Realignments of 1890 to 1896 and 1924 to 1932

Congress	Average Index of Party Likeness	Percentage of Votes with IPL ≤ 20%	Percentage of Votes with Maj. vs. Maj.	Party Unity Average on Maj. vs. Maj. Votes	
				Dem.	Rep.
1896 Realignment					
52d (1890)	61.0	10.9	45.4	76.2	79.6
53d (1892)	59.6	20.0	44.8	85.1	86.1
54th (1894)	46.1	30.3	68.5	86.9	83.2
55th (1896)	30.8	53.6	79.8	89.3	93.3
% increase or decrease, 52d–55th	−30.2	42.7	34.4	13.1	13.7
1932 Realignment					
69th (1924)	63.7	10.5	43.9	74.7	86.0
70th (1926)	61.8	9.5	48.6	80.5	81.8
71st (1928)	50.9	27.2	58.3	85.1	86.0
72d (1930)	61.0	19.5	57.7	80.9	78.6
73d (1932)	42.3	33.6	70.6	87.6	88.5
% increase or decrease, 69th–73d	−21.4	23.1	26.7	12.9	2.5

Democrats in the 1930s were 74.7 to 87.6—rises of 13.7 and 12.9, respectively. All three measures of party voting show a sharp increase over the realignment period. During the 1890s, the percentage of party votes with majority versus majority rose from 45.4 to 79.8, while the proportion of party votes with an IPL ≤20 percent rose from 10.9 to 53.6. The results for the Roosevelt realignment show the same pattern. The proportion of party votes rose from 43.9 to 70.6, while the percentage of roll calls with an IPL ≤20 percent rose from 10.5 to 33.6. Party cohesion and party voting increased rapidly during both realignments. In addition, separate studies of both these realignments (Sinclair 1977; Brady 1978) have shown that partisan voting on realignment issues was especially high. Thus, the analysis of the 1896 and 1932 realignments corroborates the general model posited in this chapter—namely, realigning elections create conditions conducive to responsible party government in the House.

COMMENTS

The major purpose of this essay was to establish an institutional linkage between critical elections and clusters of policy changes. However, another broader question was implicit in the analysis—namely, are critical or realigning elections necessary conditions for major policy changes? The results of this analysis show that, over time, there are positive relationships between partisan conflict and membership turnover in the House. Also, membership turnover is related to committee instability and majority-party strength, and each of these three variables is directly related to policy change in some area. The use of these variables allows us to speak about the conditions necessary for policy change without referring directly to critical elections. That is, elections which offer voters real alternatives often result in the election of new members and committee instability, both of which are positively related to increased majority-party strength. According to this reasoning, any election which generates a substantial turnover in membership can create the conditions necessary for approving major shifts in policy.

The 1912 and 1964 elections resulted in major policy changes, and both were characterized by substantial membership turnover. In the Eighty-ninth House (elected in 1964), members representing switched-seat districts were highly supportive of party positions and provided the votes necessary to enact the major policy changes which occurred. Committee turnover in that Congress was the highest in over fifteen years, and the level of party voting and party unity rose over five percentage points in the first session. The 1964 election, which may or may not be a realignment, brought in a number of new members who increased the cohesiveness of the majority party and facilitated passage of policy changes. Further evidence supporting the assertion that the impetus for policy changes is the new membership comes from a recent work which shows that, during the 1886 to 1966 time period, the correlation between the percentage of new members and the level of party voting is .46 (Cooper et al. 1977). That is, the effect of the new members is to create the conditions for party government and, over time, the larger the percentage of new members, the higher the level of party voting. Thus, elections characterized by a high turnover of membership seem to be a necessary but not sufficient condition for significant policy changes. It is interesting to note that the Ninety-fourth House of Representatives, with seventy-five new Democratic members, has been the most partisan Congress in recent years.

Elections which bring to the House a substantial number of new members are not sufficient to insure policy changes for a number of reasons. The most important reason is that there must be a program, either party or presidential or both, which proposes major policy changes. Another necessary condition is unified control of the presidency and the Congress. The 1920 election of Warren Harding brought to the Sixty-seventh House a large number of new members, and the percentage of party votes rose from 45 in the Sixty-sixth House to 60 in the Sixty-seventh. However, as Jones (1970) has shown, the lack of a program prohibited that Congress from distinguishing itself by passing significant policy changes. The Ninety-fourth Congress may well have passed legislation which might be considered major, but the threat and fact of a conservative president's veto prohibited shifts in policy. Clearly, presidential programs and the president's involvement, as well as uniform control of the policy-making institutions, are factors which affect the likelihood of policy shifts.

Major shifts in public policy are most likely to occur during periods when the parties and their candidates take divergent issue positions and the electorate sends to Washington a new congressional majority party and a president of the same party. Since 1896, this set of conditions has occurred only four times—1896,

1912, 1932 to 1936, and 1964—and in each instance there were major shifts in public policy or the threat of major shifts was averted. When these conditions are met, there are relatively strong connections between the electorate, the representatives, and public policy. In sum, during such periods the American system of government exhibits many of the characteristics of responsible party government. Clearly, it is during realigning eras that the sum of all these effects is highest, and thus during such eras policy change is greatest.

NOTES

1   A detailed analysis of these districts can be found in Brady (1978).

2   The model meets the necessary assumptions of time ordering. Partisan conflict as measured by party platforms occurs before the election, and the membership turnover in elections precedes the concomitant committee instability. In turn, majority-party strength in voting precedes policy changes. There is no causal arrow between partisan conflict and majority-party strength because two separate empirical tests showed the relationship was canceled when membership turnover and committee instability were controlled.

3   While it is certainly true that as an institution the House in the 1890s differed from the House in the 1930s, committees were already well defined and important. In fact, Woodrow Wilson called congressional government committee government. Thus, turnover on committees was an important component of the system. For an analysis of the House as an institution in the 1890s, see Brady (1973). For the influence of the Speaker on committees, see note 4.

4   The committee system in the 1890s was centralized under the Speaker, who had the power to appoint committees. Thus, seniority norms were more likely to be violated during this era. However, the Speaker's power to appoint in violation of seniority cannot account for a large portion of either the committee or the committee leadership turnover. The two major papers on seniority in the House, Abram and Cooper 1969 and Polsby et al. 1969, both show a lower level of seniority violation than could account for the turnover in committee membership. For example, Abram and Cooper say that on major committees only two seniority violations occurred in the Fifty-fifth House. Polsby et al. show that Speaker Reed followed seniority on thirty-six of fifty-two committee appointments and, of the sixteen violations, eleven were compensated. Both these figures are far too low to account for the 80 percent turnover.

5   The same analysis was run over the minority-party members of the two committees, and the partisan predispositions of these members increased.

The Impact of Realigning Elections
on Public Bureaucracies

KENNETH J. MEIER and KENNETH W. KRAMER

The earlier chapters in this volume have suggested that realignments set a long-term climate for policy making by one party and establish that party's policy preferences as the preferences of a majority of the electorate. The concomitant view of critical elections as the fundamental mechanism through which those preferences actually become policy makes three essential assumptions. First, public pressures and public opinion are somehow aggregated so that election winners represent a majority or plurality preference on a series of issues (Downs 1957). Second, candidates present platforms in good faith and attempt to enact their platforms if they gain public office; in short, an elected official acts on the promises made during the campaign (Pomper 1968). Third, the actions taken by elected officials while in office have an impact on public policy.

This chapter accepts the first two assumptions and examines a portion of the third. We are interested in examining the ability of bureaucracy to prevent elections from influencing the policy process. Lipset (1950), in *Agrarian Socialism*, was among the first to examine this problem. His study revealed that a popular mandate for a provincial socialist party in Canada was delayed and defeated by a coalition of conservative bureaucrats. The problems he noted are even more troublesome today. Although the description of bureaucracy as a power instrument of the first order goes back to Weber (1946), in recent times the bureaucracy's power was multiplied dramatically. The bureaucracy now plays a major role in the policy-making process from the initial drafting of a policy proposal to the implementation and evaluation of the policy (Rourke 1976; Fritschler 1975; Piven and Cloward 1971; Allison 1971; Halperin 1974; Wolman 1971). Despite the growth of bureaucratic influence and Lipset's early warning, little scholarly analysis has focused on the role bureaucracy plays in translating electoral results into public policy outputs. The purpose of this chapter is to examine the impact that elections have on public policy when the policy, at some stage, must be funneled through the bureaucracy.[1] From another vantage point, the purpose is to examine the impact of elections on public bureaucracy.[2]

The question of electoral impact on bureaucracy will be addressed in four stages. First, we shall set the bureaucracy in its political environment. Second, the ways elections can influence bureaucratic policy-making will be discussed. Third, the characteristics of bureaucracy that restrict the impact of elections on public policy will be examined. Fourth, using information gained from the first three stages, a series of testable hypotheses will be presented about the probable impact of elections, critical elections, and realignments on bureaucracy.

BUREAUCRACY AS AN OPEN SYSTEM

Bureaucracies are large-scale formal organizations that are, according to Parsons (1960; see also Katz and Kahn 1966), goal-oriented systems; that is, they pursue goals established by and for the organization. Bureaucracies can be distinguished from other goal-oriented systems by several common traits.[3] First, bureaucracies are large; a bureaucrat rarely knows all the other bureaucrats. Their large size makes it convenient for bureaucracies to operate impersonally according to rules and established procedures. Second, bureaucracies are staffed by full-time employees. Because bureaucrats derive their income from performing bureaucratically assigned tasks, they have a serious commitment to the organization and its goals. Third, the personnel processes of bureaucracy—the hiring, firing, and promoting—are based on merit, on how well the assigned tasks are performed, rather than on the basis of politics, wealth, religion, or other ascribed characteristics. Fourth, bureaucracies are instruments of rationalization; the primary mechanism promoting rationality is the specialization of bureaucrats who are coordinated by other bureaucrats who are also specialists. In fact, Weber and some of his intellectual descendants define bureaucracy as the most rational form of organization (Blau and Meyer 1971).

Our concern here is with the policy impact of public bureaucracy—that bureaucracy sanctioned as a legitimate government body.

Public bureaucracies cannot be fruitfully examined in isolation; they are open systems existing in an environment that structures their tasks and responses (Warwick 1975). Downs (1967) refers to a bureau's environment as its power setting; an abstract version of a bureau's power setting is presented in figure 10.1.

The most visible portion of a bureau's environment is the sovereigns; in the United States, these are the elected officials and their appointees. Sovereigns, the legitimate rulers of a state, possess the formal power to issue orders to the bureau. Simply because the sovereigns occupy a hierarchically superior position, however, does not mean that all interactions between the sovereign and the bureau are based on authoritative commands. As Barnard (1938) so perceptively noted four decades ago, authority comes from below; if subordinates accept a person as a superior, the superior has authority. If the subordinates reject the superior, the superior has no authority. This fact about superior-subordinate relationships means that orders, as denoted in figure 10.1, include not only directives but also bargaining and persuasion. Political power, much like presidential power, is often no more than the power to persuade (Neustadt 1960). Although figure 10.1 oversimplifies the political subsystem by omitting the interrelationships between sovereigns, a bureau receives inputs from all three political institutions—the executive, the legislature, and the judiciary. Since the different sovereign directives may not be consistent, a bureau may have substantial flexibility in responding to sovereign pressures (see below).

Other actors in a bureau's environment may be divided into dependents and coequals. The dependent actors include suppliers, beneficiaries/sufferers, and regulatees. Since suppliers are dependent on the bureau for business, they tend to support bureau actions. Beneficiaries/sufferers are those actors receiving some tangible service from the bureau: the public, interest groups, members of the legislature, and bureau employees. Beneficiaries and sufferers are likely to view a bureau in utilitarian terms (beneficiaries support, sufferers oppose). Regulatees are those members of the environment whose behavior is regulated and altered by a bureau. Their view of the bureau also depends on whether or not they benefit from such regulation.

The coequals in a bureau's environment include both allies and rivals (functional and allocational). The coequal actors may be other bureaus, private groups, private citizens, etc. In its quest for funding, for example, the National Park Service enlists as allies

FIGURE 10.1. The environment of a bureau (adapted from Downs 1967)

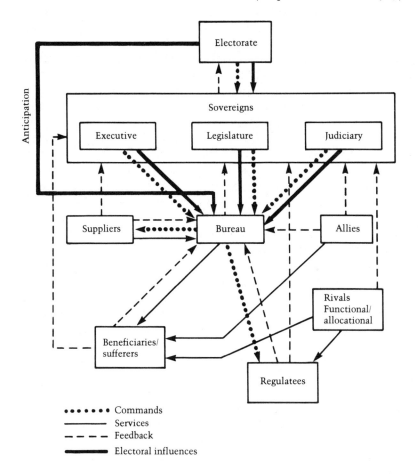

• • • • • • Commands
——————— Services
— — — — Feedback
▬▬▬▬▬▬▬ Electoral influences

the U.S. Fish and Wildlife Service, the National Wildlife Federation, and numerous other actors. Functional rivals are other organizations capable of performing similar functions; the Bureau of Reclamation and the Army Corps of Engineers are functional rivals, as are the U.S. Postal Service and the United Parcel Service. Allocational rivals are all other organizations that compete with a bureau for scarce resources (budgets, personnel, authority, etc.).

A bureau's dependents and coequals are connected to it by service or orders links, and these actors provide feedback to the political subsystem. Through these linkages a bureau can indirectly influence the sovereigns, because bureaus deliver services to a portion of the electorate.

Before discussing the methods of electoral impact in bureaucracy, three additional points should be noted about a bureau and its environment. First, none of the individual boxes in the diagram is a homogeneous unit. Within the bureau, for example, coalitions seek to gain control of the organization. Competing groups of bureau employees have different personal and policy objectives for the organization. The conflict between the lawyers and the economists over control of the Federal Trade Commission is a commonly cited example of an intraorganizational dispute over policy objectives (Hartman 1975). The multilithic nature of a bureau means that some of its actions may be not totally purposive but, rather, the result of a compromise struck between competing factions.

Second, the quantity of inputs to an individual bureau is massive. These inputs come from suppliers, beneficiaries, rivals, and allies, as well as the political sovereigns. *Electoral influences are only a small part of a bureau's total inputs* from the political subsystem and an even smaller part of the bureau's grand total inputs.

Third, the sovereigns do not own all the valuable resources. Suppliers, beneficiaries, allies, and even the bureaus themselves have access to independent sources of funds, personnel, and services. The sovereigns, in fact, are also dependent on the bureau and much of its environment. Since the bureau and its supporters provide programs the sovereigns consider essential, the former have some leverage over the latter. More crucially, a bureau's environment contains many members of the electorate who control the sovereigns' fate. Because most bureaus can influence portions of their environment, bureaus do not just respond to sovereign demands but often actively shape those demands.

THE INFLUENCE OF ELECTIONS
ON BUREAUCRATIC POLICY MAKING

Elections can influence bureaucratic policy making in at least four ways (the starred lines in figure 10.1). Two methods of impact filtered through political sovereigns are "overhead democracy" and administrative reorganization. A more direct link between a bureau and elections involves bureau members observing the political environment and anticipating the sovereigns' policy actions. A final means of electoral impact on bureaucracy is through the mechanisms of direct democracy—including initiatives, referenda, recalls, and the long ballot.

Overhead Democracy

Overhead democracy relies on the doctrine of political supremacy (Redford 1969; Hyneman 1950). According to this doctrine, political sovereigns, such as the president and Congress, are hierarchically superior to nonelected administrative officials. Overhead democracy includes the normal processes of popular control over governmental institutions, leading from the voters through political sovereigns to bureaucratic agencies and their personnel. Political sovereigns have several possible mechanisms for controlling bureaucracy—among the more important are executive direction, budgeting, and legislation and its adjuncts (oversight and the legislative veto).

At the national level, the Constitution designates the president as the head of government, and custom includes the functions of chief administrative officer in this role (Friend 1976). As chief administrator, the president occupies what Redford (1969) refers to as a strategic position; he has the authority to order bureaus to implement laws and executive orders. To supplement the power of executive direction, the president can appoint some 580 top-level officials (department heads, bureau chiefs, etc.) as well as 500 technical and 1,200 schedule C employees to monitor the bureaucracy.[4]

Studies of executive direction reveal that the president can use the formal powers of office to affect the direction of bureaucratic policy. Stanley's (1965) analysis of six agencies during the Kennedy transition found that bureau behavior could be changed by presidential appointees if the political appointee had clear goals for the agency, took immediate steps to direct the agency toward those goals, and had the strong support of the president. Zentner's (1972;

see also Nathan 1975) study of presidential transitions also found that the president must be forceful, persistent, and consistent if he is to change established behavior patterns in the bureaucracy. One of the best examples of establishing political control over a bureaucracy is the success of Robert McNamara as secretary of defense (Longley 1974).

To be effective, presidential intervention in bureau policy decisions must have the advantage of the best possible information, information equal to that of the agency. To provide such information, the presidency has been institutionalized. Employing over 2,700 people directly and many more through detailing, the president can draw on the expertise of the Office of Management and Budget, the Council of Economic Advisors, the National Security Council, the Council on Environmental Quality, and others (Nathan 1975).

Despite the president's formal powers and his ability to gather information, the bureaucracy still may have the means to thwart executive direction. Although such resistance is usually covert, during the Nixon administration the HEW bureaucracy refused to cooperate with Secretary Finch on civil rights matters and continued to press for school desegregation despite presidential orders to the contrary (Sickels 1974; Glazer 1976). The power of executive direction often means that the president has the right to *try* to persuade the bureau to do something. Neustadt, in his examination of presidential power, found that the president could command obedience only if he was unambiguously involved, his orders were clear, the orders were publicized, the recipient of the order had the resources to implement it, and the president's authority to issue the order was accepted (1960: 19). Since few instances completely fit these five criteria, the president must often spend his time convincing bureaucrats that his policies are in their own best interests.

A second mechanism of overhead democracy that political sovereigns can use to influence the bureaucracy is the budget process. A bureau can be disciplined or rewarded for past behavior by denying or granting it resources. The periodicity of the budget process means certain questions are reviewed on an annual basis, with the possibility of a clear sanction (budget cuts) for noncompliance.

The budgetary powers at the federal level are shared by the president and Congress. Since 1921, the president has prepared the budget and submitted it to Congress. Recent presidents have translated this role into a power instrument unequaled in national politics. Agencies make their initial budget request to the Office of Management and Budget (OMB), which examines the requests and cuts them according to presidential guidelines. Bureaus suffering cuts in the executive budget are prohibited by law from requesting additional money from Congress.[5] OMB's budget authority is reinforced by its legislative clearance functions—a bureau cannot send any legislation, whether or not it requires funding, to Congress without OMB clearance to insure that the legislation is in accord with the president's program.

Presidents have used their budget powers effectively to influence bureaucracy. Richard Nixon used the budgetary ax to eliminate many of the Great Society programs that he opposed; he also showed that the budget can be used to strengthen a program, as he did with cancer research. Presidential/OMB budget decisions are often the most important step in the process because other actors must respond to their initial decisions (Wanat 1974).

Congress may also use the budget to reward allies and punish enemies. At times Congress has gone so far as to eliminate programs and agencies by deleting all funds for an agency. The Subversive Activities Control Board and the Area Redevelopment Administration met such fates. Although initial studies of congressional budgeting revealed the process to be incremental (Wildavsky 1964; Fenno 1966), in the past few years inflation has forced Congress to set priorities via the budget process.

After Congress passes the budget, the president can review it again. Although he can veto a budget, vetos are unlikely since budgets for many agencies are lumped together in omnibus appropriations bills. The Budget and Impoundment Control Act of 1974, however, permits the president to refuse to spend funds, subject to congressional veto (see below). Presidents have used impoundment in the past to limit bureaucratic programs they opposed. John Kennedy, for example, impounded funds for a new bomber, and Richard Nixon impounded funds for federal pollution-control grants.

Legislation, the third mechanism of overhead democracy available to influence bureau actions, can deal with procedural or substantive matters. During the Korean War, the Whitten Amendment limited bureau hiring and promotions—an action concerning procedural matters. The Federal Energy Act of 1974, on the other hand, directed the Federal Energy Administration to "do something" about the energy crisis—an action concerning substantive matters.

Legislation is supplemented by two adjuncts to the process—oversight and the legislative veto. Congressional oversight, the investigative function of Congress, receives widespread publicity at times when investigations are newsworthy, such as the FBI and CIA hearings of the mid 1970s. Despite such spectacular hearings, oversight has a mixed record. It was used effectively in the mid 1950s to pressure President Eisenhower and the National Labor Relations Board to adopt a more balanced labor policy (Scher 1961). On the other hand, a series of hearings in the 1960s failed to convince the National Aeronautics and Space Administration that it should investigate solid fuel rockets (Kerr 1965). Recently, the oversight powers of Congress have been augmented by the transformation of the General Accounting Office into a major investigative body that conducts "program results reviews" (Fitzgerald 1975). Although oversight appears to have great potential for affecting bureaucratic behavior, most analysts feel Congress lacks the desire to rigorously oversee the bureaucracy (Ripley and Franklin 1976; Keefe and Ogul 1973).

A second adjunct to the legislative process is the legislative veto, a procedure that focuses on policy implementation. Desiring to insure bureaucratic compliance with legislative intent, yet being uncertain about specific objectives, Congress passes a law instructing an agency to do something (e.g., the Department of Energy should decide how to allocate domestic oil). Part of the initial law declares that bureau decisions must be submitted to Congress and that Congress may "veto" them within sixty days.[6] Congress has relied increasingly on the legislative veto. A recent survey by the Congressional Research Service found veto provisions in 196 pieces of legislation, 89 of which were passed since 1970 (Norton 1976). The veto is used not only on such major laws as the War Powers Act, Impoundment, and Campaign Finance Reform but also on such minor matters as the General Service Administration regulations for release of presidential papers and the HEW sex discrimination regulations.

The Creation of New Bureaus and Reorganizations
Although the above sections discuss a variety of techniques for controlling bureaucracy, all have severe limitations. A political sovereign might be unwise to force an agency to change its policies because an agency hostile to a program can find numerous ways to handicap it. As a result, alternative means of establishing or changing programs become a necessity. The easiest way to circum-

vent a hostile bureau is to create a new bureau more favorably disposed to the program in question.

To understand why many politicians often view reorganization and the creation of new bureaus as an indispensable tool for translating elections into public policy, the major reason for bureaucratic opposition to policy must be noted. Bureaus resist new or established programs because the programs conflict with the bureau's self-defined role. All bureaus define their role in the policy process, communicate this role to their members, create a set of beliefs supporting the role, and build a coherent organizational ideology around the role. The Marine Corps has defined its role as amphibious assault and attempts to project an image of toughness for the corps. The Forest Service uses various personnel practices to socialize its employees into the role of natural resource protector and to strengthen its members' attachment to the service (Kaufman 1960). One study of civil servants' attitudes revealed that a bureaucrat's agency of employment was the best predictor of his or her position on many policy issues (Meier and Nigro 1976). Bureau ideologies result in policy biases that must be considered by political sovereigns because bureau-socialized attitudes often lead bureaus to oppose presidential and congressional initiatives. Yarmolinsky, for example, found that the U.S. Army resisted the establishment of the special forces (Green Berets) because counterguerrilla activity was not part of the Army's traditional role (1971).

If an elected official is so foolish as to entrust a program to a bureau hostile to that program, that elected official must be constantly vigilant. If oversight relaxes even for a short period of time, the bureau can find ways to downgrade or eliminate the program. One solution, discovered by Franklin Roosevelt, is to create a new bureau and entrust the program to it. This tactic permits the new bureau to develop a loyalty to the program and act as its advocate. After the 1932 election, Roosevelt created a host of new agencies and staffed them with loyalists. Later, President Kennedy established a separate Peace Corps rather than entrust his pet program to the staid State Department. After the 1968 election, President Nixon, believing the Federal Communications Commission was not "objective" enough, established the Office of Telecommunications Policy to watch over the media.

A president need not create a new bureau to counter organization biases, however; he can achieve the same end through executive reorganizations. Through reorganization, a president can place

a program in an environment sympathetic to his policy preferences. Shifting pesticide-control programs, for example, from the
Environmental Protection Agency to the Department of Agriculture would mean decisions more favorable to those who wished
to use pesticides. Reorganization can be used to aid a struggling
program in other ways. By upgrading a bureau to an independent
agency or by establishing a program within the White House, programs receive increased attention, status, and resources (Seidman
1975). In sum, a president can use reorganizations to influence
policy direction, but to do so he must have a conscious reorganization strategy and not perceive reorganization as a means to economy and efficiency.

Anticipation
A third way elections can influence bureaucracies is by bureaucrats anticipating the desires of newly elected officials or candidates with a strong chance of winning. Downs (1967) argues that,
all things being equal, a bureau will seek to expand its power
base; one way to expand its power base (and possibly its jurisdiction) is by gaining support from elected officials. The rational bureau will attempt, therefore, to anticipate the policy preferences
of the newly elected officials and present proposals for programs
it feels the officials will support (as long as the programs coincide
with the bureau's perceived role in the policy process).

Bureau actions may be more complex than Downs indicates.
Since many bureaus have coalitions of bureaucrats competing for
control, the election of new political superiors may alter the power
of various coalitions within a bureau. A coalition favored by the
new sovereign will know that as a result of the election it can
appeal to potential allies outside the bureau; a disadvantaged coalition may well acquiesce rather than suffer for openly opposing the
anticipated views of a newly elected sovereign. For example, the
election of a president with a strong proenvironmental outlook
might well alter the traditional power alignments within such
agencies as the Bureau of Land Management, the Bureau of Reclamation, and the Army Corps of Engineers; internal bureau coalitions favoring environmental protection rather than development
interests should find their bargaining position strengthened within
their respective agencies. Consequently, these bureaus would
probably become more responsive to environmental concerns even
without specific White House directives.

A bureau's ability to anticipate policy changes and take appropriate action after the election is relatively clear, but a bureau can also anticipate policy changes before the election. A bureau might change policies during an electoral campaign to undercut a candidate hostile to its traditional viewpoints. The Army Corps of Engineers, for example, in order to deflect the criticisms of environmentalist candidates, might stress increased reliance on flood plain management rather than its traditional dependence on dams and other structural methods of flood control. This bureau action may be internally motivated or it may be the result of directives from an incumbent sovereign. The ability of an incumbent president to take action directly or indirectly through the bureaucracy, during a presidential campaign, is an effective method of undercutting the criticisms of an opposing candidate.

Elections may also have a cyclical effect on bureau policy making. In many urban areas, public works programs follow a cyclical pattern based on elections. Immediately after an election, such large, costly, and often controversial projects as schools, parks, and inner-city programs are proposed. As the next election nears, the workload of city government shifts from large projects to street repair and other noncontroversial items. City bureaucrats may find that certain projects can be sold to political superiors in some years but not in others.

Direct Democracy
Certain electoral events provide a more direct impact on bureaucratic activity than is possible through overhead democracy, administrative reorganization, or anticipation. More direct electoral methods of influencing the bureaucracy are provided by the initiative, the referendum, and the recall. Through the initiative, the citizens themselves are allowed to set items on the public agenda. Referenda occur when a legislative body or other officials place a matter on the public agenda and permit voters to respond via the ballot. Recall is, of course, a procedure that permits voters to remove public officials from office before their term expires.[7]

Direct democracy's methods of influencing bureaucracy are available only in certain state and local jurisdictions. Despite the limitations of scope, the contemporary use of these mechanisms is extensive. Between ten and fifteen thousand referendum-type elections are held annually in the United States, 98 percent at the local level (Hamilton 1970).

Although scholarly interest in direct democracy has a long history, the impact of these methods on bureaucracy has not been

analyzed. Almost all the studies concern questions of voting behavior, such as the relationship between turnout and election outcomes and the effect of campaign variables on electoral outcomes
(Hamilton 1970; Shephard 1975; Bone and Benedict 1975; Lutrin
and Settle 1975; Hamilton and Cohen 1974). As a result, our analysis must rest on case studies and hypothetical examples.

If the voters can affect bureau behavior by electing political
sovereigns, their impact will be at least as great and probably greater when they use electoral mechanisms directly rather than going
through the political sovereign. Many of the sovereign's resources
are available to the direct democracy voter. Using the initiative
to create new agencies is permitted in some states. In 1972, California voters created a Coastal Zone Conservation Commission
and six regional commissions charged with the responsibility of
protecting the coastal environment. The initiative was precipitated by a perceived insensitivity to the issue by California officials
and by close ties between bureaucrats and land developers.

Initiatives and referenda need not create new bureaus to affect
bureau policy making. The procedures can be used to change the
goals of a bureau or to create restrictions on its actions. Voters
may reject a school budget to show their dissatisfaction with education policy and/or costs, or they may file an initiative to reverse an
administrative decision (Hamilton and Cohen 1974). California voters indicated their concern with property taxes when they passed
Proposition 13. Although initiatives and referenda are fairly blunt
instruments, they can elevate a policy issue from a narrow subsystem to the broader electoral system.

The impact of a recall election should be different from the impact of initiatives. A recall election has the same impact as a
regular election; if the recall is successful, the official is replaced
and relationships with bureaucrats are disturbed. Even an unsuc-
cessful recall attempt indicates to the bureaucracy that the incumbent is weak and can be opposed. The impact of recall elections,
then, depends a great deal on the reasons for the recall and the
causes of electorate dissatisfaction.

Although not usually considered in the same category as the
initiative, referendum, and recall, another electoral feature prevalent at the state and local level—the "long ballot"—also affects
bureaucratic activity. The potential for electoral impact on bureaucracy increases in situations where voters select several executive
officials. In long ballot jurisdictions, voters can choose a wide array
of elected officials. In Texas, for example, voters elect the follow-

ing people (in addition to the governor, lieutenant governor, state legislators, and judges): attorney general, treasurer, comptroller, land commissioner, agriculture commissioner, members of the Railroad Commission (which regulates the oil and natural gas industries), and members of the State Board of Education. Although the selection of such a large number of executive officials may result in much uninformed voting, the long ballot permits campaigns on specific issues, such as oil and gas regulatory problems or changes in the educational system. Whether or not the issues presented are policy specific, the long ballot permits the voters' preferences to reach the bureaucracy directly rather than through the chief executive or the legislature. For example, the 1972 Texas general election replaced an attorney general who put a low priority on environmental and consumer protection laws with one who promised to enforce such laws vigorously. The replacement of right-wing Republican Max Rafferty as the state superintendent of education with a black, liberal Democrat in California brought a different emphasis in state educational policy. Although we lack systematic examinations of the impact of the long ballot on the policy activities of the bureaucracy, enough examples exist to contend that the long ballot alters bureaucratic environments and, thus, affects bureau behavior.

BUREAUCRATIC CONSTRAINTS ON ELECTORAL INFLUENCES

Although elections may affect bureaucratic behavior through several avenues, bureaus are not passive instruments at the mercy of their environments (Rourke 1976)—they are complex organizations with goals and purposes of their own, and they often independently possess the means to achieve their goals. This section examines the characteristics of bureaucracy that restrain electoral influence on policy outputs. The restraints listed in this section apply to all electoral influences in the previous section except the creation of new bureaus.

Rational Bureaus Respond Slowly

A rational bureau responds slowly to pressures from the environment. As the result of previous accommodation of environmental pressures, most bureaus reach a state of equilibrium with their environment that permits the bureau to survive and permits some of its environmental demands to be met. A bureau responds slowly to new pressures from the environment, especially electoral pressures, for several reasons (Downs 1967). First, the information present in the bureau's environment, as depicted in figure 10.1, is overwhelming. Inputs into the bureau far exceed its ability to receive communications, decode the communications, and act on the messages. Bureaus are organizations that attempt to maximize action in pursuit of their goals, not organizations that received communications. A bureaucratic organization, therefore, restricts its information so that it can perform other, more important tasks.

Second, being overly sensitive to the environment can be dangerous for a bureau. If the environment of a bureau is constantly changing, quickly responding to environmental demands may be counterproductive—the environment will likely change again, forcing a responsive bureau to reverse itself publicly. A rational organization waits until the environment reaches a consensus about bureau objectives before acting. This aspect of slow response is especially important with electoral influences, since tenured civil servants view electoral influences as short-term phenomena subject to change with the next election.[8]

Third, bureaus must build coalitions of support for their action (Rourke 1976; Allison 1971; Thompson 1967). Although coalitions sometimes form before environmental demands peak, usually the time necessary to build a supportive coalition for the new action will delay the bureau's response. The large size of bureaus means coalitions will change slowly.

The rational, slow response of a bureau dampens the impact of electoral influences, because the impact of all environmental influences is restricted and electoral influences are only one type of influence.

Size
The larger the bureau, the more difficulty the elected official will have in controlling or even having an impact on it.[9] The relationship of bureau size to the influence of elected officials is a function of the number of policy-making positions in the bureaucracy. In a small city of 200,000, for example, no more than one or two levels of policy-making officials exist.[10] Often the chief executive can appoint or at least interact personally with all the policy makers. The Department of Defense, however, has as many as ten or twelve levels of policy-making officials. Since the number of policy-making levels increases with the size of the bureau, elected

officials lose influence because they appoint and interact with only the top few.[11] Career personnel, who will fill the other policy positions, are less sensitive to political demands. Since these career officials must still be given some discretion to accomplish their tasks, the influence of elections and elected officials is tempered.

Professionalism

Mosher (1968) and Price (1965) have noted the increased professionalization of the federal civil service. The federal government is the nation's largest employer of scientists, engineers, doctors, and social scientists. Because professionals are socialized to the norms of their profession, professionalism is a restraint on electoral influences. A lawyer approaching a policy problem will likely take a legal approach.[12] A scientist may well direct her or his attention from what is necessary to what is scientifically interesting. An economist in the Department of Labor may act as an economist first and an employee of the Department of Labor second.

Professionalism, thus, affects a bureaucrat's decisions by providing an alternative set of rational decision criteria. These criteria temper the impact of elections because politics is perceived as the opposite of science (Price 1965). Most scientists will object if political considerations force a decision inconsistent with their professional beliefs. The greater the professionalization of a bureau, therefore, the smaller the impact of elections.

The Merit Principle

The greater the merit system coverage in a bureaucracy, the smaller the impact that elections will have on bureau-related policy. Two aspects of the merit principle restrict the influence of elections—job tenure and the norm of neutrality. Job tenure means a bureaucrat is secure in her or his position and cannot be removed for partisan reasons.[13] Security means a bureaucrat can covertly resist an elected official's policy proposals because the elected official cannot rely on the normal ultimate threat (dismissal from office) to gain compliance.[14]

The merit principle also establishes a norm of neutral administration. Although we know policy administration is not a neutral process, the belief of many is that it reduces the legitimacy of political influence. Nothing weakens a proposed policy innovation more than being labeled a political move. The stronger a jurisdiction's merit system, the weaker the influence of elections on bureau policy making. This factor is important because the merit principle and its application vary widely by jurisdiction; the federal government and some states have almost universal coverage, while other states have fewer than 10 percent of their employees covered by merit regulations.[15]

Clientele Relationships

Many political decisions in the United States are made not by the major political institutions but, rather, by what Freeman (1965) refers to as subsystems. Bureaus, interest groups, and congressional committees combine in self-sufficient groups to set policy. Since bureaus can deliver services but need resources, since interest groups can deliver political support but need services, and since congressional committees can grant resources but need political support, a unified subsystem can become self-sufficient. Subsystems are common in agricultural policy, health research, public works, transportation policy, defense contracting, and many other policy areas.

Major political actors such as the president or the entire Congress rarely influence subsystem politics except under extraordinary circumstances. Intervention in subsystems is infrequent because the costs of intervention are high and the rewards are low. Successful intervention usually results in hostile subsystem actors who will oppose the successful intervenor on other issues, and it usually results in minor changes because the scope of each subsystem is relatively narrow.

Successful intervention, moreover, is unlikely because subsystems are isolated from each other, thus permitting them to operate autonomously. A sovereign must deal with subsystems one at a time. Subsystem politics also facilitate strong ties between the bureau and its clientele, thus reducing the impact of the electoral system. By gathering political support from all or most of the interests concerned with the bureau, a bureau usually has sufficient political support to thwart political directives inconsistent with clientele demands.[16]

The Cohesion of Bureau Personnel

The more cohesive a bureau's personnel, the more that bureau can resist outside pressures, especially pressures from the political sovereigns. If a bureau can present a monolithic face to the outside community, elected officials cannot play one coalition in the bureau against the others to gain leverage. Although most bureaus contain factions competing for control, some bureaus are more successful than others in resolving policy disputes internally. Cohesion is directly related to a bureau's organizational ideology. If the members of a bureau develop a common view of the bureau's role and its approach to the problems facing it, bureau personnel become more cohesive.[17] The armed services, for example, have had moderate success in defining their roles in national defense and have occasionally prevented others from adopting some policy options (Allison 1971). The resistance of the U.S. Marines to a recent Brookings Institution proposal that it abandon its traditional role of amphibious assault clearly demonstrates the unifying power of a bureau's ideology.

In summary, the characteristics of bureaucracy that limit the influence of political sovereigns are rational slow response, size, professionalism, the merit principle, clientele relationships, and cohesion. To be successful, an electoral change must do one of two things: it must remove some of the bureaucratic obstacles to change, or it must concentrate in areas where the resources of bureaucracy are fewest.

THE IMPACT OF CRITICAL ELECTIONS

The above discussion has included several implicit hypotheses about the impact of elections on bureaucracy. In the following sections, some explicit hypotheses about elections and bureaucracies will be discussed.

One: the impact of a critical election on a bureaucracy will, all things being equal, be greater than the impact of another type of election. Critical elections have some characteristics that permit political sovereigns to overcome bureaucratic obstacles to policy change. First, as Brady in this volume, and Brady and Lynn (1973) have carefully demonstrated, one mechanism for translating election results into policy outputs is the influx of newly elected officials in large numbers. They find that, the more new members elected to Congress, the more new legislation is passed. Critical elections, which cause a high turnover of politicians, destroy subcommittee and clientele relationships that the agency develops over decades. A bureau is forced to deal with newly elected officials without the aid of its old friends who went down to defeat.

Second, if the critical election is a landslide, as one would expect, the newly elected sovereigns interpret their election as a mandate. This legitimacy and the size of the electoral landslide are effective means of overcoming an organization's usual tendency to restrict information from the environment.

Third, critical elections are characterized by issue salience and high turnout (Burnham 1970). The concern with issues will likely replace many of the old order with zealots in either elected or appointed positions. The new zealots with sufficient political support can alter a bureau's ideology by rewarding only "acceptable" behavior and denying resources for unacceptable behavior. If used with sufficient force over an extended period of time, these actions can also break up clientele relationships.[18]

THE IMPACT OF REALIGNMENT

Two: The impact of a political realignment on bureaucracy will be cumulative with each passing election. Realignment, the altering of political coalitions as a result of critical elections, permits the advantage of time to pass from the bureaucrat to the politician. During normal political times, the bureaucrat can outwait the politician because the bureaucrat has job tenure (McGregor 1974). But, realignment means the political majority and its policy objectives will remain consistent over a long period of time. If realignment means that sympathetic politicians are replaced by politicians hostile to the bureau, a bureau must learn to live with this new environment.

Realignments also provide the opportunity to alter the recruitment patterns of the bureaucracy, as the Democrats did after the New Deal realignment. Government employment normally attracts people with policy perspectives similar to the current government. For example, the federal government is staffed primarily with liberal Democrats (Aberbach and Rockman 1976); the New York state bureaucracy, on the other hand, is dominated by moderate Republicans. Changing recruitment patterns can be the greatest single source of policy change. If a coalition can alter recruitment patterns to support the realignment viewpoint, many of the other bureaucratic constraints become minor obstacles.

The time provided by realignments also permits the altering of bureau ideologies. By replacing people and structuring behavior, the rare cases of change—for example, when the National Labor Relations Board was changed from a vehement proindustrial labor board to a more balanced board in the 1950s—will become more frequent (Scher 1961). Finally, with a longer time period, elected sovereigns have the potential to alter clientele relationships permanently through the creation of new bureaus or reorganizations that force the bureaucracy to respond to a different clientele. If, for example, a new conservative coalition desired to change the direction of federal work force training to a more probusiness perspective, all job programs could be transferred to the Department of Commerce. The job programs either would become more responsive to Commerce Department clientele or would suffer years of decay and decline.

OTHER HYPOTHESES

Three: The impact of elections on bureaucratic policy making will be greater in state and local jurisdictions than it will be at the federal level. The constraints that bureaucracy can place in the way of political sovereigns are greater at the national level despite the greater formal powers of the federal politician. At the state level, bureaucracy is much smaller, so that the chief executive usually appoints a greater percentage of the policy-making posts. Bureaucracy at the state and local level is not nearly as professionalized as at the federal level. To be sure, large states, such as California and New York, have highly professionalized bureaucracies, but professionals have not penetrated policy-making posts in these states as effectively as they have at the federal level. Finally, the merit system norms are not as strong in most states as they are at the federal level, where the president can appoint only a few thousand bureaucrats. Some states have fewer than 10 percent of the civil service under merit regulations, making the bureaucracy much more responsive to political pressure. If one is seeking to find elections with an impact on bureaucratic policy making, the ideal place to look is the state- and local-level bureaucracies, especially in small, patronage-oriented states.

Four: The impact of an election on a bureaucracy will be greater, all things being equal, if the policy preferences of the elected officials are consistent with the bureaucracy's ideology. Neustadt's (1960) argument that the president's major power is the power of persuasion underscores this hypothesis. Agencies must be persuaded that a given policy is in their own best interest. If elected officials hold beliefs consistent with a bureau's ideology, their ability to persuade that bureau to take action on electoral issues is enhanced.[19]

Five: The bureaus most subject to electoral influences are those lacking strong political support. According to Rourke (1976), two major factors contributing to an agency's political support are its clientele support and its expertise. Agencies lacking clientele support or expertise, such as the current Selective Service System, have few arguments or resources they can marshal against political officials. Politically powerful agencies, such as the Department of Defense and the National Institutes of Health, can usually weather eight years of a hostile presidency by mobilizing their allies elsewhere.

Six: Elections will have the greatest impact on new agencies, all other things being equal. New agencies are particularly vulnerable to electoral influences for several reasons. A new agency has not had the time to socialize its employees to a consistent ideology concerning the agency's role in the policy process. Building clientele support among interest groups and members of Congress is also time-consuming. Most new agencies confront a skeptical if not a hostile environment. Finally, developing a professional recruitment system cannot be done quickly, especially when the agency needs new types of professionals (such as experts in environmental engineering or transportation planning). Professionalization, clientele support, and ideology are all resources a bureau can use to blunt the policy initiatives of political sovereigns, and older agencies usually have had the time to develop advantages in each of these areas.

THE POLICY AREAS

The national policy-making process is not uniform and consistent; it varies by both actors and procedures among substantive policy areas (see Lowi 1972). For example, a distributive policy area, such as agricultural subsidies or health research, is characterized by strong bureaus and interest groups with most decisions taking place in subsystems rather than in the major political institutions. Questions of redistributive policy (taxes, social security, etc.) are usually decided by the major political institutions through the legislative process. Given such variations in the policy process, examining the impact of elections on bureaus in different policy areas should be a fruitful exercise.

Seven: Electoral impacts on bureaucracy will be strongest in foreign policy. Foreign policy bureaus are generally weak because they cannot develop strong clientele support (foreign nations are notoriously poor clientele) and because any expertise they claim is expertise that many others are willing to contribute directly to the president. As a result foreign policy bureaus, such as the State Department, are sometimes ignored; recent presidents have built their personal State Departments within the National Security Council. Since the president is recognized as the sole voice of the nation in foreign policy, the role of bureaucracy is reduced to one of advice and implementation. Given the weak bureaus and the preeminent role of the president, bureaucracies can only rarely deflect electoral influences in the area of foreign policy.[20]

Eight: In defense policy, the impact of elections on bureaucratic policy making will be strong, through not as strong as in foreign policy. The military services have many of the resources that bureaucracies use to resist electoral inputs—size unequaled in the federal government, access to the most advanced expertise available, and powerful clientele among defense contractors and members of Congress. If the president and the Congress are divided on military policy, the military can use these resources to thwart electoral intentions. For example, the military services were able to use their allies quite effectively to receive funding for a bomber denied by President Kennedy (Yarmolinsky 1971), though they were not as successful under the Carter administration. The McNamara experience, on the other hand, shows that the military bureaucracy can be subjected to civilian control if the Secretary of Defense has skilled aides and full support of the president. Under these conditions, presidential influence on the military may almost equal his influence in foreign policy.[21]

Nine: In distributive policy making (agriculture subsidies, business support, health research, etc.), elections will have little impact on the bureaucracy. Distributive politics is the area of national politics where clientele relations are strongest. The clientele support of such agencies as the Army Corps of Engineers, the Agriculture Research Service, the Bureau of Reclamation, and the National Institutes of Health is unrivaled by bureaus in other policy areas. Couple this support with the professionalization of these agencies, dominated as they are by scientists, economists, engineers, and doctors, and distributive bureaus are effectively insulated from electoral politics. Political sovereigns are likely to have influence only when disputes cannot be settled within the policy subsystem and a group appeals to the sovereign for help (Schatt-schneider 1960). Since most distributive subsystems are extremely adept at resolving disputes at the subsystem level, even critical elections will rarely affect existing distributive policy bureaus.

Ten: In regulatory policy (transportation, drug, and safety regulations), the impact of elections on bureaus will be minimal at best. Regulatory policy is characterized by the same problems as distributive policy (strong clientele relationships, some professionalism, lack of conflict) plus a major structural problem. Most, though by no means all, regulation is done by *independent* regulatory commissions. Commissioners serve overlapping terms and must be bipartisan to provide some independence from political pressures. Given the special position that the independent regulatory commission holds in the eyes of Congress, electoral influences, especially those channeled through the president, will likely have little impact. Even in the early 1970s, with great pressure to "reform" regulation and with consensus that current regulatory policy was inadequate, political decisions have little impact on regulatory policy.

Regulatory agencies, however, may be more receptive to long-term political changes than are distributive agencies. A single president, if reelected, can usually replace an entire regulatory commission. If consistent appointments are made over a long period of time, the election can affect regulatory policy as it did for the National Labor Relations Board in the 1950s (Scher 1961). Unfortunately for this form of control, regulation is rarely salient to most presidents long enough to generate several consistent appointments.

Eleven: All things being equal, the impact of elections on bureaucracies involved in redistributive policy (welfare, housing, social security) will be moderate, greater than the impact on distributive and regulatory bureaus but less than the impact on defense and foreign affairs bureaus. Redistributive policy in the United States is characterized by intense conflict at the congressional and presidential level for a period of years, culminating in the passage of legislation (Marmor 1973; Steiner 1966; Piven and Cloward 1971).

Redistributive legislation is normally set out in great detail so that administrative discretion is reduced to a minimum. The Social Security Administration, long characterized as a redistributive agency with little discretion despite its size (Schick 1971), administers a series of laws that run almost three hundred pages in the U.S. Code. Bureaus such as this tend not to be affected by normal elections because these elections do not have enough impetus to change basic legislation. Critical elections, however, if focused on a redistributive policy area, can have a profound impact on redistributive bureaus.

DISCUSSION

The study of electoral impacts on bureaucratic policy making is long overdue. Although some scholars have theorized about the difficulties elected officials have in controlling bureaus (Mosher 1968; Redford 1969), the systematic study of elections as an input into the bureaucratic process has been ignored. Since bureaucracy can marshal an impressive array of obstacles to prevent a political sovereign from influencing policy making, electoral influences on bureaucracies may be significant only after critical elections or during periods of realignment. Bureaus will, of course, be affected somewhat by most elections, since elections change the opportunities available to enterprising bureaucrats; but in most cases the bureau will act to avoid or act to minimize change and will be successful at it. Only critical elections have the potential of so changing a bureau's environment that nonincremental action is possible.

Although this essay has attempted to present some significant hypotheses to guide research in the area of elections and bureaucracies, some major problems must be surmounted before many hypotheses can be evaluated. The primary problem is that few good indicators of the direction and quality of bureaucratic policy making exist. To evaluate the relative impact of an election on several bureaus, policy output indicators that are comparable across agencies are needed. Until such indicators are developed, most research will of necessity be limited to case studies. The problem of data does not mean that we cannot empirically analyze the impact of elections on bureaucracies. One method of affecting bureaucracies is through reorganization and the creation of new bureaus. The above hypotheses suggest that the number of new bureaus created should increase significantly after critical elections, a hypothesis that can be tested with available data.

The most promising area in which electoral influences on bureaucracy might be studied is state and local government. At the state level, bureaus often lack the political and professional impediments to political influence that characterize national bureaucracies. Critical elections in the fifty states are bound to occur more frequently than do such elections at the national level. Numerous critical elections must be analyzed to assess fully the impact of such elections on bureaucratic policy making. Our knowledge of elections and their influence on bureaucracy, therefore, will progress at a more rapid pace if the locus is states and localities rather than the federal government.

NOTES

Note: We would like to thank David W. Brady, Richard Trilling, and Larry Hill for their helpful comments on earlier versions of this chapter.

1 Elections, of course, can have a direct impact on public policy when the elected officials do not need to rely on bureaucracy to implement the policy or when the discretion in implementing the policy is minimal. Recent congressional changes in the social security program, for example, required little bureaucratic assistance in implementation because the program requires little bureaucratic discretion.

2 This chapter also addresses another set of questions with a long tradition of research—that of public administration and democracy (see Redford 1969; Mosher 1968). If elections influence bureau policy making, political control over bureaucracy is feasible (e.g., overhead democracy). This question is much discussed, but no analysis has yet attempted to delineate the circumstances under which political control becomes a reality.

3 The traits discussed here are taken from a variety of sources. The discussion draws heavily on the early work of Weber (1946) and the later work of Downs (1967).

4 Schedule C employees are political appointees placed at middle levels in the bureaucracy. Created during the Eisenhower administration, schedule C positions serve two functions. They permit the president some limited patronage, and they can be filled by loyalists, thus giving the president additional sources of information. The creation of the Senior Executive Service in 1979 should give the president additional leverage.

5 Agencies and congressional committees have found subtle ways to let Congress know how much an agency requested from the OMB. In effect, an agency with strong congressional support can "request" more money than the OMB allotted.

6 The veto comes in a variety of forms. Vetoes may specify veto by the entire Congress, one house of Congress, a committee of Congress, or even a committee chairperson. A negative veto requires Congress to reject an action; an affirmative veto means actions are void unless Congress affirms them. The time period for congressional action varies by statute. For a fuller discussion of the legislative veto, see Cooper (1956).

7 These three products of the Progressive Era exemplify what has traditionally

been termed "direct democracy," although the degree of directness varies considerably among different forms of each mechanism. Price (1975) has identified four major forms of initiative: (1) constitutional initiative, which permits citizens to amend the Constitution or city charter; (2) direct initiative, which allows citizens to enact or amend laws by themselves; (3) indirect initiative, which requires final approval by the legislative body after approval by the voters; and (4) advisory initiative, in which voters express a nonbinding opinion on a proposed law. Similar variations of the referendum exist. Recall also has direct and indirect forms where the voters may directly remove an official or may simply set in motion the process for removing an official.

8 Often the bureaucratic reaction to presidential initiatives at the national level is "this too shall pass." Presidents are viewed as temporary occupants of their position, unlike civil servants, who were there long before the incumbent president and will be there after he leaves.

9 We assume, of course, that the elected official desires some influence over a bureau. Since the desire to influence a bureau is also positively related to the size of the bureau, actual control over a bureau is probably curvilinearly related to its size.

10 We found in earlier studies of two metropolitan areas that policy-making posts were limited to the top two or three levels of the city bureaucracy. Even in a city of 200,000, most bureaucrats delivered services directly to citizens rather than making policy.

11 We assume that the individual official in a large bureau exercises as much discretion as one in a small bureau. In an agency such as the Social Security Administration, where most decisions are specified in law, large organizations can be controlled by a few appointments.

12 Professionalized approaches may well be harmful. The abundance of lawyers in regulatory agencies has led to a judicialization of procedures, according to Davis (1969). As a result, regulatory agencies have slowed and failed to anticipate new problems.

13 A recent decision by a Chicago district court extended some job tenure rights to nonpatronage public employees. The consequences of this decision may be to restrict the politician's options further in dealing with the bureaucracy. On the other hand, Heclo's (1977) description of executive politics indicates that, with enough effort and patience, one can fire any high-level civil servant.

14 The resistance must be covert, since open insubordination is grounds for dismissal even under the most stringent merit principles. With enough pressure, elected officials might be able to make the civil servant pursue certain policies, but the influences of implementation are subtle and have a wide impact. A recent example of this is cited in Glazer (1976). In opposition to direct White House orders, the HEW bureaucracy applied increasing pressure on southern school districts to desegregate.

15 Merit regulation does not necessarily mean that the bureaucrat is selected according to some ability to perform a job. A recent study of the federal service (Pincus 1976) found over half of the civil servants entered under noncompetitive procedures. Onondaga County, New York, has gained a reputation for appointing politicians to administrative posts and giving them an exam, often several times, until they finally pass it.

16   All other things being equal, clientele support is maximized when the clientele
is large, the clientele is cohesive, the clientele is competitive (that is, there
is more than one group so the bureau is not captured by a single interest),
the clientele is geographically dispersed, the clientele has some prestige in the
community, and the clientele does not have several additional points of access
to politics other than the bureau. See Rourke (1976) for a discussion of these
points.

17   The need to develop an organizational ideology grows out of several other characteristics of bureaucracy. Bureaucracies are goal-oriented systems; as a result,
their goals provide the core for an ideology. The full-time nature of employees
permits bureaus to socialize their members by withholding and granting rewards.

18   Critical elections also increase the probability of creating new bureaus. Normally the reason for the creation of a new bureau is a new program. New
programs are easier to press for, according to Brady and Lynn (1973), immediately after critical elections, when many new people are elected because they
supported new policies.

19   This hypothesis indicates that a conservative president will have little impact
on the federal bureaucracy. Any initiatives of such a president will immediately be viewed with skepticism. Despite all the articles on the powers of the
Nixon presidency, Nixon was unable to effectively change the direction of the
bureaus administering many social programs (see Nathan 1975).

20   We realize that this hypothesis contradicts much of the recent literature on
bureaucracy and foreign policy (see Halperin 1974; Destler 1972; Warwick
1975). We agree with Art (1973) that many of these findings are overstated,
especially if the influence of foreign policy bureaus is compared to that of
domestic policy bureaus.

21   One reason for effective presidential control might be the norms of the military
itself. The military services are much like bureaucracies in the pure Weberian
sense—they carry out orders exceptionally well. If the military can be convinced that the political sovereigns have the military's best interests in mind
or if they can be convinced that resistance is futile, then they may be very
subordinate to the sovereigns' wishes.

The Supreme Court's Role in Critical Elections

DAVID ADAMANY

Although lively, the debate over the Supreme Court's role in critical election periods is still in a primitive state. Two roles have been asserted for the Court, and a third has apparently escaped attention. First, do the justices play a special policy-making role in the aftermath of critical elections? Second, what implication about the Court's role during critical election periods should be drawn from the legitimacy-conferring function often attributed to it? On the one hand, it has been argued that the Court is a stabilizing force because it wraps a cloak of legitimacy around highly controversial policies of the new majority coalition installed by a realigning election. On the other hand, the view has been advanced that the justices, mainly carrying over from the old regime, delegitimate the policies of the new majority coalition, at least in the immediate aftermath of a realigning ballot (Adamany 1973: 820–843). No attention has yet been paid to a third role the Supreme Court might play in critical elections: its potential, as a policy-making center in the majority-party coalition, for shaping the coalition's stance on those high-intensity issues which provoke critical elections. This chapter elaborates upon these several, sometimes conflicting, theories about the Supreme Court's role during critical election periods and portrays in very broad strokes the evidence relevant for selection among them.

We have previously defined a critical election as one marked by a substantial shift in long-term voter allegiances. Campbell and his colleagues have extended the definition to include the transfer of control of the national government to a new majority-party coalition, which they have called a realigning election (1960: 531–538). This extension requires recognition of a second class of critical elections, which Pomper has dubbed converting elections (1967: 535–538). In a realigning election, existing policy is rejected and the out party wins a mandate to make policy. In converting elections, however, the preexisting majority party remains in power and its policy, while provoking shifts in voters' allegiance, endures. For discussion of national policy making in critical elections, the dichotomy between realigning and converting elections, as distinct subsets of critical elections, is therefore important. Indeed, it is a central thesis of this essay that, although the Supreme Court has a similar role during the prelude to both kinds of critical elections, its impact on national policy is usually greater and more enduring in converting elections.

THE LEGITIMATING FUNCTION
OF THE SUPREME COURT

At the outset, a distinction must be made between the Supreme Court's legitimacy and its legitimating function. Both involve public confidence in the Supreme Court, arising not from the substance of policy decisions but from popular belief that those exercising power under rules of law and in accordance with their traditional authority have a right to do so. This public belief has been characterized as "symbolic legitimacy" to distinguish it both from "content legitimacy" (public approval of an institution arising from approval of its specific policies) and from effectiveness (public confidence in an institution stemming from its perceived success in meeting societal problems) (Adamany 1973: 801–802; Johnson 1967: 9–15).

Supreme Court legitimacy adheres in the Court and does not require it to do something else. Such legitimacy may shield the Court from attack by others in the political arena. The legitimacy-conferring function requires, by contrast, that the Court not merely have legitimacy but that it transfer legitimacy to other institutions, to public policies, to regimes, or to other government officials.

Black and Dahl assert, for instance, that the Court's constitutional validation of policies enacted by the popular branches might transfer legitimacy not only to those policies but, ultimately, to the regimes promulgating them (Black 1960: chap. 3; Dahl 1957: 293–294). The late Alexander Bickel suggested, similarly, that judicial approval of policies on constitutional grounds not only engendered popular consent for them but also had the subtler consequence of "adding a certain impetus to measures that the majority enacts rather tentatively" (1962: 29–33, 68–72, quoted passage on pp. 30–31).

Murphy and Tanenhaus have specified three conditions necessary for the Court to fulfill a legitimacy-conferring role: (1) the public must have knowledge of the Court and its major decisions, (2) the public must recognize and accept that it is a proper judicial function to interpret and apply the polity's fundamental principles, especially the Constitution, and (3) the public must have confidence that the justices carry out their work in an impartial and competent manner (1968b: 359).

Public opinion studies have consistently shown that very few Americans know of the Court's decisions (Murphy and Tanenhaus 1968a: 34–35, 1968b: 360, 1976: 6; Dolbeare and Hammond 1968: 20–21; Kessel 1966: 171–174; Adamany 1977: 12). At most, about 40 percent of those polled were able to specify actions taken by the Supreme Court, and the vast majority of them recalled only one subject of decision. At least as important, virtually all public knowledge is about Supreme Court decisions striking down acts of other officials. There is not the slightest evidence of public knowledge about the Court's affirmations of the policies of other officials. Yet the Court's asserted legitimacy-conferring function necessarily turns on the justices' validation of policies, not on their disapproval of them.

Public opinion studies also show that not more than half of the population meets the second condition for the Court's legitimating function: recognition and acceptance that it is a proper judicial function to interpret and apply the polity's fundamental principles, especially those of the Constitution (Murphy and Tanenhaus 1968b: 365; Kessel 1966: 174; Adamany 1977: 21–24). Casey tends to confirm the earlier conclusion that relatively few Americans identify the Court as an interpreter of the Constitution. Only 8 percent of his Missouri respondents gave Constitution-related answers when asked about the "Supreme Court's main job in government." Including all answers relating to law enforcement, legal interpretation, and the constitutional review of laws brings that total to only 38 percent (1974: 392–394). Hence, even using the most generous measure, it cannot be said that the public recognizes the Court's constitutional role.

The public apparently has a mixed view about the Supreme Court's impartiality (*Gallup Opinion Index* 1967: 16; Johnson 1967: 165). Several surveys show large minorities of the population suspecting that the Court favors special interests. Other surveys have shown the Court falling behind the Congress and the president in public confidence. Recent polls have, however, shown increased public confidence in the Court, and its ranking relative to other governmental institutions has improved markedly (Dennis 1975: 22–23, table 10; Adamany 1977: 16–17).

Surveys are available for so short a time period that it is difficult to know what to make of these changing currents of public confidence in the Supreme Court. One earlier study suggested that attitudes toward the Court are influenced by partisan affiliation. When a Republican president occupies the White House, support for the Court rises among Republicans. During Democratic presidencies, however, Republican attitudes toward the Court become more unfavorable. There is some evidence from the Eisenhower and Nixon years that changes in poll support for the Court were caused primarily by such shifts among Republicans (Dolbeare and Hammond 1968; *Gallup Opinion Index* 1973: 9).

Partisan confidence in the Court would not, of course, add to its legitimacy-conferring capacity. Those who need to be symbolically reconciled to government policies are those who disagree with the substance of them—usually the supporters of the out party. Yet, if confidence in the Court is rooted in partisan affiliation, judicial decisions affirming disfavored policies will not reconcile out-party adherents to them, precisely because their party does not control the government.

Only a very small percentage of the public apparently holds attitudes consistent with the legitimacy-conferring function asserted for the Supreme Court. Those who had knowledge of the Court's decisions, recognized and accepted judicial review, and were confident that the justices carried out their duties in an impartial and competent manner constituted only 12.8 percent of a national sample in 1965 (Murphy and Tanenhaus 1968b: 378). Using survey questions likely to elicit somewhat more supportive public responses, a 1976 study nonetheless found that only 17 percent of the Wisconsin public met the three conditions for judicial legitimation of policies, regimes, or institutions (Adamany 1977: 30).

Perhaps the legitimacy-conferring function of the Supreme Court is misdirected when aimed at the general public. In many aspects of American politics, it is the "elite" or "activist" segment of the population that performs important tasks or holds significant attitudes. Judicial legitimation may operate only among these narrow, but politically significant, sectors of the population. Knowledge of judicial decisions is certainly greater among the activist stratum (Dolbeare and Hammond 1971: 17–20; Murphy and Tan-enhaus 1970: 22; Casey 1974: 406; Adamany 1977: 12), but even their information is rather shallow, with few activists knowing of more than one Supreme Court decision (Adamany 1977: 12). There is, moreover, no evidence that political activists are aware of Su-preme Court decisions approving governmental decisions; like the general population, their attention seems riveted on cases which invalidate national or state policy. Invalidating decisions obvious-ly does not confer legitimacy, and such knowledge of judicial ac-tivity does not therefore confirm the Supreme Court's legitima-cy-conferring capacity among politically active sectors of the population.

Political elites apparently have a higher recognition than the general public of the Supreme Court's duty of constitutional re-view (Murphy and Tanenhaus 1968b: 366–367; Casey 1974: 400, 408–409). A Wisconsin survey showed, for instance, that 37.5 per-cent of political activists but only 21.5 percent of politically in-active respondents recognized the Supreme Court's constitutional role (Adamany 1977: 21). Moreover, political activists show greater commitment than the politically inactive to the creed that the justices decide cases "strictly on the basis of what the Constitu-tion says" rather than to the more realistic notion that jurists exercise discretion and promulgate policy preference in reaching decisions (Adamany 1977: 22–23). Political activists have greater general confidence in the Supreme Court than do the politically inactive; they evaluate its specific decisions more favorably; and they give it more support in policy disputes with Congress and the president (Adamany 1977: 13–16, 25–28; Murphy and Tanen-haus 1970: 22). Finally, 30 percent of political activists met the three conditions for judicial legitimation of policies, institutions, or regimes; only 12.8 percent of the general public did so (Adamany 1977: 29–30).

The sum of this evidence tends to show that the Supreme Court's legitimacy-conferring capacity is somewhat higher among political elites than among the general public. But even here the Court's authority falls far short of including even a majority of those surveyed. This scarcely lends support to the assertion that the justices can assure widespread public acceptance for policies, in-stitutions, or regimes by handing down decisions which sustain them and their actions.

One other exploration is important in assessing the Supreme Court's legitimacy-conferring authority among political activists.

The ideology of both political activists and the general public has been shown to color their attitudes toward the Supreme Court. Those who hold liberal political attitudes or take liberal positions on national issues are more likely to evaluate the Court favorably; conservatives express greater reservations about the Court (Murphy et al. 1973).

Ideological evaluations of the Supreme Court tend, however, to be more pronounced among political activists than among the general public. Studies of congressional administrative assistants, Princeton University students, and the attentive public (i.e., those survey respondents who were most knowledgeable about the high court) found that liberals strongly supported the Court, while conservatives gave it low ratings (Murphy and Tanenhaus 1970). Similar ideological cleavages were found by Dolbeare and Hammond between local liberal and conservative activists (1969: 4) and were confirmed in a survey of Wisconsin residents (Adamany 1977: 18).

The importance of these findings is obvious: if evaluation of the Supreme Court turns upon the convergence between its policies and the ideological preferences of political activists, the Court's legitimating function will have force mainly among those who already agree with its policies. The justices will, then, have very little authority to confer legitimacy on policies, institutions, or regimes among those who disagree with its policies. Yet it is precisely among those who lose the conflict over policy that legitimation is most important, for it is the losers who must be reconciled in order to maintain a stable political system.

This long excursion into the Supreme Court's asserted legitimacy-conferring function is not, as it may initially seem, irrelevant to defining the justices' role in critical election periods. Suppose for a moment that the Supreme Court does confer legitimacy upon policies, institutions, and regimes by its validating decisions. The justices would then be in a position to reconcile minorities to policies and regimes they oppose. This would be of the utmost importance during critical election periods. Realigning elections initiate sweeping new policies and bring a new party leadership to power. The social, economic, and political issues or conditions that precipitate abrupt, large-scale changes in partisan allegiance and voting also demand of newly installed political leaders that they act dramatically and decisively. Instead of slow, incremental policy change, the national government is likely to embark upon major new programs.

These programs will be especially unacceptable to the nation's minority party and its leadership, for their insistent opposition to change while they controlled government was a major catalyst of realignment. Moreover, they will find it difficult to accept the authority of the newly installed national leadership, because it will include large numbers of those who for years were thought incapable of guiding the nation and were, therefore, rejected at the polls. Alienation from national policy and leadership will therefore be higher during realignments than at other periods.

If the Supreme Court confers legitimacy, its role in promoting acceptance of policies and leadership would be vitally important to national stability in the aftermath of a realignment. Black has made precisely this point. The Supreme Court's endorsement of the New Deal after 1937 was, he argues, essential for reconciling the large minority whose reservations went beyond the merits of Rooseveltian policy to the constitutionality of the New Deal program (1960: 56–69). A similar task fell to the justices in other great periods when the leadership and policies of government changed in response to electoral upheaval (ibid.: 69–86).

The Supreme Court might play a somewhat similar role following converting elections. Here important factions in the majority party bolt to the opposition because they cannot accept the dominant coalition's stance on highly salient and intensely felt issues. At the same time, some in the minority party decamp to the majority coalition for similar reasons. In the fashion of all fratricidal struggles, those who have been forced from their traditional partisan homes by such emotional issues will feel especially bitter against their erstwhile brethren. Moreover, powerholders who have forsaken office to shift to the minority party will find it difficult to accept the authority of former electoral opponents who have assumed those offices as they attached themselves to the majority coalition.

A stable democracy must reconcile and accommodate dissenters in electoral periods characterized by such emotional issues, party divisions, and changes in officeholding. The Supreme Court would assume towering importance in the political process if its decisions, by validating the policies and anointing the leaders of new majority-party coalitions formed by realignment and conversion, served to reconcile embittered and alienated minority factions.

The evidence does not, however, support such a characterization of the Supreme Court's role. There is little in the survey data that confirms the Court's legitimacy-conferring capacity, either among the general public or among minority-party activists, who are likely to be especially embittered about the shifts in policy and power-holding that follow critical elections. Those who have character-ized the Supreme Court as a balance wheel which stabilizes the American polity in the aftermath of critical elections have simply not proven their case.

Assume, however, for the sake of argument that the Supreme Court did have the capacity to confer legitimacy upon policies and leaders. There remains the stark prospect that in critical elec-tion periods this authority would backfire, producing results exact-ly contrary to those usually predicted. The new majority political coalition forged by realignment usually inherits a Court fully staffed by the opposition party. "At every turn in national policy where the cleavage between the old order and the new was sharp, the new President has faced a judiciary almost wholly held over from the preceding regime (Jackson 1941: 315). Even if vacancies occur at average intervals of twenty-two months, the president who leads a newly established majority party will not win work-ing control on a nine-member Court during the period of deepest national crisis, when he and his congressional allies are enacting major new programs. And it is plausible that there will be fewer opportunities than usual for presidential appointment if justices of the displaced majority party tend to cling to their seats (Ada-many 1973: 821–825).

If the Supreme Court, dominated by men and ideas of the re-jected party coalition, opposes the policies and programs of the president and the Congress installed by realignment, the power to confer legitimacy becomes the power to deny legitimacy. Thus, at moments of crisis and realignment, the Court's opposition to the popular branches may go beyond checking their actions to undermining their legitimacy. As the new president and Congress gradually appoint justices who agree with them, the Court will eventually validate the policies of the elected departments, but, for minority-party leaders and their followers, this may have the appearance more of judicial surrender to superior force than of legitimation of the new regime (Adamany 1973: 842, 844).

The scenario during converting election periods may follow a different course. If the Supreme Court is dominated by justices from the wing of the majority party that prevails in intraparty conflict, the policies of the newly constituted majority coalition will be validated and, therefore, legitimated. But, if a majority of the justices are sympathetic to that wing of the dominant party that loses the intraparty contest and bolts to the minority party, the reconstituted majority coalition will find the judicial branch hostile to its program. And, of course, such judicial opposition would delegitimate their policies.

Subsequent sections of this chapter will detail the nature of policy making in the aftermath of critical elections. They will tend to show that conflict between the president and Congress, on the one hand, and the Supreme Court, on the other, has indeed characterized realigning election periods but has not usually marked the aftermath of converting elections. Although survey data do not support the view that the Supreme Court has a legitimacy-conferring capacity, the implications of postrealignment conflict are stark for those who insist on attributing such a role to the Supreme Court. The justices become a force for instability as they oppose and delegitimate the policies and leaders of majority-party coalitions newly created by the electorate in response to highly salient and intense social, economic, and political issues confronting the nation.

SUPREME COURT POLICY MAKING IN THE AFTERMATH OF REALIGNING ELECTIONS

The Supreme Court and Popular Sovereignty

Political scientists have been concerned about the Supreme Court's policy-making role in the aftermath of realigning elections. It is necessary, at the outset, to acknowledge that realignments are usually the product of electoral changes stretching over several elections. As we discovered in chapter 2, the concept of a "realigning period" is probably more apt in speaking about electoral behavior than is the designation "realigning election." On the other hand, policy analysis and concerns for regime legitimacy necessarily focus on the transition in government authority, not on the crosscurrents of electoral behavior throughout a realigning period. So it may indeed be correct, for these purposes, to begin analysis from the occurrence of a "realigning election"—that is, from the moment during the realigning period when shifts in electoral allegiance have gathered such force that a new lawmaking majority is installed in both the presidency and the Congress.

The Supreme Court typically stands as a barrier against the "constituent act," which, as Burnham points out, is the significance of realignments in American democracy (1970: 9–10). First, if the justices have a legitimating function (which is doubtful, as indicated above), their usual mode in the years following a re-aligning election is to delegitimate the new regime and its policies. Second, the Court typically succeeds in preventing the lawmaking majority from fully effecting its policy objectives, although it cannot block the majority from putting major new programs into place.

Burnham has argued that realigning elections are the primary instruments of domestic sovereignty and of tension management in the American polity (1970: 9–10, 175–183). Change, he says, moves at a rapid pace in the nation's social and economic sectors. But fragmented, decentralized government, combined with coalitional political parties, defeats substantial change in the public sector. Tensions mount over long periods and, finally, when large segments of the electorate see themselves menaced by existing conditions, a flash point is reached. Sweeping electoral realignments occur, and a new lawmaking majority embarks on policies consistent with the needs of the freshly created electoral majority.

Realigning elections therefore become the instrument for voters in a democratic polity to set "the outer boundaries of policy in general, though not necessarily of policies in detail" (Burnham 1970: 10). The specific formulation of policy within those general boundaries lies, of course, with elected elites. In addition, realignments are the means by which decentralized, status quo government structures are periodically forced to "catch up" with fast-paced changes in the nation's private sector.

If Burnham's speculations are correct and if, additionally, the Supreme Court typically stands, as I have suggested, against the full realization of the forces unleashed during realigning periods, then the judiciary must be harshly judged from a democratic perspective. Further, it must be evaluated as a force which threatens the viability of the American polity by preventing government from keeping pace with the major developmental trends occurring elsewhere in society.

The Sources of Conflict

The Supreme Court's nay-saying role during realignments is not invariable; rather, it turns upon the assumption that the justices will stand in opposition to the new lawmaking majority. While this is the usual situation, it is not inevitable. First, it requires that the justices sitting at the time of a realigning election be adherents of the policies of the old regime. This seems plausible enough, since the justices were appointed by presidents and confirmed by Senates who were part of the old dominant majority coalition. And history bears this out. The Federalist court was hostile to the Jeffersonian regime; Lincoln inherited an unfriendly Democratic Court; and the "Old Court" invalidated a large number of the New Deal's most sweeping reforms.

Second, the old regime's justices must continue to serve on the Court for some duration after the realigning election occurs. Presidents named in realigning elections have on the average had a slightly greater opportunity than other chief executives to make appointments to the Supreme Court. But, because these appointments tended to occur near the end of their terms and because the preexisting membership of the Court was so heavily dominated by justices of the old regime, the appointees of realigning presidents constituted a majority, if at all, only very late in the second terms of those chief executives. Hence, during the critical years immediately following a realigning election, the lawmaking majority is indeed faced with a Supreme Court composed primarily of justices who were part of the old regime (Adamany 1973: 823–825).

The Nature of Conflict
There is some tendency to oversimplify the nature of conflict that occurs between the Supreme Court and the elected branches following a realigning election. Funston has suggested that the incidence of Supreme Court invalidations of federal laws, especially those enacted within the prior four years, is substantially higher in realigning periods than at other times. Further, he has argued that such conflict is even greater if the Court's review of federal laws is examined beyond the realigning period up to the time at which the new lawmaking majority succeeds in naming a majority of justices (1975: 804–807).

Systematic analysis of Supreme Court invalidations of federal laws during realigning periods does not, however, support Funston's conclusions. First, Funston examined Supreme Court cases during periods of *electoral* realignment. During the Civil War realignment, for instance, he analyzed decisions from 1852 to 1860. But, as Beck has pointed out, "by using the years in which the realignment is taking place, Professor Funston has included many years in which the 'emerging majority' had not yet become a legislative majority" (1976: 931). Plainly, judicial invalidation of legislation enacted before the electoral realignment had installed the new majority party in the seats of power cannot accurately be viewed as Supreme Court opposition to that party's policies. To return to our example, Funston erred by selecting cases in the period from 1852 to 1860 because the Civil War realignment did not bring the emerging Republican coalition to national power until 1861.

Second, and more important, Funston's analysis, which averages all Supreme Court invalidations of federal legislation in all realigning periods over the total number of years in those periods, distorts reality. A disproportionate number of these decisions occurred during the New Deal period, and only when this large number of cases is averaged over all realigning periods does judicial invalidation of national policy appear consistently high. To put it another way, the Supreme Court did not strike down national laws with any extraordinary frequency during realigning periods other than the New Deal era (Canon and Ulmer 1976: 1215–1218).

Nagel suggests a different measure of conflict—the incidence of bills introduced to curb the Court or the number of such measures reported from congressional committees (1969: 260–264). His division of American history into high- and low-frequency Court-curbing periods does not closely correspond either to the commonly accepted periods of electoral realignment or to the time periods following realigning elections. Such limited overlap between his periods of high Court-curbing activity and realigning periods as does occur is too imprecise to support firm conclusions. Hence, Nagel defines one Court-curbing period as 1858 to 1869 and another as 1935 to 1937. The former fully overlaps the Civil War realignment; the latter encompasses only two years of the New Deal conflict, which, at a minimum, must be defined as beginning in March 1933 and ending with the demise of the Court-packing plan in 1937.

Conflict between the elected branches and the Supreme Court is susceptible more to traditional narrative and descriptive analysis than to more fashionable quantitative measures. Judicial invalidation of national legislation is, of course, important. So is the frequency of Court-curbing activity in Congress. And so is the incidence of Supreme Court nullification of state laws which may reflect policies of the new national majority party acting in state legislatures. The Supreme Court's decision in *Home Building & Loan Ass'n* v. *Blaisdell*[1] could be interpreted as a favorable judicial response to state-level Democratic policies to mitigate the effects of the Depression, and *Morehead* v. *Tipaldo*[2] might be seen as judicial hostility to state economic regulations consonant with the philosophy of the New Deal coalition. No one has, as yet, seen fit to consider judicial invalidations of state laws as a measure of conflict between the Supreme Court and the new national majorities emerging from realigning elections (Casper 1976: 57–60). Beyond such quantitative measures, however, are more qualitative indicators of conflict. Dahl has spoken of the necessity to discriminate between judicial invalidations "involving legislation that could reasonably be regarded as important from the point of view of the lawmaking majority and those involving minor legislation" (1957: 287). In addition, rhetoric and belief may be as important in spurring conflict as are actual legal or constitutional assaults by one branch upon another. Justice Chase's fiery hostility to the Republicans was plainly a source of conflict between the Jefferson administration and the Marshall Court, but who can measure it quantitatively? And Jackson's veto of the Bank Charter Bill, based upon a presidential interpretation of the Constitution, was regarded as an encroachment upon the Court's prerogatives.

Conflict Following Realigning Elections
Conflict between the elected departments and the Supreme Court followed the realigning elections of 1800, 1828, 1860, and 1932.[3] The nation's first realignment was marked by bitter hostility between the Federalist judges and the Republicans in Congress and the executive (Warren 1926a: chaps. 4–6; Scigliano 1971: 31–33). The stage for conflict in 1801 was set early by the judiciary's previous denial of state confiscation of British debts and its validation of President Adams' carriage tax, by the justices' approval on circuit of the Alien and Sedition acts and their heatedly partisan charges to grand juries, and finally by the service of certain justices on foreign missions and as secretary of state. The Circuit Court Act of 1801, the midnight appointments, and the reduction of the Supreme Court from six to five members to deny Jefferson an early appointment added fuel to the fire.

The conflict continued after the Jefferson administration had taken office. Lower courts assailed the administration's policies. The Supreme Court's decision in *Marbury* v. *Madison*[4] not only asserted the power of judicial review but enunciated the doctrine that presidential cabinet officers were subject to mandamus. The Jeffersonians perceived a similar "invasion of presidential prerogatives" when Chief Justice Marshall twice issued subpoenas to the president in the Burr case. Indeed, the whole course of the Burr trial seemed a repudiation of Jefferson: the issuance of habeas corpus to Burr's codefendants, the narrow judicial definition of treason, the setting of bail for Burr, and the exclusion of most government evidence.

The Jeffersonian response by impeachment of Chase (Lillich 1960), repeal of the Circuit Court Act, revision of the judicial calendar so as to force a lengthy adjournment of the Supreme Court, and removal of the hapless Pickering (Turner 1949) gave vent to the hostility felt by the administration party toward the Federalist judiciary.

The conflict between Jackson and the Supreme Court, similarly, took many different forms (Warren 1926a: chaps. 19–20; Longaker 1956). Wide publicity giving an erroneous report that Marshall had disparaged General Jackson during the 1828 campaign set the stage for conflict between the two branches (Beveridge 1919: 463–465, 519–551). The Court's decisions in disputes between the Indian tribes and Georgia stirred further conflict, since they differed from Jackson's views and the president took no steps to vindicate the Supreme Court's orders despite Georgia's resistance. Jackson's two battles to name Roger Taney to the Court were viewed as Court packing, and criticism of the Court's nationalist bent by administration members of Congress was taken as an expression of the president's own position. Jackson's message vetoing a new charter for the Bank of the United States was widely seen as an assertion that, when exercising his veto, the president may interpret the Constitution differently from the Supreme Court and that he may refuse to execute statutes he deems unconstitutional.

As in previous realigning periods, the stage for conflict following the 1860 election was set prior to that realignment (Warren 1926b: chaps. 26–27). The *Dred Scott*[5] decision and the Court's series of orders to the Wisconsin judiciary in the *Booth* cases,[6] overruling that state's position that the Fugitive Slave Law was unconstitutional, deeply embittered Republicans (Beitzinger 1957; Heffernan 1969). For most of the decade following the 1860 election, the Court either upheld the Republican administration or abstained from deciding controversial issues (Warren 1926b: chaps. 28–30). In the former class fell the *Prize* cases,[7] a series of decisions upholding national financial and tax measures to support the war effort, and the dictum in *Texas* v. *White*[8] that the Reconstruction Acts were constitutional. In the latter category were the Court's refusals to pass on the constitutionality of Reconstruction in *Mississippi* v. *Johnson*[9] and *Georgia* v. *Stanton*,[10] the Court's avoidance of the issue of military jurisdiction to try civilians,[11] and the justices' acquiescence in congressional paring of their own authority in *Ex parte McCardle*.[12]

Far overshadowing these acts of judicial validation and restraint were those cases in which the Court set its face against the president and Congress. Chief Justice Taney's issuance of a writ of habeas corpus in *Ex parte Merryman*[13] precipitated one of the few instances in American history of overt and unambiguous presidential defiance of the judiciary (Randall 1926: 120–124, 157–163). The Court's unanimous pronouncement in *Ex parte Milligan*[14] that military commissions could not constitutionally try civilians where the civil courts remained open precipitated violent criticism in Congress and the country. So did the Court's decisions striking down loyalty oaths for professional persons and for practice in the federal courts.[15] The refusal of the justices, led by Chief Justice Chase, to sit in the southern circuits as long as military government continued in the vanquished states brought still further abuse, which was heightened because Chase's posture delayed the treason trial of Jefferson Davis until 1868. The Court's short-lived decision invalidating the Legal Tender Acts was the last of the judicial provocations of the Republican leadership (Warren 1926b: chap. 31).[16]

The intensity of the conflict between the judiciary and the Republicans in the executive and legislative departments was reflected not only in bitter criticism but in Lincoln's defiance of Taney and in the congressional denial of judicial authority in *Ex parte McCardle*. The size of the Court was altered, first to prevent Andrew Johnson from making appointments and then to allow President Grant to select sound Republicans who would support legal tender and other party policies (Ratner 1935). And new circuit judgeships were created to assure that the lower courts would also be reliably Republican.

More than any realigning election in American history, the Democratic victory of 1932 was followed by judicial nullification. Almost four decades of judicial intervention preceded the conflict (Swindler 1969: chaps. 12–14, 17). After 1896, the justices had used the due process clauses and a narrow interpretation of the commerce and taxing powers to invalidate legislation aimed at curbing business, redistributing the wealth, and advancing social welfare. Progressive forces in the nation had sought in vain to curb judicial power. In 1930, they bitterly fought the appointment of Chief Justice Charles Evans Hughes (Swindler 1969: 297–299), and two years later they blocked President Hoover's nomination of Judge John J. Parker to the Supreme Court (Grossman and Wasby 1971: 347–352).

Some decisions following the 1932 realignment favored New Deal policies: the Minnesota mortgage moratorium was upheld,[17] New York's milk price control scheme was approved,[18] the TVA passed constitutional muster,[19] and national legislation taking the country off the gold standard was sustained.[20] But these decisions were overshadowed as the justices rained blows on the New Deal and its legislative program. Pensions for railway workers were struck down.[21] So was the NRA.[22] So was the Frazier–Lemke Federal Farm Bankruptcy Act.[23] So was the Agricultural Adjustment Act.[24] So was the Guffey Coal Act.[25] So was the Municipal Bankruptcy Act.[26] In all, twelve New Deal laws were invalidated—eight of them involving relatively important policy issues (Dahl 1957: 287). These decisions wiped out federal attempts to regulate wages and hours, to institute collective bargaining, to support farm prices, to relieve the ravages of farm foreclosures, and to prevent the financial collapse of local governments. In addition, the Court reaffirmed its earlier decisions invalidating state minimum wage laws.[27]

President Roosevelt's reaction to judicial dismantling of the New Deal remained mild enough throughout his first term. In 1937, however, he proposed his famous Court-packing bill (Swindler 1970: 59–80). Reaction in the press, in the Congress, and finally in the country was hostile. The steam was taken out of the Court-packing drive when, on a single day, the Court reversed itself by sustaining minimum wage laws,[28] a new federal farm bankruptcy act,[29] and a measure promoting collective bargaining in the railroad industry.[30] Later the Wagner Act, establishing collective bargaining across the nation, was sustained.[31] Finally, the justices found the taxing and spending powers broad enough to sustain unemployment compensation and old-age pensions.[32] The New Deal sustained, the Senate sent the Court-packing bill to its death by recommending it to a hostile Judiciary Committee on a vote of seventy to twenty.

The Consequences of Conflict

It is tempting to portray the consequences of these conflicts in the simplest way. If one believes—as I do not—that the Supreme Court has a legitimacy-conferring capacity during the long periods when it stands as part of the lawmaking majority, then it follows that during the periods of conflict after realignments it has a delegitimating role. Its approval of majority policies legitimates them and their sponsoring regime. But its disapproval, whether expressed by invalidatiqns or other manifestations of judicial displeasure, delegitimates a new regime. And such delegitimation occurs at a time of crisis, when the legitimacy of government is already shaken and when the new regime bears a heavy burden to reestablish public confidence.

Similarly, if one focuses solely on judicial invalidations of laws enacted by the newly emergent lawmaking majority—as Funston does—one is led to understate the policy-making implications of postrealignment conflict between the elected departments and the Court. As Canon and Ulmer (1976) have shown, the incidence of judicial review was unusually high only during the New Deal realignment. In other realigning periods, the Court would be adjudged, by the relatively low incidence of judicial review, to have had a very slight effect on national policy making.

The consequences of conflict are, however, susceptible to a more subtle analysis. The leaders of the new lawmaking majority, often harboring deep hostility toward the Court because of its prerealignment decisions, take office expecting the justices to block their programs. They resent, furthermore, that they cannot immediately place their own men in the desirable seats of judicial authority. Relatively few incidents of apparent judicial hostility, not necessarily limited to invalidations of federal laws, are perceived as confirming the prediction that the justices of the old regime will cripple the programs of the new. And, in some realigning periods, such manifestations of judicial hostility have been more than few in number or slight in importance.

Before the realigning period closes, judicial provocations are deemed grave enough to warrant attacks upon the Court. These may be public criticism in Congress, from the president, and by administration supporters. But, in three of four realigning periods, these attacks went much further—including impeachments, changes in the Court's size and jurisdiction, abolition or creation of new lower courts or judgeships, and revision of the Court's calendar.

It is here that the Supreme Court's own legitimacy and standing in the American constitutional system—as opposed to some asserted legitimacy-conferring function—become important. The ideological vanguard of the new majority coalition, and usually the presidential wing of that party, launches assaults on the Court, on its membership, jurisdiction, size, and structure. Other elements in the coalition may now hold back, either because they disagree with the farthest reaches of policy sought by the coalition's vanguard or out of respect for the Court's place in American politics. The public, too, including supporters of the new majority party, hesitates. It is most likely to be troubled by the presidential assault upon the Court, a legitimate institution in its eyes.

The majority coalition in the government and in the country is diverted from its program of substantive policies to a quarrel, often inspiring internal disunity, about issues of constitutional structure and organization. The standing of the president and of other coalition leaders is certain to be tarnished as they confront the Court. Some voters withdraw their allegiance to the new majority party; others simply lose their ardor for the leaders of the coalition. In government, the vanguard of the lawmaking majority finds itself separated from other leaders who share the party label.

The consequences of conflict for both legitimacy and policy making become clear. The standing of the presidential wing of the party is diminished, and the legitimacy of the presidency itself may suffer. More important, the controversy over the Court diverts attention from substantive reform issues. And, finally, division in both the electoral and the governmental wings of the majority party over the counterattack on the judiciary diminishes the coalition's ability to act in concert on other matters.

Although the Court soon capitulates to the new majority, some of that coalition's reform thrust is already lost. Division and disunity have taken their toll. And the extraordinarily large electoral and governmental majorities, as well as the high intensity of ideological zeal, which uniquely follow in the immediate aftermath of realigning elections are dissipated. The Supreme Court stands as a reef on which the vessel of reform runs aground.

Burnham may be correct to characterize realignments as "constituent acts" which temporarily concentrate sufficient political power to force rapid change in governmental policies that brings them into line with the unfettered and rapid developments that have already occurred in the nation's social and economic sectors. But this political development always remains incomplete, because the concentration of political power is broken on the issue of judicial review. And, by the time that issue is resolved, not by permanent revisions in judicial power but rather by eventual presidential appointment of a majority of justices from the new coalition, the forces of reform in the nation and the government have spent themselves.

THE SUPREME COURT ON THE PATHWAY TO CRITICAL ELECTIONS

A Speculative Approach

Most scholarly attention has been devoted to the Supreme Court's role during or after realignments. This concern arises from the visible and important conflicts that have arisen from the Court's adherence to the philosophies of an old regime after the people have given their mandate to a new majority coalition. At the main crossroads in American history, the Court has been, in Jackson's words, "the check of a preceding generation on the present one; a check of conservative legal philosophy upon a dynamic people, and nearly always the check of a rejected regime on the one in being" (1941: 315).

Sundquist is one of the few students of realignment politics to focus on the dynamics that produce realignments, rather than on realignments themselves or their aftermaths (1973: chaps. 2, 3, 13). He argues that a new issue or cluster of issues emerges which threatens the existing lines of policy and party division in the nation. And, "if the issue remains unresolved and public concern continues to grow, the polar forces will increase and each of the major parties will become a battleground for the three forces contending for control—the two polar blocs and the centrists who are trying to prevent the party from being torn apart. The outcome of the struggle determines the timing of the realignment, its scale, and the form it takes" (ibid.: 27).

The conduct of party leaders influences whether a realignment will occur at all and, if it does, what shape it will take. It is in this context that Dahl's insights about the Supreme Court's role in the dominant coalition are most persuasive. "As an element in the political leadership of the dominant alliance," he argues, "the Court of course supports the major policies of the alliance." Ordinarily the Court's policy making is confined, then, "within the somewhat narrow limits set by the basic policy goals of the dominant alliance" (1957: 293–294). During long eras of stable rule by a dominant coalition, "the main task of the Court is to confer legitimacy on the fundamental policies of the successful coalition." But "there are times when the coalition is unstable with respect to certain key policies; at very great risk to its legitimacy powers, the Court can intervene in such cases and may even succeed in establishing policy" (ibid.: 294).

Dahl's insight points the way to understanding the Supreme Court's role in shaping realignments. The emergence of new, cross cutting issues tends to create instability in the major-party coalitions. The reaction of party leaders, as Sundquist points out, determines whether and how a critical election will occur. The Supreme Court, as a center of power within the dominant coalition, has an uncharacteristic leadership opportunity in such an unstable situation. It may take a centrist role, hoping that the coalition will avoid the polarizing issue and maintaining existing electoral lines intact. Or it may lend its support to one side or the other on the cross cutting issue. In that case, it may help shape the party's posture as it goes to the country on the issue or issues that foster a critical election.

One more insight helps define the Supreme Court's role in those tumultuous periods leading up to critical elections. Scigliano has argued that "the Constitution intended that the Supreme Court and the President would be not infrequently aligned against Congress. There is . . . a natural affinity between the judicial and executive powers . . . Both branches are involved in executing the law, in expounding it, and in applying it to specific cases" (1971: 8). Further, both the executive and the judicial departments originally had a common fear of the legislative branch, which the framers created as the strongest department (ibid.: 7–10). Finally, and perhaps most important, the president names the justices, ordinarily without major resistance from the Senate, and, through the decades, he has been careful to name them in his own image (ibid.: 115–124).

If one views the presidential wing of the dominant party as having a stable base of support within the party and the electorate during the long eras between critical elections, then one expects also that the justices named by succeeding presidents of the same party will usually share a coherent executive perspective on crucial national issues. Hence, as new issues create the potential for a critical election, the Supreme Court will ordinarily side with the presidential wing of the party in shaping a strategy for dealing with those issues.

The role of the Supreme Court and the success of its policies during the prelude to critical elections are, therefore, complex. It may take a stance on newly emerging issues, seeking to influence the majority coalition's posture. Or it may refrain from acting. When it does act, it will usually join the presidential wing of the party. The enduring success of its policies depends on the strategy adopted by the political leadership of the incumbent majority coalition, including the justices, to face newly emerging issues. If the leadership adopts a position inconsonant with the rising tide of public sentiment in the country, a realignment follows and repudiation of the party's policies (including those promulgated by the Court) occurs. If the party's stance gains as many or more supporters as it loses, a converting election occurs in which the party's policies are vindicated and it maintains control of government, albeit with a changed electoral base.

The Supreme Court does not necessarily play a crucial role in establishing the strategy with which an incumbent political elite faces new issues in a critical election period. It may, for instance, avoid decision on fiery issues facing the nation. Or it may adhere to a centrist position, attempting to forestall any party polarization on new issues. Or it may cast its lot with the faction whose response to those critical issues does not prevail within the party. Mainly, however, the Court, joined as it is to the presidency, will take the same position as the executive wing in the party; and those two powerful forces, together, will ordinarily prevail in shaping a party position on newly emerging issues which so arouse voters as to reshuffle long-standing party loyalties.

Judicial Policy as a Prelude to Realignment

The Supreme Court had scarcely established its policy-making authority as the realignment of 1800 approached. If that election is seen as a shift of power from the nation's mercantile interests, particularly in the Middle Atlantic and New England states, to planters and agrarians in the South and West, the Court must be regarded as having had little influence in shaping that realignment. At the very most, the justices' approval on circuit of the Alien and Sedition acts and perhaps their approval of national authority in the carriage tax case reenforced the dominant faction within the Federalist party.

The 1828 election has been regarded as diminishing the political influence of powerful financial interests and of the national government while increasing the strength of agrarians and of the states. It may also have signaled a shift of power from the Northeast to the South and West. The Supreme Court had steadily been a protector of major financial interests and a proponent of national power. The *Dartmouth College* case[33] and *McColluch* v. *Maryland*[34] remain leading examples of the judiciary's stance. The Court's nationalist and private property preferences undoubtedly stiffened the resolve of the conservative wing of the Democratic-Republicans and had special impact within that party because the coalition was so loosely joined. The Court's decisions helped create an identity for the national regime that made it more vulnerable to attack from the emerging agrarian and state sovereignty forces in the nation, but the level of judicial activity was relatively slight. One must therefore be cautious not to overstate the Court's role in shaping the policy of the national regime as the 1828 election approached.

The Court's role was much more apparent as the nation hurtled toward the realignment of 1860 and ultimately to civil war. The justices plainly aligned themselves with the presidential wing of the Democratic party, which had successively nominated "northern men of southern principles." Schmidhauser analyzed the justices' response to cases involving slavery, the national commerce power, and corporations from 1837 to the Republican victory in 1860 (1961: 617–629). The question whether the national government or the states had jurisdiction over commerce was vitally linked to the other two issues. The South favored interpretations of the commerce power that respected the internal policy power of the states, both to allow the transit of slaves to be regulated by the southern states and to permit those states to impose controls on northern corporations which were deemed threatening by the rural and agricultural South. Seven of the twelve Democrats who served on the Supreme Court during the period leading up to the 1860 realignment voted with the South on these issues, four Democrats voted a "moderate" position, and one voted the northern position. The four Whigs, by contrast, voted a consistently northern view.

The composition of the Court in 1860, before the death of Peter V. Daniel of Virginia in that year, was eight Democrats and one Whig and, more important, five justices from the South and border states and four from the North (Adamany 1973: 823–824). Whether *Dred Scott*[35] and the *Booth* cases[36] were attempts to suppress the slavery issue, as the Court's apologists suggest, or a judicial policy preference for slavery, there can be little doubt that the justices strengthened the hand of the proslavery wing of the Democratic party and heightened the public perception that the Court favored the South in the deepening tension between the sections. A presidential and judicial leadership setting that tone led the Democratic party to division and defeat in 1860, as its policies were repudiated at the polls.

The Supreme Court's role in shaping the posture of a national coalition was most evident in the decades preceding the realignment of 1932. The presidential wing of the Republican party became increasingly conservative. In Congress, a coalition of Democrats and progressive Republicans adopted some policies expanding national regulation of the economy and extending social welfare programs. A number of state governments went even farther in adopting programs hostile to the business and financial interests favored by the presidential wing of the GOP. The Court's nullification of the income tax, of state and federal wage and hour laws, of legislation regulating business practices and prices, and of laws encouraging the growth of labor unions gave the upper hand to the conservative presidential wing of the Republican party (Swindler 1970: chaps. 12–14). And it was in that posture that the GOP, despite a vigorous progressive wing, faced a changing electorate and the debacle of the Depression. The presidential and judicial leadership together dominated the Republican party, and the policies they set were repudiated in the realigning period that began in 1924 and culminated in the Democratic victories of 1932 and 1936.

In three of the nation's four realigning periods, the Supreme Court did exert influence within the majority-party coalition. In all three, it supported the presidential wing of the party, although its role prior to 1828 was slight. And, in each case, the Court helped shape majority-party policies that did not respond to a changing electorate and that were subsequently repudiated in realigning elections.

Judicial Policy and Converting Elections
Pomper identifies the elections of 1836, 1896, and 1960 to 1964 as converting elections (1967: 562). In addition, Burnham points out a sharp break in voting patterns in 1874 and 1876 (1970: 15–20). It is possible that the 1836 and 1876 elections mark the beginning of the stable phases of the Jacksonian and Civil War realignments, respectively. On the other hand, in both years the base of electoral support of the dominant coalition shifted significantly, while the majority party retained control of government. Such

shifts are precisely the definition of a converting election. And such changes in the electoral coalition supporting the majority party would ordinarily be explained as a response to the policies adopted by the leaders of that party.

The converting election of 1836 signaled the decline of Jacksonian strength in the South and its increase in the North, including New England. The Jacksonian movement was basically agrarian and populist. Southern planters supported Jackson in 1828 because of their hostility toward New England business and political interests, the endorsement of Jackson by William H. Crawford, who spoke for their interests as secretary of the treasury and as a 1824 presidential candidate, and the belief that as a fellow slaveholder Jackson would share their interests. Jackson's small vote in New England reflected regional allegiance to John Quincy Adams and the continuing power of the mercantile and professional elites in a section still marked by deference politics (Binkley 1962: 125–141).

In 1836, the southern planters abandoned Van Buren and the Democrats (Binkley 1962; McCormick 1967: 100–101). Their reaction was only partly regional. Jackson's acceptance of the Tariff Act of 1832 and his belligerent Proclamation against Nullification clearly established Democratic party policies that were unacceptable to southern elites. In New England, artisans and agrarians joined the Democratic ranks as the Bank Veto and the rejection of internal improvements established the antibusiness posture of the Jacksonian party.

In all of this, the Supreme Court played virtually no role. Until Marshall's death in 1835, the Court adhered to the nationalist and private property tenets that had been its hallmark since the Federalist era. After 1835, Roger Taney would lead the Court toward greater deference to state power and a looser construction of the contract clause. But the Court then acted as a vehicle for the established policies of the Democratic coalition, not as a center of political leadership shaping the policies upon which the party would enter a critical election period.

Similarly, it was the presidential wing of the dominant party that shaped policy and strategy in the converting election of 1876. The infamous "bargain of '76" gave the Republicans enough electoral votes to put Rutherford B. Hayes in the White House. But it also marked the abandonment of the Republican commitment to civil rights. And it doomed efforts to establish a viable Republican party in the South, built on military force, carpetbag and scalawag political leadership, the votes of black freedmen, and the support of whites outside the plantation counties. In place of a civil rights program and a southern electoral strategy, the Republican executive leadership was not prepared to commit the GOP to probusiness policies and a northern and western political coalition (Ladd 1970: 150–152).

This sharp turnabout in Republican policy occurred without significant participation by the Supreme Court. The justices had, of course, struck down federal and state laws, aimed at former Confederates, requiring loyalty oaths for professional licensing and admission to the federal bar.[37] And, in 1876, the Court invalidated two sections of the act of May 31, 1870, intended to protect the right of blacks to vote (Warren 1926b: 602–603).[38] But the judiciary's main role in sealing the bargain of '76 and promoting the new probusiness policies of the national Republican coalition occurred only in the aftermath of the critical election of 1876.

After the bargain of 1876, the Republican administration virtually abandoned its civil rights program and its strategy of building a viable Republican party south of the Mason-Dixon line (Ladd 1970: 135–140). The Supreme Court moved in concert with this policy, striking down parts of the Ku Klux Klan Act of 1871[39] and of the Civil Rights Acts of 1875[40] (Warren 1926b: 612–614) and endorsing, in 1896, racial segregation in public facilities.[41] During the same period, the Court joined the presidential and senatorial wings of the Republican party in securing the interests of the nation's emerging industrial, transportation, and financial interests. The justices thus participated in setting the party policies that would shape the converting election of 1896.

Westin has described the judiciary's decisions protecting railroad and corporate interests against state and national legislation intended to aid farmers and workers (1953: 3–42). The justices stood steadfast against every attempt to repudiate municipal bond indebtedness, even where such debts had been incurred to support the internal improvement schemes of unscrupulous speculators who never built the promised railways, canals, and other public projects. Farmers were, of course, heavily burdened by such debts, since property taxes were levied to meet the obligations. The Court also rejected government attempts to reclaim lands conditionally granted to railways or to obtain compensation for timber taken from such lands, even when those corporations failed to meet grant conditions requiring a regular schedule of railway construction. State attempts to compel railways to lease lands to Farmers' Alliance grain elevators, which were intended to prevent price gouging by private elevators, and state legislation regulating railway rates were struck down by the Court. Finally, in 1895, the Court invalidated the income tax,[42] weakened the Sherman Anti-Trust Act by giving a narrow interpretation to congressional power under the commerce clause,[43] and upheld the conviction of Eugene Debs for violation of an *ex parte* judicial order forbidding union activities in the Pullman strike as a conspiracy violating the Sherman Act.[44]

The Supreme Court had no small role in establishing the balance of power within the Republican party as the GOP approached the converting election of 1896. Supported by judicial decisions, the industrial Northeast and Midwest overwhelmed the agricultural West, "sound money" triumphed over silver and paper currency, and the interests of business were favored over the concerns of agrarians. Conservatives dominated both national policy making and the Republican-party structure in 1892 and 1896. Finally, the western agrarians were forced out of the Republican party, taking refuge first in the Populist party and then in the Democratic party. The Supreme Court had participated in shaping the Republican position on the issues of industrialization, tariffs, government regulation of railroads and utilities, and monetary policy. In the converting election of 1896, these issues sharply divided the two parties; and the conservative position was vindicated at the polls and in a reshuffling of party and voter coalitions that endured until the Great Depression.

The years preceding 1964 and continuing through 1968, when new electoral allegiances became firm, saw the Supreme Court play a decisive role in shaping party policies that led to a converting election. The justices aligned themselves with the liberal wing of the Democratic coalition in the controversy over civil rights and on the "social issue" (Scammon and Wattenberg 1970). Both issues divided the Democratic party and the nation. With the Supreme Court's support, the liberal faction largely captured control of the Democratic party. Conservatives dominated the Republican apparatus as the GOP struck its posture on these issues. When the electoral dust settled, a larger percentage of the American electorate declared themselves independent and the voting coalitions of both major parties had changed substantially. Despite this reshuffling, the Democrats remained the dominant party.

In the 1950s and 1960s, the Supreme Court was aligned with the northern presidential wing of the Democratic party on civil rights, and it had a decisive influence in overcoming the entrenched resistance of the party's southern wing to any policy that promoted racial equality and desegregation. President Truman's civil rights commission and the civil rights plank of the 1948 Democratic platform were the first significant shifts away from Franklin Roosevelt's moderate policy on race relations, which respected the long-standing influence of the Solid South within the Democratic coalition (Sundquist 1973: 315–317). The Dixiecrat bolt of 1948 and the firm hold of southern Democrats on congressional leadership positions temporarily forced national Democratic leaders to back off from their strong stance on civil rights. It was the Supreme Court's decisions striking down desegregation in public schools and in other public facilities that maintained the civil rights impetus within the Democratic party.[45] When the Democrats in Congress finally succeeded in passing civil rights legislation in 1957, 1960, 1964, and 1965 and 1967, the justices sustained these measures against constitutional challenge (Swindler 1970: chap. 13).[46]

The "social issue"—despite its poor definition—also divided American politics. The Supreme Court sharpened these divisions by its decisions favoring criminal defendants' rights (Fellman 1976), school prayers,[47] and sexual activity—particularly contraception and abortion.[48] The liberal wing of the Democratic party, conspicuously associated with the presidency, was held publicly accountable for these policies. Congressional Republicans maintained a steady drumbeat of criticism against both the president and the justices, but the Republican party's unmistakable identification with the "conservative" stance on these issues was etched into public consciousness by the successive presidential campaigns of Barry Goldwater and Richard Nixon.

The electoral impact of these issues is clearest in the South. Southern whites became more conservative. They abandoned the Democratic party to become more independent, a posture which made them readily susceptible to the appeals of conservative Republican candidates (Ladd and Hadley 1975: 135–145, 153). Eisenhower and Nixon carried the southern periphery in 1952 and 1956. And, as the civil rights movement reached high tide in 1964, Goldwater scrambled previous party-voting patterns by sweeping the Deep South (Sundquist 1973: 314–319, 355–369). In 1968 and 1972, the Republican national ticket won both the Deep South and the border states (Ladd and Hadley 1975: 151–156). Jimmy Carter's 1976 victory in those regions affirmed the competitive nature of their politics, for his southern success rested on overwhelming majorities among black voters joined by only minorities of traditionally Democratic whites. The South has also become competitive in voting for governor, senator, and representative (Sundquist 1973: 333–335). The new electoral division in the South pits a Democratic party consisting of moderate whites and newly enfranchised blacks against a Republican electorate composed of urban and rural whites conservative on race, economic, and social welfare questions, defense, and the emerging life-style issues (Ladd and Hadley 1975: 156–177; Nie et al. 1976: 247–256).

Outside the South, the Democrats gained votes and the Republicans lost adherents. Issues of race and life style alienated working-class Democrats from the party of Roosevelt (Ladd and Hadley 1975: 233–246), but the Democrats more than compensated for these losses by appeals to the newly created postindustrial middle and upper-middle classes, who are mainly liberal on civil rights and on economic, defense, and life-style issues (Ladd and Hadley 1975: 195–220, 233–240). Overall, northern white Protestants became more liberal and more independent, often voting Democratic. Blacks became more Democratic nationwide; and Jews and Catholics, concentrated in the North and West, became slightly more independent than formerly but continued to vote mainly Democratic (Nie et al. 1976: chap. 14). Sundquist's analysis shows that, as the Democrats gained strength in the North, the eighteen most Republican states, like the South, became more competitive (1973: 333–335).

In short, the liberal posture of the Democratic party's dominant wing, including the Supreme Court, on issues of race and life style prompted dramatic shifts in voter allegiance. By 1964, and continuing in 1968, these policies prompted a substantial conversion of voters. While the electorate became somewhat more independent and the nation more thoroughly competitive in all sections, the two parties became more ideologically distinct, with the Democrats in a more striking liberal posture and the Republicans in a clearer conservative stance. The series of Supreme Court decisions on civil rights, defendants' rights, school prayers, and sexual privacy helped precipitate this redrawing of voter allegiances and reenforced it once underway.

In two of the nation's four converting election periods, the Supreme Court played a significant role. In both, it joined the presidential wing of the majority party to change the basic policies of the dominant coalition. The Court's conservatism on economic issues after 1876 contributed to shaping a party stance that, in

1896, consolidated a new Republican majority in the nation. Western agrarians who left the party where more than offset by new Republican voters in the industrial states of the East and Midwest. Similarly, in the 1950s and 1960s, the Court's decisions on racial desegregation, defendants' rights, and life-style issues reenforced the Democratic party's liberal wing and helped spur voter shifts both North and South. The Democratic majority has become more evenly distributed across the nation, as has the strength of the Republican opposition.

CONCLUSION

The Supreme Court's role in critical election periods is far more complex than formerly believed. It is doubtful that the Court has a legitimacy-conferring capacity, but, if it does, the justices may well play a delegitimating role in the aftermath of realignments. It seems more likely, however, that friction between the Supreme Court and the newly emerging lawmaking majority provokes the elected branches to assault the Court, the last bastion of the old regime. Such an assault weakens the new majority coalition as the public draws back from an attack upon an institution possessing its own legitimacy, as the party elite divides over a question of constitutional structure, and as the energies of the party's ideological leadership are diverted from substantive policies to conflict with the Court.

The justices may play a more creative role in shaping party policies as a majority coalition becomes unstable in response to emerging, crosscutting political issues. Usually the Court will join the party's presidential wing in formulating a response to such issues. In three of the four realigning periods, the Court has played a significant role in shaping majority-party policies that ultimately led to repudiation and realignment at the polls. In two of the four converting periods, the Court joined the dominant party's presidential wing to shape party policies that would reshuffle voter loyalties around new issues but would leave the party with a new majority coalition that vindicated those policies.

NOTES

1   290 U.S. 398 (1934).
2   298 U.S. 587 (1936).

3   There are some differences among scholars in defining realigning elections. In general, I have followed the analysis of Thomas Jahnige and Gerald Pomper. I have marked 1800 as the onset of the Jeffersonian party system; Jahnige more vaguely described the period from 1789 to 1828 as the Federalist-Jeffersonian party period, and Pomper does not consider this early party realignment because it occurred before the popular balloting on which his analysis is based. In addition, I mark the realignment as occurring at the first election in a period when control of the government shifted from a dying party coalition to a newly emerging party. Jahnige and Pomper sometimes select the second election in a series if the discontinuities from past voter allegiance become more pronounced at that polling. Their technique may very well be correct for electoral analysis, but for policy analysis a realignment occurs when the newly emerging party wins control of government, not when its electoral base becomes stabilized. Finally, I follow Pomper's analysis rather than Jahnige's by classifying 1896 as a converting election instead of a realigning poll.

4   5 U.S. (1 Cranch) 137 (1803).

5   60 U.S. (19 How.) 393 (1857).

6   62 U.S. (21 How.) 506 (1859).

7   67 U.S. (2 Black) 635 (1862).

8   74 U.S. (7 Wall.) 197 (1870).

9   71 U.S. (4 Wall.) 475 (1867).

10   73 U.S. (6 Wall.) 50 (1867).

11   *Ex parte Vallandigham*, 68 U.S. (1 Wall.) 243 (1864).

12   74 U.S. (7 Wall.) 506 (1869).

13   17 F. Cas. 144 (No. 9,487) (C.C.Md. 1861).

14   71 U.S. (4 Wall.) 2 (1866).

15   *Cummings* v. *Missouri*, 71 U.S. (4 Wall.) 277 (1867); *Ex parte Garland*, 71 U.S. (4 Wall.) 333 (1867).

16   *Hepburn* v. *Griswold*, 75 U.S. (8 Wall.) 603 (1870); the Court overruled itself in *Knox* v. *Lee*, 79 U.S. (12 Wall.) 457 (1871).

17   *Home Building & Loan Ass'n.* v. *Blaisdell*, 290 U.S. 398 (1934).

18   *Nebbia* v. *New York*, 291 U.S. 502 (1933).

19   *Ashwander* v. *TVA*, 297 U.S. 288 (1936).

20   *Norman* v. *Baltimore & O.R.R.*, 294 U.S. 240 (1935); *Nortz* v. *United States*, 294 U.S. 317 (1935); *Perry* v. *United States*, 294 U.S. 330 (1935).

21   *Railroad Retirement Board* v. *Alton R. R.*, 295 U.S. 330 (1935).

22   *Schecter Poultry Corp.* v. *United States*, 295 U.S. 495 (1935).

23   *Louisville Joint Stock Land Bank* v. *Radford*, 295 U.S. 555 (1935).

24   *United States* v. *Butler*, 297 U.S. 1 (1936).

25   *Carter* v. *Carter Coal Co.*, 298 U.S. 238 (1936).

26   *Ashton* v. *Cameron Water Improvement District No. One*, 298 U.S. 513 (1936).

27   *Morehead* v. *Tipaldo*, 298 U.S. 587 (1936).

28   *West Coast Hotel* v. *Parrish*, 300 U.S. 379 (1937).

29   *Wright* v. *Vinton Branch*, 300 U.S. 440 (1937).

30   *Virginia Railway Co.* v. *System Federation R.E.D.*, 300 U.S. 515 (1937).

31 *NLRB* v. *Jones & Laughlin Steel Corp.*, 301 U.S. 1 (1937).

32 *Helvering* v. *Davis*, 301 U.S. 619 (1937).

33 17 U.S. (4 Wheat.) 518 (1819).

34 17 U.S. (4 Wheat.) 316 (1819).

35 60 U.S. (19 How.) 393 (1857).

36 62 U.S. (21 How.) 506 (1859).

37 *Cummings* v. *Missouri*, 71 U.S. (4 Wall.) 277 (1867); *Ex parte Garland*, 71 U.S. (4 Wall.) 333 (1867).

38 *United States* v. *Reese*, 92 U.S. 214 (1876).

39 *United States* v. *Harris*, 106 U.S. 629 (1882).

40 The *Civil Rights* cases, 109 U.S. 3 (1883).

41 *Plessey* v. *Ferguson*, 163 U.S. 537 (1896).

42 *Pollock* v. *Farmers' Loan & Trust Company*, 158 U.S. 601 (1895).

43 *United States* v. *E. C. Knight Co.*, 156 U.S. 1 (1895).

44 *In re Debs*, 158 U.S. 564 (1895).

45 *Brown* v. *Board of Education*, 347 U.S. 483 (1954). The *Brown* case was followed by a series of summary and *per curiam* decisions striking down racial segregation in various other public facilities. For a list of these decisions, see Lockhart et al. 1970: 1206.

46 *Heart of Atlanta Motel, Inc.* v. *United States*, 379 U.S. 241 (1964), and *Katzenbach* v. *McClung*, 379 U.S. 294 (1964) (sustaining the Civil Rights Act of 1964); *South Carolina* v. *Katzenbach*, 383 U.S. 301 (1966) (sustaining the Voting Rights Act of 1965).

47 *Engel* v. *Vitale*, 370 U.S. 421 (1962); *School District* v. *Schempp*, 374 U.S. 203 (1963).

48 *Griswold* v. *Connecticut*, 381 U.S. 479 (1965), and *Eisenstadt* v. *Baird*, 405 U.S. 438 (1972) (contraception); *Roe* v. *Wade*, 410 U.S. 113 (1973), and *Doe* v. *Bolton*, 410 U.S. 179 (1973) (abortion).

PART IV

The Impact of Realignment on Policy

12

The Federal Income Tax and the Realignment of the 1890s

CHARLES V. STEWART

> In my former speech I pointed out that the proposed [income] tax is inequitable, inquisitorial, and sectional, and will in time of peace subject the people to methods that were well nigh intolerable in time of war.—Jacob Gallinger, April 20, 1894[1]

> I have never brought myself to believe that an income tax is an unjust tax, and today I cordially give my assent to the proposition that, supplemental to the duties that are imposed in the bill under consideration, an income tax is a very proper mode of raising additional revenue.—Jacob Gallinger, August 27, 1913[2]

Senator Gallinger uttered his first evaluation of income taxation during a time often labeled as "populist," his second at the high tide of "progressivism." These periods of social and political ferment have long attracted eminent students from many disciplines (McConnell 1966; Hofstadter 1955; Burnham 1974b; Converse 1974; Rusk 1974; Marquette 1974). By common consent, the two decades taken together represent America's first attempt to cope through government with an obvious economic transformation. While historians have often claimed to focus on the time frame for its own sake, political scientists have found it fascinating because so much of the texture of today's political life seems traceable to this initial response to industrial development. A few examples might include the use of regulatory commissions, allegedly to control big business; the extension of the techniques of direct democracy, allegedly to break the stranglehold of "corrupt interests" on government and tending to undercut such political intermediaries as parties; and the introduction of new forms of taxation, allegedly to bring growing burdens in line with the ability to pay them.

If the two decades possess commonalities, Jacob Gallinger's conversion on income taxation highlights some obvious differences. Since in fact the income tax is just one of several reforms on which political elites did an about-face, earlier scholarship tended to interpret the period by placing populism and progressivism in a comparative framework. While able studies of both eras continue to appear, efforts to draw out their similarities and differences through explaining the behavior of men like Gallinger now seem passé.[3] While understandable, the demise of this research focus is unfortunate; probing the differing responses of American political elites to demands for change offers a rich insight into the inner workings of the American political system.[4] Thus, after a brief discussion of methods, this chapter will plead for the power of realignment concepts as a means to revitalize these comparative efforts.

THE METHOD OF ANALYSIS

If the critics of earlier comparative efforts made one point, it is that "reform periods" are exceedingly complex, with no analytical constructs lying in readiness for immediate employment. Certainly the older concept of "movement" has proven far too unwieldy (Filiene 1970). Nevertheless, similar difficulties surround any interesting problem, and the comparative method is a long-established basic research strategy under such conditions (Lijphart 1971).

This method's first requirement is specificity: what is under comparison and why? Granted that no institution can be a perfect microcosm, this study will assume that the American Congress is a worthwhile focal point, behavior there reflecting significant forces at work within the larger society.[5] Given this assumption, I will compare legislative responses to one issue, income taxation, in the twenty-year period between 1893 and 1913.

The discussion begins with a brief historical review which serves to highlight two apparent anomalies in the process of formulating tax policy in the 1893 to 1913 period.[6] First, the price of placing income taxation on the congressional agenda in 1893 was intense conflict, both between and within parties, especially the Democratic. This conflict had largely abated as early as 1898. Second, the income tax which became a permanent part of the revenue system in 1913 was much like the one enacted in 1894, despite the decreased rancor, the broad bipartisan endorsement, a considerably more stable economic environment, the passage of twenty years, and the successful ratification that year of a constitutional amendment authorizing such taxation. These two observations serve as the focal point of the analysis.

After the historical review, the analysis section explores several possible explanations for the observed anomalies. In barest outline, socioeconomic change made inevitable some alteration in the American tax system. The income tax came to be the preferred reform. To understand the specifics of its enactment, however, it is necessary to appreciate the political context into which this reform was injected. This intervening variable, the political context, is thus the key to explaining both the history of the income tax and the larger differences between populist and progressive reform. Hence, the remainder of this essay will adumbrate the changing political context, which hinged on the realignment of 1896, link it to the observations, and suggest significant implications.

HISTORY OF THE ISSUE

America's first federal income tax, inspired by the Civil War and launched amidst generally favorable public opinion, was instituted in 1861 (Ratner 1942a: 67). After several revisions and increasing public dissatisfaction, the experiment came up for renewal in 1870. Previously opposed, Democrats now voted to keep the tax. Republicans were split; the majority pushed for repeal, but prestigious party members such as Senators Sherman and Morton favored retention (ibid: 126). A complex series of Senate votes, culminating in the passage of a revenue bill on July 14, 1870, resulted in the tax being extended but doomed it to extinction. The last taxes levied under the law were paid in the year 1871, and the matter seemingly died. Almost every Congress thereafter witnessed attempts to reinstitute this fiscal device, however, and in the Fifty-third, 1893 to 1895, the effort turned serious (Blakely and Blakely 1940: 9).

Consolidating a trend begun in 1890, the 1892 elections ended with a huge Democratic majority lodged in the House of Representatives (218 to 127 Republicans and 11 Populists) and a sizable one in the Senate (44 to 38 and 3). Democratic commitment to reverse the Republican high tariff policy was, of course, clear and of long standing, and many expected it to receive primary attention. President Cleveland, however, decided to maintain the gold

TABLE 12.1. Positions Taken in Debate on Income Taxation Related to Party Identification and Region, Fifty-third Congress

Region	Opposed			Moderate[a]			Favorable		
	Dem.	Rep.	Pop.-Fus.	Dem.	Rep.	Pop.-Fus.	Dem.	Rep.	Pop.-Fus.
Northeast	16	23	0	3	3	0	1	0	1
East Midwest	1	7	0	2	4	0	22	3	0
West Midwest	0	4	0	0	1	0	12	0	8
South	0	0	0	3	0	0	26	0	0
Border	1	0	0	1	0	0	11	0	0
West	0	3	0	2	2	0	1	0	2
Total	18	37	0	11	10	0	73	3	11

Note: I have followed the following definitions of "region": Northeast: New England, Delaware, New Jersey, New York, Pennsylvania; East Midwest: Illinois, Indiana, Michigan, Ohio, Wisconsin; West Midwest: Iowa, Kansas, Minnesota, Missouri, Nebraska, North Dakota, South Dakota; South: Alabama, Arkansas, Florida, Georgia, Louisiana, Mississippi, North Carolina, South Carolina, Texas, Virginia; border: Kentucky, Maryland, Oklahoma, Tennessee, West Virginia; and West: all other states.

[a] The moderate category consists of members commenting on the measure without making their position unequivocal.

standard as his first priority, so only after a bruising "free-silver" battle and the onset of a severe depression did attention turn to raising governmental revenue. Convinced that lowering the tariff would necessitate additional revenue, Cleveland suggested imposing "a small tax upon incomes derived from certain corporate investments" (Richardson in Ratner 1942a: 174); but with their big majority other Democrats were determined, in the name of social justice, to reestablish a personal and corporate income tax. These other Democrats eventually prevailed. A combination income, inheritance, and corporation tax, with a uniform 2 percent rate and an individual exemption of $4,000, was attached to the pending revenue bill. This combination, soon to be labeled the Wilson-Gorman Tariff, was successfully guided through the House and Senate, becoming law without Cleveland's signature in August 1894.

The important fact is not simply that an income tax was imposed but that the process of its enactment exposed a sharp split in both major parties. While relatively few Republicans chose to disagree openly with their party's stance of hostility toward the revenue bill, an open rupture developed in the majority party, albeit partially masked by fairly harmonious roll-call voting.[7] For example, on the critical decision to join the income tax to the general tariff bill, Democratic members of the House Ways and Means Committee split six to five (*Washington Post* 1893: 1). Contemporary news accounts, moreover, asserted that virtually the entire Democratic House delegations of New York, Connecticut, New Jersey, Delaware, and Pennsylvania were openly hostile to the income tax (*Washington Post* 1894a: 1, 1894b: 1). Even congressional speeches, tailored with an eye to the upcoming elections, were considerably less consensual than actual voting. Table 12.1, classifying the congressmen who commented on the income tax, shows that partisanship was but one dimension of the contest. Representation of the Northeast, for example, was a better predictor of one's debating position than party identification.[8]

The actual content of these speeches is perhaps the best example of this inflamed feeling. In the case under consideration, for example, forty-two of the fifty-five opponents framed their position around supposedly eternal principles. They asserted that income taxation was inherently unacceptable; the federal government should under no condition, save extreme peril, employ this fiscal device. Proponents tended to be equally unrestrained, freely predicting an end to the Republic should enactment fail. Maneuvering room, in short, was not sought.

This furor did not cease with the final passage; opponents took their case to the Supreme Court. While this body's path to a decision, *Pollock* v. *Farmers' Loan & Trust Company*, is tortuous indeed, its conclusion can be easily summarized. By May 1894, a divided Court, harangued on the imminence of socialism and class welfare, had decided first that a federal tax on rents on incomes from real estate was unconstitutional unless apportioned as a direct tax and, second, that since one key section of the 1894 income tax law was thereby invalidated, all the sections should be held invalid. This case immediately achieved and held for years thereafter the status of a *cause célèbre*, the polarized response itself gauging the passion engendered by this attempt to tax incomes. On one side, papers such as the *New York World*, the *St. Louis Post-Dispatch*, the *Detroit Free Press*, and the *Augusta Chronicle* saw in the decision a confirmation of America's domination by corporations and plutocrats. Many others, such as the *New York Sun*, felt differently: "The wave of socialistic revolution has gone far, but it breaks at the foot of the ultimate bulwark set up for the protection of our liberties. Five to four the Court stands like a rock" (*Literary Digest* 1895: 125–126).

In less than three years, however, during debates over financing the Spanish-American War, this question of employing an income tax was resuscitated. This time the Democrats spoke with one voice. In the House, every Democrat and Populist present, 130 in all, supported Joseph Bailey's amendment substituting an income tax for the Republican-sponsored bond issue. In fact, a major speech endorsing the income tax was delivered by a Democrat from New York City, the hotbed of opposition to the 1894 tax (McClelland 1898). In the Senate, Democrats unanimously backed Senator Morgan's attempt to put an income tax amendment on the way to ratification. Presumably the consensus was not forced, since the reporter covering the party caucus found that "all seemed favorable to an income tax" (*Washington Post* 1898: 4).

At the same time that the Democratic party found it could unite behind income taxation, opposition to the tax within the GOP was much more restrained. Probing into Republican speeches on taxation in 1898 uncovers few principled attacks on the concept itself, a maneuver typical of prior addresses. Most simply argued that, with the Spaniards at our gates, the country could not afford the time for another Supreme Court test—it needed money immediately. Two Republican members of the Ways and Means Committee stated that they, like many of their colleagues, saw considerable merit in income taxation and would support such legislation under other conditions (Dolliver 1898; Grosvenor 1898). Remarks by the most prominent of Republican officeholders further illustrate that, if attitudes in that party had not changed as rapidly as among Democrats, they had clearly moderated. Theodore Roosevelt, for example, spoke kindly about such taxes several times, most notably in his annual message to Congress in 1906:

> The National Government has long derived its chief revenue from a tariff on imports and from an internal or excise tax. In addition to those, there is every reason why, when next our system of taxation is revised, the National Government should impose a graduated inheritance tax and, if possible, a graduated income tax. (Roosevelt 1906: 4)

Roosevelt's handpicked successor, William Howard Taft, also approached the matter in a spirit of compromise. Accepting his party's presidential nomination in 1908, he commented:

> In my judgement, an amendment to the Constitution for an income tax is not necessary. I believe that an income tax, when the protective system of customs and the internal revenue tax shall not furnish income enough for governmental needs, can and should be devised which, under the decisions of the Supreme Court, will conform to the Constitution. (Taft 1908: 2)

Even with the discontent stemming from the sharp Panic of 1907, Taft went on to defeat his opponent, William Jennings Bryan, handily, running well ahead of his fellow Republicans in practically every state (Mowry 1958: 57–59). Moreover, the GOP, though slipping a bit in its strength, maintained control of both Houses: 219 to 172 and 60 to 32. What would come out of this mandate was less clear, a clue emerging when the newly inaugurated president decided to confront the growing demand within his own party for downward tariff revision. Immediately summoning Congress to a special session, he called for an overhaul of the country's revenue system. In light of Taft's campaign oratory and a clear budgetary deficit, the question of an income tax was destined to play a prominent role in the ensuing brouhaha.

The legislative product of this special session, the Payne-Aldrich Tariff, has attracted considerable scholarly attention. In barest outline, Sereno Payne guided a bill through the House of Representatives with dispatch. Although refusing to employ an income tax, he did consent to attaching an inheritance tax as a revenue producer. Payne's counterpart in the Senate, Nelson Aldrich, made progress more slowly, unable to steamroller enough of his opposition. The income tax became a focus for several grievances, and ultimately the Republican leadership chose to compromise. Rather than an inheritance tax, there would be a corporation tax, acknowledged by Aldrich to be a type of income tax.[9] Congress would then send an income tax amendment to the states with its nearly unanimous blessing, final ratification of the Sixteenth Amendment not coming until 1913.

This contest differed considerably from its two predecessors. As in 1898, Democrats united behind the income tax, apparently the only thing upon which the party caucus, called to devise tariff strategy, could agree (*Washington Post* 1909b: 1). New, however, was the large number of open income tax advocates in the GOP. While no roll-call votes were recorded in the House, and only ten Republican senators could be induced to vote favoring an immediate income tax, probably at least half of the party's representatives were sympathetic. This intraparty dispute spilled over into the newspapers as well as into the private correspondence of the participants (*Washington Post* 1909a: 1, 1909c: 4; Lodge 1925: 337–339). Positions taken in debate bear out this point.

As table 12.2 illustrates, Republicans from all sections were now more willing to pay the tax lip service. Concomitantly, the rhetoric continued to deescalate, indicating that the visceral emotions prevalent earlier had vanished. Only two congressmen expressed vituperative objections, with advocates also tending to be mild and straightforward. One side asserted the need for a more flexible revenue source; the other pressed respect for the Supreme Court. Senator Charles Dick of Ohio, classified as a moderate, delivered what was probably the majority Republican position. To Senator Dick, an income tax held no real menace either to the country or to the protective tariff system. He asserted not only that the tax was "equitable" and "easily collected" but that "I would have voted for an income tax had I been reasonably certain that it would have been declared constitutional by the Supreme Court" (1909: 4958–4959).

Even before assuming office in 1909, President Taft had realized that a spirit of dissension was tearing at his party and had expected the new tariff to be healing (Taft 1909). Instead, for a complex of reasons, the breach between Republican-party factions widened while Democratic strength resurged. In eclipse since 1896, the opposition party captured control of the House in the next election and, in the three-cornered contest of 1912, both branches and the presidency. Under a much heralded reform banner, President Wilson entered Washington, enjoying majorities Democrats last saw in 1892: 290 to 127 to 17 (Progressives and all others) and 51 to 45.

As in 1909, the incoming president gave first priority to restructuring the national revenue system. However, now that the Sixteenth Amendment was ratified and the Democrats were in power, the relevant question regarding taxing incomes was not "whether?" but "how much?" There was, in other words, going to be an income tax; less clear was how radical or conservative it would be. Opinion on degree turned out to be distinctly nonpartisan.

Both Cordell Hull, author of the new income tax bill, and Oscar Underwood, chairman of the House Ways and Means Committee, long-time advocates of income taxation, wanted a slow start, apparently even preferring ungraduated rates (*New York Times* 1913: 2). Thus, the measure first reported was moderate indeed. The minimum personal exemption of $4,000 remained, high enough to exclude all but a few Americans.[10] Rates, while now progressive, were hardly onerous, rising to a maximum of 4 percent for those fortunates earning more than $100,000 annually. Attempts were made to increase the levy by Republicans and Progressives, a proposal to end at 70 percent being the most extreme of several rejected.

The Democratic Senate leadership was equally cautious. John Sharp Williams, enthusiastic backer of the 1894 tax and now floor manager, met every attempt to increase progressivity with a homily on the merits of moderation (*Congressional Record* 1913: 3772). In this body, however, as in 1909, bipartisanship was more productive, as Republicans aided dissident Democrats in elevating the top rate to 7 percent. Progressives in both parties hoped to go still further, but Finance Committee Chairman Furnifold Simmons obtained President Wilson's support for moderation.[11] Further pressure evaporated for want of Democratic votes, and the final version of the Underwood-Simmons Tariff was signed on October 3, 1913.

Most obvious in this debate is the general consensus; virtually all congressmen agreed that income taxation was an acceptable, even desirable fiscal tool. Table 12.3 reveals nearly unanimous verbal endorsement of such taxation, indicating that Senator Gallinger of Vermont, quoted earlier, was not unique among conserva-

TABLE 12.2. Positions Taken in Debate on Income Taxation, Sixty-first Congress

Region	Opposed		Moderate		Favorable	
	Democrat	Republican	Democrat	Republican	Democrat	Republican
Northeast	0	7	1	11	5	0
East Midwest	0	1	2	7	14	3
West Midwest	0	1	0	7	0	7
South	0	0	3	0	26	0
Border	0	0	2	2	13	1
West	0	1	0	5	3	2
Total	0	10	8	32	61	13

TABLE 12.3. Positions Taken in Debate on Income Taxation, Sixty-third Congress

Region	Opposed			Moderate			Favorable		
	Dem.	Rep.	Progr.	Dem.	Rep.	Progr.	Dem.	Rep.	Progr.
Northeast	1	8	0	0	1	0	7	6	3
East Midwest	0	2	0	0	2	0	17	8	3
West Midwest	0	0	0	0	0	0	12	18	1
South	0	0	0	0	0	0	11	0	0
Border	0	0	0	0	0	0	8	3	0
West	0	2	0	0	2	0	3	7	4
Total	1	12	0	0	5	0	58	42	11

tive Republicans. On one Senate roll call, for example, every single Republican present, thirty-two in all, voted for an amendment pushing rates above those provided for the pending bill. Like Gallinger, Henry Cabot Lodge, opposed to the tax in 1894, endorsed this proposition with a short speech (1913: 3832).

Less noted in contemporary and subsequent scholarship has been the strong moderating role played by Wilson and the congressional leadership. The sizable bloc of Republicans, eager to join with their counterparts in the Democratic party to push for higher rates, indicates that differences between parties on this issue were no greater than differences among members of the same party. The Democratic leadership suppressed this potential alliance, however, so that the opposition to moderate rates remained effectively divided by party label.

This historical view highlights several points meriting further elaboration. Congressional response to the issue of taxing incomes remained unchanged in some respects. At an obvious level, the formal terms of the bill introduced each session were essentially identical.[12] Less patent, those most enthusiastic about employment of an income tax tended to represent more rural, less industrialized constituencies where its burden would be light. New, however, was the fact that strong proponents formed a sizable bloc in both major parties. Moreover, after 1894 they had almost no opponents on the principle that incomes might be taxed. Virtually no one thereafter engaged in the denunciations which characterized the 1894 debate. Since a number of these former fulminators, such as Jacob Gallinger, had participated across time, perceptions of the dangers inherent in the taxing of incomes clearly had altered, at least among the political elite. Finally, although united behind enacting an income tax, the major parties were divided on an equally important issue: how high its rates should be. The remainder of this essay will focus on two questions that summarize this history. What altered the perceptions of the former opponents of income taxation? Why was the 1913 tax not designed to be much more progressive in impact, given the much more favorable environment in which it was considered?

ALTERNATIVE EXPLANATIONS

First, mere maturation is the most obvious answer to these questions. Individuals adapt to change slowly, the argument goes. Income taxation was frightening at first because, although needed, it was new; once people grew accustomed to the notion, hostility abated. Such dynamics certainly have some explanatory power. However, changes in attitudes do not occur randomly or with equal consequence, and emphasis on the passage of time cannot explain such important changes. Why did the Democrats, for example, coalesce on the issue earlier than the Republicans? Moreover, when does one begin marking time's passage? The United States had had an income tax in 1870. Political behavior was more, not less, explosive twenty-four years later. Finally, if truly significant, "growing comfort with a new concept" should have resulted in the 1913 tax's being considerably more progressive than its 1894 counterpart.

Second, a similar type of explanation relates to the return of economic prosperity. Everyone knows that passions are close to the surface in hard times, so the rancor aroused by tax questions in 1894, the pit of a major depression, should not be surprising. Again this consideration is of obvious importance, but, like maturation, it does not explain many specifics: "who acted how?" and "why change among some and not others?" Why, for example, did midwestern Republicans change positions before northeastern Republicans? Moreover, other economic cycles since 1870 had not produced similar responses to income taxation. Finally, this explanation does not account for the fact that the specific bill passed in stable times was much the same as the one passed in hard times. The politics of the 1890s, in short, was more than the politics of depression.

Prosperity, like maturation, in other words, can be considered as an environmental factor. Obviously, altered conditions create demands for new policies: policies usually provoke conflict when first proposed. However, this generalization is inadequate for digging deeply into an individual case. In fact, demands for change do arise which are ignored forever. Others are transmuted before becoming law. Perhaps less obviously, a specific change can induce competing, almost irreconcilable pressures (Rakoff and Schaefer 1970).

Third, a better understanding of responses to this specific issue entails joining a close look at Congress itself with key developments in the larger society. Such a merger focuses attention on the political context in which political behavior occurs. Unfortunately resistant to precise measurements, this concept has as its major component the relationships between politically relevant external conditions and the constituency structure of existing political parties. The central explanation for both continuities and discontinuities in congressional responses to income taxation, in other words, lies in the interaction of the era's predominant secular trend, rapid industrialization, with the electoral composition of political parties.[13]

American political parties are, at first glance, too decentralized to warrant the attribution of such influence; appeals to party loyalty, for example, seldom seem to bind anyone. However, at the national level, it is this attenuated party discipline itself which necessitates the careful weighing of electoral bases. Many factors shape legislative behavior, but few representatives long ignore the interests of mobilized voting blocs in their districts (Miller and Stokes 1963; Hedlund and Friesma 1972). Hence, when party leaders, eyeing national campaigns, have sole charge of framing legislation, as was the case with the revenue bills of this period, constituency makeup clearly becomes a powerful determinant of the policy process. The relationship is not static, of course, but varies with the environmental conditions affecting electoral decisions, both directly and by their impact in converting latent groups into active ones. It is in this respect that industrialization comes into the equation, although full appreciating its role requires first a discussion of the dynamics of American electoral alignments, focusing on the 1893 to 1913 period.

One hallowed justification for political parties is as a means to assist the electorate in influencing the policy direction taken by its elected representatives. Each party, theoretically, offers appropriate but distinct solutions to current problems. A free, open election gives representatives belonging to the winning party a mandate to implement its stated solutions. In this framework, parties are, in essence, collections of like-minded voters, each with a distinct perspective on the problems facing the country. There will be obvious differences between such voters, but on the central issues of the campaign, differences between them will be less significant than differences between them and members of rival parties. This similarity greatly aids their representatives in implementing policies designed to deal with the problems at issue.

How does such a view apply to the politics of the two decades under study? While acknowledging the enormous benefits industrial growth spawned by the turn of the century, few observers today would deny that high prices were being paid. Some benefited greatly, others less so—still others were quite literally destroyed. Since this distribution of costs and benefits was obviously affected by governmental decisions, political debate might have revolved around the matter of allocation. In such a scenario, political parties would logically have coalesced around the great transformation as the central fact affecting all Americans' life fortunes. One party could have appealed to those basically satisfied with the current variant of economic change and the other to those more dissatisfied, with each offering policies consistent with its constituency base to cope with the situation.

Although historians have often assumed such a realignment of forces to be only reasonable, modern electoral studies reveal that enormous obstacles would block the way. In a country as diverse as the United States, for example, issues will obviously have differing salience for different voters. Institutional considerations, however, contain probably even greater barriers. For a variety of reasons, Americans tend to vote as they have in the past, even after the original reasons for their partisanship have faded away.[14] As a result, party divisions come to bear little relation to current concerns. On these, party constituencies overlap, so that giving any new issue paramount importance would most likely entail cutting across existing party distinctions.[15] Suggestions to simply reorient the party system to reflect new realities, while perhaps rational, will provoke understandable hostility, particularly from established political elites. By definition they have their stakes in the existing system and will consequently oppose suggestions to endorse new policies to deal with new developments when linked to realignment pressure. Such resistance will probably be in proportion to the threat that the reorientation poses to a given representative's power base.

Less vested ideological underpinnings also help make intense anxiety predictable around periods when realignment seems likely. Blurred distinctions between party constituencies on current issues, especially economic ones, have generally been viewed in America not simply as normal but as ideal. Until very recently, for example, most political analysts glorified a system of overlapping constituencies, arguing that only when both parties contended for the center ground on divisive issues was our form of government secure (Sundquist 1973: chap. 14; Lipset 1970). Such convictions are deeply rooted in our political culture, traceable at least to the architects of the federal constitution, who perceived American society as "disharmonious," highly susceptible to being rent by a single cleavage, especially one with an economic component (Smith 1965).

However, overlapping constituencies obviously inhibit the ability of party-oriented voters to register opinions on current issues. Hence, at certain periods in the nation's history, all-encompassing parties become intolerable; and suppressed tensions explode, shattering and rearranging party boundaries. For example, in the antebellum period, repeated attempts were made to depoliticize issues growing out of the regional existence of slavery. In large part, these efforts by established political elites were based on the knowledge that the major parties, Whig and Democratic, contained significant constituencies on both sides of any conceivable dimension of slave-related controversies (Sundquist 1973: chap. 4). For a variety of reasons, however, the politically relevant attitudes of sufficient people became hot enough to melt away old allegiances. A new party, the Republican, was formed, consisting of groups which could take some positive positions on this searing question without undue risk of political self-destruction.

Of course, this process of shaking loose old party ties does not have to result, as in 1854, in a new party. Party names could remain the same while party composition, and hence issue orientation, would alter significantly. Hypothetically, in the 1850s blocs of Whig slave sympathizers could have found a happy home as Democrats, while their opponents could simply have begun voting Republican.

This chapter argues that a polarized voter realignment similar to the hypothetical one sketched above seemed to be a distinct possibility in the 1890s. Lured by the apparent impact of hard times, a significant element of the Democratic party elite hoped to reshuffle the American electorate in order to deal with what it saw as pressing problems. This elite projected that American voters would divide somewhere along the continuum between those enriched by the current version of industrial change and those crushed by it. They saw that the Democratic party, through its stands on issues like the income tax, would be composed of the latter, presumably larger group. Their rallying point would not, incidentally, be to oppose industrial change but to redirect its flow of costs and benefits somewhat. The Republican opposition refused to acknowledge such a subtlety, claiming its misguided foes were out to destroy rather than to modify the modern system. Many were convinced by the Republican argument, and ultimately the attempt to realign along such lines aborted.

Democratic party attachment to agrarian-based policy change continued after 1896 but without its association to what today might be called a class-based electoral strategy. With the class-based strategy, Democratic economic policy demands stimulated emotion because they were perceived as part of a plan to bring about more comprehensive economic change. After 1896, this expanded scope no longer seemed credible, allowing quite similar economic policies to be viewed as moderate, incremental changes in the established order.[16] Thus, the central political fact of the 1890s was not hard times but, rather, the possibility that hard times would precipitate a party free of major internal divisions over issues affecting the economy. The central political fact of the Progressive Era was that such a political realignment was no longer the goal of any significant segment of the political elite.

To summarize the preferred explanation, the major difference between the political contents of populist (1892 to 1896) and progressive (1908 to 1913) tax reform is that political elites perceived in the former the seeds of a major party realignment along an economic axis. They saw that the income tax would nurture this development, the fruit of which would be a two-party system capable of more directly representing social and economic cleavages related to industrial change. Propositions aimed at modifying existing economic arrangements, in their view, would not inevitably divide each party against itself. The possibility of such a realignment passed with the election of William McKinley in 1896. For a variety of reasons, the less fortunate in industrialized areas declined to join the party captured in their name by the agrarian dissidents.[17]

This transformation in the perspective of political elites toward the possibility of realignment holds the key to understanding the two anomalies highlighted in the introduction to this essay. The hypertrophied reaction in 1894 to a 2 percent tax on the incomes of less than 1 percent of the population makes sense because it was linked to restructuring the Democratic party in support of more fundamental change. Furthermore, the denouement of this potential alliance explains why the tax enacted again, almost twenty years later, in much more stable times, was but slightly more robust than its populist shade. Cross cutting cleavages, realigning pressures being absent, worked to insure that an income tax, made inevitable by changing economic conditions, would be moderate, both in its substance and in the process of its enactment.

SUPPORTING EVIDENCE

Before marshaling more direct evidence in support of this conclusion, let me first consider which parts need to be buttressed. That massive movements in the constituency base of the party system were taking place in the early 1890s and not in 1898, 1908, or 1913 now seems beyond debate (Sundquist 1973: chaps. 7, 8). Moreover, such fluctuations would be of obvious concern to political leaders potentially affected by them (ibid.: 277–278). Furthermore, the severe economic distress of the early 1890s makes reasonable the assertion that sensible politicians would believe that voting behavior could be made to relate to economic concerns. Finally, that class-based parties did not develop seems beyond the need for elaborate proof.

Instead of these points, the key facts demanding further support are two. First to be demonstrated is that in 1894 the income tax was a crosscutting issue, that it was associated with pressures for a party realignment, and that the character of the realignment might well have facilitated the formation of additional and perhaps more radical redistributive legislation. Second, further evidence must demonstrate that the issue of higher income tax rates did cut across party lines in 1913, that this cleavage was related to economic development, and that the issue of income taxation per se was less divisive at that time because it no longer threatened to crystallize an alliance productive of more fundamental economic reform. Support for these propositions can be generated simultaneously through examining three types of evidence: elite perceptions, correlations of industrial development and party strength; and location of support and opposition to the tax.

Elite Ideation
Scratching any politically sensitive person in the 1890s would expose a belief that the success or failure of the Democratic/Populist alliance in 1896 would bear on the established economic order. Perhaps the best evidence of the primacy of such concerns among the elite is the summaries of traditional historians, who based

their conclusions predominantly upon careful analysis of elite rhetoric. Here, for example, is a fairly typical comment:

> For the first time in 30 years [1896] the country divided roughly along class and sectional lines, and the electorate was confronted with a clean-cut issue. And that was not merely the money issue, but the more fundamental one of the control of the government by the business interests of the East or the agrarian interests of the South and West. (Morison et al. 1970: 191)

It would be hard to find similar interpretations of the election in 1908 or even 1912, when Theodore Roosevelt headed another threat to the two-party system. Roosevelt's Progressive party did indeed promise major reform (Scott 1959). However, the party's appeal to a substantial middle- and upper-class constituency suggests that we should not conceive of it in the same light as Bryan's party of 1896. The chairman of the Progressive party's National Executive Committee, for example, was George W. Perkins, erstwhile partner of J. P. Morgan and Company and a director of both the United States Steel Corporation and the International Harvester Company.

Clearly, the Democratic party in 1896 seemed to menace the status quo considerably more than the Progressive party did in 1912, but was the income tax associated with this threat? In 1894 and not thereafter, the tax did in fact seem to be viewed as tied to building a coalition committed to a series of economic reforms. Reading through the three tax debates after 1894, for example, reveals few such perceptions expressed. In 1894, however, forty-three of the fifty-five legislators opposing the tax emphasized their fear of what shortsighted economic policy would come next, should the coalition get its way on the income tax.[18] Moreover, the opponents of the tax within the Democratic party did not contest that the income tax would produce a party realignment. Rather, they argued in effect, with considerable vigor (and foresight), that the realignment would be a disaster for the party, not to mention for them personally. In this light, Senator David B. Hill, the most strident opponent, concluded an income tax indictment consuming thirteen pages of the *Congressional Record* with his central concern:

> Those who insist upon injecting into this bill [an income tax] should realize that it means the loss of the control of this Senate . . . it

means the loss of the next House of Representatives, it means the loss of the electoral votes of New York, New Jersey and Connecticut, and probably every Northern state; and finally it means the loss of the next Presidency and all that implies. They should recollect that this income tax feature is just regarded in New York and many other Northern states as a scheme of spoliation, an unwarranted sectional attack upon their citizens of means. (1894: 3568)

As final evidence for the primacy of such concerns, it is interesting to shift the focus back to Nelson Aldrich, trying, in 1909 to get a revenue bill through a Senate in which his party held an almost two to one majority. He had hedged his position on an income tax, and Senator Bailey, his Democratic antagonist, began to entertain those present by recalling Aldrich's unrestrained condemnation of such taxation in 1894 and queried the motives for his conversion. A brief exchange followed:

Aldrich: Whenever the income tax proposition here appeared in this body . . . it has appeared here advocated by Populists or by others who sympathized with them in a desire to redistribute the wealth of the United States by this method.
Bailey: Was it supported only by such?
Aldrich: At the time which I mentioned [1894], I think I can say it was supported only by such.
Bailey: But not now?
Aldrich: Not now, I think. (*Congressional Record* 1909: 1536–1537)

Electoral Behavior

Did this rhetoric have a realistic root? In 1896, William Jennings Bryan watched the "plutocrats" stalk out of the Democratic convention. He did not try to block their departure, convinced that it would facilitate the attainment of his oft-stated goal of "capturing the common man" (Coletta 1964: 161). Lacking survey data, we will never know how well founded his hopes really were. My argument is simply that elites perceived this goal as realizable by 1893 or 1894 but not so after 1896. In addition to rhetoric, some behavioral evidence that the voting of that period related to economic concerns is provided by table 12.4, which consists of state-level correlations of degree of industrial development with Democratic party strength. These aggregate correlations have obvious methodological problems as conclusive evidence.[19] In addition, the degree of industrial development is far from being an ideal measure of those constituencies gaining from the current variant

TABLE 12.4. Correlations of Industrial Development with Party Strength

	1892	1894	1896	1898	1900
Democratic	+.09	+.01	−.49	−.21	−.27
Third party	−.57	−.62	−.25		

of industrial development. The pattern of correlations does, however, tend to support the idea that voting behavior in 1896, more so than before or after that date, seemed related to economic concerns. Had the Democrats won in that year, the constituency base of its elected representatives would probably have supported attempts by the federal government to change the distribution of costs and benefits of the industrial process. In short, the rhetoric cited previously did have a realistic root.

Evidence presented earlier demonstrates that many participants sensed in the income tax debates this larger struggle to reorient the Democratic party. Again election returns provide some indication that stated perceptions, such as those of Senator Hill, were realistic. Democratic opposition to the income tax was not random; it was concentrated in the industrializing northeastern states. With the declining Democratic appeal to this region, only two of its fifty Congressmen were able to win their next election. The rest were defeated, chose not to run, or were denied renomination by their party. If purged, however, their position was vindicated in 1896; the Democratic party did not achieve national power with its apparent commitment to redistribution policy.

Facing this failure, the Democratic party quickly began to repair its eastern fences. Its agrarian-based policy commitments were stripped of their redistributive trappings. Richard Coker, the Tammany boss who lobbied hard against the tax in 1894, converted six years later to both Bryan and the income tax.[20] Senator Hill, though defeated at the polls, found a role managing the presidential campaign of Alton B. Parker in 1904 (Bass 1961: 246).

The final evidence that the cleavage stimulated by populism remained quiescent in the Progressive Era comes from comparing party membership to the income tax coalitions in 1913. Since the Democratic party did not expose its historically obvious divisions to the public, the nature of its disagreements over the rate structure cannot be ascertained. Divisions on this question among Republicans was, however, more open. Scaling this opposition in the Senate by means of factor analysis and correlating it with the mea-

(Continued)

1902	1904	1906	1908	1910	1912
−.16	−.13	−.19	−.19	−.11	−.12
					+.22

sure of industrial development used previously yield the relatively high negative correlation of −.63.[21] Again, while not conclusive, such a finding does indicate that the constituencies represented by each party were not distinct along an economic dimension, a point also supported by table 12.4. Hence, questions relating to industrial development raised at this time would inevitably divide each party against itself at least as much as they would divide one party against the other.

In summary, given the decentralized structure of American political parties, realignment along an economic axis was a dead issue with the 1896 election of McKinley and the return of prosperity. As a result, the intraparty cleavage over the proper response to industrialism remained into the Progressive Era. While many have stressed the conservative/liberal divisions in both parties at this time, few have linked the split to the realignment of 1896 or have examined its policy implications. Implications for the income tax, at any rate, are clear. In 1913, two blocs, each of which had much in common with the losing side in 1896, pushed for higher tax rates. The fact that these blocs were in separate parties tended to insure that an income tax would be passed with lower rates, even if with less conflict.

IMPLICATIONS

The Democratic party in 1896 seemed to threaten the established order. By 1912 the same party, endorsing the same policies, no longer had this image. The basic reason is that these same reforms were sponsored by different coalitions with different aims. Social scientists have long debated how radical the spirit of 1896 really was—specifically, whether it had a class base (Woodward 1976: 28–29). This essay has argued that the potential was present for class-based parties, such as were gestating at the same time in Europe. Had the Populist/Democratic coalition been successful in electing a president in 1896, a very different political response to the pressures of industrial change would have been possible.

Progressive reform, on the other hand, lacked this class dimension. In other words, while America differed greatly along selected measures of industrial development, variation between the two parties, after 1896, was significantly less than variation within each.

These facts of party structure have broad implications for the shape of the political economy emerging in the Progressive Era.[22] When congressional leaders have an active role in forming legislation, the end result tends to be a compromise which reflects the balance of interests represented by their party (Jackson 1974: 6140). The tariff bills of this period, and by extension their income tax component, have long been acknowledged as products of such intraparty "log rolling."[23] Less well developed, however, has been the importance of how electoral logs happen to be split into parties. If one party consists primarily of the economically disadvantaged, for example, economic policies will be shaped quite differently than if each party represented a broad spectrum of economic groups.

It is in this regard that the major lines of electoral cleavage in the Progressive Era had significant policy implications. Certainly, had all the income tax radicals in 1913 been in the same party, rather than being separated by party membership, the ultimate tax structure would have had quite a different cast. That the party system of the period was not so oriented was in many ways due to the frustrated realignment of the nineties. Since the productive Sixty-third Congress constructed a number of other economic policies, notably the Federal Trade Commission and the Federal Reserve System, this Progressive Era party system, and its link to Populism, merits further elaboration.

As a related point, political parties have long been justified by democratic theorists as vehicles for translating very efficiently the popular will into government policy. Realignment concepts were initially advanced in part as a means of defending the party system's capacity to play this role (Key 1959). In one sense the 1896 realignment bears out the theory, albeit with an ironic twist: a conservative realignment permitted popular demands for income taxation to be realized. The cross cutting of economics and party membership provided conservatives with the security necessary for a diplomatic conversion. On the other hand, the price for this comfort, in addition to delay, was a less robust tax than desired by the majority of the population.

At another level, the arguments of this chapter highlight the value of emphasizing the political context. The importance to the policy process of such environmental factors as economic prosperity or rapid industrialization is generally mediated by such variables as the constituency base of the party system. Because such structural variables are normally quite stable, not to mention hard to measure, they are often underestimated as important factors in studying policy formation.

NOTES

1 *Congressional Record* 26, April 20, 1894, p. 3893.

2 *Congressional Record* 50, August 27, 1913, p. 3813.

3 This generalization is relative, of course. So-called radical historians maintain a more intense interest in the subject. Kraditor (1972) presents a stimulating call to examine reform movements as a way to probe the nature of ruling-class hegemony.

4 The last major work to contrast populism and progressivism as a way to study the dynamics of American reform was Hofstadter's *The Age of Reform* (1955). The rapid fall from grace of this Pulitzer prize–winning study has probably discouraged further comparative analysis.

5 Zemsky (1975: 75) argues that this generalization is even more true for earlier legislatures.

6 In all four Congresses examined, votes on the general revenue bills under consideration were virtually identical to voting patterns on the income tax, when they were recorded. Hence, discussing income tax policy is a good way to understand larger tariff questions (Stewart 1974: chaps. 1, 2, 3).

7 The Rice Index of Cohesion for tariff roll calls was .85 in the House and .94 in the Senate for the Democrats. For the income tax alone, the Senate mean score is .88.

8 Considering only party supporters and opponents from table 12.1 and collapsing the categories into northeast and nonnortheast result in a phi of .55 versus one for a classification based on party of .46.

9 Aldrich (1909). Almost all the income tax moderates in the Republican party made this argument even more explicitly.

10 It had been estimated in 1894 that only 85,000 Americans, .14 percent of the population, had annual incomes above $4,000 (Miller 1894).

11 Letter from Furnifold Simmons to Woodrow Wilson requesting his assistance, September 4, 1913. Wilson replied the same day; Simmons thanked him on the fifth. Woodrow Wilson Papers, Library of Congress, Series 2, Reel 50.

12 This fact was pointed out repeatedly during debate in 1913 by Progressives and Republicans who openly advocated higher rates. The major difference in 1913 was the addition of a Progressive rate structure. However, Underwood

acknowledged that this was added for symbolic rather than revenue purposes. He noted that raising the basic rate by one-half of a percentage point would have had more effect. The income tax as a whole was projected to bring in less than 10 percent of the government's revenue (1913: 1255).

13 Industrialism is defined in the conventional way as sustained economic growth associated with major and continual changes in material technology. See Wrigley (1972: 266). The state-level measure of industrial development used throughout is Hofferbert's (1968). It was provided in machine-readable form by the Inter-University Consortium for Political and Social Research, University of Michigan, as were the roll-call data used here.

14 Both Sundquist (1973) and Burnham (1970) document the existence of long periods of such partisanship. I am not, of course, arguing that "issues" are absent from American politics but, rather, that the policy response to a demand for "reform" cannot be understood without reference to party constituency structure and, most especially, to perceptions of movements in it.

15 I am following definitions used by Rae and Taylor (1970: 90) in equating "crosscutting" and "overlapping" cleavages as opposed to reinforcing ones. Here, for example, the party and industrial cleavages reinforce each other.

16 Tubbesing (1975) asserts that realignments are in fact caused by redistributive policies which are frustrated. The argument here is that the same policy may or may not be viewed as redistributive, depending upon the political context in which it is considered.

17 The standard explanation is that ethnocultural identities were stronger to such voters than were economic ones. Republicans in 1896 successfully portrayed the issue as being for or against industrial development, rather than for or against a different allocation of its costs and benefits. See, for example, Kleppner (1970), McSeveney (1972), and Jensen (1971). This last work has, however, been criticized on methodological grounds. See Wright (1975).

18 This conclusion is based on an extended analysis of the rhetoric of all those discussing the issue in Congress. Only two opponents, for example, argued that income taxation was wrong because it taxed those "most fit." The others simply worried about what would come next (Stewart 1974: chap. 4).

19 The state-level measure of party strength is the index "Composite B" computed by David (1970). The conventional Pearson's (product moment) correlation coefficient was used. I am making the assumption that representatives of less industrialized states were less sensitive to the needs of the industrializing sector of the economy and more sensitive to its dangers. Obviously, the findings are subject to the ecological fallacy. See the discussion by Lichtman (1974).

20 *New York Times* (1894: 2) and Stoddard (1913: 219–220) point to the conversion, ascribing it to Croker's "sublime ignorance of national affairs."

21 The industrial score was correlated with the tariff factor loading of each state's Republican senator. Unfortunately, the Democratic party did not divide openly on the tax question, so no comparison can be made (Stewart 1974: 124).

22 Kolko (1963) and Weinstein (1968) give two forceful attempts to explain this new relationship between government and the economy. Contemporary scholarship tends to hold that their "radical" viewpoint characterizes the nature of this relationship better than its causes. This essay is in this vein, arguing that significant "causes" lie in the somewhat less teleologic developments

affecting party structure. It can be argued, of course, that a kind of "elite consensus," reinforced by constitutional arrangements, frustrated the emergence of class-based parties, and hence a more fundamental response to economic development, in the Progressive Era. See Burnham (1970: 79). One of Burnham's later essays stresses more accidental factors such as mass immigration (1975b).

23 In addition to the classic tariff studies by Taussig and Schattschneider, see Fleming (1972). Like most successful congressional leaders, Underwood owed his power to his ability to put together, by bargain and compromise, a measure which would maximize party support.

13

Partisan Realignment and Tax Policy: 1789–1976

SUSAN B. HANSEN

This chapter examines the impact of realigning elections on U.S. tax policy from 1789 to the present. Recent research emphasis on incremental tax policy changes at state and local levels does not account for major changes in the sources, levels, or distribution of federal taxes. One recent study (Winters 1976) concluded that tax policy is effectively insulated from such elements of popular control as parties and elections. From a historical perspective, however, party and electoral changes have profoundly affected tax policy, even when alternative causes for tax changes, such as war, economic development, and demand for new services, are considered.

The focus here is on the policy implications of institutional changes resulting from realignments. Linkage between collective choice-making procedures and opposition to taxes is postulated, building on Downs' (1960) theory concerning taxation in democracies. Unified control of government by a single political party proves to be a key component of tax policy making at both state and federal levels. Unified party control also offers a parsimonious explanation for the consequences of realigning elections for other policy areas. In recent years, however, the impact of electoral change on policy has been greatly reduced. The weakening of the major parties and the increased role of the federal executive have contributed to our present system of taxation without representation and have led to the current taxpayers' revolt by referenda, exemplified by the passage of California's Proposition 13.

TAXES AND POLITICAL ECONOMY

For political scientists, taxation in a democracy raises several interesting and significant questions concerning representation, political obligation, and the role of government in the economy and society. If taxes are as unpopular as most opinion polls indicate, why do people support political systems which constrain their freedom by imposing taxes? Under what political conditions can democratically elected politicians impose new taxes? How can governments raise taxes and still retain popular support? These problems are especially crucial at the national level, where the option of "exit" to a more congenial tax environment is costlier than at state or local levels.[1]

Taxation plays a central role in political economy. Tax policy affects economic growth, business cycles, the proportion of private wealth and income allocated to the public sector, and the distribution of collective costs and benefits. Despite its importance, the politics of taxation has received relatively little attention from either economists or political scientists. Students of economics and public finance have been interested more in the impact of taxes on the economy than in questions of political support for taxes. Empirical studies abound in the analysis of policy outputs and governmental expenditures, but the econometric models and methods developed there have seldom been applied to changes in levels or sources of taxation.

Economic historians have suggested three factors to account for historical changes in tax systems: economic development, war, and demand for new services. Thus, Musgrave (1969) argues that economic structure determines the sources and amount of revenue which can be raised. Simple taxes on land, mines, or agriculture may be imposed in underdeveloped extractive economies. Trading nations can raise revenue from tariffs. But more sophisticated taxes (payroll, income, sales) require a money economy, an industrialized population, and a complex administrative system and thus appear at later stages of economic development. Further, tax revenues in nations among the American states tend to increase with urbanization and industrialization (Dye 1966: chap. 7).

Peacock and Wiseman (1961) stress the importance of wars in tax development. Extraordinary demands are imposed on a political system, so that new sources of revenue must be considered. Inflation or borrowing may of course be used instead of taxes, but Peacock and Wiseman argue that new taxes are likely to be imposed in wartime because citizen opposition to them may be diminished by patriotism. Their United Kingdom data suggest that those new taxes persist long after peace has returned—that both taxing and spending are displaced to new and higher plateaus by wars.

A third theory of tax development stresses demand for new services. Thus, Britain's adoption of an income tax was linked to the introduction of social security in 1906; gasoline taxes in the U.S. came into use to meet demands for roads for the new automobiles. At a broad comparative level, these patterns describe changes in revenue patterns quite well. But they do not take into account the political factors which determine how a policy responds to the economic choices posed by war, economic development, or the need for new services. Collier and Messick's analysis of social security adoptions may explain a considerable portion of the variance across countries, but one cannot fail to note that the U.S. is one of the furthest outliers on a regression line based on agricultural employment (1975: 1309). Heidenheimer et al. (1975) examined revenue policies in seven highly developed western democracies and noted considerable variation in tax sources and burdens. Clearly, political factors should be considered to explain these residual patterns.

Taxes distribute the burden of government across different social or economic groups and as such represent the outcome of complex political bargaining. Further, tax policy decisions must be made by political actors operating under legal and electoral constraints. Aggregate measures of political variables can be added to the usual economic explanations, but feeding random political variables into a correlation matrix will not suffice.[2] A more general theory concerning the politics of tax outcomes is needed. The literature on realignment and the writings of the economist Anthony Downs suggest such a theory.

REALIGNMENT AND TAX POLICY: THEORY

Periodically in American history, critical elections have ushered in realignments in parties and voting patterns and have changed the political agenda. For two reasons, realigning elections should alter the relationship between elections and tax policy. First, the social or economic crisis which precipitates realignment may change perceptions of revenue needs: "politics as usual" could not deal with war (1860), with depression (1893, 1932), or with the tariff problems and governmental surpluses of the 1830s. Second, realigning elections have changed the nature of political opposition and support and thus could affect politicians' calculus of social forces favoring or opposing changes in the financing of government.

Most empirical analyses of political realignment have focused on the behavior of the American electorate. The central finding is that realignment is a response to a major social or economic crisis, when the electorate undergoes a large-scale transformation in its durable political attachments. In realigning elections, the coalitional base of the party system shifts (in Sundquist's terms) to a new axis. Burnham and others have documented these shifts with aggregate data on voter turnout, registration, and voting behavior (Burnham 1970; Sundquist 1973), and Seligman and King, in chapter 8, note major shifts in elite recruitment patterns.

But—then what? Are changes in the electorate and in government personnel followed by changes in the political agenda and in policy outputs and outcomes? Based on the small amount of research that has been done on these aspects of realignment, the answer must be "not necessarily." As Trilling and Campbell note in the introduction to this volume:

> The process may be aborted anywhere along the way—because the severity of the crisis ebbs by itself, or because party leaders waffle on the critical issues long enough to deny meaningful choice to voters, or because electoral change lacks the clarity and magnitude to transform the party system, or because institutional factors cause personnel turnover or policy change to lag substantially behind social and economic and electoral change, or because entrenched officials effectively engage in obstructionism, or because subsequent social and electoral conditions offset or reverse the realignment.

Sundquist's various scenarios for party realignment also suggest a multiplicity of possible outcomes. In several cases, the results may well be stalemated under our system of divided government and fragmented parties. Third parties could win a substantial proportion of votes or seats, the major parties could shift but divide the control of offices, or different parties might control different states or regions within our federal system. There is no a priori theory to suggest that major shifts in federal or state policy will follow a realigning election or a realigning era, even if the political agenda and the political decision makers change. And, if changes do occur, the analyst must ascertain whether electoral change was the proximate cause, because factors in the domestic or international environment (such as war or economic development) may produce policy changes which have little to do with the politics of realignment.

Even though the diffuse "theory" of realignment is of little help in predicting policy outcomes, there is empirical reason to believe that realigning elections will have more impact on public policy than "normal" elections. First, party polarization around some issue (old or new) has occurred during realigning elections, as suggested by Ginsberg's analysis (1976) of changes in the salience and direction of party stands on seven major issues from 1840 to 1968. Downs' spatial model (1957) would predict party convergence on issues in attempts to build majority support, but for several reasons this has not occurred during critical elections: the electorate may be changing, new elites may take over a party and impose a new agenda, the country may be undergoing a social or economic crisis. All these factors make strategic calculation of party stands difficult, especially in the days before mass survey techniques enabled politicians to calculate modal preferences with any accuracy.

Second, realigning elections have produced large and one-sided shifts in the control of government. The years following 1800, 1828, 1860, 1896, and 1932 (as well as the exceptional period following the nonrealigning election of 1920) are characterized (as table 13.1 demonstrates) by a phenomenon otherwise rare in American political history: control of the House, the Senate, and the presidency for extended periods by members of the same political party.[3] In these high-stimulus elections, a switch of party alignments has been accompanied by a one-sided surge in support for one particular party. This of course does not guarantee unified control of government; the Supreme Court, the bureaucracy, and state governments may remain out of phase for years thereafter, and factional divisions may persist within the Congress (e.g., the southern Democrats who opposed Roosevelt and the New Deal).[4] Nevertheless, formal political control of the decision-making machinery of the federal government has been firmly in the hands of one political party by larger majorities and for longer periods of time after realignment than during the periods between critical elections.

This striking fact suggests that realignments may indeed affect policy outputs and outcomes because the machinery to do so is in the hands of one party. Advocates of responsible parties (such as Schattschneider 1942) have long argued for a system of party government which would facilitate public policy making. If their prognosis is correct, unified control of governments should produce changes in public policy. But divided control of government is even less likely to be associated with major policy changes, because of the greater need for compromise to insure that neither party gets the credit for policy leadership. If one can rely on Ginsberg's elaborate coding of federal statutes and his multiplicative

TABLE 13.1. Periods of Unified Political Control of Presidency and
Congress, 1791–1981

Date	Party	Years
1791–1793	Federalist	2
1795–1801	Federalist	6
1801–1825	Democrat-Republican	24
1829–1841	Democrat	12
1841–1843	Whig	2
1845–1847	Democrat	2
1853–1855	Democrat	2
1857–1859	Democrat	2
1861–1869	Republican/Unionist	8
1873–1875	Republican	2
1881–1883	Republican	2
1889–1891	Republican	2
1893–1895	Democrat	2
1897–1911	Republican	14
1913–1919	Democrat	6
1921–1931	Republican	10
1933–1947	Democrat	14
1949–1953	Democrat	4
1953–1955	Republican	2
1961–1969	Democrat	8
1977–1981	Democrat	4

measures (criticized by Neuman and Hicks 1977), it appears that
new legislation has occurred corresponding to those elections usually defined as realigning (although the passage of laws does not
mean that changes in policy outputs will occur). Brady, in chapter
9, shows *why* critical elections are associated with policy changes
by analysis of the internal structuring of the House. Perhaps the
unified control of government may offer a further explanation.[5]

If political realignment suggests major changes in taxes, the
work of Downs (1960), based on "normal" politics, suggests why
marginal and incremental changes more typically characterize tax
policy. Downs' analysis rests on two key assumptions. The first is
obvious: tax burdens are unpopular. The second is certainly plausible: tax burdens are more salient to citizens than are the benefits
each person is supposed to receive from collective goods. He then
argues that rational politicians will be reluctant to raise taxes (or
impose new ones) because their perceived costs will outweigh any

benefits that might be provided by these taxes. Further, in an earlier work (1957), Downs argued that parties tend to converge on highly salient issues (such as tax policy) or to avoid the issue altogether. Thus, the amount of collective goods provided in democracies is less than optimal; politicians fear electoral retribution for tax increases and are constrained to avoid or hide them. Politicians of both parties have incentives to avoid making taxation an election issue and to keep budgets low.[6]

These theoretical considerations are generally supported by empirical analyses of state and local tax policy making. Taxes are raised (if at all) incrementally, indirectly, even deviously in order to minimize political fallout (Meltsner 1971: Fisher 1969). Sharkansky notes little difference in parties' positions on tax issues and suggests that economic or administrative criteria are paramount (1969: 19). Winters' (1976) longitudinal analysis of redistribution considered spending as well as taxation, but he found that political variables such as party competition, Democratic control, or the powers of the governor had little impact on redistribution ratios of tax burdens to benefits in the American states. Economic and demographic factors have generally proved to be better predictors of state tax policies than political variables.

The existing state and local studies have focused on a short time span and on incremental changes. If one looks at revenue patterns over all of U.S. history, however, a very different pattern emerges. First, taxes have increased from less than 1 percent of the GNP in 1789 to over 30 percent today, and dramatic increases are apparent even if one uses constant dollars or revenue per capita. Second, tax sources have shifted not once but several times from the tariff, to excise taxes, to the income tax, to increased reliance on payroll taxes.

Third, state tax patterns have also changed. State and local tax rates have increased faster than federal taxes, although they have remained fairly stable as a percentage of the GNP (Mosher and Poland 1964: 61–72). And, since 1900, almost all states have come to rely on income, sales, and excise taxes rather than property taxes for their revenues, considerable financial innovations which Walker's 1969 study did not consider. What extraordinary circumstances could explain these dramatic and nonincremental changes in tax policy? What factors have led politicians to implement policies fraught with such apparent political peril? Analyses such as Winters' or Sharkansky's, based only on recent and limited time periods, cannot help us answer these questions.

Downs' approach suggests some answers, however, because he focuses on two factors crucial for tax policy formation: the salience of the issue and the intensity of support for or opposition to it. His key assumptions are probably realistic for "normal" elections at the present time. But these can be restated as constants, and they become the basis of a series of hypotheses linking political realignment with changes in tax policy.

First, the salience of taxes to voters should have been much lower in the nineteenth and early twentieth centuries, when federal taxes were largely indirect and amounted to less than 5 percent of the GNP. Since World War II, however, almost everyone must file a federal income tax return; and federal, state, and local taxes account for more than 30 percent of the GNP. Tax policy is potentially a much more dangerous campaign issue today than it was during earlier periods of realignment.

Second, as specific social problems or demands become more salient, taxes should appear less onerous. As Peacock and Wiseman (1961) suggest, people may pay taxes more willingly during war, because they perceive a direct link between their economic sacrifices and policy outcomes (peace, victory), than in peacetime, when many more issues crowd the political agenda; Buchanan (1967) makes a similar argument with respect to earmarked taxes. The major social crises precipitating realignment may therefore have decreased popular opposition to changes in tax policy.

Third, voters' opposition to new taxes should be more salient to political candidates if they face competition for office. During realigning periods, old political alliances crumble, and the lopsided victories for the dominant party should give elected officials greater freedom to implement changes in tax policy.

Finally, politicians face opposition not only at the polls but also within legislatures and among different branches of government. A legislature controlled by the same party as the executive may well produce tax policies different from those of a divided government. Downs' analysis stresses voters' opposition to taxes and focuses on the cost/benefit calculations of individual political actors. This must be supplemented by consideration of collective decision-making processes in parties and legislatures and by an examination of institutionalized political opposition.

An analysis of the politics of taxation should help us examine the complex relationship between realignment and public policy. Tax issues figured prominently in each critical election and thus can be used as a basis for systematic comparison and analysis over time. Further, the policy results of changes in tax laws are readily observable: the *Historical Statistics of the United States* provides figures on all government revenues, by source, from 1789 to the present. One must of course use these data with caution, recognizing that systematic material on tax incidence, or taxation as a proportion of the GNP, is not available before 1900 and that the analysis of tax incidence even today is a difficult problem for econometricians (Pechman and Okner 1974). But, while estimates for a particular source of revenue in any given year may not be precise, economic historians have generally found these data useful for comparisons across time.[7]

In the remainder of this essay, I will first examine historical variation in the size and source of federal revenues. I will then consider the relative saliency and polarization of tax issues, as indicated by political party platforms from 1844 to the present. Do politicians, as Downs suggests, converge on tax questions or avoid the controversy altogether? Or, as Ginsberg's analysis indicates, do parties sometimes take opposing positions on such issues as taxation, offering the electorate a clear choice? And are they more likely to do so during periods of realignment?

Third, I will analyze two aspects of political opposition in those periods when major tax changes were made at the state and federal levels: party cohesion on legislative roll calls and party control of the executive and legislature. Major tax changes should coincide with minimal opposition, if Downs' analysis of individuals' reelection calculus fits the collective decision-making process. As I shall show, this is indeed the case, and it is the major reason for the link between realignment and tax policy. Finally, I shall discuss some reasons why tax policy making in recent years has become increasingly insulated from parties and electoral politics, producing a system of taxation without representation.

SIZE AND SOURCE OF THE FEDERAL TAX BURDEN, 1790–1970

Figure 13.1 shows the percentage of total revenue derived from various sources from 1790 to 1970. Until World War I, revenue from customs duties was the principal source, supplemented by income from the sale of public lands and from excise taxes (used briefly before 1800 and during the War of 1812 and extensively after the Civil War). The individual and corporate income taxes

FIGURE 13.1. Sources of federal revenue, 1790–1970

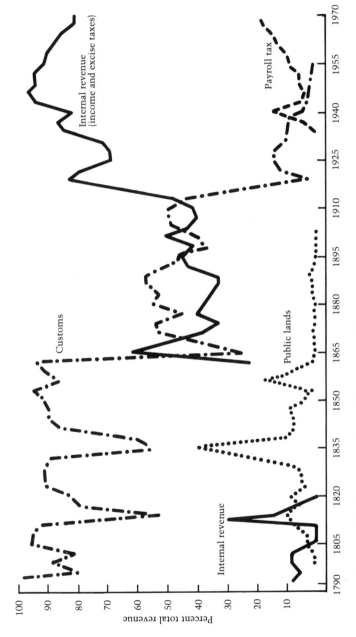

SOURCE: *Historical Statistics of the United States* 1975: tables Y567–Y568.

FIGURE 13.2. Total federal revenue, 1791–1970 (Log~n~), in constant dollars

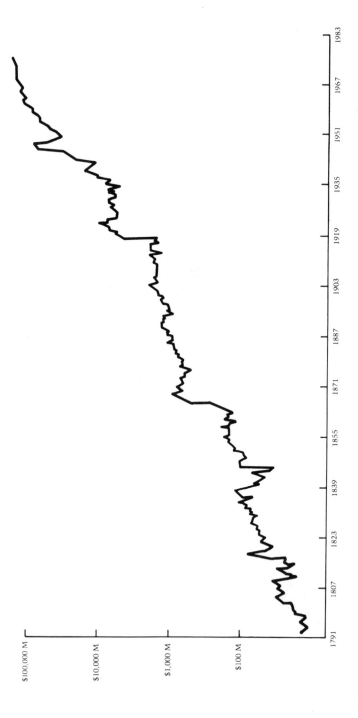

were introduced briefly during the Civil War to meet the revenue needs of the Union. These taxes became the principal source of federal revenue after the passage of the Seventeenth Amendment. Payroll taxes earmarked for social security began in 1936 and have increased in importance up to 1970.

Changes in the sources of federal revenues have accompanied dramatic increases in the *amount*, from $4 million in 1791 to over $193 billion in 1970 (fig. 13.2). Generally sharp increases occurred during wars, but the 1830s and 1930s also witnessed growth in revenue. However, the country has grown, too, in size, wealth, and population. Inflation has also been considerable since 1790. If one examines the trend in revenue in constant dollars on a per capita basis, the curve is much flatter: wartime peaks are followed by long periods of very little growth in revenue, with downward trends during the 1830s and 1840s, the 1870s and the 1920s.

From an economist's viewpoint, data on revenue should indicate the proportion of the gross national product allocated to the public sector, because of the role played by government in fiscal policy and economic growth. No reliable GNP data are available before 1870, but Trescott (1957: 62, 68) estimates that only about 1 to 2 percent of the GNP was allocated to the public sector during this period for either revenue or expenditures, except for a brief surge of 3 to 5 percent during the War of 1812 and an increase to 10 to 14 percent during the Civil War. This reflects the prevalence of a philosophy of minimal federal government spending during much of that period.[8] Up until the Civil War, internal taxes (income or excise) were generally unnecessary; federal government requirements in defense, postal service, pensions, the debt, and Indian affairs could be financed largely out of customs and land sales (Dewey 1934; Howe 1896) (although customs duties were of course passed on to consumers).

After the Civil War, the federal government returned to a more limited role. Although population and productivity grew rapidly during that period, federal revenue as a percentage of the GNP actually *declined* until World War I (fig. 13.3). Revenues increased sharply during that war and also (as I shall describe below), during the Depression, against the advice of economists and political conservatives. The proportion of the GNP going to the federal government soared during World War II and has remained high since then.[9]

How well do the economists' theories account for these trends in U.S. federal taxes? The "war" model has considerable merit:

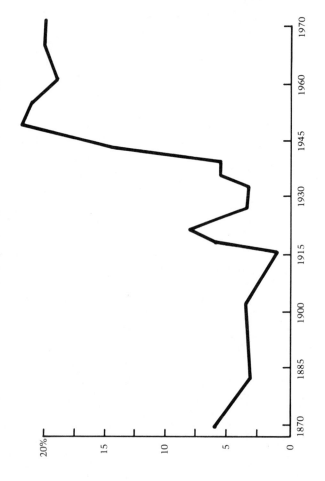

FIGURE 13.3.   Federal revenue as a percentage of the GNP, 1869–1970

revenue amounts certainly increased during the major wars in our history (1812, Civil War, World Wars I and II) and tended to stay high after each war. In the nineteenth century, tariff revenue declines precipitously during war, an added incentive to develop new revenue sources. War periods account for the largest deviations from the trend line. But, as Tussing and Henning (1974) have shown for the twentieth century, such changes are not attributable to war alone—domestic spending and population also increased. They conclude that Peacock and Wiseman's "displacement effect," suggesting higher levels of taxing and spending after wars, does *not* hold up very well for the U.S.

The "economic development" model also has some merit: the sources of U.S taxes follow the pattern of increasing administrative complexity (tariff, excise, income, payroll) suggested by Musgrave (1969), and the sequence of revenue changes in the U.S. is similar in order (if not in timing) to that of other industrialized countries. Growth in revenues has also paralleled American economic growth, and the largest negative residuals from the trend line (plotting growth in revenues over time) occurred during the Depression.

These economic models account for changes in revenue amounts better than changes in revenue sources. Moreover, they cannot explain several puzzling patterns: why is revenue as a percentage of the GNP lower in the U.S. than in comparable western nations (Heidenheimer et al. 1975: 228), and why did it decline during the 1870 to 1910 period of rapid economic growth (fig. 13.3), contrary to Wagner's Law? Why were excise taxes (in fact, most internal revenue) abolished from 1800 until the Civil War, except for a brief period after the War of 1812? No pressing revenue needs account for the passage of income taxes in 1894 and 1909; and, as already noted, the adoption of social security, financed by payroll taxes, lagged considerably behind that predicted for the U.S. on the basis of other countries' experiences.

To answer such questions, we now turn to an examination of political factors influencing the size, source, and distribution of federal revenue.

PARTY PLATFORM STANDS ON TAXES

Downs predicted that tax policy would not be salient in the electoral context and that parties or candidates would converge on revenue issues. An analysis of party platforms offers one way to examine the relative salience and party polarization over time on an issue such as tax policy. The role of platforms in national elections has varied widely since they came into use in the 1840s, and one may of course debate whether these documents, the product of bargaining among factions and leaders in the national organizations, provide any guidelines to the activities of the party in office or to electoral strategy. Several analyses have suggested that parties' platforms *do* have some policy relevance, however (Ginsberg 1976; Pomper 1968), so a careful examination of changing party positions on tax issues seems in order.

To indicate the salience of revenue as an issue in a particular year, the number of sentences which mentioned any form of taxation was counted in each major-party platform and in the platforms of third parties which garnered at least 5 percent of the vote in a national election.[10] Party positions on tax issues were coded + for each of the following: advocacy of redistribution of wealth; support for higher taxes; support for increased federal spending and a greater role for government in the economy.[11] I also coded + for party support for "sound money" and the maintenance of the gold standard, since either policy would make tax burdens more onerous. Opposite positions on each of these dimensions were coded −, and party conflict on an issue is indicated if opposite signs are shown for a particular issue in a given year.

The results (table 13.2) indicate that, with few exceptions, tax issues were salient to at least one party in most years and were not mentioned at all in only a few instances. Further, salience showed a clear curvilinear trend, peaking in the late nineteenth century. This pattern was almost entirely due to one issue: the tariff. This was a major source of federal revenue until 1910, and the Democratic and Republican parties were polarized on that venerable issue over a seventy-year period, with each devoting a substantial part of its platform to it. A qualitative shift occurred after World War II, when fewer references (mostly negative) to taxes appear. Downs' predictions thus hold up better for the recent past than for earlier periods. Perhaps as federal taxes become more salient to citizens with the expansion of the direct federal tax on incomes, they became less attractive to party leaders as a political issue.

Party polarization on issues other than the tariff, however, was less common. Generally both favored lower taxes, but there were exceptions to this: a party would sometimes advocate "sufficient revenue" to meet the needs of government (Democrats, 1872, 1936) or to reduce the public debt (Republicans, 1896, 1920). Contrary to what Downs would have us believe, the party advocating higher taxes actually won the presidency in four of those five years (1872, 1896, 1920, 1936, and 1972), when the parties differed on this issue. On some occasions, at least, higher taxes were preferred to the alternatives (inflation, soaring national debt, unstable economy) by a particular party and (apparently) by a majority of the electorate as well.

The parties differed only occasionally on particular types of taxes or on questions of redistribution; usually such issues were mentioned by only one party platform. As Stewart outlined in the previous chapter, the Democrats, joined by the Populists, Progressives, and Socialists, did favor a progressive income tax after 1896; Republicans (except for the Mugwumps) generally opposed it in Congress, but this conflict did not appear in their platform. New taxes (excise, sales, death, or inheritance) were mentioned only occasionally in the platform, although we know from other sources that these (especially Henry George's single tax) were objects of controversy in the nation as a whole. Likewise, currency problems received little mention, even though (as the 1896 Democratic platform stated) "hard" currency, national banking, and the gold standard all served to make tax bills more onerous.

This analysis does not indicate that tax issues were significantly more salient or more polarized at those times than in the interim periods. The parties did take different positions on revenue questions in the critical elections of 1860 and 1896, and, as will be discussed below, they also disagreed sharply in 1800 and 1828. In 1928 to 1932, however, the parties offered little choice to the voters, except on the perennial tariff question. The Democratic platform urged that "something" be done about the state of the economy. But national social security was not mentioned, nor were tax increases, nor was progressive taxation, nor closing tax loopholes for the rich. Roosevelt pledged to reduce taxes and balance the budget. No wonder Marriner Eccles said, "Given later developments, the campaign speeches often read like a grave misprint, in which Roosevelt and Hoover speak each other's lines" (Paul 1954: 171).

As I shall show below, substantial changes in tax policy did correspond to periods of realignment (including 1932) and were necessitated by the economic crises or wars which accompanied or precipitated the realignments. The importance of these other is-

TABLE 13.2. Party Platform Positions on Revenue Issues, 1844–1976

Year	No. of Tax Sentences			Tariff	Income Tax	Excise Tax	Redistribution	Size of Tax Burden	Gov't in Economy	Currency
	D	R	Other							
1844	1[a]	1		W+				D−	D−W+	D−
1848	3	0						D−	D−	
1852	1	1		W+				D−	D−W+	D−
1856	1	0						D−	D−R+	D−
1860	0	2	B, C (0)[b]	R+					D+R+	
1864	0	0							R+	
1868	3	2		D+			D+	D−R−		
1872	1	3		R+		R+		D+R−	D−	
1876	2	1		D−R+				D−		
1880	1	1		D−R+					R+	D−R+
1884	7	4		D−R+		D−		D−	R+	D−R−
1888	8	3		D−R+		R−		D−		R−
1892	3	2	P (2)	D−R+	P+			D−P−	D+R+P+	D−R+P−
1896	6	7		D−R+			D+	D−R+	D−R+	D−R+
1900	12	14		R+				D−R−	D+R+	D+R+
1904	10	11		D−R+	D+		D+	R−	D+R+	R+
1908	8	8		D−R+			D+		D+R+	D+R−

Year									
1912	8	8	BM (11)	D−R+		D+			D−R−
1916	4	9		D−R+				D+	R+
1920	5	7	Pr (3)	D−R+		Pr+	D−R+	R−	
1924	19	18		D−R+	D+Pr+		D−R−Pr−	R+	
1928	15	16		D−R+	D+R+	D+	D−R−	D+	
1932	3	15		D+R+	R+		D−	D−R−	D+
1936	3	17		D−R+	D+R−		D+R−	D+R−	
1940	3	7		R+	D+R−		R−	D+R−	
1944	1	8		R+		D−	R−		R+
1948	5	5		R+		D−	D−R−	D+R+ᶜ	D+
1952	10	10			D+	D−	D−R−		
1956	8	4		D−R−	D−	D−			
1960	9	2		D−	D−	D−	D−R−		
1964	5	7		D−R+	D−R+	D−	D−R−		
1968	15	3	AIP (7)	D−R+AIP+	D−	AIP−	D−R−		
1972	27	13				R+D+	R+D−		
1976	20	12				R+	R−		

ᵃ 1844 to 1852, W = Whig party.

ᵇ Third parties receiving at least 5 percent of the vote: P = Populist, BM = Bull Moose, Pr = Progressive, AIP = American Independent party, B = Breckenridge Democrats, C = Constitutional Union.

ᶜ By this date, both parties supported a larger role for government in the economy, though they disagreed on many details.

sues may have reduced the relative salience of taxes, thus reversing Downs' assumption (reasonable for periods of "normal" politics) that tax burdens would be more salient than any benefits they would finance. Thus, the party controlling the government could change tax sources or amounts with less fear of electoral retribution.

REALIGNMENT AND TAX POLICY: EVIDENCE

As figures 13.1 to 13.3 suggest, several changes in revenue, sources, and amounts have corresponded to periods of realignment. Thus, excise taxes vanished when the Jeffersonian Democrats took over from the Federalists. Land sales and tariff revenues soared under the Jacksonians. Income taxes were adopted in 1860 and 1892, also critical realignment periods, and the payroll tax appeared during the New Deal. Each of these new taxes shifted the costs of government to different groups in society. I will now examine more closely some reasons why critical elections (as opposed to the "normal" operation of parties and elections) have affected tax policy.

This account will focus on four variables: the salience of tax issues, party polarization over revenue, the actions taken by the newly dominant majority coalition, and the policy impact of those actions. I will compare the politics of realignment with tax politics during the periods between critical elections and also with other factors affecting tax policies: wars, economic growth, and revenue needs.

Tax Policy after the First Realignment

Tax questions figured prominently in national politics from the beginning. The first bill introduced into the House of Representatives was a revenue bill, and the first party system in the United States was based partly on profound conflicts over the appropriate financial program for the new nation. Hamilton and the Federalists proposed sound financial measures on the Continental model to pay off the war debt and establish the credit of the U.S.: national assumption of all debts, establishment of the first Bank of the United States, and excise taxes to finance the new government. The Jeffersonians felt that excise taxes, payable in coin or currency, were inappropriate for a barter economy, and they were convinced that the moneyed classes would benefit from Federalist banking and revenue measures. Excise taxes were thoroughly unpopular among people who had just rid themselves of British taxes, and the Jeffersonians were able to turn this discontent (evidenced by the Whisky Rebellion) to their own political advantage (Ratner 1942b: 27).

When the Federalists lost Congress as well as the presidency in 1800, the result was predictable: "complete abolition of all of the taxes so laboriously established by Hamilton and his successors" (Howe 1896: 34) until the War of 1812 necessitated the imposition of taxes on consumer goods to provide revenue lost as the war cut income from the tariff. Although revenue from this was reduced by war and the Embargo Acts, Jefferson and his successors clearly differed from the Federalists regarding tax policy, and after 1800 they were able to abolish excise taxes, use land sales to help settlers, and keep the tariff lower (as desired by southern planters and western farmers) than Hamilton and the eastern industrialists might have desired (Paul 1954: 7). It seems clear, therefore, that the realigning election of 1800 produced changes in federal tax policy which accorded with the philosophy of the victors. The War of 1812, however, necessitated a temporary departure from that philosophy.

Jacksonian Democracy and Tax Policy

Changes in both revenue and expenditures occurred during the Jackson and Van Buren administrations. Revenue from the tariff and from sales of land increased sharply. The federal debt was retired completely in 1835, and in fact the treasury reported large surpluses from 1834 on.

But realignment did little to produce these changes. Although the Jacksonian Democrats tried to change the level and distribution of the federal tax burden, they lacked the fiscal and administrative means to do so. The dilemma was noted by Schlesinger (1946): the Jeffersonian philosophy of support for the interests of the common people (modified by the Jacksonians to include urban laborers as well as yeoman farmers) required Hamiltonian means to achieve its ends. But Jackson was limited by his strict constructionist philosophy of limited federal intervention in the economy, banking, and social investment.

How did this anomaly come about? Two conditions that I have established for the policy impact of elections were met. First, Jackson (and Van Buren after him) scored impressive victories, and the Democrats controlled both houses of Congress from 1829 until

1841. Further, the Jacksonian Democrats' ideas on taxation differed markedly from those of the opposition (which included National Republicans, Anti-Masonites, and Whigs). They opposed taxation for internal improvements and the infamous 1828 "Black Tariff," because high tariffs (the principal source of revenue) would have reduced the money capital of farmers. Jackson also favored reducing land prices and held that the public lands should not be made a source of revenue but should be sold at nominal cost to settlers (Dewey 1934: 218). Finally, Jackson and Van Buren were "hard money" advocates, compared to the Whigs, who favored easy money and the generous use of bank credit for financing of such internal improvements as roads and canals. The Jacksonians opposed the Second Bank of the United States and issued the Specie Circular of 1835 to 1837, because they assumed (mistakenly) that soft money benefited speculators and the rich at the expense of farmers and workers.

Despite their apparent political advantages, the Jacksonians had either no effect on revenues or precisely the opposite effect from that intended. The major reason for this was a lack of understanding of fiscal and monetary policy. Although Jackson possessed the formal political power to change the laws regarding federal revenue, his unstable political coalition of southern planters and New England industrialists probably would not have held together to support such changes.[12] Southerners and Westerners were strongly opposed to protectionism, but many compromises had to be engineered to gain sufficient support from other regions to pass the measure, and its major tariff reductions were scheduled far into the future.

Neither Jackson nor the Southerners were willing to reopen debate on the issue for fear of even higher tariffs. Thus, throughout Jackson's administration, revenue from the tariff remained embarassingly high, because revenue derived from the tariff depended far more on business conditions than on the reductions in duties imposed on imports of 1830, 1832, and 1833. The same was true of land sales, which soared due to easy credit, population growth, and increased value and accessibility of western lands.

Although the overflowing treasury was not due to Jackson's policy choices, he took steps to decrease revenues: requiring land payments in specie, recalling federal bank loans so as to distribute federal funds among state "pet" banks, and distributing the treasury surplus to the states. But the consequences were disastrous, and the resulting severe economic depression fell most heavily on the small farmers and urban workers who had supported Jackson. Bank failures in Europe and crop failures in the U.S. aggravated the dismal situation, and economic problems helped defeat the Jacksonians in 1840.

The Jacksonians lacked economic knowledge of the causes of business-cycle fluctuations and of the government's responsibility for them. But, even if their economic theory had been more advanced, one must doubt whether they would have been willing to expand the powers of the federal government into regulation of the economy, or if they could have rallied the necessary political support from their southern populist–strict constructionist coalition.[13] Many elections would take place before persons opposed to the dominance of business interests would again attempt to shift the tax burden from consumers to producers.

Tax Policy in the Civil War Period

Major changes in government revenue occurred during and after the Civil War. Some of these (wartime income and excise taxes) were clearly due to the compelling need for revenue during the war, when sea blockades hindered trade and cut tariff revenue. These measures were repealed soon after the war, however. But the political history of wartime increases in tariff rates and their longevity after Appomattox suggest that a major switch back to a protective tariff occurred. This was the result not of the war but of Republican hegemony in Washington from 1860 until 1878, the outcome of the realigning elections of 1854 to 1860.

The Republican-sponsored changes began in 1858, when the Republicans gained control of the House of Representatives. The highly protectionist Morrill Tariff passed the House during the 1859 to 1860 session. This was not war legislation but an effort to attract Republican presidential votes in the upcoming presidential election in such protectionist states as Pennsylvania (Taussig 1966: 158) and to supplement revenue lost in the business panic of 1857.

After the Republicans gained control of the Senate in 1860, the bill passed that chamber before a single shot was fired in the South. The author of the act, Morrill, became chairman of the House Ways and Means Committee, and practically every month of the ensuing war saw tariff increases. Most of these high tariff duties remained in effect until 1892, when the Democrats finally regained control of the national government.

Two major changes in revenue were introduced during the Civil

War: a progressive income tax and an inheritance tax. These, however, did not result from the 1860 election; neither party proposed them until the precarious state of Union finances made new sources of revenue mandatory, and both received support from Republicans as well as Union Democrats. It appears that the rich and the Republican party accepted a progressive tax on incomes as the lesser of two evils. The financial condition of the North was so unstable, due to war losses, inflation, and the suspension of specie payments, that those in business realized that their investments would be better protected if taxes were raised.

As soon as the financial emergency of the war abated, however, the true colors of the Republican majority and the wealthy emerged. Income from stocks, bonds, and land sales was eliminated from the income tax (a forerunner of modern "capital gains" exclusions). The progressive rate structure was abandoned in 1867, and the income tax was repealed altogether in 1872. According to Ratner, President Grant's opposition to the income tax was "explained by his wish to strengthen his hold on the support of the great moneyed interests in the Presidential election of 1872" (1942b: 96).

Three of my conditions for the policy impact of elections on revenue were therefore met after 1860: the parties differed (the Republicans had a strong protectionist plank in their 1860 platform), the Republicans controlled the government, and legislative changes were made. The impact of the high tariffs on total revenue was not immediately noticeable for two reasons. First, the war cut into tariff revenue. Second, tariffs as a proportion of total government revenue actually declined, since many new (and usually regressive) excise taxes were introduced. But the industries which supported the tariff certainly benefited from it: revenue from the tariff increased from 1866 on. This did *not* happen, as Taussig posits, because "all feeling of opposition to high import duties almost entirely disappeared" (1966: 166). Rather, it was the Democrats opposed to the tariff who all but vanished from the national government. The new Republican majority favored generous pensions for war veterans (who were, of course, mostly Republicans: Sanders 1976) and spending on internal improvements, especially railroads. Increased revenues from the new taxes underwrote those policies. These revenues were so large relative to the demand for their use that even the Republicans considered reforming or reducing tariff rates in the 1870s, but of course tariffs were more likely to be cut on items for which there was no domestic producers' lobby (Taussig 1966: 178–180).

Post–Civil War taxes clearly suited the needs of the growing industrial elite. Revenues declined as a percentage of the GNP: business profits could thus be directed toward investment or consumption, not toward the public sector or higher wages. Taxes fell much more heavily on consumption than on production, and excise taxes on liquor and tobacco, adopted for moral as well as revenue purposes, were in fact highly regressive (Trescott 1957: 66). Individual and corporate income and profits were not taxed, and high investment rates no doubt contributed to economic development. But farmers and urban workers had to pay the social and economic cost. Growing protest against high tariffs, hard money, and lack of credit laid the basis for the next period of realignment.

The 1894 Income Tax: Aborted Realignment

Support for an income tax continued after the 1861 tax was repealed. Revenue needs were *not* a major factor (Paul 1954: 27). Its advocates saw an income tax not only as an alternative to high tariff rates but as a means to redistribute income and to stop the piling up of pensions. The agrarian protest parties had long argued that government power should be used to control the economic monopoly on behalf of the public. The Populists had included an income tax plank in their national platforms, stressing its value as a means of redistributing wealth, and, beginning about 1890, substantial numbers of people within the Democratic party (including Bryan) agreed with this view. Republicans strongly disagreed, and the vote on the bill was highly partisan. But the bill (part of the Wilson-Gorman bill to reduce tariffs) passed largely because in 1894 Democrats controlled the presidency and both houses of Congress for the first time since the Civil War.

Was this a result of realignment? Certainly some of Burnham's state data suggest that major changes in state voting patterns, as indicated by t-tests or his "discontinuity variable," began in 1892 or 1894, not 1896 (Burnham 1970: 22–23, table 2.4) and populists and other agrarian reformers carried many central and western states in the "prairie fire" of 1890. Sundquist, however, argues that 1892 was a deviating, not a realigning, election and did not produce fundamental shifts in party loyalty (1973: 145). But he also suggests that the severe depression of 1893, when a Democratic administration was in power, seriously hindered the efforts of the Populists and reform Democrats to consolidate their new majority. Also, the Supreme Court, dominated by Republicans, reversed a century of precedents to rule that a tax on incomes was a direct tax and therefore unconstitutional.[14] And the tax may have contributed to the Republican victory in 1896. Fearful of its reappearance, the Republicans outspent Bryan by at least $3.5 million to $650,000. Employers, the media, and the clergy were enlisted in the fight against the threat of social revolution posed by the income tax and by Bryan (Ratner 1942b: 217ff.).

The 1894 income tax may be viewed as a consequence of two of my preconditions for policy consequences of elections: differing party stands on the issue and a shift to unified control of the government by one party (the Democrats). But the Democrats held control for only two years and did not control what proved to be a crucial branch of government. The 1896 realignment is the only one in American history *not* accompanied by a shift in control of government. The basis of Republican votes was certainly somewhat different after 1896 than before, but they remained the majority party. A consequence of the realignment of 1896 was not only a delay in consideration of the income tax in any form but also a return to high tariffs (the McKinley Tariff of 1898) as a means of financing the federal government.

Taxation in the New Deal: Inverted Realignment
Political realignment contributed substantially to the major changes in taxes which occurred during the New Deal. Federal revenue increased sharply over 1920 levels, in constant dollars, per capita, and as a percentage of the GNP. Individual and corporate income tax rates were increased. After 1934, the tariff became an instrument of foreign policy, largely controlled by the president, instead of a domestic policy debated in Congress, and a payroll tax on employers and employees was introduced to finance the new social security system.

These tax changes, like the New Deal policies of deficit spending and government intervention in the economy, were clearly the responsibility of the overwhelming Democratic control of the national government. But New Deal policy was never presented to the electorate as the basis of choice in the 1932 election: as already mentioned, the party platforms differed little. The major revenue changes were largely initiated by the Roosevelt administration and underwent substantial changes in the nominally Democratic Congress. Further, although these policies were intended to aid the economic recovery and to shift the burden of government from the poor and middle classes to the rich, many of them had precisely the opposite effect. The evidence in fact suggests that New Deal policies prolonged the recession and made the tax burden more regressive.

The history of the New Deal revenue policy suggests a delicate political balancing act. The administration had liberal and labor support, but Roosevelt moved cautiously in many areas so as not to frighten off business investment.[15] In Congress, some Democrats supported the demands for redistribution voiced by Huey Long and the Townsendites. But in 1933 other House Democrats proposed what even Republicans called a "soak the poor" plan to increase taxes on small salary and wage earners, and in 1936 Southerners opposed many aspects of social security. Very few conservative Democrats suffered defeat in the 1932 and 1936 Democratic landslides. Their presence in Congress guaranteed trouble for Democrats who favored lower and less regressive taxes, since many of them gained leadership positions because of increasing reliance on seniority (Brady 1973).

Even if these complex political considerations had not been present, economic confusion in this pre-Keynesian era produced policies whose impact differed greatly from their stated purpose. The Revenue Act of 1935, for example, increased taxes on the rich and on corporations. Liberals who urged even higher rates failed to realize that a considerable portion of corporate taxes are shifted to consumers. Taxes were *increased* every year from 1933 through 1938 to finance growing federal expenditures, but the economic impact of such increases was to decrease disposable income, remove money from the economy, and thus slow recovery (Trescott 1957; Brown 1956). The impact on redistribution was minimal (Lambert 1970). Also, several New Deal taxes were in fact regressive. The agricultural adjustment program was based on a "wickedly regressive processing tax" (Trescott 1957); the social security tax was levied only on the first $3,000 of income and was coupled with a deflationary reserve program. Congress also amended the Social Security Act to insure that the unemployment program would be administered at the state level, and the states varied widely in their distribution of unemployment benefits, with the poor states predictably providing the least assistance. Finally, many states, strapped for revenue, imposed new and regressive sales taxes which "diminished purchasing power more seriously than the Federal income tax" (Paul 1954: 245).

Unlike Jackson, Roosevelt was willing to use federal resources to counter the effects of business cycles. But, as with Jackson, he lacked both the political power and the economic theory to enable him to realize his policy goals. The realignment of 1928 to 1932 gave the New Dealers the power to make many changes in federal tax policy, but they did not fully control Congress, the Supreme Court, or state governments. It is therefore not surprising that the impact of the New Deal was not as great as its supporters had hoped or as its conservative opponents had feared.

TAX POLICY CHANGES BETWEEN REALIGNMENTS

Some changes in tax sources and amounts have occurred between realignments. These are attributable either to wars or to unified control of the national government by one political party. One of the ironies of American history is that one party has controlled the federal government during our major wars (1812, Civil War, both world wars, Korea, Vietnam), so that it is difficult to determine the independent effect of party control and war demands on tax policy.

Revenues have been increased (through deficit spending or the imposition of new taxes) during every war in which the U.S. has engaged since 1789. Revenue and expenditure levels have moved to new plateaus after wars. But considerable portions of the war-based taxes have been repealed or greatly reduced as soon as the wars ended, except for the high tariff following the Civil War, which (as described above) was not due to the war itself. Wars have not produced lasting changes in *sources* of revenues, but they provide the simplest explanation of changes in *amounts* of revenues. New sources of taxes and changes in tax incidence, however, are better explained by political factors. A partial exception may be the introduction of withholding in 1943, which resulted in a dramatic increase in the proportion of Americans filing federal tax returns[16] and gave the national government automatic access to wages and wage increases (Hughes 1977: 207). This also occurred under a unified government but under wartime conditions and with considerable Republican support. Administrative, political, and financial conditions were all involved.

Unified control of the national government has consistently been associated with tax policy changes. The Democrats were able to make some reductions in the tariff whenever they gained control of the national government during the nineteenth century (bills of 1846, 1857, and 1886 especially). Nevertheless, the tariff remained the major source of federal revenue throughout this period, except when the Civil War interrupted trade. Since Democrats also controlled Congress and the presidency in 1913, the first tax bill passed under the Seventeenth Amendment had progressive rates rather than the flat rates the Republicans preferred. When the Republicans regained control in the 1920s, Harding, Coolidge, and Treasury Secretary Mellon reversed this pattern: they eliminated the wartime "excess profits" tax, devised such new loopholes as the oil depletion allowance, and raised tariff rates, all over the protests of the Progressives and Democrats in Congress (Paul 1954: 128–132). They also delayed implementation of social security (Waltman 1976).

A major tax change which did *not* coincide with realignment of the major parties was the passage of a federal income tax amendment (as a provision of the Payne-Aldrich Tariff) in 1909. Republicans controlled both Congress and the presidency, but the major factor here was the strength of the Progressives in *both* parties and in the White House. If one accepts Sundquist's view, this was a realignment in the composition of both parties which was nevertheless contained within the framework of the existing party system (1973: 158–162). The process began with Theodore Roosevelt, who shocked his party in 1906 by advocating "the adoption of some such scheme as that of the progressive income tax on all fortunes" (Ratner 1942b: 260) and gained fame as a trustbuster. Democratic Progressives gained seats in the previously Republican East, Republican Progressives in the West and Midwest. Many conservative Republicans also came to support an income tax, rather than continuation of high tariff rates, because during the 1890s the U.S. shifted from being a debtor to a creditor nation (Bauer et al. 1963: 18).[17] A country which was now a net exporter of manufactured goods quickly found the protective tariff a hindrance to trade. And, beginning in 1901, reciprocal provisions for bilateral trade agreements with such countries as France and Great Britain began to appear in tariff legislation. In short, a protective tariff was no longer economically necessary nor politically desirable. Another source of revenue had to be found, and the income tax was the most obvious alternative.

In the final House vote on the income tax amendment, fifty-five insurgent Republicans abstained because they saw the amendment as a strategy to defeat the income tax through a long ratification process in state legislatures and preferred a direct act of Congress (Ratner 1942b: 301ff.). But a vote against the measure would have guaranteed defeat of the tax. Progressive Republicans and Democrats held the balance of power in Congress and thus assured a significant change in the source of federal revenue, although changes in the popular basis of party support and in the economy contributed to this far-reaching innovation.

RECENT TRENDS IN THE POLITICS OF TAXATION

This analysis has suggested that parties and elections have significantly shaped the development of U.S. tax policy, apparently contradicting recent empirical studies as well as Downs' theories concerning taxes and electoral strategy. Two recent trends in American history may account for this anomaly, however: the decline of political parties and the progressive depoliticization of tax policy making. Political parties have long served as a means, however minimal, of producing cooperation in policy making across different levels and units of government. But party strength has varied considerably throughout American history, reaching its peak during the 1890s. A major legacy of the Progressive Era was a general weakening of the party system, at least partially attributable to the "reforms" they introduced (nonpartisan election, direct primaries, voter registration requirements). As a result, the realignment of 1932 was far more diffuse than its predecessor (Burnham 1970: 91–110), and Burnham suggests that the "onward march of party decomposition" has made future realignments less likely. Unified party control of government today is likely to be far removed in practice from the "responsible party" model.

These developments have affected tax policy making as well. Opposition to tax changes should be less effective if it is diffuse rather than structured, whether in the electoral arena or in legislatures.[18] At the same time, advocates of tax policy innovation may be stymied by lack of organizational ability to initiate effective changes in the size, source, or distribution of the tax burden.

Party voting patterns on major revenue bills have varied considerably from the Jacksonian era to the present. As table 13.3 shows, party cohesion on tax issues (as measured by Rice's index) was substantially higher in the nineteenth century, especially in the House of Representatives. It peaked in the 1890s with the vote on the 1894 income tax, declined somewhat with Republican insurgency in the Progressive Era (vote on the income tax amend-

TABLE 13.3. Party Votes on Tax Bills, House of Representatives, 1833–1975

Tax Bill	Rice Index of Party Cohesion Republicans	Democrats
Compromise tariff of 1833	.49[a]	.51
1861 income tax	.52[b]	.58
1894 income tax	1.00	.84
1909 income tax	.73	.85
1936 social security	.54	.91
1969 Vietnam surcharge	.22	.33
1972 to index social security[c]	.25	.02
1975 tax cut	.14	.64

[a] Includes Whigs and Anti-Masons.
[b] Includes Whigs and Unionists.
[c] Amendment to bill raising federal debt ceiling.

ment), increased slightly during the New Deal, but has declined steadily since. Some recent tax bills have been almost unanimously bipartisan (the Investment Tax Credit of 1967, for example, passed 386 to 2), while others were conflictual within rather than between parties (Vietnam surcharge, 1975 tax cut).

Factors other than party have become more important in tax policy formulation, so that even unified party control of the federal government is unlikely to produce major or predictable changes in federal revenue patterns. Perhaps not coincidentally, this pattern began to develop very shortly after the Seventeenth Amendment imposed direct federal income taxes on the American public. As taxes became more salient to citizens, individual politicians were motivated to find ways to insure that tax increases would not be linked to their political careers or positions on federal issues. O'Connor (1973: 67–73) further suggests that business and conservative forces represented in the Republican party were alarmed by the prospect of a dominant populist or liberally oriented party and took steps (creation of the Bureau of the Budget, city-manager government, Internal Revenue Service) to minimize the impact that any party could have on taxes on wealth or corporate profits.

An early step in this process was the fiscal dividend derived from progressive income tax rates: the government could reap an ever growing share of revenue from inflation and economic growth without changing tax rates. A second step was the creation of the Bureau of the Budget in 1921, when accountants and statisticians in the Budget Office in the executive branch began to take responsibility for coordinating taxing and spending decisions away from Congress. Since the 1920s, the Internal Revenue Service has been granted considerable authority to prescribe tax rules and regulations.

This trend continued in the 1930s. Congress delegated a major element of distributive policy (the tariff) to the executive but gained respite from the intense conflict generated over tariff rates. The Social Security Administration set up an independent trust fund operating at least in part on actuarial principles. Attempts to fund the reserves through general revenues have been stoutly resisted, from Conservative Coalition members in the 1930s down to Representative Al Ullman today. Benefits are now indexed to the cost of living and are due to legal entitlements, not legislative discretion. Such a system entails so little political risk that it is no wonder that increases in social security taxes as well as benefits are generally by nonpartisan votes. The House Ways and Means Committee still has a role to play in making tax policy, but there nonpartisanship is the norm, and most members are insulated from electoral control by seniority, incumbency, and the resulting large margins of victory in their districts (Manley 1970).

These national trends are reflected at state and local levels. City-manager governments, relying on uniform sales taxes and "businesslike" assessment procedures, have made local taxing less responsive to political demands and social needs (Lineberry and Fowler 1967). Many states have also adopted progressive income taxes and budget bureaus. Federal programs such as revenue sharing have also limited the impact that state parties or elections can have on either revenue or expenditures (Winters 1976).

Since the Keynesian revolution, tax policy has become an instrument of economic stabilization, left to the experts in the Treasury Department and the Council of Economic Advisers. Tax decisions are made far more on the basis of inflation and unemployment rates (determined by complex statistical procedures insulated from the political process: de Neufville 1975; Pierce 1971) than by demands for expenditures or for redistribution. Congress (over Nixon's objections) passed the Economic Stabilization Act of 1970, giving the president unprecedented authority over taxation and economic policy. This action made political sense, removing Congress even further from political fallout over taxes. The experts may be unable to use fiscal policy effectively to regulate the economy (Shultz and Dam 1977), but they have become increasingly less vulnerable to political control.

CONCLUSION

This analysis has shown that party control of government has been an important explanation for changes in federal tax policy. In American history, unified party control of the legislature and executive has shown a strong pattern of association with critical elections defined in terms of electoral shifts, and the economic crises so often associated with periods of realignment also contribute to demands for changes in the size and source of tax burdens. Tax changes between realignments have also coincided with unified control of the presidency and Congress. But realigning periods have been associated with larger tax changes than have interim years, perhaps because other political or economic considerations reduced the relative salience of tax questions.

These results are further strengthened by a study of tax innovations at the state level (Hansen 1978). State adoptions of sales and income taxes were more likely when the governor and legislature were controlled by the same party, and one-party states initiated these innovations many years earlier than more competitive states.

Two important caveats must be stressed, however, because party dominance is a necessary but hardly sufficient criterion for tax policy making. First, a party may be nominally in control but divided internally in many respects. On a highly disaggregated, distributive issue such as the tariff, or revisions in the Internal Revenue Code, party unity is not likely. Thus, even when Democrats controlled Congress before and after the Civil War, they were unable to make large downward revisions in tariff rates. Tariff reduction was a collective good with little political support: it was far easier politically to extend protection than to reduce rates (Bauer et al. 1963: 15–17). But efforts to impose entirely new sources of revenue cannot be so easily compromised within parties. Higher party unity should therefore prevail when new sources of revenue are being considered than when older ones are being adjusted.

Second, Downs' theory of budget making in democracies stressed that popular opposition to taxes would give parties little incentive to advocate tax changes or increases and that rational political actors would tend to avoid the issue altogether. But the salience of tax questions has varied throughout American history. Federal taxes have become more salient to the electorate since greatly increased tax rates and near universal withholding were instituted during World War II. Thus, recent platforms of both parties ritually call for lower taxes. In earlier years, parties differed as to the sources and amounts of federal taxes, and parties in Congress were more highly polarized on revenue issues than is now the case. Under those conditions, unified control of the national government produced changes in tax policy. But this is less likely today, as parties have weakened and the tax process has become more insulated from political control. Downs' tax policy model based on political opposition must be expanded to allow for historical variation in its key parameters.

The intractability of some aspects of tax policy to political control constitutes another limitation on the role of the party in tax policy making. The impact of tax changes depends on many factors, such as the state of the economy, the international situation, or the state of economic theory. Thus, while Democrats and Republicans differed on the tariff throughout most of the nineteenth century, income derived from the tariff depended on war, depressions, and the trade policy of other nations and was only marginally affected by changes in rates. Similarly, governments before the New Deal lacked the tools and the knowledge to do much about business cycles. Even though the parties differed concerning the causes and consequences of business cycles, successful manipulation of the economy was largely a matter of luck, and the tax policies pursued by Roosevelt and Jackson were entirely inappropriate to their policy goals.

Calls for across-the-board tax increases or decreases are generally heeded today because of widespread acceptance of the role of fiscal policy in regulating the economy. But substantive tax reform that would affect the distribution of wealth in society is not a strong possibility in a society which lacks a labor or socialist party and which limits participation within the party system by those lower-status persons who would have the most to gain from redistributive taxation. A state-level analysis by Winters (1976) finds that changes in party control of governments have no effect on redistribution. This result must be expected in a system which has largely isolated taxation and economic policy from party and electoral conflict.

Despite the predominant role of political and administrative elites in tax policy making, American taxpayers have a long history of resistance to objectionable taxes. Direct action has often been used if redress through the existing political system was not attainable. Historically, this has been the case with the Boston Tea Party, the Whisky Rebellion, and the resistance of generations of moonshiners to federal revenue agents. In the current context, referendum voting is the means most readily available to citizens to control the upward spiral of taxes. This populist taxpayers' revolt began in the 1960s with increased rates of rejection of school bond issues and has expanded recently to support for limitations on state taxes, such as California's Proposition 13. Although both parties are converging on the tax cut bandwagon, the current tax rebellion had its roots outside the party system, and one must seriously question whether political parties can discover or implement solutions to the current crisis in government finance. Taxation by referendum is thus a logical consequence of a weakened party system which has produced taxation without representation.

NOTES

1   Hirschman (1970) discusses exit, voice, and loyalty as three possible responses people may make to organizational or political demands. As Niskanen (1971: 19) notes, greater political representation and support may result from movement to congenial political units than from the operation of politics within units.

2   See Tarschys (1975) for discussion of financial and tax-related perspectives on Wagner's Law and the growth of public expenditures. Pryor (1968) attempts a quantitative cross-cultural analysis. But the political variables for which he was able to find comparable data (such as party competition and voter turnout) had no theoretical linkage to government taxing or spending and, not surprisingly, accounted for little of the variance in either.

3   Campbell's "surge and decline" theory of electoral change (1966b), based largely on survey data from the recent past, also appears to fit aggregate electoral data from earlier periods.

4   Brady (1973) has contrasted the strong leadership and party unity that prevailed after 1896 with the dispersion of power characteristic of the period since the New Deal and the rise of the Conservative Coalition.

5   Riker's (1962) theory of political coalitions suggests that a large majority for one legislative party may result in low cohesion and policy making characterized by stalemate and compromise. But this theory does not appear to fit congressional behavior after periods of realignment: very high party-unity scores

prevailed after 1896 and from 1933 through 1936. See also the discussion and references in Hardin (1976).

6   Niskanen (1971) and Buchanan and Tullock (1962) describe processes internal to bureaucracies which may result in larger-than-optimal budgets. But larger budgets may *not* require tax increases, especially when a nation has a progressive income tax, a flexible debt ceiling, and the ability to print money (Hughes 1977: 224). The issue here is the amount of taxes, not budgets.

7   See Trescott (1957: 80–81) and the notes to the tables on revenue in *Historical Statistics of the United States* (1975 edition) for a discussion of the reliability of these revenue data for different time periods. Both sources conclude that these data are the best estimates currently available.

8   As Hughes (1977) has shown, the federal government took an active role in the U.S. economy since colonial times. But much of this activity was regulatory and did not involve spending much money: the states invested more heavily in capital-intensive internal improvements, especially before 1860.

9   GNP and total revenues were transformed into constant (1967) dollars using two overlapping wholesale price indexes (tables E23, E52) from *Historical Statistics of the United States* 1975, since no Consumer Price Index or other GNP deflator is available before 1900.

10 I abandoned my initial plan to compute salience as the percentage of all platform sentences devoted to taxes because the size of party platforms had changed dramatically from five or so sentences before 1860, to fifty to one hundred up through 1912, to two or three hundred sentences in recent years as the scope of the federal government has increased. One must seriously question Ginsberg's (1976) constant-over-time salience measures (based on paragraphs).

11 Before the Depression, coding on this variable was fairly simple, since neither party urged increases in the scope of the federal government. After that time, both parties did (usually the Democrats more than the Republicans), but no attempt was made to code distinctions among the many programs mentioned in the increasingly long and complex party platforms.

12 The nascent political parties of this period were divided regionally and ideologically: the Rice Index of Cohesion on the 1833 tariff was only .51 for the Jacksonian Democrats.

13 Trescott (1957) notes that such deficit spending may have eased the impact of the Depression, but such a "Keynesian" policy was hardly intentional: it simply resulted from a lag between federal revenues and expenditures. Nor did it absolve the Jacksonians from the responsibility of creating the Depression in the first place.

14 See Ratner (1942b: 193ff.) for a detailed discussion of the political and legal ramifications of the Supreme Court's ruling on the 1894 income tax.

15 See Lambert (1970) for an analysis of Roosevelt's strategy in revenue matters during the New Deal.

16 The number of returns filed rose from seven million in 1939 to forty-four million in 1943, imposing direct federal taxes on a majority of Americans for the first time in U.S. history (*Historical Statistics of the United States* 1975: 1110).

17 The change in the balance of trade was noted in the 1900 Republican party

platform, but its economic and political significance did not affect party policy for several years. See Stewart (1976) for an analysis of other reasons for changes in Republicans' attitudes toward the tariff and income tax.

18 As Buchanan noted "the institutions through which costs and benefits are presented to the private citizen may affect his choices" (1967: 5). Market choice (correspondence between private costs and benefits) does not apply to collective, political choice processes. Individuals thus reduce information costs by choosing among parties, candidates, or other fiscal choice-making institutions.

Notes on Contributors

DAVID ADAMANY graduated from Harvard College and Harvard Law School. He obtained his Ph.D. in political science at the University of Wisconsin. Since 1977, he has been vice-president for academic affairs and professor of political science at California State University, Long Beach. He is the author or coauthor of *Financing Politics* (1969), *Campaign Finance in America* (1971), *The Borzoi Reader in American Politics* (1972), *Political Money* (1975), and *American Government: Democracy and Liberty in the Balance* (1976), as well as numerous articles on constitutional law, the judicial process, American politics, and campaign finance.

DAVID W. BRADY, professor and chairman, Department of Political Science, University of Houston, received his Ph.D. from the University of Iowa. He has published articles and monographs on congressional behavior, public policy, and political parties. His major publications include *Party Voting in a Partisan Era* (1973) and articles in the *American Political Science Review, British Journal of Political Science,* and others. At present, he is working on a book entitled *Critical Elections in the U.S. House of Representatives.*

BRUCE A. CAMPBELL, associate professor of political science and research associate in the Institute for Behavioral Research at the University of Georgia, received his Ph.D. from the University of Michigan. He has taught there for several summers in the program of the Inter-University Consortium of Political and Social Research. His current research lies in two areas: partisanship and voting in the contemporary South and political socialization of adolescents and young adults. He is a frequent contributor to scholarly journals and has recently published *The American Electorate,* a book on mass political behavior.

PHILIP E. CONVERSE is Robert C. Angell Professor of Political Science and Sociology at the University of Michigan, where he received his Ph.D., and program director at the Center for Political Studies at Michigan's

Institute for Social Research. He has been associated since 1956 with the sequence of national election studies at the institute and is coauthor of *The American Voter, Elections and the Political Order* and author of numerous articles on political behavior.

SUSAN B. HANSEN received her Ph.D. in political science from Stanford University. She has worked at the National Opinion Research Center, Washington State University, and the University of Illinois in Urbana and is currently at the University of Michigan in Ann Arbor. She has published several articles concerning the policy consequences of citizen participation and is now completing a monograph on the politics of taxation.

MICHAEL R. KING, associate professor of political science and senior research associate, Institute for Policy Research and Evaluation, Pennsylvania State University, received his Ph.D. from the University of Oregon. His research has focused primarily on political parties and state legislatures. He is coauthor of *Patterns of Recruitment: A State Chooses Its Lawmakers* and author or coauthor of articles on the historical development of American political parties and on legislative behavior.

KENNETH W. KRAMER received his Ph.D. from Rice University and is an assistant professor of political science at Angelo State University. His research interests focus on environmental policy and policy implementation. He has contributed articles in these areas to professional journals and edited volumes.

ROBERT G. LEHNEN, professor of public and environmental affairs at Indiana University, is a graduate of the University of Iowa; he has taught at the University of North Carolina and the University of Houston as well as the University of Michigan. He is currently active in research regarding the measurement and analysis of public opinion as it relates to public policy issues and is a frequent contributor to scholarly publications. He is the author of *American Institutions, Political Opinion and Public Policy* (1976).

LAWRENCE G. McMICHAEL received his Juris Doctor degree from the School of Law at Duke University. He is presently practicing law with Dilworth, Paxson, Kalish, Levy and Kauffman in Philadelphia.

GREGORY B. MARKUS, assistant professor of political science, received his Ph.D. from the University of Michigan in 1975 and has been at the University of Michigan since that date. He is also affiliated with the Center for Political Studies, Institute for Social Research. His current research focuses on dynamic models of sociopolitical behavior, in areas ranging from human intellectual development to mass public opinion.

KENNETH J. MEIER received his Ph.D. from the Maxwell School at Syracuse University and is currently assistant director of the Bureau of Government Research and an assistant professor of political science at the University of Oklahoma. He is the author of *Politics and the Bureaucracy*, as well as professional articles on representative bureaucracy, regulation, agricultural policy, interest groups, and voting behavior.

DAVID H. NEXON received his Ph.D. from the University of Chicago in 1974. He has published articles and book reviews in the *American Political Science Review*, the *Sage Yearbook of Political Studies*, and the *Columbia Journalism Review*. Research interests include political parties, voting behavior, and health care financing and organization. He is currently on the staff of the Office of Management and Budget.

LOUIS M. SEAGULL received his Ph.D. from the University of Chicago. He is the author of two books, *Southern Republicanism* (1975) and *Youth and Change in American Politics* (1977). He has also served as assistant professor of political science at the University of Pennsylvania and in advertising research positions with Young and Rubicam and Doyle Dane Bernbach. He is currently an associate professor of marketing at Pace University in New York City.

LESTER G. SELIGMAN, professor of political science, University of Illinois, Champaign-Urbana, received his Ph.D. from the University of Chicago. He is particularly interested in research on political elites, comparatively and in the U.S. He has published widely on the theory of elite recruitment, on executive leadership, and on realignment and its recruitment and policy consequences. He has been working on a comparative study of the institutionalization of presidential roles. He is also engaged in research that links presidential selection and presidential coalitions.

CHARLES V. STEWART received his degree at the University of North Carolina at Chapel Hill. He is assistant professor of political science at Meredith College and teaches in the general area of American politics. His research interests lie in the field of law and social change. His recent papers have discussed the Bakke case, citizen regulatory agencies, and federal courts.

RICHARD J. TRILLING obtained his Ph.D. in political science from the University of Wisconsin-Madison in 1970. He is currently affiliated with Rockwell International in Durham, North Carolina, and is working toward his master's degree in computer science. He is author of *Party Image and Electoral Behavior* as well as articles on American political behavior and data base administration.

Bibliography

ABERBACH, J. D., and B. A. ROCKMAN
1976 "Clashing Beliefs within the Executive Branch: Data on the Nixon Administration Bureaucracy." *American Political Science Review* 70: 456–468.

ABRAM, M., and J. COOPER
1969 "The Rise of Seniority in the House of Representatives." *Polity* 1: 52–85.

ABRAMSON, P.
1975 *Generational Change in American Politics.* Lexington, Mass.: D.C. Heath.
1976 "Generational Change and the Decline of Party Identification in America: 1952–1974." *American Political Science Review* 70: 469–478.

ACHEN, C. H.
1975 "Mass Political Attitudes and the Survey Response." *American Political Science Review* 69: 1218–1231.

ADAMANY, D.
1973 "Legitimacy, Realigning Elections and the Supreme Court." *Wisconsin Law Review* 1973: 790–846.
1977 "Public and Activists' Attitudes towards the United States Supreme Court." Paper presented at the annual meeting of the American Political Science Association, Washington, D.C.

ALDRICH, N.
1909 *Congressional Record* 44: 4232.

ALLARDT, E., and S. ROKKAN, eds.
1970 *Mass Politics.* New York: Free Press.

ALLISON, G. T.
1971 *Essence of Decision: Explaining the Cuban Missile Crisis.* Boston: Little, Brown.

ART, R. J.
1973 "Bureaucratic Politics and American Foreign Policy." *Policy Sciences* 4: 467–490.

BARNARD, C. I.
1938   *The Functions of the Executive.* Cambridge, Mass.: Harvard University Press.
BASS, H. J.
1961   *I Am a Democrat: The Political Career of David Bennett Hill.* Syracuse: Syracuse University Press.
BAUER, R. A., I. de S. POOL, and L. A. DEXTER
1963   *American Business and Public Policy.* New York: Atherton Press.
BECK, P. A.
1976   "Communication—Critical Elections and the Supreme Court: Putting the Cart after the Horse." *American Political Science Review* 70: 930–932.
1977   "Partisan Dealignment in the Post-War South." *American Political Science Review* 71: 477–496.
BEITZINGER, E.
1957   "Federal Law Enforcement and the Booth Cases." *Marquette Law Review* 41: 7–32.
BERELSON, B. R., P. F. LAZARSFELD, and W. N. McPHEE
1954   *Voting.* Chicago: University of Chicago Press.
BEVERIDGE, A.
1919   *The Life of John Marshall.* Vol. 4. Boston: Houghton Mifflin.
BICKEL, A.
1962   *The Least Dangerous Branch.* Indianapolis: Bobbs-Merrill.
BINKLEY, W.
1962   *American Political Parties.* 4th ed. New York: Alfred A. Knopf.
BIOGRAPHICAL DIRECTORY OF THE AMERICAN CONGRESS 1774–1961.
1961   Washington, D.C.: G.P.O.
BIOGRAPHICAL DIRECTORY OF THE AMERICAN CONGRESS 1774–1973.
1973   Washington, D.C.: G.P.O.
BIRCH, A. H.
1971   "Children's Attitudes and British Politics." *British Journal of Political Science* 1: 519–520.
BISHOP, G. F., A. J. TUCHFARBER, and R. W. OLDENICK
1978   "Change in the Structure of American Political Attitudes: The Nagging Question of Question Wording." *American Journal of Political Science* 22: 250–269.
BLACK, C.
1960   *The People and the Court.* Englewood Cliffs, N.J.: Prentice-Hall.
BLACK, M., and G. RABINOWITZ
1974   "An Overview of American Electoral Change: 1952–1972." Paper presented at the annual meeting of the Southern Political Science Association, New Orleans.
BLAKEY, R. G., and G. BLAKEY
1940   *The Federal Income Tax.* New York: Longmans, Green.
BLAU, P. M., and M. W. MEYER
1971   *Bureaucracy in Modern Society.* 2d ed. New York: Random House.

BOGUE, A. G., ed.
1975 *Emerging Theoretical Models in Social and Political History.* Beverly Hills, Calif.: Sage.
BOGUE, A. G., J. M. CLUBB, C. R. McKIBBIN, and S. A. TRAUGOTT
1976 "Members of the House of Representatives and the Process of Modernization, 1789–1960." *Journal of American History* 63: 275–302.
BONE, H. A., and R. C. BENEDICT
1975 "Perspectives on Direct Legislation: Washington State's Experience, 1914–1973." *Western Political Quarterly* 28: 330–351.
BOYD, R. W.
1969 "Presidential Elections: An Explanation of Voting Defection." *American Political Science Review* 63: 498–514.
1972 "Popular Control of Public Policy: A Normal Vote Analysis of the 1968 Election." *American Political Science Review* 66: 429–449.
BRADY, D. W.
1973 *Congressional Voting in a Partisan Era: A Comparison of the Mc-Kinley Houses to the Modern House.* Lawrence: University of Kansas Press.
1978 "Critical Elections, Congressional Parties and Clusters of Policy Changes." *British Journal of Political Science* 8: 79–99.
BRADY, D. W., and P. ALTHOFF
1974 "Party Voting in the U.S. House of Representatives: Elements of a Responsible Party System." *Journal of Politics* 36: 753–775.
BRADY, D. W., and N. B. LYNN
1973 "Switched-Seat Congressional Districts: Their Effect on Party Voting and Public Policy." *American Journal of Political Science* 17: 528–543.
BRODY, R. A.
1975 "Change and Stability in Partisan Identification: A Note of Caution." Manuscript, Stanford University, Stanford, California.
1977 "Stability and Change in Party Identification: Presidential to Off-Years." Paper presented at the annual meeting of the American Political Science Association, Washington, D.C.
BROWN, E. C.
1956 "Fiscal Policy in the Thirties: A Reappraisal." *American Economic Review* 46: 857–879.
BUCHANAN, J. M.
1967 *Public Finance in Democratic Process: Fiscal Institutions and the Individual Choice.* Chapel Hill: University of North Carolina Press.
BUCHANAN, J. M., and G. TULLOCK
1962 *The Calculus of Consent.* Ann Arbor: University of Michigan Press.
BUDGE, I.
1971 "Support for Nation and Government among English Children: A Comment." *British Journal of Political Science* 1: 389–392.

BURNHAM, W. D.
1964   "The Alabama Senatorial Election of 1962." *Journal of Politics* 26: 798–829.
1965   "The Changing Shape of the American Political Universe." *American Political Science Review* 59: 7–28.
1968   "American Voting Behavior and the 1964 Election." *Midwest Journal of Political Science* 12: 1–40.
1969   "The End of American Party Politics." *Transaction* 7: 12–22.
1970   *Critical Elections and the Mainsprings of American Politics.* New York: W. W. Norton.
1974a   "Rejoinder." *American Political Science Review* 68: 1050–1057.
1974b   "Theory and Voting Research: Some Reflections on Converse's 'Change in the American Electorate.'" *American Political Science Review* 68: 1002–1023.
1975a   "Insulation and Responsiveness in Congressional Elections." *Political Science Quarterly* 90: 411–435.
1975b   "The United States: The Politics of Heterogeneity." In R. Rose, ed., *Electoral Behavior*, pp. 653–725. New York: Free Press.
BURNS, J. N.
1963   *The Deadlock of Democracy.* Englewood Cliffs, N.J.: Prentice-Hall.
BUTLER, W. H.
1966   "Administering Congress: The Staff Role." *Public Administration Review* 26: 3–24.
CAMPBELL, A.
1966a   "A Classification of Presidential Elections." In A. Campbell, P. E. Converse, W. E. Miller, and D. E. Stokes, *Elections and the Political Order*, pp. 63–77. New York: John Wiley & Sons.
1966b   "Surge and Decline: A Study of Electoral Change." In A. Campbell, P. E. Converse, W. E. Miller, and D. E. Stokes, *Elections and the Political Order*, pp. 40–62. New York: John Wiley & Sons.
CAMPBELL, A., P. E. CONVERSE, W. E. MILLER, AND D. E. STOKES
1960   *The American Voter.* New York: John Wiley & Sons.
1966   *Elections and the Political Order.* New York: John Wiley & Sons.
CAMPBELL, B. A.
1977a   "Change in the Southern Electorate." *American Journal of Political Science* 21: 37–64.
1977b   "Patterns of Change in the Partisan Loyalties of Native Southerners: 1952–1972." *Journal of Politics* 39: 730–761.
CANON, B., and S. S. ULMER
1976   "Communication—the Supreme Court and Critical Elections: A Dissent." *American Political Science Review* 70: 1215–1218.
CASEY G.
1974   "The Supreme Court and Myth: An Empirical Investigation." *Law & Society Review* 8: 385–419.

CASPER, J.
1976 "The Supreme Court and National Policy Making." *American Political Science Review* 70: 50–63.
CASSEL, C. A.
1977 "Cohort Analysis of Party Identification among Southern Whites: 1952–1972." *Public Opinion Quarterly* 41: 28–33.
CHAMBERS, W. N., and W. D. BURNHAM, eds.
1967 *The American Party System.* New York: Oxford University Press.
CITRIN, J.
1974 "Comment: The Political Relevance of Trust in Government." *American Political Science Review* 68: 973–988.
CLAUSEN, A.
1973 *How Congressmen Decide: A Policy Focus.* New York: St. Martin's.
COLEMAN, J. S.
1974 *Youth.* Chicago: University of Chicago Press.
COLETTA, P. E.
1964 *William Jennings Bryan: Political Evangelist.* Vol. 1. Lincoln: University of Nebraska Press.
COLLIER, D., and R. E. MESSICK
1975 "Prerequisites versus Diffusion: Testing Alternative Explanations of Social Security Adoption." *American Political Science Review* 69: 1299–1315.
CONGRESSIONAL RECORD
1909 Vol. 44: 1536–1537.
1913 Vol. 50: 3772.
CONVERSE, P. E.
1963 "On the Possibility of Major Political Realignment in the South." In A. P. Sindler, ed., *Change in the Contemporary South*, pp. 195–222. Durham: Duke University Press.
1964 "The Nature of Belief Systems in Mass Publics." In D. E. Apter, ed., *Ideology and Discontent*, pp. 206–261. Glencoe, Ill.: Free Press.
1966 "The Concept of a Normal Vote." In A. Campbell, P. E. Converse, W. E. Miller, and D. E. Stokes, *Elections and the Political Order*, pp. 9–39. New York: John Wiley & Sons.
1969 "Of Time and Partisan Stability." *Comparative Political Studies* 2: 139–171.
1972 "Change in the American Electorate." In A. Campbell and P. E. Converse, eds., *The Human Meaning of Social Change*, pp. 263–337. New York: Russell Sage Foundation.
1974 "Comment." *American Political Science Review* 68: 1024–1027.
1975 "Public Opinion and Voting Behavior." In F. I. Greenstein and N. W. Polsby, eds., *Handbook of Political Science*, vol. 4, pp. 75–169. Reading, Mass.: Addison-Wesley.

1976   *The Dynamics of Party Support*. Beverly Hills, Calif.: Sage.
CONVERSE, P. E., and G. MARKUS
1979   "Plus Ça Change . . . : The New CPS Election Study Panel." *American Political Science Review* 73: 32–49.
CONVERSE, P. E., and R. PIERCE
1970   "Basic Cleavages in French Politics and the Disorders of May and June, 1968." Paper presented at the 7th World Congress of Sociology, Varna, Bulgaria.
COOPER, J.
1956   "The Legislative Veto: Its Promise and Its Perils." In C. J. Friedrich and S. E. Harris, eds., *Public Policy*, vol. 7, pp. 128–174. Cambridge, Mass.: Harvard Graduate School of Public Administration.
COOPER, J., D. W. BRADY, and P. A. HURLEY
1977   "The Electoral Basis of Party Voting: Patterns and Trends in the U.S. House of Representatives, 1887–1969." In L. Maisel and J. Cooper, eds., *The Impact of the Electoral Process*, pp. 133–165. Beverly Hills, Calif.: Sage.
CRESPI, I.
1977   "Attitude Measurement, Theory and Prediction." *Public Opinion Quarterly* 41: 285–294.
DAHL, R.
1957   "Decision-Making in a Democracy: The Supreme Court as a National Policy-Maker." *Journal of Public Law* 6: 279–295.
DAVID, P.
1970   *Party Strength in the United States: 1872–1970*. Charlottesville: University of Virginia Press.
DAVIDSON, R. H.
1969   *The Role of the Congressman*. New York: Pegasus.
DAVIDSON, R. H., D. M. KOVENOCK, and M. O'LEARY
1966   *Congress in Crisis: Politics and Congressional Reform*. Belmont, Calif.: Wadsworth.
DAVIS, K. C.
1969   *Discretionary Justice*. Baton Rouge: Louisiana State University Press.
DE NEUFVILLE, J. I.
1975   *Social Indicators and Public Policy*. New York: Elsevier.
DENNIS, J.
1966   "Support for the Party System by the Mass Public." *American Political Science Review* 60: 600–615.
1975   "Mass Public Support for the U.S. Supreme Court." Paper presented at the annual meeting of the American Association for Public Opinion Research, Itasca, Ill.
DENNIS, J., L. LINDBERG, and D. McCRONE
1971   "Support for Nation and Government among English Children." *British Journal of Political Science* 1: 25–48.

DESTLER, I. M.
1972 *Presidents, Bureaucrats and Foreign Policy.* Princeton: Princeton University Press.
DeVRIES, W., and V. L. TARRANCE
1972 *The Ticket-Splitter.* Grand Rapids, Mich.: W. B. Eerdmans.
DEWEY, D. R.
1934 *Financial History of the United States.* New York: Longmans, Green.
DICK, C.
1909 *Congressional Record* 44: 4958–4959.
DOBSON, L. D., and D. ST. ANGELO
1975 "Party Identification and the Floating Vote: Some Dynamics." *American Political Science Review* 69: 481–490.
DOLBEARE, K., and P. HAMMOND
1968 "The Political Party Basis of Attitudes Toward the Supreme Court." *Public Opinion Quarterly* 32: 16–30.
1969 "Local Elites, the Impact of Judicial Decisions, and the Process of Change." Paper presented at the annual meeting of the American Political Science Association, New York.
1971 *The School Prayer Decisions.* Chicago: University of Chicago Press.
DOLLIVER, J.
1898 *Congressional Record* 31: 4306.
DOWNS, A.
1957 *An Economic Theory of Democracy.* New York: Harper & Row.
1960 "Why the Government Budget Is Too Small in a Democracy." *World Politics* 12: 541–563.
1967 *Inside Bureaucracy.* Boston: Little, Brown.
DUNCAN, O. D.
1975 *Introduction to Structural Equation Models.* New York: Academic Press.
DYE, T.
1966 *Politics, Economics and the Public.* Chicago: Rand McNally.
EASTON, D.
1965 *A Systems Analysis of Political Life.* New York: Wiley.
FABRICANT, S.
1952 *The Trend of Government Activity in the United States since 1900.* New York: National Bureau of Economic Research.
FELLMAN, D.
1976 *The Defendant's Rights Today.* Madison: University of Wisconsin Press.
FENNO, R.
1966 *The Power of the Purse.* Boston: Little, Brown.
1973 *Congressmen in Committees.* Boston: Little, Brown.
1977 "Congressmen in their Constituencies: An Exploration." *American Political Science Review* 71: 883–917.

FILIENE, P.
1970 "An Obituary for the Progressive Movement." *American Quarterly* 22: 20–34.
FIORINA, M., D. W. ROHDE, and P. WISSEL
1975 "Historical Change in House Turnover." In N. Ornstein, ed., *Congress in Change: Evolution and Reform*, pp. 24–57. New York: Praeger.
FISCHEL, J.
1973 *Party and Opposition: Congressional Challengers in American Politics*. New York: David McKay.
FISHER, G.
1969 *Taxes and Politics: A Study of Illinois Public Finance*. Urbana: University of Illinois Press.
FITZGERALD, M. J.
1975 "The Expanded Role of the General Accounting Office." *The Bureaucrat* 3: 383–400.
FLACKS, R.
1971 *Youth and Social Change*. Chicago: Markham.
FLANIGAN, W. H., and N. H. ZINGALE
1974a "The Measurement of Electoral Change." *Political Methodology* 1: 49–82.
1974b "Measures of Electoral Competition." *Political Methodology* 1: 31–60.
FLEMING, J. S.
1972 "Re-establishing Leadership in the House of Representatives: The Case of Oscar W. Underwood." *Mid-America* 54: 234–250.
FREEMAN, J. L.
1965 *The Political Process: Executive Bureau–Legislative Committee Relations*. New York: Random House.
FRIED, R. C.
1976 *Performance in American Bureaucracy*. Boston: Little, Brown.
FRITSCHLER, A. L.
1975 *Smoking and Politics: Policy-Making and the Federal Bureaucracy*. 2d ed. Englewood Cliffs, N.J.: Prentice-Hall.
FUNSTON, R.
1975 "The Supreme Court and Critical Elections." *American Political Science Review* 69: 795–811.
GALLUP, G. H.
1940 *Pulse of Democracy*. New York: Simon & Schuster.
THE GALLUP OPINION INDEX
1967, 1973, 1974 Princeton: Princeton Opinion Press.
GATLIN, D. S.
1975 "Party Identification, Status and Race in the South, 1952–1972." *Public Opinion Quarterly* 39: 39–51.
GINSBERG, B.
1972 "Critical Elections and the Substance of Party Conflict: 1844–

1968." *Midwest Journal of Political Science* 16: 603–625.
1976 "Elections and Public Policy." *American Political Science Review* 70: 41–49.

GLAZER, N.
1976 *Affirmative Discrimination*. New York: Basic Books.

GLENN, N. D.
1972 "Sources of the Shift to Political Independence: Some Evidence from a Cohort Analysis." *Social Science Quarterly* 53: 494–519.

GROSSMAN, J. B., and S. WASBY
1971 "Haynsworth and Parker: History Does Live Again." *South Carolina Law Review* 23: 345–359.

GROSVENOR, C.
1898 *Congressional Record* 31: 4418.

HALPERIN, M. H.
1974 *Bureaucratic Politics and Foreign Policy*. Washington, D.C.: Brookings Institution.

HAMILTON, H. D.
1970 "Direct Legislation: Some Implications of Open-Housing Referenda." *American Political Science Review* 64: 124–137.

HAMILTON, H. D., and S. H. COHEN
1974 *Policy-Making by Plebiscite: School Referenda*. Lexington, Mass.: Lexington Books.

HAMMOND, J. L.
1977 "Race and Electoral Mobilization." *Public Opinion Quarterly* 41: 13–27.

HANSEN, S. B.
1978 "The Politics of State Tax Innovation." Paper presented at the annual meeting of the Midwest Political Science Association, Chicago.

HANUSHEK, E., J. E. JACKSON, and J. F. KAIN
1974 "Model Specification, Use of Aggregate Data, and the Ecological Correlation Fallacy." *Political Methodology* 1: 89–107.

HARDIN, R.
1976 "Hollow Victory: The Minimum Winning Coalition." *American Political Science Review* 70: 1202–1214.

HARRIS, P. M. G.
1969 "The Social Origins of American Leaders: The Demographic Foundations." In D. Fleming and B. Bailyn, eds., *Perspectives in American History*, vol. 3, pp. 159–344. Cambridge, Mass.: Charles Warren Center for Studies in American History, Harvard University.

HARTMAN, A.
1975 "Representative Bureaucracy." Paper presented at the annual meeting of the American Political Science Association, San Francisco.

HECLO, H.
1977 *A Government of Strangers*. Washington, D.C.: Brookings Institution.

HEDLUND, R., and P. FRIESMA
1972   "Representatives' Perceptions of Constituency Opinion." *Journal of Politics* 34: 730–752.
HEFFERNAN, N. S.
1969   "The Judicial Civil War: The Wisconsin Supreme Court and Its Battle with Federal Authority (1854–1869)." Paper presented to the Madison Literary Society.
HEIDENHEIMER, A. J., H. HECLO, and C. T. ADAMS
1975   *Comparative Public Policy.* New York: St. Martin's.
HEISE, D. R.
1969   "Separating Reliability and Stability in Test-Retest Correlation." *American Sociological Review* 34: 93–101.
HILL, D. B.
1894   *Congressional Record* 26: 3568.
HIRSCHMAN, A. O.
1970   *Exit, Voice, and Loyalty.* Cambridge, Mass.: Harvard University Press.
HOFFERBERT, R.
1968   "Socio-economic Dimensions of American States: 1890–1960." *Midwest Journal of Political Science* 12: 401–418.
HOFSTADTER, R.
1955   *The Age of Reform.* New York: Alfred A. Knopf.
HOWE, F. C.
1896   *Taxation and Taxes in the United States under the Internal Revenue System 1791–1895.* New York. Crowell.
HUGHES, J. R. T.
1977   *The Governmental Habit.* New York: Basic Books.
HUITT, R.
1954   "The Congressional Committee: A Case Study." *American Political Science Review* 48: 340–365.
1961   "Democratic Party Leadership in the Senate." *American Political Science Review* 55: 333–344.
HYNEMAN, C. S.
1950   *Bureaucracy in a Democracy.* New York: Harper & Brothers.
JACKSON, J. E.
1974   *Constituencies and Leaders in Congress: Their Effects on Senate Voting Behavior.* Cambridge, Mass.: Harvard University Press.
JACKSON, R. H.
1941   *The Struggle for Judicial Supremacy.* New York: Alfred A. Knopf.
JAHNIGE, T. P.
1971   "Critical Elections and Social Change." *Polity* 3: 465–500.
JENNINGS, M. K., and R. NIEMI
1975   "Continuity and Change in Political Orientations: A Longitudinal Study of Two Generations." *American Political Science Review* 69: 1316–1335.

JENSEN, R.
1971 *The Winning of the Midwest.* Chicago: University of Chicago Press.
JOHNSON, R. M.
1967 *The Dynamics of Compliance.* Evanston, Ill.: Northwestern University Press.
JONES, C. O.
1970 *The Minority Party in Congress.* Boston: Little, Brown.
JONES, S. L.
1964 *The Presidential Elections of 1896.* Madison: University of Wisconsin Press.
KATZ, D., and R. KAHN
1966 *The Social Psychology of Organizations.* New York: Wiley.
KAUFMAN, H.
1960 *The Forest Ranger.* Baltimore: Johns Hopkins University Press.
KEEFE, W. J., and M. S. OGUL
1973 *The American Legislative Process.* 3d ed. Englewood Cliffs, N.J.: Prentice-Hall.
KENISTON, K.
1968 *The Young Radicals: Notes on Committed Youth.* New York: Harcourt, Brace.
KERR, J.
1965 "Congress and Space: Overview or Oversight." *Public Administration Review* 25: 192.
KESSEL, J. H.
1966 "Public Perceptions of the Supreme Court." *Midwest Journal of Political Science* 10: 167–191.
1968 *The Goldwater Coalition.* Indianapolis: Bobbs-Merrill.
KEY, V. O., JR.
1949 *Southern Politics.* New York: Random House.
1955 "A Theory of Critical Elections." *Journal of Politics* 17: 3–18.
1958 *Politics, Parties and Pressure Groups.* 4th ed. New York: Crowell.
1959 "Secular Realignment and the Party System." *Journal of Politics* 21: 198–210.
1966 *The Responsible Electorate.* Cambridge, Mass.: Harvard University Press.
1967 *American State Politics: An Introduction.* New York: Alfred A. Knopf.
KING, M. E., and L. G. SELIGMAN
1974 "Critical Elections, Congressional Recruitment and Public Policy." Paper presented at the annual meeting of the Midwest Political Science Association, Chicago.
1976 "Critical Elections, Congressional Recruitment and Public Policy." In H. Eulau and M. M. Czudnowski, eds., *Elite Recruitment in Democratic Politics: Comparative Studies across Nations*, pp. 263–299. New York: Halstead Press.

KLEPPNER, P.
1970   *The Cross of Culture.* 2d ed. New York: Free Press.
KOLKO, G.
1963   *The Triumph of Conservatism.* New York: Free Press.
KRADITOR, A.
1972   "American Radical Historians on Their Heritage." *Past and Present* 56: 136–153.
KRAFT, J.
1958   *Profiles in Power.* New York: New American Library.
LADD, E. C., JR.
1970   *American Political Parties.* New York: W. W. Norton.
LADD, E. C., JR., and C. D. HADLEY
1973   "Party Definition and Party Differentiation." *Public Opinion Quarterly* 37: 21–34.
1975   *Transformations of the American Party System.* New York: W. W. Norton.
LADD, E. C., JR., C. D. HADLEY, and L. KING
1971   "A New Political Realignment?" *Public Interest* 23: 46–63.
LAMB, K. A.
1972   "Plotting the Electorate's Course in Dangerous Waters." *Political Science Reviewer* 2: 39–65.
LAMBERT, W. F.
1970   "New Deal Revenue Acts: The Politics of Taxation." Ph.D. dissertation, University of Texas at Austin.
LANG, K., and G. LANG
1975   "Televised Hearings: The Impact Out There." In R. E. Pynn, ed., *Watergate and the American Political Process,* pp. 71–79. New York: Praeger.
LEHNEN, R. G.
1976   *American Institutions, Political Opinion, and Public Policy.* Hinsdale, Ill.: Dryden Press.
LEUCHTENBURG, W. E.
1963   *Franklin D. Roosevelt and the New Deal.* New York: Harper & Row.
LICHTMAN, A.
1974   "Correlation, Regression and the Ecological Fallacy: A Critique." *Journal of Interdisciplinary History* 4: 417–433.
LIJPHART, A.
1971   "Comparative Politics and the Comparative Method." *American Political Science Review* 65: 682–693.
LILLICH, R.
1960   "The Chase Impeachment." *American Journal of Legal History* 4: 49–78.
LINEBERRY, R., and E. P. FOWLER
1967   "Reformism and Public Policies in American Cities." *American Political Science Review* 61: 701–716.

LIPSET, S. M.
1950   *Agrarian Socialism.* Berkeley and Los Angeles: University of California Press.
1960   *Political Man.* Garden City, N.Y.: Doubleday.
1970   "Political Cleavages in 'Developing' and 'Emerging' Politics." In E. Allardt and S. Rokkan, eds., *Mass Politics,* New York: Free Press.
LITERARY DIGEST
1895   June 1, pp. 125–126.
LOCKHART, W., Y. KAMISAR, and J. CHOPER
1970   *Constitutional Law: Cases, Comments, Questions.* 3d ed. St. Paul: West Publishing Co.
LODGE, H. C.
1913   *Congressional Record* 50: 3832.
1925   *Selections from the Correspondence of Theodore Roosevelt and Henry Cabot Lodge.* New York: Charles L. Scribner's Sons.
LONGAKER, R.
1956   "Andrew Jackson and the Judiciary." *Political Science Quarterly* 71: 341–364.
LONGLEY, C. H.
1974   "McNamara and Military Behavior." *American Journal of Political Science* 18: 1–21.
LOWI, T. J.
1972   "Four Systems of Policy, Politics and Change." *Public Administration Review* 32: 298–310.
LUBELL, S.
1965   *The Future of American Politics.* 3d ed. New York: Harper.
1970   *The Hidden Crisis in American Politics.* New York: W. W. Norton.
LUTRIN, C. E., and A. K. SETTLE
1975   "The Public and Ecology: The Role of Initiatives in California's Environmental Politics." *Western Political Quarterly* 28: 352–371.
McCLELLAND, G. B.
1898   *Congressional Record* 31: 4363.
McCONNELL, G.
1966   *Private Power and American Democracy.* New York: Alfred A. Knopf.
McCORMICK, R. P.
1967   "Political Development and the Second American Party System." In W. N. Chambers and W. D. Burnham, eds., *The American Party System,* pp. 90–116. New York: Oxford University Press.
McGREGOR, E. B., JR.
1974   "Politics and the Career Mobility of Bureaucrats." *American Political Science Review* 68: 18–26.
MacKAYE, W. R.
1963   *A New Coalition Takes Control: The House Rules Committee Fight of 1961.* New York: McGraw-Hill.

MacRAE, D., JR., and J. A. MELDRUM
1960   "Critical Elections in Illinois: 1888–1958." *American Political Science Review* 54: 669–683.
1969   "Factor Analysis of Aggregate Voting Statistics." In M. Dogan and S. Rokkan, eds., *Quantitative Ecological Analysis in the Social Sciences*. Cambridge, Mass.: MIT Press.

McSEVENEY, S.
1972   *The Politics of Depression*. New York: Oxford University Press.

MANLEY, J.
1970   *The Politics of Finance*. Boston: Little, Brown.

MANNHEIM, K.
1952   "The Problem of Generations." In Paul Kecskemeti, ed., *Essays on the Sociology of Knowledge*, pp. 276–320. London: Oxford University Press.

MARGOLIS, M.
1977   "From Confusion to Confusion: Issues and the American Voter (1956–1972)." *American Political Science Review* 71: 31–43.

MARMOR, T. R.
1973   *The Politics of Medicare*. Chicago: Aldine.

MARQUETTE, J. F.
1974   "Social Change and Political Mobilization in the United States: 1870–1960." *American Political Science Review* 68: 1058–1074.

MATTHEWS, D. R.
1960   *U.S. Senators and Their World*. Chapel Hill: University of North Carolina Press.

MATTHEWS, D. R., and J. W. PROTHRO
1964   "Southern Images of Political Parties: An Analysis of White and Negro Attitudes." In S. Leiserson, ed., *The American South in the 1960's*. New York: Praeger.
1966a   "The Concept of Party Image and Its Importance for the Southern Electorate." In M. K. Jennings and L. H. Zeigler, eds., *The Electoral Process*. Englewood Cliffs, N.J.: Prentice-Hall.
1966b   *Negroes and the New Southern Politics*. New York: Harcourt, Brace.

MAYHEW, D.
1973   "Congressional Elections: The Case of the Vanishing Marginals." *Polity* 6: 295–317.

MEIER, K. J., and L. C. NIGRO
1976   "Representative Bureaucracy and Policy Preferences." *Public Administration Review* 36: 458–469.

MEISEL, J.
1973   *Working Papers on Canadian Politics*. Enlarged edition. Montreal: McGill-Queen's University Press.

MELTSNER, A.
1971   *The Politics of City Revenue*. Berkeley and Los Angeles: University of California Press.

MILLER, A. H.
1974 "Political Issues and Trust in Government: 1964–1970." *American Political Science Review* 68: 951–972.
MILLER, J.
1894 "Letter to Benton McMillin." *Congressional Record* 26: 293.
MILLER, W. E., and T. E. LEVITIN
1976 *Leadership and Change.* Cambridge, Mass.: Winthrop.
MILLER, W. E., and D. E. STOKES
1963 "Constituency Influence in Congress." *American Political Science Review* 57: 45–56.
MORISON, S. E., H. S. COMMAGER, and W. E. LEUCHTENBURG
1970 *The Growth of the American Republic.* Vol. 2. New York: Oxford University Press.
MOSHER, F. C.
1968 *Democracy and the Public Service.* New York: Oxford University Press.
MOSHER, F. C., and O. F. POLAND
1964 *The Costs of American Government.* New York: Dodd, Mead.
MOWRY, G. E.
1958 *The Era of Theodore Roosevelt.* New York: Harper & Row.
MUELLER, J. E.
1970 "Presidential Popularity from Truman to Johnson." *American Political Science Review* 64: 18–34.
1971 "Trends in Popular Support for the Wars in Korea and Vietnam." *American Political Science Review* 65: 358–375.
1973 *War, Presidents and Public Opinion.* New York: John Wiley & Sons.
MURPHY, W., and J. TANENHAUS
1968a "Public Opinion and the Supreme Court: The Goldwater Campaign." *Public Opinion Quarterly* 32: 31–50.
1968b "Public Opinion and the United States Supreme Court." *Law and Society Review* 2: 357–384.
1970 "The Supreme Court and Its Elite Publics." Paper presented at the annual meeting of the International Political Science Association, Munich.
1976 "Patterns of Public Support: A Study of the Warren and Burger Courts." Paper presented at the annual meeting of the International Political Science Association, Edinburgh.
MURPHY, W., J. TANENHAUS, and D. KASTNER
1973 *Public Evaluations of Constitutional Courts: Alternative Explanations.* Beverly Hills, Calif.: Sage.
MUSGRAVE, R. A.
1969 *Fiscal Systems.* New Haven: Yale University Press.
MYERS, W. S., ed.
1934 *The State Papers and Other Public Writings of Herbert Hoover.* Vol. 1. New York: Doubleday, Doran.

NAGEL, S. S.
1969   *The Legal Process from a Behavioral Perspective.* Homewood, Ill.: Dorsey Press.
NATHAN, R. P.
1975   *The Plot That Failed.* New York: John Wiley and Sons.
NEUMAN, W. L., and A. HICKS
1977   "Public Policy, Party Platforms, and Critical Elections: A Reexamination." *American Political Science Review* 71: 277–280.
NEUSTADT, R. E.
1960   *Presidential Power.* New York: John Wiley and Sons.
NEWCOMB, T. M.
1943   *Personality and Social Change.* New York: Dryden.
NEW YORK TIMES
1894   January 26, p. 2.
1913   March 23, p. 2.
NEXON, D. H.
1970   "Hacks, Fanatics, and Responsible but Dense Voters." M.A. paper, University of Chicago.
NIE, N. H., and K. ANDERSON
1974   "Mass Belief Systems Revisited: Political Change and Attitude Structure." *Journal of Politics* 36: 540–591.
NIE, N. H., S. VERBA, and J. R. PETROCIK
1976   *The Changing American Voter.* Cambridge, Mass.: Harvard University Press.
NISKANEN, W. A., JR.
1971   *Bureaucracy and Representative Government.* Chicago: Aldine-Atherton.
NORTON, C. F.
1976   *Congressional Review, Deferral and Disapproval of Executive Actions.* Washington, D.C.: Congressional Research Series.
O'CONNOR, J.
1973   *The Fiscal Crisis of the State.* New York: St. Martin's.
OLESZEK, W.
1969   "Age and Political Careers." *Public Opinion Quarterly* 33: 100–102.
OLSON, M.
1971   *The Logic of Collective Action.* Boston: Harvard University Press.
ORFIELD, G.
1975   *Congressional Power: Congress and Social Change.* New York: Harcourt, Brace, Jovanovich.
PARSONS, T.
1960   *Structure and Process in Modern Societies.* Glencoe, Ill.: Free Press.
PATTERSON, T. E., and R. D. McCLURE
1976   *The Unseeing Eye.* New York: G. P. Putnam's Sons.

PAUL, R. E.
1954 *Taxation in the United States*. Boston: Little, Brown.
PEABODY, R., and N. W. POLSBY
1963 "The Enlarged Rules Committee." In R. Peabody and N. Alsby, eds., *New Perspectives on the House of Representatives*, pp. 359–394. Chicago: Rand McNally.
PEACOCK, A. T., and J. WISEMAN
1961 *The Growth of Public Expenditures in the United Kingdom*. Princeton: Princeton University Press (National Bureau of Economic Research).
PECHMAN, J. A., and B. A. OKNER
1974 *Who Bears the Tax Burden?* Washington, D.C.: Brookings Institution.
PHILLIPS, K.
1969 *The Emerging Republican Majority*. New Rochelle, N.Y.: Arlington House.
PIERCE, L. C.
1971 *The Politics of Fiscal Policy Formation*. Pacific Palisades, Calif.: Goodyear.
PINCUS, A.
1976 "How to Get a Government Job." *Washington Monthly* 8: 22–27.
PITKIN, H.
1965 "Obligation and Consent, I" *American Political Science Review* 59: 990–999.
1966 "Obligation and Consent, II." *American Political Science Review* 60: 39–52.
PIVEN, F., and R. A. CLOWARD
1971 *Regulating the Poor*. New York: Pantheon.
POLSBY, N. W.
1969 "An Emerging Republican Majority?" *Public Interest* 17: 119–126.
POLSBY, N. W., M. GALLAHER, and B. S. RUNDQUIST
1969 "The Growth of the Seniority System in the U.S. House of Representatives." *American Political Science Review* 63: 787–807.
POMPER, G.
1967 "Classification of Presidential Elections." *Journal of Politics* 29: 535–566.
1968 *Elections in America: Control and Influence in Democratic Politics*. New York: Dodd, Mead.
1972 "From Confusion to Clarity: Issues and American Voters, 1956–1968. *American Political Science Review* 66: 415–428.
1975 *Voter's Choice*. New York: Dodd, Mead.
1977 "The Decline of Partisan Politics." In L. Maisel and J. Cooper, eds., *The Impact of the Electoral Process*, pp. 13–38. Beverly Hills, Calif.: Sage.

PRICE, C. M.
1975 "The Initiative: A Comparative State Analysis and Reassessment of a Western Phenomenon." *Western Political Quarterly* 28: 243–262.

PRICE, D. K.
1965 *The Scientific Estate.* New York: Oxford University Press.

PRICE, H. D.
1968 "Micro- and Macro-Politics: Notes on Research and Strategy." In O. Garceau, ed., *Political Research and Political Theory*, pp. 102–140. Cambridge, Mass.: Harvard University Press.
1971 "Critical Elections and Party History: A Critical View." *Polity* 4: 236–242.

PRYOR, F. L.
1968 *Public Expenditures in Communist and Capitalist Nations.* Homewood, Ill.: Richard D. Irwin.

RAE, D., and M. TAYLOR
1970 *The Analysis of Political Cleavages.* New Haven: Yale University Press.

RAKOFF, S. H., and G. F. SCHAEFER
1970 "Politics, Policy and Political Science: Theoretical Alternatives." *Politics and Society* 1: 51–77.

RANDALL, J. G.
1926 *Constitutional Problems under Lincoln.* Urbana: University of Illinois Press.

RANNEY, A.
1962 "The Utility and Limitations of Aggregate Data in the Study of Electoral Behavior." In A. Ranney, ed., *Essays on the Behavioral Study of Politics*, pp. 91–102. Urbana: University of Illinois Press.

RATNER, S.
1935 "Was the Supreme Court Packed by President Grant?" *Political Science Quarterly* 50: 343–358.
1942a *American Taxation.* New York: W. W. Norton.
1942b *A Political and Social History of Federal Taxation 1789–1913.* New York: W. W. Norton.

REDFORD, E. S.
1969 *Democracy in the Administrative State.* New York: Oxford University Press.

RePASS, D. E.
1971 "Issue, Salience and Party Choice." *American Political Science Review* 65: 389–400.

RICHARDSON, J. D.
1898 *Messages and Papers of the Presidents.* vol. 9. Washington, D.C.: G.P.O.

RIESMAN, D., in collaboration with R. DENNEY and N. GLAZER
1969 *The Lonely Crowd.* New Haven: Yale University Press.

RIKER, W.
1962 *The Theory of Political Coalitions.* New Haven: Yale University Press.

RIPLEY, R. B., and G. A. FRANKLIN
1976 *Congress, the Bureaucracy and Public Policy.* Homewood, Ill.: Dorsey Press.

ROOSEVELT, T.
1906 "Annual Message." *New York Times,* December 5, p. 4.

ROSE, R.
1975 "On the Evolution of Public Policy in the European State." Paper presented at a conference on comparing public policy, Warsaw.

ROURKE, F. E.
1976 *Bureaucracy, Politics, and Public Policy.* 2d ed. Boston: Little, Brown.

RUSK, J. G.
1974 "Comment." *American Political Science Review* 68: 1028–1049.

SANDERS, H.
1976 "Pensions and Politics 1875–1896." Manuscript, University of Illinois.

SCAMMON, R. M., and B. J. WATTENBERG
1970 *The Real Majority.* New York: Coward-McCann.

SCHATTSCHNEIDER, E. E.
1942 *Party Government.* New York: Holt, Rinehart & Winston.
1960 *The Semi-Sovereign People.* New York: Holt, Rinehart & Winston.

SCHER, S.
1961 "Regulatory Agency Control through Appointment: The Case of the Eisenhower Administration and the NLRB." *Journal of Politics* 23: 667–688.

SCHICK, A.
1971 "Toward the Cybernetic State." In D. Dwight, ed., *Public Administration in a Time of Turbulence,* pp. 214–233. Scranton: Chandler.

SCHLESINGER, A. M., JR.
1946 *The Age of Jackson.* Boston: Little, Brown.
1957 *The Crisis of the Old Order, 1919–1933.* Boston: Houghton Mifflin.

SCHMIDHAUSER, J. R.
1961 "Judicial Behavior and the Sectional Crisis of 1837–1860." *Journal of Politics* 23: 615–640.

SCHREIBER, E. M.
1971 "Where the Ducks Are: Southern Strategy vs. Fourth Party." *Public Opinion Quarterly* 35: 157–167.
1973 "Vietnam Policy Preferences and Withheld 1968 Presidential Votes." *Public Opinion Quarterly* 37: 91–98.

SCIGLIANO, R.
1971 *The Supreme Court and the Presidency.* New York: Free Press.

SCOTT, A.
1959   "The Progressive Era in Perspective." *Journal of Politics* 21: 685–701.
SEAGULL, L. M.
1971   "The Youth Vote and Change in American Politics." *Annals of the American Academy of Political and Social Science*, pp. 88–96.
1975   *Southern Republicanism.* New York: Schenkman.
1977   *Youth and Change in American Politics.* New York: New Viewpoints.
SEIDMAN, H.
1975   "Politics, Position and Power." 2d ed. New York: Oxford University Press.
SEITZ, S. T.
1974   "Social Unrest and Critical Elections: Periodicity in American History." Paper presented at the annual meeting of the American Political Science Association, Chicago.
SELIGMAN, L.
1970   *Recruiting Political Elites.* New York: General Learning Press.
SELLERS, C.
1965   "The Equilibrium Cycle in Two-Party Politics." *Public Opinion Quarterly* 29: 16–38.
SHARKANSKY, I.
1969   *The Politics of Taxing and Spending.* Indianapolis: Bobbs-Merrill.
SHEPHARD, W. B.
1975   "Participation in Local Policy Making: The Case of Referenda." *Social Science Quarterly* 56: 55–70.
SHIVELY, W. P.
1971–72   "A Reinterpretation of the New Deal Realignment." *Public Opinion Quarterly* 35: 621–624.
SHULTZ, G., and K. DAM
1977   *Economic Policy beyond the Headlines.* Stanford: Stanford Alumni Association.
SICKELS, R. J.
1974   *Presidential Transactions.* Englewood Cliffs, N.J.: Prentice-Hall.
SINCLAIR, B.
1977   "Party Realignment and the Transformation of the Political Agenda." *American Political Science Review* 71: 940–953.
SMITH, D. G.
1965   *The Convention and the Constitution.* New York: St. Martin's.
SMITH, F.
1964   *Congressman from Mississippi.* New York: Pantheon.
SNIDERMAN, P. M., W. R. NEUMAN, J. CITRIN, H. McCLOSKY, and J. M. SHANKS
1975   "Stability of Support for the Political System: The Initial Impact

of Watergate." *American Politics Quarterly* 3: 437–457.

SORAUF, F.
1968 *Party Politics in America.* Boston: Little, Brown.

STANLEY, D. T.
1965 *Changing Administrations.* Washington, D.C.: Brookings Institution.

STEINER, G. Y.
1966 *Social Insecurity.* Chicago: Rand McNally.

STEWART, C. A.
1974 "The Formation of Tax Policy in the United States, 1893–1913." Ph.D. dissertation, University of North Carolina.
1976 "Tax Policy 1893–1913: A Case Study of Conflict and Consensus." Manuscript, University of North Carolina.

STIMPSON, J. A.
1976 "Public Support for American Presidents: A Cyclical Model." *Public Opinion Quarterly* 40: 1–21.

STODDARD, L.
1913 *Master of Manhattan: The Life of Richard Croker.* New York: Longmans.

STRONG, D. S.
1963 "Durable Republicanism in the South." In A. P. Sindler, ed., *Change in the Contemporary South,* pp. 174–194. Durham: Duke University Press.
1971 "Further Reflections on Southern Politics." *Journal of Politics* 33: 239–256.

SULLIVAN, J. L., and R. E. O'CONNOR
1972 "Electoral Choice and Popular Control of Public Policy: The Case of the 1966 House Elections." *American Political Science Review* 66: 1256–1268.

SUNDQUIST, J.
1966 *Elections and Policy in the Eisenhower, Kennedy and Johnson Years.* Washington, D.C.: Brookings Institution.
1973 *Dynamics of the Party System: Alignment and Realignment of Political Parties in the United States.* Washington D.C.: Brookings Institution.

SWINDLER, W.
1969 *Court and Constitution in the 20th Century: The Old Legality 1889–1932.* Indianapolis: Bobbs-Merrill.
1970 *Court and Constitution in the 20th Century: The New Legality 1932–1968.* Indianapolis: Bobbs-Merrill.

TAFT, W. H.
1908 "Acceptance Speech." *New York Times,* August 20, p. 2.
1909 "Letter to Horace Taft." William Howard Taft Papers. Library of Congress, series 8, vol. 5, June 27.

TARSCHYS, D.
1975 "The Growth of Public Expenditures: Nine Modes of Explanation."
Scandinavian Political Studies 10: 9–31.
TAUSSIG, F. W.
1966 *The Tariff History of the United States.* New York: Capricorn
Books. (Originally published by G. P. Putnam, 1892.)
THOMPSON, J. D.
1967 *Organizations in Action.* New York: McGraw-Hill.
TRESCOTT, P. B.
1957 "Some Historical Aspects of Federal Fiscal Policy 1790–1956." In
U.S. Congress, Joint Economic Committee, *Federal Expenditure
Policy for Growth and Stability,* 85th Congress, 1st session, pp.
60–83. Washington, D.C.: G.P.O.
TRILLING, R. J.
1975a "Party Image and Partisan Change." In L. Maisel and P. M. Sacks,
eds., *The Future of Political Parties,* Sage Electoral Studies Yearbook, vol. 1, pp. 62–100. Beverly Hills, Calif.: Sage.
1975b "Party Image and Electoral Behavior." *American Politics Quarterly* 3: 284–314.
1976a "The Electoral Mechanics of Realignment." Paper presented at
the annual meeting of the Social Science History Association,
Philadelphia.
1976b *Party Image and Electoral Behavior.* New York: Wiley-Intersci-
ence.
TUBBESING, C. D.
1975 "Predicting the Present: Realignment and Redistribution." *Polity*
7: 478–504.
TURNER, L. W.
1949 "The Impeachment of John Pickering." *American Historical Review* 54: 485–507.
TUSSING, A. D., and J. A. HENNING
1974 "Long-Run Growth of Nondefense Government Expenditures in
the United States." *Public Finance Quarterly* 2: 202–222.
UNDERWOOD, O. W.
1913 *Congressional Record* 50: 1255.
UNITED STATES, BUREAU OF THE CENSUS
1931 *Unemployment.* Vol. 1. Washington, D.C.: G.P.O.
1932 *Population.* Vol. 3, Pt. 2. Washington, D.C.: G.P.O.
1950 *Historical Statistics of the United States: Colonial Period to 1945.*
Washington, D.C.: G.P.O.
1961 *Historical Statistics of the United States: Colonial Times to 1957.*
Washington, D.C.: G.P.O.
1975 *Historical Statistics of the United States: Colonial Times to 1970.*
Bicentennial edition, pts. 1 and 2. Washington, D.C.: G.P.O.

WAHLKE, J. C.
1971   "Policy Demands and System Support: The Role of the Represented." *British Journal of Political Science* 1: 271–290.
WALKER, J.
1969   "The Diffusion of Innovation among the American States." *American Political Science Review* 63: 880–899.
WALTMAN, J. L.
1976   "Linkage Politics and Public Policy: An Analysis of the American Social Security and Income Tax Adoptions." Ph.D. dissertation, Indiana University.
WANAT, J.
1974   "Bases of Budgetary Incrementalism." *American Political Science Review* 68: 1221–1228.
WARD, J. F.
1973   "Toward a Sixth Party System? Partisanship and Political Development." *Western Political Quarterly* 26: 385–413.
WARREN, C.
1926a *The Supreme Court in United States History.* Vol. 1: 1789–1835. Boston: Little, Brown.
1926b *The Supreme Court in United States History.* Vol. 2: 1836–1918. Boston: Little, Brown.
WARWICK, D. P.
1975   *A Theory of Public Bureaucracy.* Cambridge, Mass.: Harvard University Press.
WASHINGTON POST
1893   January 3, p. 1.
1894a January 6, p. 1.
1894b January 25, p. 1.
1898   April 30, p. 4.
1909a March 25, p. 1.
1909b April 15, p. 1.
1909c May 19, p. 4.
WEAVER, D. H., M. E. McCOOMBS, and C. SPELLMAN
1975   "Watergate and the Media: A Case Study in Agenda-Setting." *American Politics Quarterly* 3: 458–472.
WEBER, M.
1946   *From Max Weber: Essays in Sociology.* H. H. Gerth and C. W. Mills, eds. and trans. New York: Oxford University Press.
WEINSTEIN, J.
1968   *The Corporate Ideal in the Liberal State.* Boston: Beacon Press.
WENCES, R.
1969   "Electoral Participation and the Occupation Composition of Cabinets and Parliaments." *American Journal of Sociology* 75: 181–192.

WESTIN, A.

1953   "The Supreme Court, the Populist Movement, and the Campaign of 1896." *Journal of Politics* 15: 3–41.

WHITE, W. A.

1965   *A Puritan in Babylon: The Story of Calvin Coolidge.* New York: Capricorn Books.

WILDAVSKY, A.

1964   *The Politics of the Budgetary Process.* Boston: Little, Brown.

WILEY, D. E., and J. A. WILEY

1970   "The Estimation of Measurement Error in Panel Data." *American Sociological Review* 35: 112–117.

WILSON, W.

1885   *Congressional Government.* Boston: Houghton Mifflin.

WINTERS, R. T.

1976   "Party Control and Policy Change." *American Journal of Political Science* 20: 597–636.

WOLFINGER, R. E., and R. E. ARSENEAU

1974   "Partisan Change in the South, 1952–1972." Paper presented at the annual meeting of the American Political Science Association, Chicago.

WOLMAN, H.

1971   *Politics of Federal Housing.* New York: Dodd, Mead.

WOODWARD, C. V.

1976   "The Promise of Populism." *New York Review of Books* 23: 28–29.

WRIGHT, J.

1975   "The Ethno-Cultural Model of Voting." In A. G. Bogue, ed., *Emerging Theoretical Models in Social and Political History,* pp. 35–56. Beverly Hills, Calif.: Sage.

WRIGLEY, E. A.

1972   "The Process of Modernization and the Industrial Revolution in England." *Journal of Interdisciplinary History* 3: 225–259.

YANKELOVICH, D.

1974   *The New Morality.* New York: McGraw-Hill.

YARMOLINSKY, A.

1971   *The Military Establishment.* New York: Harper & Row.

ZEMSKY, R.

1975   "American Legislative Behavior." In A. G. Bogue, ed., *Emerging Theoretical Models in Social and Political History,* pp. 57–75. Beverly Hills, Calif.: Sage.

ZENTNER, J. L.

1972   "Presidential Transitions and the Perpetuation of Programs: The Johnson-Nixon Experience." *Western Political Quarterly* 25: 5–15.